John MacHale, Thomas MacHale

**Sermons and discourses**

John MacHale, Thomas MacHale

**Sermons and discourses**

ISBN/EAN: 9783742837417

Manufactured in Europe, USA, Canada, Australia, Japa

Cover: Foto ©Andreas Hilbeck / pixelio.de

Manufactured and distributed by brebook publishing software (www.brebook.com)

John MacHale, Thomas MacHale

**Sermons and discourses**

# SERMONS AND DISCOURSES

BY THE LATE

## MOST REV. JOHN MAC HALE, D.D.

*ARCHBISHOP OF TUAM*

EDITED BY

### THOMAS MAC HALE, D.D., Ph.D.

DUBLIN
M. H. GILL & SON, 50 UPPER SACKVILLE STREET
1883

# PREFACE.

THE volume now published contains select Sermons and Discourses delivered by the late Most Rev. John Mac Hale, D.D., Archbishop of Tuam, while Professor in the College of Maynooth, and during the course of a long apostolic career in the Church of Ireland. These Sermons and Discourses are arranged in the following order:

  I. Great truths of religion.
  II. Detached moral subjects.
  III. Festivals.
  IV. Subjects for special occasions.
  V. Discourses in the College of Maynooth.

In the four sermons, viz., iv., vi., xviñ., xix., in this collection, preached in Rome, in the church of Gesù e Maria, in the Corso, during the winter of 1831-1832, and translated into Italian by the

Abbate de Luca, now Cardinal Bishop of Palestrina, as well as in other discourses, the Archbishop vigorously combats the folly of those persons who, while they love religion in its barren form, abhor its practical effects; who, pretending to be followers of a crucified Saviour, ridicule the austerity and mortification inculcated by His religion; and while they glory in manifesting their belief in the principles of a religion inculcating the abandonment of the pleasures of the world, and the mortification of the unruly passions, fail not to represent as superstitious the laws of fasting, abstinence, and self-abnegation.

In the nineteenth discourse the Archbishop, considering the varied and conflicting fortunes of the "Eternal City," and taking a comprehensive view of the designs of the Almighty with respect to the Church of Rome, the parent and teacher of all other churches, conclusively establishes the necessity of a divinely ordained bond of Catholic union in the person of the Sovereign Pontiff, on which is founded the uniform, mutual, and universal communion of the members of the Church of Christ, and from which may legitimately be deduced the doctrine that the Roman Pontiffs, like the Catholic Church, are the unerring expounders of the dogmatical and moral truths of divine revelation.

In the following interesting passage, extracted from an unpublished discourse, delivered on the occasion of announcing the great jubilee granted by Pope Leo XII., in the year 1826, to the universal Church, we find the prerogatives of the successors of St. Peter urged by the Archbishop with his accustomed vigour: "Is this the voice of Peter which has just reached our ears? Has the supreme Pastor, to whom Christ committed the care of His fold, condescended to speak to this little and distant portion of his flock? Yes, Peter has spoken through the mouth of Leo, and it is to us a consolation that, after the lapse of fourteen hundred years, we can still repeat the language of the Fathers of the Council of Chalcedon, who, on hearing the letter that was addressed to them by the first and greatest of the Leos, unanimously exclaimed: 'Peter has spoken through the mouth of Leo, and his authority still lives in the person of his successor.' It is to us a consolation that notwithstanding the number of the flock of Peter which the wolf has snatched or scattered, we still recognise and hear the voice of the good shepherd, who, in the language of the Redeemer, 'knoweth His own sheep, and inviteth the rest to place themselves in the unity of the same fold under the guidance of one Pastor.' What a source of joy and triumph that we constitute a portion of that sacred edifice whose foundation was laid by divine Wisdom on a rock, which has neither yielded to the decay of time nor the violence of the tempest, but has stood a striking attestation of the truth of Christ's promises, equally unshaken by the waves that are beating against its foundation and the winds that are rushing against its summit, mocking the successive tides of error that are breaking in from around its base, and standing a majestic monument of the Omnipotence that has sustained it. Bound, as many of us have been, in the chains of sin, and excluded from the favour of the Almighty, how ought we not to rejoice that Peter, to whom Christ gave the power of loosing sins, as well as the keys of the kingdom of heaven, when in the person of his successor He offers to strike off the fetters in which we have been bound, and to unlock the portals of heaven for our admission. Do I dwell on the prerogatives of the Roman Pontiff for the purpose of controversy? If by controversy is meant the desire of irritating, far be from me the unhallowed wish. No; from the chair of truth no sound but that of genuine charity should go forth; and the Church is a place in which a truce ought to be given to the passions of mankind. No; but I mention them, rather for the purpose of healing than of fomenting irritation, and of removing that ignorance under which many, and some of them Catholics, have laboured. Often have I preached here, and I have not obtruded the subject of controversy. But being about to commence a series of instructions on the recommendation of this letter, and to set on foot a practice which derives its sanction from Rome, what is more natural, and perhaps for some more necessary, than that I should explore the purity of that channel through which Christ's doctrine is transmitted, and show that it is immediately connected with that divine source which pours forth the living waters. This is the reason why I dwell upon this topic. To answer the secret interrogatories of those who may ask: Who is this Leo, or for what purpose does he address his instructions to this distant country? He is the living representative of him whom Christ thus addressed after the glorious confession of His Divinity: 'Blessed art thou, Simon Bar-Jona, because flesh and blood hath not revealed it to thee, but My Father who is in heaven. And I say to thee that thou art Peter, and upon this rock I will build My Church, and the gates of hell shall not prevail against it.'[1] He is the successor of him to whom Christ the Sovereign Truth thus solemnly declared: 'And I will give to thee the keys of the kingdom of heaven: and whatsoever thou shalt bind upon earth, it shall be bound also in heaven: and whatsoever thou shalt loose on earth, it shall be loosed also in heaven.'[2] He is the successor of him, the ardour of whose love Christ, having tried by the repeated interrogatory of Peter, 'Dost thou love me?' rewarded by the ample commission of feeding His whole flock: 'Feed my lambs, feed my sheep:' words which embrace the entire of His fold within his jurisdiction. Had these texts not been clearly recorded in the divine Scriptures, I must confess that I should not feel surprised that those who pretend to follow its exclusive guidance

---

[1] S. Matt. xvi.      [2] S. Matt. *ibid*.

should controvert the supremacy of the Roman Pontiff. But that those, who read this language in the Bible, should persist in rejecting such evidence speaks a humiliating, and, I will add, an instructive lesson of the strong force of early prejudice. To illustrate this observation, let anyone forget for a moment the bias of his youth, and take up the book in which he finds the same individual uniformly preferred to the rest of the Apostles. One time called the rock on which the Church was to be erected, another time invested with the keys of the kingdom of heaven, and again appointed to feed not only the lambs but the sheep, would it not be his natural conclusion that either there was no significancy in language or that Peter was constituted the chief Pastor of the Church? The more the meaning of those texts is unfolded the more the first impression which they convey is confirmed. In one place the Church is characterised as an edifice which the powers of hell cannot shake, because St. Peter is its solid and immovable foundation. To him are also given the keys of the kingdom of heaven; and are you ignorant that in the customs of every country the delivery of the keys is the emblem of the amplest authority? The keys were formerly a part of the marriage ceremony to denote that the husband, by giving the keys to his bride, shared with her the dominion of his household. When a city is surrendered to a conqueror, the most significant symbol by which his power is recognised is to deliver to him the keys; and we know that when his Majesty visited this kingdom his jurisdiction was acknowledged by the ceremony of receiving from the chief the keys of the gate of his capital. Giving the keys to Peter was a metaphorical mode of language, it is true; but it was a metaphor always expressive of supreme authority, and therefore, unless it be in our power to torture language out of its ordinary meaning, the text which is preserved in the Bible of Christ, promising to Peter the keys of the kingdom of heaven, will attest to the end of time his supreme jurisdiction.

"Christ was not content to call him the rock on which His Church was to repose, nor to promise him the keys of the kingdom of heaven; but, as if to put his power beyond the possibility of cavil, He tells him, after His resurrection, to feed His lambs and to feed His sheep. What is the meaning of these words? It is hardly necessary to explain to you that in the whole compass of human language there are none so expressive of absolute dominion. When Christ wishes to characterise His own dominion over His disciples, He expresses it by the image of a good shepherd who leadeth forth his sheep, adding that the sheep follow him because they know his voice. Now, this office of Supreme Pastor He transferred upon Peter, and if we wish to be ranked among the sheep we must hear his voice and follow him. The word is expressive not only of absolute sway, but likewise implies the meek and provident care which characterises the office of shepherd, to keep his flock from the noxious, and to lead them to the most wholesome pastures. It was the word by which kings were formerly designated; and it is remarkable that when the first of profane writers wished to extol the power of him who was appointed the chief of the assembled forces of Greece, the most complimentary epithet he chose was that of pastor of his people.

"Again, if you read over the Gospels with attention, you find Peter appearing first on every occasion; of all the Apostles, he is the first to confess the faith, as well as the first to express his obligations of love. Peter was the first of the Apostles to whom Christ appeared after His resurrection, as he was the first to bear testimony to this fact before the people. We find him first, when there was question of electing an Apostle in the place of Judas; the first, who confirmed the faith by a miracle; the first, to convert the Jews; the first, in receiving the Gentiles, in the person of Cornelius; in short, the individual who represents on all occasions the college of the Apostles. 'Is the Church,' says the holy Francis of Sales, 'likened unto an edifice? Peter is constituted its foundation. Will you represent it under the figure of a family? You behold the Redeemer paying the tribute as its head, and after Him comes Peter as His representative. Is the Church called a bark? Peter is the pilot, and it is our Saviour who instructs him. Is the doctrine by which we are called from the gulf of sin represented by a fisher's net? It is Peter who casts it; it is Peter who draws it; the other disciples lend their aid, but it is Peter who presents the fishes to our Redeemer. Is the Church represented by an embassy? Peter is at its head. Do you prefer the figure of a kingdom? Peter carries the keys. In fine, if it is shadowed under the symbol of a flock and a fold, Peter is their shepherd and universal pastor under Jesus Christ.'"

The panegyric of St. Patrick was also delivered in Rome, in the Church of St. Isidore Agricola, now, as then, served by the Irish Fathers of the Order of the glorious St. Francis of Assisi.

The Discourses delivered at the National Synod of Thurles, in 1850, and at the Provincial Synods of Tuam, in 1854 and 1858, as well as the Sermons on Education—a theme with which the Archbishop's literary labours may be said to have commenced and ended—a burning question, we may add, still unsolved, owing more to Irish servility and corruption than to British bigotry and intolerance, cannot fail to attract attention.

On the colonisation of distant lands by Irishmen, now more than ever warmly advocated by friends and foes of the Celtic race, the Archbishop's opinion forcibly urged in Discourse xxvii. is likely to be variously appreciated when considered from different points of view.

The Ecclesiastics to whom the four last Discourses were addressed at the close of the academical years of 1822, 1823, 1824, 1825, in the College of Maynooth, have in a great measure disappeared from the ranks of the Irish Clergy for a better and more lasting inheritance; still the salutary admonitions they contain, and the principles they inculcate, cannot but secure for them a share of favourable attention.

# CONTENTS.

| NO. | | PAGE |
|---|---|---|
| | Preface | v |
| I. | Importance of Salvation | 1 |
| II. | Mortal Sin | 15 |
| III. | The danger and folly of the hope of a Death-bed Repentance | 25 |
| IV. | On Death | 37 |
| V. | On Purgatory | 50 |
| VI. | On Penance | 60 |
| VII. | The Sacrament of Penance | 75 |
| VIII. | On Pride | 86 |
| IX. | Prosperity: its dangers | 97 |
| X. | On the Love of God | 107 |
| XI. | Christmas Day | 118 |
| XII. | On the Passion of Our Lord | 130 |
| XIII. | St. Patrick's Day | 148 |
| XIV. | Pentecost Sunday | 170 |
| XV. | The Assumption of the Blessed Virgin | 180 |
| XVI. | All Saints | 192 |
| XVII. | The General Judgment | 207 |
| XVIII. | Preaching of St. John the Baptist | 222 |
| XIX. | The Reprobation of the Jews | 234 |
| XX. | On False Prophets | 254 |

# CONTENTS.

| NO. | | PAGE |
|---|---|---|
| XXI. | On Education | 265 |
| XXII. | Charity Sermon for Children | 283 |
| XXIII. | Charity Sermon for Widows and Orphans | 296 |
| XXIV. | Charity Sermon for Female Penitents | 307 |
| XXV. | Laying the Foundation Stone of a Church | 317 |
| XXVI. | The Dedication of a Church | 324 |
| XXVII. | The Dedication of a Church | 341 |
| XXVIII. | The Consecration of a Church | 358 |
| XXIX. | The Consecration of a Bishop | 374 |
| XXX. | The Profession of a Nun | 395 |
| XXXI. | The Synod of Thurles (1850) | 408 |
| XXXII. | The Opening of the Tuam Synod (1854) | 420 |
| XXXIII. | Tuam Synod (1858) | 434 |
| XXXIV. | Funeral Oration on the Most Rev. Dr. Cantwell, Bishop of Meath | 446 |
| XXXV. | Address to the Theological Students of the College of Maynooth, 1822 | 455 |
| XXXVI. | Address to the Theological Students of the College of Maynooth, 1823 | 471 |
| XXXVII. | Address to the Theological Students of the College of Maynooth, 1824 | 487 |
| XXXVIII. | Address to the Theological Students of the College of Maynooth, 1825 | 503 |

# SERMONS AND DISCOURSES.

## IMPORTANCE OF SALVATION.

"Seek first the kingdom of God and His justice, and all these things shall be added unto you."—LUKE xii., 31.

To dissipate those cares which, unfortunately, interfere with man's salvation, and to direct his exclusive attention to that end for which he was created, was the object of the Redeemer in addressing to His disciples the foregoing language. By unfolding to their view the wonderful providence of the Almighty over the animal and vegetable creation, even to the lilies of the field, He rebukes their unnecessary concern for the provision of this world, and reminds them of that heavenly kingdom to which they should continually aspire. Were we to take a minute and extensive survey over the entire range of society, it would seem that to provide a suitable establishment in this world were man's first duty, and that his salvation were a matter of subordinate importance. Although early instructed in the truths of religion, though taught to lisp even from his infancy, that to know and love and serve God on earth, and afterwards to enjoy Him in heaven, is the whole end of man, he soon forgets the end of his creation in the business or pleasures of the world, content to exchange for its enjoyments his claims to a divine inheritance. Were he destined for no higher felicity, such conduct might be pardonable. Were no adequate reward proposed to stimulate him to exertion, he might, perhaps, not be unreasonable in reposing in the enjoyments of life. Were not irretrievable misery the consequence of not attaining the happiness for which he was created, his folly might still excite less surprise and awaken less commiseration. But, through an erroneous estimate of happiness, to forfeit a kingdom, not of earth, but of heaven, and to incur, by the forfeiture of that kingdom, never-ending misery, is an instance of human blindness such as only a Man-God could sufficiently deplore. And are we really promised a kingdom as the reward of our fidelity? Yes; Christ solemnly assures us of this truth while He adds after the words quoted in my text: "Fear not, flock; for it hath pleased your Father to give you a kingdom." This is the kingdom for which we were all created and which we must all attain, or be eternally miserable; this is the one thing necessary, without which the possession of the whole world would be utterly unprofitable. To give, then, a subject which is the nearest to the most important interests of your souls, all that attention it requires, I shall first explain the importance, or rather the necessity, of salvation, and then point out the means by which it is attainable.

Let each one in this congregation put himself the question: What is the constant occupation of his life? and the answer of all will be, however they may stray in its pursuit, that it is a continual struggle for the attainment of happiness. This is the secret spring of all his desires. It accompanies him by day; it intrudes itself by night; it mixes with every business and amusement of his life, and is so intimately intertwined with his entire nature, that to be divested of the desire of happiness, he must cease to enjoy existence. Hence we value any object in proportion as it satisfies this irresistible propensity of our hearts; and we avoid with an instinctive sensibility whatever could diminish that enjoyment which is the study of our lives. To exhort you, therefore, to the general pursuit of your own happiness, or, in other words, your own interest, would be a superfluous labour, since there is none among you who is not prompted to it by the active consciousness of his own mind—a principle far more irresistible than any exhortation. But as, unfortunately, there are many who centre that happiness where it is not be found, it is the duty of the christian preacher to correct their erroneous notions and recall their wandering thoughts to the only object of their creation. Man's happiness, then, can never be consummated but by the enjoyment of his God, and nothing less than God Himself can satisfy the immensity of his desires. For this truth, too, I will appeal to the conviction of your own bosoms. Was there ever one to whom the widest range of enjoyment was laid open, that yet met an object that could fill the vast capacity of his soul? No. Is he ambitious of honours? The attainment of the desired object of his wishes only gives fresh impulse to his ambition; and instead of indulging that happy repose for which he panted, he is tempted to advance, and at every step his prospects expand with his elevation. Is he desirous of riches? They are esteemed by few but in as far as they are instruments of ambition or of pleasure. And should he place that happiness in the indulgence of sense, the melancholy experience of the voluptuary will attest that pleasure, instead of appeasing, has only irritated the vehemence of his passions, which grow more importunate by indulgence, until his feeble frame, which he has converted into an instrument of happiness, falls a victim to the intensity of a desire, which, as it was not destined to satisfy, it was unable to sustain. Solomon was the man on whom the treasures of nature seem to have been bestowed in greatest profusion; yet what did he find but vanity and vexation of spirit. If such were the feelings of Solomon, the richest of the sons of men in wealth and knowledge, does it not seem to be an awful warning to those who place their happiness in the world? What a melancholy object thus to contemplate the most favoured votaries of the world, toiling from infancy to manhood, and from manhood to old age, treausring up disappointment as the reward of their labours; and, instead of departing in peace, as if they attained their object, sinking into the grave, and dragging with them the long and heavy chain of hopes frustrated, proving the truth of the language of St. Augustine: "We were created for Thee, O Lord, and our hearts cannot rest until they rest in Thee." Here, then, is the term of our repose, the enjoyment of our God; and whatever has not a reference to that object, instead of being a blessing, is the greatest curse with which man can be afflicted. Hence the awful importance of the words of our Redeemer: "What profiteth a man if he gain the whole world and lose his own soul; or what can a man give in exchange for his soul?"[1] In this short sentence of our Divine Redeemer we read the most interesting lesson that was ever addressed to man —the indispensable necessity of salvation. Yes; the indispensable necessity; because no other word could convey a sufficient idea of the interest which our salvation involves. A thing may be important, and yet not indispensable. Thus a man might be benefited by such an important station in life; yet it is not absolutely necessary. He might derive important advantages from the aid of friends; but he can absolutely dispense with

[1] S. Matt. xvi. 26.

their assistance. Nothing, in fine, that is transitory can be absolutely necessary; and hence honours, friends, riches, stations, are all only relative necessities, the creatures of an hour, and not of absolute necessity, because life itself must pass away. But salvation is not only important, but absolutely necessary, since it embraces everything that man can hope; and since, by forfeiting that salvation, nought is left him but the dreadful alternative of misery unutterable in its endurance, interminable in its continuance, and aggravated through all eternity by the horrors of despair. This is the reason why Jesus Christ, whose soul calmly contemplated those fleeting vanities that engage the attention of man, and surveyed that immeasurable felicity which alone is worthy of the immensity of our desires, broke out into this significant language : " What profiteth it a man if he gain the whole world and lose his own soul?" Had we the same strong perceptions of the illusions of life and of the happiness of eternity which our Redeemer had, we should practically feel the justness of the sentence, and, instead of courting those objects, of which the possession might divert us from our destination, we should tremble for the danger to which we might be exposed. Every other obligation would then yield to the imperative commands of this one thing necessary. Hence, honours, pleasures, friends, would be cheerfully sacrificed were they to interfere with that one thing necessary, which man, in charity to himself, can never consent to sacrifice, and which he cannot forfeit without plunging himself into misery, which all the sympathy of friends cannot mitigate, and all the honours and pleasures of life cannot retrieve. Is there anyone who, after the longest and most prosperous life, could reflect without shuddering on the prospect of eternal torments ; or is there a human being who would consent to enjoy for a short period the most extensive share of wealth or power that ever fell to the lot of mortal, and then to be hurled into a fire kindled before his view, with a certainty that it never was to be extinguished? Such a spectacle would appal the strongest heart, and subdue the most violent ambition.

As far as experience can confirm them, the words of our Saviour are attested by the experience of mankind. Many of those who have been most successful in securing the possessions of the world confessed their folly at their death; and, in their unavailing repentance, often exhibited the horrors of their reprobation. You have already heard the language of Solomon, who, while he seems to have reached the goal beyond which human prosperity could never extend, stands likewise an awful monument of its vanity and its danger. We have other examples in the inspired writings, of which I shall content myself with two awful instances. The one of Herod Agrippa, who was raised to the throne of Jerusalem through the favour of the Roman emperors, and who scrupled not to sacrifice the interests of religion and the dictates of his conscience to those to whom he owed his elevation. But the vengeance of heaven soon overtook him in his career. For the Scripture assures us that, having arrogated to himself the honour which he owed to the Almighty, he was struck by the angel of the Lord at the moment that he was saluted by the acclamations of the people, and eaten up with worms—a sad and terrible end of one who had exchanged his soul for the possession of the world. Another example, still more striking, is exhibited in the fate of Antiochus, King of Syria, whose wishes were all anticipated by his obsequious courtiers, and who possessed every object that could seem to confer happiness on man. Yet, amidst this apparent prosperity, and in the very frenzy of his triumphs, the hand of God falls heavy upon him; and in the midst of a disease too loathsome for utterance, and torture too excruciating for conception, he pines out his accursed spirit in alternate paroxysms of blasphemy and despair. "Into how much tribulation am I come, and into what floods of sorrow wherein now I am: I that was pleasant and beloved in my power."[1]

But it may be said that the dangers of kings and the great ones of the earth are too remote to interfere with your salvation. I have adduced them as the most striking exemplifications of the words of Jesus Christ: "What doth it profit a man if he gain the whole world and lose his own soul." For if all must acknowledge, on a review of their lives, that the glory and opulence which these men enjoyed were but a poor compensation for the miserable end to which they conducted them, what possible apology can be offered by any other mortal in bartering for a still more trifling price the interests of his salvation? What other necessity can be pleaded comparable to that of his soul? You may have difficulties to encounter peculiar to the situation in which you are placed. Every station, I acknowledge, has its dangers; and if wealth exposes its votaries to the indulgence of pride and sensuality, poverty is subject to the temptations of envy and injustice. Whatever your station may be, you will doubtless plead the necessity of providing for its wants, and making a suitable establishment for your children. Yes; but if, in making such a provision, you sacrifice your soul, who can remunerate you for a loss which the world itself could not redeem? Be not, then, deceived; there is no other necessity but that of salvation. Whatever other duty, whatever other connection, might threaten to come in contact with this paramount obligation must be instantly sacrificed, though the consequence should be the loss of fortune, friends, parents, nay, of life itself. Be not startled; it is the doctrine of Jesus Christ that I preach. "He that

[1] 1 Mach. vi. 11.

loveth father or mother more than me is not worthy of me; and he that loveth son or daughter more than me is not worthy of me. And he that taketh not up his cross and followeth me is not worthy of me. He that findeth his life shall lose it, and he that shall lose his life shall find it."[1] It is not, therefore, by mere inference that we conclude that every tie which could endanger salvation must be rent asunder. No, it is the language of the Redeemer Himself, who thus continues: "Do not think that I came to send peace upon earth. I came not to send peace but the sword. For I came to set a man at variance against his father, and the daughter against her mother, and the daughter-in-law against her mother-in-law."[2] Within the range of duties and connections in which you may be engaged, are there any duties that come nearer to your bosoms, or any connections that are so strongly entwined around your heart, as those domestic ones mentioned in the Gospel? Yet to attain the one thing necessary we must be divorced from those objects, if that one thing cannot be obtained without such a separation. Nay, He goes further and insists that we must not only cut off the connections of those who are dear, but even amputate our own members should they become dangerous to our souls. "And if thy right eye scandalise thee, pluck it out and cast it from thee: for it is expedient for thee that one of thy members should perish rather than thy whole body be cast into hell. And if thy right hand scandalise thee, cut it off and cast it from thee: for it is expedient for thee that one of thy members should perish rather than thy whole body go into hell."[3] But why speak of the dear and tender ties of kindred, or the nearer connection of the members of our own frame, which must be severed, when life itself must be sacrificed to the salvation of our souls? "And fear ye not them that kill the body, and

[1] S. Matt. x. 37, 38, 39.  [2] S. Matt. x. 34, 35.  [3] S. Matt. v. 29, 30.

are not able to kill the soul; but rather fear him that can destroy both soul and body into hell." [1]

The prospect of death or torture, it is true, is calculated to make us tremble; but had we a lively sense of the eternal interest of our souls, the fear of death and torments would give way to the overwhelming apprehension of losing the kingdom of heaven. Hence St. Paul, to whose vision was unfolded a glimpse of those mysteries of bliss which it is not given to human tongue to utter, breaks out into this ardent and rapturous expression of divine love: "Who then shall separate us from the love of Christ? shall tribulation, or distress, or famine, or nakedness, or persecution, or the sword?" [2] What an astonishing impression of the activity of divine love! The apostle represents to himself whatever is most terrible in human suffering, and supposes himself to be its victim. Though devoured by hunger, burning with thirst, and shivering with nakedness, the object of persecution and the sport of every element, in short, though assailed by all the terrors of this world and the other, he beholds, undismayed, their combined hostility, and exclaims, "Who shall separate us from the love of Christ?" Nay, more, full of confidence in the grace of God, he proceeds: "For *I am sure* that neither death, nor life, nor angels, nor principalities, nor powers, nor things present, nor things to come, nor might, nor height, nor depth, nor any other creature, shall be able to separate us from the love of God, which is in Christ Jesus our Lord." [3]

If you are deeply impressed with the necessity of salvation, you must be equally so to know the means by which so great a blessing may be secured. Were an enterprising prince or leader to propose to his followers the possession of a flourishing kingdom as the reward of their fidelity, with what ardour would not

[1] S. Mat. x., 28.   [2] Rom. viii., 35.   [3] Rom. viii., 38, 39.

numbers throng around his standard? With what impatience would they not learn the conditions of their service, and what peril and fatigue would they not cheerfully encounter to obtain their promised reward? And all this labour is cheerfully undergone, even with the chance of a disappointment, to obtain a prize insecure in its possession, and transient in its duration. Yet to obtain a kingdom of such value as neither eye hath seen, nor ear hath heard, nor hath it entered into the heart of man to conceive, how few are willing to labour, though none that seriously labour shall be disappointed? Unlike those who combated in the ancient games, of whom one only received the prize, all who run in the Christian race may be rewarded. "Yet they refrained from all things," as the Apostle says, "though they laboured only for a corruptible crown;" and shall not we imitate their example who labour for "an incorruptible one?"[1] So true is the language of Scripture, that "the children of this world are wiser in their generation than the children of light."[2] Son of man, how long will you love vanity? or how long will you continue to prefer the perishable interests of this world to those of your immortal soul? Leave, therefore, the subordinate care of those things which Christ assures us will be added unto you, and seek first the kingdom of God and His justice—the kingdom of God as the end, and His justice as the means by which you must arrive at its possession. If, therefore, you are truly solicitous for your salvation, you must practise this justice which is commanded you by Christ, and fulfil the precepts of the law. There is no other road to heaven. When a young man addressed himself to our Redeemer to learn what he should do to enter into life, Christ replied: "If you wish to enter into life, keep the Commandments."[3] Whoever wishes to share in the re-

---

[1] 1 Cor. ix. 25.   [2] S. Luke, xvi. 8.   [3] S. Matt. xix. 17.

wards proposed by his leader to the companions of his toils and victories must first secure them by his fidelity in his service. Now we are soldiers of Jesus Christ, and therefore if we disobey His commands or desert His standard, we cannot hope to participate in the glory of His kingdom. Is not this the natural relation between a general and his soldiers, that while he who fights is entitled to the rewards of victory, the deserter is not only excluded but also consigned to punishment? Now, the life of man is compared to a warfare in Scripture. The apostle exhorts us to "labour as good soldiers of Jesus Christ."[1] This labour he qualifies by the name of a contest, and gives the name of "a crown of justice" to the reward. As our fidelity, or negligence, then, in the service of Christ is to be the measure of our reward or punishment, is it not incumbent upon us to have His commandments continually before our eyes; Follow, therefore, the precept which Moses thus addressed to the Hebrew people: "Hear, O Israel, the Lord our God is one Lord. Thou shalt love the Lord thy God with thy whole heart, and with thy whole soul, and with thy whole strength. And these words which I command thee this day, shall be in thy heart; and thou shalt tell them to thy children, and thou shalt meditate on them sitting in thy house and walking on thy journey, sleeping and rising. And thou shalt bind them as a sign on thy hand, and they shall be and shall move between thy eyes."[2] Yes, let them move before your eyes, not like a stationary and inanimate object which may not excite the senses, but like a living object, moving wherever you turn, and still arresting your attention. Such must be your diligent study of the law, if you desire to be saved.

Tell me not that it is only the religious or the recluse that are capable of such unremitting application to the

[1] 2 Tim. ii. 3; iv. 8.   [2] Deut. vi. 4, 5, 6, 7, 8.

law. It was promulgated not for the Levites alone but also for the entire body of the Israelites, and if we pretend that we are more freed from the obligation of loving God than the Jews, we misunderstand the precepts and become a reproach to the profession of our religion. Do not tell me that it is not in the nature of man to bestow such incessant and undistracted attention on the study of the law. The words which I have quoted prove its practicability. If God commands obedience to His law, He commands them also to treasure it up in their hearts. "And these words which I command thee this day shall be in thy heart." Now, whatever is seated in the heart and dear to our affections requires no effort to recall it to our attention. It obtrudes itself unsought, it is entertained with pleasure and parted with with regret, and when we seem least conscious of its influence it gives a silent but a strong impulse to the whole current of our thoughts and actions. Was it ever necessary to exhort a tender and a pious mother to be solicitous for the safety of her offspring? Is it necessary to exhort a man to a thrifty prudence who devotes his mind to the accumulation of a fortune? No, wherever our treasure is thither the affections of the heart are invariably attracted. If, therefore, your treasure is in heaven there your thoughts will be habitually directed, without deranging the ordinary occupations of your life.

Now the kingdom of God is compared unto a treasure hidden in a field, which a man having found, he goes and sells all that he has and purchases the field.[1] And again it is likened to a pearl of great value, discovered by a merchant, who sold all his possessions to purchase the precious treasure. Think you did they find it painful to be constantly turning their attention to the object of their hope, or did they shrink from the difficulties

[1] S. Matt. xiii. 44.

they would encounter in its accomplishment. No, it was this anxious attention that crowned their efforts with success, and alleviated the toil which might have been otherwise unsupportable. In like manner, I tell you that unless you look upon the kingdom of heaven as your treasure you will never come to its possession, because you will not exert the vigilance by which so great a treasure may be secured. Without this vigilance you will be surprised into frequent violations of the commandments, nor will you perform those good works by which St. Peter exhorts us to make our election sure.

Since, then, you are doubtless impressed with a full sense of the importance of salvation, and since the misfortune of Christians in neglecting this only concern is owing less to ignorance than to inattention, let me exhort you as you value the dearest interests of your soul to awaken at length to the dangers with which you are surrounded. Had you any security that your life would be prolonged to a certain period, and that you would be favoured with the grace of repentance, your confidence might be less censurable. But when, instead of such an assurance, we know that the hour of death is doubtful, I have not language to convey my feelings of the folly of that man who trusts the only affair for which he was created to so awful an uncertainty. "Watch ye therefore because you know not what hour your Lord will come. But this know ye, that if the good man of the house knew at what hour the thief would come he would certainly watch, and would not suffer his house to be broken. Who, thinkest thou, is a faithful and wise servant whom his Lord hath appointed over his family to give them meat in season? Blessed is that servant whom when his Lord shall come He shall find so doing. Amen, I say to you, he shall place him over all his goods. But if that evil servant shall say my Lord is long a-coming, and shall begin to strike his fellow-servants, and shall eat and drink with drunkards, the Lord of that servant shall come in a day that he hopeth not and at an hour that he knoweth not, and shall separate him and appoint his portion with the hypocrites; there shall be weeping and gnashing of teeth."[1]

If there are any among you who, like the wicked servant, might have thought your Master tardy in coming, and under this false security might have forgotten your obligations, I beseech you to profit of his awful punishment. Now, at least, your Lord is coming. This is the day on which the Church announces His coming in the flesh to prepare us for His last coming, and on which the voice of an inspired Apostle mingles in the noise of a falling world, to awaken us from the slumbers of sin and death and arouse us to repentance. Now is the hour, he says, to rise from sleep. Yes, my dearly beloved, it is the hour; the kingdom of God is at hand, the axe is now laid to the root. The patience of God has waited long that the tree might bring forth fruit. But if it is barren, after being so often watered with the dews of heaven, its end must be to be cut down and cast into the fire. May God avert this dire calamity. With the same Apostle, I hope better things. You will not, I trust, suffer the approaching season to pass away without bringing forth fruit worthy of penance. Perhaps it is the last season that the judgment of Jesus Christ might be announced to you. And that ere it returns again you should hear the tremendous reality of that judgment of which but a feeble echo is conveyed in the mysteries of this day. And will you stake your eternal happiness for some precarious advantage of which you may be deprived before the expiration of another year? Go, then, and throw yourselves at the feet of your Redeemer, while He visits you in mercy,

[1] S. Matt. xxiv. 42-51.

and efface your sins by a timely repentance, that when He comes, in the terrors of His justice, He may fix your portion with the blessed servant who is always awaiting the coming of his Lord. Amen.

---

## MORTAL SIN.

*"But of the tree of knowledge of good and evil thou shalt not eat: For in what day soever thou shalt eat of it thou shalt die the death."*—GEN. ii. 17.

SUCH is the precept by which God wished to prove the fidelity of Adam, and such the punishment which He denounced against the infraction of His law. To impress upon your mind an idea of mortal sin, I wish to lead you back to its first origin, and point out from the inspired writing its nature and its punishment. From the language of my text you perceive that sin is nothing less than a violation of God's commands, and a disobedience to His authority; and that death is the lot of all who are guilty of such disobedience. Hence, though the name of mortal sin may strike us with little horror, it is the greatest evil with which man was ever afflicted. To convince you of this truth, which it is most important for you to study, I shall endeavour in this discourse to lay open the enormity of mortal sin, as well from the nature of the guilt which it involves as the misery which is its consequence, in order to stir up your vigilance against the approaches of a monster whose contact is death, and whose punishment is eternal fire.

To convince you of the guilt involved in mortal sin only meditate on the majesty of Him who is offended, contrasted with the littleness of the individual who offers Him the injury. It is a principle founded on reason, and recognised by the laws of every society, that every personal injury borrows fresh aggravation from the dignity of the individual against whom it is directed. Thus an offence offered to an equal becomes more heinous if a superior is insulted; and if the majesty of the throne is violated the culprit is doomed to expiate the offence with his blood. Transferring, then, this principle of sound and incontestible argument to the present subject, how enormous must be the malice of an offence committed by a slave against his master, a subject against his king, a reptile of the earth against the majesty of heaven, a man against his God. If an act of treason to a temporal monarch is punished with instant death, how inconceivable must be the malignity of that treason with which the creature of a moment assails his Eternal Creator, and dares, as he is borne down the tide of time, to fling his impotent but blaspheming defiance against the eternal and immovable throne of the Almighty, who, in the language of the Prophet, "stood and measured the earth, whose brightness is as the light, and whose glory covers the heavens, who in His anger treadeth the earth under foot, and in His wrath will astonish the nations. Before whom the deep put forth its voice, and the great body of the waters passed away: at whose sight the nations melted, and the hills of the world were bowed down beneath the journeys of His eternity."[1]

Be astonished, O ye heavens! at the audacity of man, who presumes by an act of disobedience to insult that King before whom the pillars of heaven tremble. No; there cannot be exaggeration in describing the magnitude of an offence which is infinite, and which literally attempts to dethrone the Almighty, and annihilate His

[1] Habacuc iii.

power. In every deliberate crime of which the sinner is guilty there is a comparison formed in his mind between two objects—the friendship of God and the indulgence of his lawless desire—and an unnatural preference given to the object of his passion. By such an election he freely consents to forfeit the favour of his God, and imitates the perfidy of the Jews, who consented to crucify Jesus, and release the murderous Barabbas. Hence, while he dishonours God by violating his law, he entertains a secret but positive hatred to the Divine Majesty. You may startle at such an assertion, and imagine that the most malignant disposition could not entertain feelings so diabolical. But let the sinner sound the depths of his own heart, and explore its dark recesses, and he will discover the feelings of hatred against God lurking in its corruption. In disobeying the law of God, he feels an inward mutiny against the rigour of the authority that checks him, and, of course, a desire to be relieved from its severity. His impatience of restraint makes him wish that there was neither immortality to be hoped nor punishment to be dreaded; and since the existence of another life, and its rewards and punishments, are the results of God's counsels, one cannot wish to abolish the existence of the one without impeaching the wisdom of the other; and since the impeachment of God's wisdom would be equivalent to a denial of the divinity, you behold how the sinner's hatred of God breathes the blasphemous desire of annihilating His existence. Call not, then, the habitual violation of God's law by the name of human weakness. No, it involves more daring guilt. It hurls defiance against heaven itself, and as far as the impotent will of man could consummate the deed, it would depose from His throne the sovereign majesty of the Almighty. Hence, sinners are characterised in Scripture by the name of enemies of God. "With the arm of Thy strength Thou hast scattered Thy enemies."[1] "For behold Thy enemies, O Lord! for behold Thy enemies shall perish, and all the workers of iniquity shall be scattered."[2] "A fire shall go before Him, and shall burn His enemies round about."[3] "Therefore, saith the Lord the God of Hosts, the Mighty One of Israel: Ah! I will comfort Myself over My adversaries, and I will be avenged of My enemies."[4] These and similar epithets with which sinners are characterised in Scripture reveal to us the hostile dispositions which animate those who despise the precepts of their God. Mortal sin comprehends, therefore, whatever there is of guilt in disobedience, aggravated by every circumstance of enormity which can be conceived in the immeasurable distance between God and man.

But it is not disobedience alone to a superior of infinite power that constitutes its malice, but likewise ingratitude to the best of benefactors. The omnipotence of God should awe us into reverence, His infinite goodness should melt us into love. But mortal sin is as insensible to the kind attractions of gratitude as it is deaf to the impressions of terror. As our Creator, God has the strongest claims on our duty, and those claims are still strengthened by the exhaustless mercies of redemption. Those claims are all forgotten, and the sinner not only lifts his arm against that God who brought him into existence, but what is more, against that God who rescued him from the punishment to which his first disobedience had consigned him. Was there indignity or ingratitude ever like unto that of the Christian, not only insulting the unspeakable majesty of God, but insulting the mercy which expiated that offence, and, in the language of St. Paul, "Crucifying again

---

[1] Ps. lxxxviii. 11. [2] Ps. xci. 10. [3] Ps. xcvi. 3. [4] Isai. i. 24.

Christ unto himself, trampling on His blood, and making a mockery of Him?"[1]. Such prevarication, which in every Christian is a grievous transgression, must be deepened in its enormity in proportion to the abundance of his lights and the profusion of his graces. And hence to you, who have been particularly favoured by the Almighty, and so often refreshed by the blood of His only Son, how justly might the Redeemer address Himself: "If my enemy had reviled me, I would verily have borne with it; but thou, a man of one mind, my guide and my familiar, who didst take sweetmeats together with me."[2] That you should transgress His commands, and aggravate your disobedience by the most hardened ingratitude is a crime for which language affords no term to express its enormity. Be not, then, surprised if the inspired writers pour out the most vehement denunciations against those who are guilty of mortal sin, declaring that "Death and bloodshed, strife, and sword, oppressions, famine, and afflictions, and scourges are created for the wicked."[3] And again, "that God shall rain snares upon sinners, and that fire and brimstone and storms of winds shall be the portion of their cup;"[4] that "He shall scoff at a sinner when He sees his day of destruction come on,"[5] and that "the sword of sinners shall turn into their hearts;"[6] that "the arms of sinners shall be crushed and broken, and they shall wither and dry up like hay from the face of the earth; that the day of the Lord shall come, a cruel day, and full of indignation, wrath, and fury, to make desolate the earth, and to crush in pieces the sinners within her."[7] Never would a merciful God have dictated to his prophets such tremendous threats against sinners if sin was only an act of weakness, and if it did not involve the most deliberate

[1] Heb. vi. 6. [2] Ps. liv. 13, 14, 15. [3] Eccl. xl. 9, 10. [4] Ps. x. 7.
[5] Ps. xxxvi. 13. [6] Ps. xxxvi. 15. [7] Isai. xiii. 9.

malignity against His own nature; and why such hatred of the Almighty against sin? Because His goodness is infinite, and since He loves that goodness with an infinite love, He hates the opposite evil with an infinite aversion: and hence until man's weak reason can sound the infinite ocean of the divine goodness, it is in vain that he can hope to fathom the dreadful abyss of sin, or conceive a sufficient idea of its horrors.

But since the weakness of man's nature is such that he is more struck by the contemplation of punishment than by abstract reasoning on the guilt and enormity of sin, I shall next place before your view some of the most striking chastisements with which God has attested in every age, and will attest to the end of time, His hatred of that monster. Scarce did sin enter into the world than the earth was struck with malediction, and we are told by the Almighty that the thistles and thorns with which it is covered have been the fruit of Adam's transgression. But the barrenness of the earth, or the labour to which man was doomed were not its bitterest effects. No; wars, strifes, plagues, and famines, and all the evils which have since afflicted the world, have followed in its desolating train. Turn your eyes to the history of the Deluge, which swept the human race, with the exception of a single family, from the surface of the earth, and what do you read in that awful catastrophe but the enormity and vengeance of mortal sin? Yes, "the earth was corrupted before God, and filled with iniquity, and all flesh had corrupted its way."[1] "The Spirit of God remained not in man,"[2] and the flame of concupiscence had spread to such extent, and raged with such fury that its fierceness could not be extinguished but by the waters of the Deluge. Again, what is it that drew down on the cities of Sodom and Gomorrha the burning vengeance

[1] Gen. vi. 11.   [2] Gen. vi. 3.

of heaven? Mortal sin. "The cry of their iniquity was grown loud before the Lord,"[1] says the inspired writer, " and the Lord rained upon Sodom and Gomorrha brimstone and fire,"[2] and the desolation that is still on the cursed spot reveals to every beholder a living and perpetual monument of God's hatred to their transgressions. To attest His horror for sin God cut off at once fourteen thousand of the Israelites at the foot of Mount Sinai; and at another time the earth yawned beneath their feet, and swallowed up the mutinous Levites, who insulted the majesty of God in the person of Aaron His sacred minister. In short, numberless are the instances in which God's patience was provoked to pour out upon sinners, even in this life, the vial of his indignation. But if you wish to have something like an adequate idea of the terrible evils of mortal sin, go in spirit to the regions of the damned, and contemplate the sufferings that are there endured by its miserable inhabitants. Among those who are doomed for ever to be the victims of penal fire, are legions of spirits once bright with the effulgence of glory, and transformed in a moment, by the deadly venom of mortal sin, into fiends of darkness, and bearing about them for ever a load of guilt which no penance can efface, and no torments can extinguish. Ask the millions of souls that are now plunged into the bottomless abyss, what is it that hurled them into that place of torture, and, in the language of the Wise man, they will reply, " repenting and groaning for anguish of spirit, we wearied ourselves in the way of iniquity and destruction, . . . and now we are consumed in our wickedness. Such things as these the sinners said in hell."[3] You behold, then, that iniquity is the cause of their destruction, and that their wickedness will be the fuel which will feed for ever the fire with which they

[1] Gen. xix. 13.    [2] Gen. xix. 24.    [3] Wisd. v. 3, 7, 14.

will be burnt, without ever being consumed. Oh! frightful monster of mortal sin, which thus constitutes the torment of the damned, enduring the action of an intense and eternal fire, and still retaining its malignity undiminished, and which alone so forms the misery of that dreary place, that if it could cease to be the abode of sin, hell itself would lose all its horrors. But if neither the view of all the chastisements which God inflicted on sin in this life, or of those which are reserved for the reprobate in the other, be sufficient to impress on your souls a detestation for its commission, turn your eyes to the sufferings of your Redeemer, and they will read to you an awful lesson of its boundless malignity. God might have alternately rained water or fire from heaven to punish the sins of mankind. Hell, through its wide extent, might be crowded with all the members of the human race, and be furnished with tortures the most intense in their endurance, and eternal in their continuation; yet, such accumulated woes would still be only the expiation of creatures which could not convey to our minds such an idea of sin as the sufferings of a Divine Victim. Contemplate, then, your Redeemer, stretched in the Garden of Olives, rolling in a flood of agony, deserted, as if by His Eternal Father, who pronounced Him His well-beloved Son, praying that the bitter chalice might pass from Him, and still left to drink it to the dregs, an object of God's malediction until He expiated by His blood that sin which was laid on Him, and then, if you have any feeling, you may perceive the infinite malice of that sin which, as long as it was sustained by Jesus Christ, made Him the object of God's wrath, and made the Man-God the object of God's vengeance. Oh! how we should shudder at the contact of a monster which God so abhors as to have punished His only-begotten Son because of its imputation. Who, after such an example of God's hatred for sin, can be surprised that it is punished with eternal torments? Who can wonder that the very name of mortal sin made the saints tremble; or that the pious mother of St. Lewis used to tell her son that she would rather see him expire at her feet than commit one mortal sin? It is impossible to have faith and to meditate with any attention a mortal sin without coming to the resolution of sacrificing the whole world, and suffering any loss, rather than offend God by its commission. You may call poverty, famine, pestilence, disease, by the name of evils; they are only relative evils, and often do they become the instruments of God's mercy; but mortal sin is the one only essential evil, since the fall of man the fruitful source of every other, which renders man necessarily miserable, and without which he is necessarily happy.

Would to God that you could conceive the hideousness of a soul possessed by mortal sin, and then would you labour to be freed from its frightful contagion. While animated by the Spirit of grace the soul is an object of complacency in the sight of heaven. Nay, it becomes "the temple of God, and the Spirit of God resideth there,"[1] filling it with peace, charity, and the other virtues which are called by the apostle "The fruit of the Spirit."[2] But when that temple of God which is holy is violated by sin, all its beauty is defaced; all the grace with which it was clothed instantly disappears, and instead of being an object of God's complacency, it is threatened with destruction. "But if any man violate the temple of God, him shall God destroy."[3]

No longer informed by that "spirit which quickeneth,"[4] according to the language of our Redeemer, the soul

[1] 1 Cor. iii. 16.   [2] Gal. v. 22.   [3] 1 Cor. iii. 17.   [4] S. John, vi. 64.

becomes dead; all its life and energy are gone, and unless again animated by the divine breath which called it into existence, it remains inert to every other impulse, and a loathsome object in the sight of the Almighty. If it is torn from the stem of that vine on which it must be engrafted to draw forth the nutriment of grace and life, it immediately withers and decays, and becomes fit only to be cast into the fire.[1]

Dreadful punishment! And are there none among you this moment in that melancholy state who have lost that beauty in which you have been enrobed by the grace of baptism, and whose souls, after having been the temples of the Holy Ghost, have become the residence of impure spirits. Oh! if you are conscious that you are in that state of hostility to your God, endeavour, I beseech you, to awaken from your deadly lethargy, and to drive that monster from your heart by which you have been so long enchained. Yes, sin repeatedly indulged, begets a habit which enchains our will and requires the strong grace of God to break its links asunder. The time of mercy is not yet past. "The Almighty wills not the death of a sinner, but that he be converted and live."[2] If, then, mortal sin has had long possession of your souls, and that you find your energy so impaired by its violence as to feel yourselves unable to shake off its oppressive weight, call upon that Spirit which once but moved over the waters and gave them fecundity and life, and, like Lazarus, whom it awoke from the tomb, it will restore your spirit from the grave of death and sin to vigour and animation. When once released from its horrid embraces never more plunge into the abyss, nor even approach its vicinity; but follow the advice of Ecclesiasticus: "My dear son, hast thou

[1] S. John. xv. 6.     [2] Ezech. xxxiii. 11.

sinned? Do so no more; but for thy former sins also pray that they may be forgiven thee. Flee from sins as from the face of a serpent; for if thou comest near them they will take hold of thee. The teeth thereof are the teeth of a lion killing the souls of men. All iniquity is like a two-edged sword; there is no remedy for the wound thereof."[1] Such is the salutary caution with which the Wise man exhorts us to expiate the past and to guard against future offences, and with which I propose to conclude the instruction of this day. Endeavour to imitate the royal Psalmist, who was so struck with remorse for having by mortal sin offended the Almighty, that he watered his couch with his tears, saying, "Rebuke me not, O Lord, in thy indignation, nor chastise me in thy wrath. . . . There is no peace for my bones because of my sins, . . . and my groaning is not hidden from Thee."[2] "Turn away thy face from my sins, and blot out all my iniquities, and restore unto me, O God, the joy of my salvation, and my tongue shall extol Thy justice."[3] Amen.

## THE DANGER AND FOLLY OF THE HOPE OF A DEATH-BED REPENTANCE.

"Because you have despised all my counsel, and neglected my reprehensions, I also will laugh in your destruction, and will mock you when that shall come to you which you feared."—PROV. i. 25, 26.

OF all the awful truths contained in the inspired writings, there is none so calculated to strike us with terror as that which is contained in the words I have just quoted. It dissipates at once a delusion as fatal in its consequences as it is daring in its conception—the presumptuous hope of a death-bed repentance—by solemnly assuring us that

[1] Ecclus. xxi. 1, 2, 3 4.  [2] Ps. xxxvii.  [3] Ps. l. 11, 14.

God, instead of indulging the hopes of sinners, will laugh at their destruction.

Notwithstanding the repeated earnestness with which this and similar denunciations are addressed to Christians, still they cling with the same blind confidence to the fallacious expectation of conversion. It is in vain they are told God's predictions will not be falsified, and that His wisdom will not be overreached by the crafty designs of man. It is in vain they are told that those truths are becoming every day more terrible by deriving fresh strength from the melancholy testimony of experience: it is in vain that they behold the sinner on the bed of death, exhibiting heartrending evidences of the truth of this prediction: this striking impression is soon effaced from their minds, and they rush forward with the same presumptuous temerity to a certain danger from which they were warned to no purpose by the deplorable fate of those who went before them. To caution you against an illusion which has worked the eternal ruin of thousands, I shall endeavour in this discourse to lay open the folly of a reliance on a deathbed repentance, by proving, that those who abuse the proffered favours of the Almighty during life are seldom visited with the grace of reconciliation in their last hour.

It is remarked by St. Augustine that of all the temptations by which the enemy of our salvation assaults and vanquishes our innocence, there is none so frequent or so successful as that by which he persuades us to delay our conversion. Of the force and justice of this remark himself affords a striking illustration, since no one felt more forcibly, or described more feelingly, the difficulties of the violent struggle that arises between the invitations to repentance and the victim of passion. Having spent his youth in the indulgence of every lawless desire, he felt the chains of his passions becoming heavier as he advanced in years, and it is therefore no wonder that he should be considered a most competent authority when he denounces the folly of those who defer their conversion in the vain hope that all the difficulties which they now encounter will yield to the influence of time. Let but the enemy of our souls fill us once with this fatal presumption, and he becomes almost assured of our inevitable ruin. The shortness and uncertainty of life, the frequency of sudden and unprovided deaths, the loss of God's grace, which is the punishment of our infidelity, and the almost irresistible violence which our passions acquire from repeated indulgence, are obstacles that ordinarily occur in the way of repentance, and mock the presumptuous hope by which the sinner calculated on his conversion. Hence, the Wise man tells us, to show us the necessity of an early and unremitting devotion to the service of God: " In the morning sow thy seed, and in the evening let not thy hand cease. . . . If a man live many years and have rejoiced in them all, he must remember the darksome time and the many days; which when they shall come, the things passed shall be accused of vanity. Rejoice, then, O young man, in thy youth, and let thy heart be in that which is good: and know that for all those God will bring thee unto judgment. Remove anger from thy heart, and put away evil from thy flesh; for youth and pleasure are vain. Remember thy Creator in the days of thy youth before the time of affliction come, and the years draw nigh of which thou wilt say, they please me not. Before the sun, and the light, and the moon, and the stars be darkened, when the keepers of the house shall tremble, and the strong men shall stagger."[1] Such is the salutary advice by which the inspired writer exhorts us to the service of

---

[1] Eccles. xi., xii.

God if we wish to be freed from those terrors by which the strongest are shaken at the hour of death. How different is the conduct pursued by the habitual and presumptuous sinner who, in his youth, is utterly thoughtless of his God, expecting that the hour of death, instead of being one of terror and remorse, will bring with it all the calm and placid confidence of pardon and reconciliation. Inconceivable presumption! thus to live as if time and the grace of God were gifts which were at man's disposal, and to turn the mercies of the Almighty into instruments of fresh guilt rather than into opportunities of repentance, to waste that youth, and health, and vigour which should be consecrated to Him who gave them, in the service of sin, and then to hope that God should be pleased with the impure relics of a life worn away in the service of corruption. How justly might we apply to them the words of the Prophet: "I have burned part of it in the fire, and I have baked bread on the coals thereof. I have broiled flesh, and have eaten, and of the residue thereof I shall make an idol."[1] Thus they, in like manner, would feign employ their lives, and reserve for the service of their Creator that portion which is only fit for eternal fire. Instead of listening to the tender invitations by which Christ exhorts them to "give Him their hearts," they spurn His admonitions, trample upon His graces, nay, convert those graces into instruments of new offences against God, realising the language with which, through the mouth of Isaias, he reproaches the perfidy of the Jewish people: "Thou hast made me to serve in thy sins, and wearied me with thy iniquities."[2] Ungrateful sinners thus to requite, by a daring perseverance in sin, the merciful forbearance of heaven! "Is this what you return to the

---

[1] Isai. xliv. 16, 17.    [2] Isai. xliii. 24.

Lord, O foolish and unwise people?"[1] Mistaking God's patience for a total inattention to their own transgressions, their presumption becomes every day more foolish, and "because sentence is not immediately executed upon the wicked, therefore the sons of men commit evil without fear."[2] But what still aggravates their guilt is the impious resolution of practising as if a deception on the Almighty, and of hoping to combine the indulgence of their passions in this life with the possession of eternal happiness in the other. God, however, has formally declared, "that eternal misery shall be the portion of the wicked, and that they shall invoke Him, and that He shall not hear them."[3] Yet, in spite of such awful menaces, they resolve to unite the pleasures of sin and the joys of heaven, and to surprise the vigilance of the Almighty by a hollow and hypocritical conversion, at the hour of their death. Yes, a hollow and hypocritical conversion, since that conversion must be deemed such which is the result, not of aversion to sin, but the impossibility of enjoying it longer. God, however, is not to be imposed upon by such presumptuous mockery. To avenge such premeditated insult He will withdraw His graces from the hardened sinners, and give them over to the dreadful punishment of impenitence and reprobation. While in the frenzy of their presumption they say in their hearts: "We have struck a bargain with death, and made a compact with hell," He dissipates their folly by assuring them: "Your bargain with death shall be made void, and your contract with hell shall not stand."[4] Alas! the effect of this tremendous threat is but too frequently experienced by the daring sinner who promises to himself that he shall close a career of iniquity by a seasonable repentance.

[1] Deut. xxxii. 6.   [2] Eccles. viii. 11.   [3] Prov. i. 28.   [4] Isai. xxviii. 15-18.

And no wonder, since they have so repeatedly shut their ears against the grace of Almighty God, one time speaking to them in the accents of the tenderest mercy: "Come to me all you that labour and I shall refresh you;"[1] and at another time addressing itself to their fears: "Delay not to be converted to the Lord, and defer it not from day to day, for his wrath shall come on a sudden, and in the time of his vengeance he will destroy thee."[2] Although the delaying sinner finds it painful to apply a remedy to the first symptoms of his disorders, yet he preposterously hopes that it will be easy to heal them when habit has festered them still more and confirmed their inveteracy. He feels it difficult to free himself from the first links of sin by which he is bound, while he is yet in his full vigour, and yet he imagines that when that vigour is wasted by infirmity and decay he shall be able to rise with a giant's strength and throw off its intolerable pressure. Preposterous man! Sin acquires strength as he becomes weaker, and at the time when he fancied he might loosen himself from its embrace he finds himself bound from head to foot in the coils of its chain, which years were only lengthening, and which no power can break except a miracle of grace which he has no right to expect from that God whom he had so often and so wantonly insulted. This folly of the persevering and presumptuous sinner is beautifully illustrated by a reference to the lives of the Anchorets of the desert. We are told that on a certain occasion an angel revealed to one of those holy men the infatuation of a foolish man who, having hewn down wood and tied it into a bundle, and laid it on his back, found it too heavy for him to carry. Having cast it down again he added still to its weight, and again attempted the

---

[1] S. Matt. xi. 28.   [2] Eccles. v. 8, 9.

burden. But finding it more oppressive than before, he threw it down in a rage and still doubled the quantity in the vain hope of rendering it lighter. When the hermit expressed his surprise at such folly the angel told him that the folly at which he wondered was but a striking image of the conduct of sinners who, finding it painful to resist one or two vices in the commencement, strengthen their force by the indulgence of many others, and defer their conversion as if the burden of sin were to become lighter by the accumulation of fresh iniquities. O infatuation! never to be sufficiently lamented, which realises in the sinner the language of Job: "God hath given him place for penance, and he abuses it into pride."[1] In vain does the minister of God thunder in his ears the folly of his presumption and the danger of delay. He persists in his obduracy, and looks forward to a death-bed repentance as the plank of his salvation. Treacherous delusion! And if I have so long detained you on the preceding part, it is to convince you by the repeated testimonies of God Himself of the fallacy of such hopes, which are as generally frustrated as they are rashly entertained.

Without insisting on the numberless unforeseen casualties that suddenly cut off the sinner in the career of his iniquity, and mock all his expectations of repentance; without adverting to those ordinary occurrences of alarming deaths which, though they seem to be the result of the ordinary laws of nature, are yet perhaps the silent and terrible inflictions of God's vengeance. Let us suppose that the hardened and persevering sinner does not fall a victim to those chastisements, and that he dies what is generally termed a natural death. Do you imagine that such an event will secure his

[1] Job, xxiv. 23.

reconciliation? Ah! little do you know of the infirmities of nature, and the confusion into which it is thrown by the dread of dissolution, if you think that that fatal hour is the time for settling the mighty account of your salvation. The commencement of his sickness he may devote to the arrangement of his temporal concerns, reserving the weighty account of his sins to the nearer approach of death. As long as he is indulged with the hope of recovery so long he protracts his sincere conversion, retaining an attachment for some sinful object from which death alone can separate him. Deceived by the officious cruelty and treacherous consolations of his friends, he clings to the hope of life even when hope is gone, and even should they honestly warn him of his danger, he cherishes the pleasing delusion to the last moment of his existence. Thus though his death may seem natural, he still dies in his sins the secret victim of a fatal delusion, to which in vengeance for his past iniquity he was, like Achab, abandoned by the Almighty. "And there came forth a spirit, and stood before the Lord and said: I will deceive him; and the Lord said to him: Thou shalt deceive and shall prevail, go forth and do so."[1] Tremendous chastisement! Yet such is the general end of the lives of the wicked. They may have received the sacraments, which from their perverse disposition lose all their efficacy on their corrupted soul. They may in the eyes of men die a tranquil death, while in the eyes of the Almighty their tranquillity is but the effect of the deceitful spirit of error which went forth to hide from them the view of their own iniquity, and thus seal their reprobation.

If, however, they die not the dupes of the spirit of error, they generally become the more appalling victims

[1] 3 Kings, xxii. 21, 22.

of despair. If faith is not utterly extinguished in their souls, it is only to give them a fuller and more frightful view of the horrors of their situation. Having at length arrived at that fatal term which they fancied would afford an easy transition to repentance and to heaven, they find themselves at the foot of that summit of virtue from which they once incautiously descended, and which it is not in their power to regain, and ready to be hurled into an abyss which it is impossible to avoid. There is no alternative. To remain stationary is not now in their choice. To retrace their guilty steps and ascend again the painful steep of innocence from which habits of sin had dragged them, is beyond the power of human nature enfeebled by disease. Hurled through life by the impetuosity of his passions from one precipice to another, his natural tendency is to the lowest abyss of hell if the arm of the Almighty arrests not the unhappy victim. Startled at the dangers which now yawn before his eyes he calls on God for mercy. But God long since assured him: "Because I called and you refused; I stretched out my hand and there was none that regarded; you have despised all my counsel and neglected my reprehensions; I also will laugh in your destruction, and will mock when that shall come to you which you feared. When sudden calamity shall fall on you, and destruction as a tempest shall be at hand; when tribulation and distress shall come upon you, then shall they call upon me and I will not hear; they shall rise in the morning and shall not find me, because they have hated instruction and received not the fear of the Lord, nor consented to my counsel, but despised all my reproof; therefore, they shall eat the fruit of their own way, and shall be filled with their own devices."[1] Good

---

[1] Prov. i. 24-31.

God! Can anything equal the presumption of those who calculate on God's aid at the hour of death after such terrible denunciations. Were they encouraged by a positive assurance of God's pardon, though their ingratitude would be still great, there might be grounds for their presumption, but when God Himself now declares " they will call on me and I will not hear," their impiety in persevering in sin can be equalled only by their infatuation.

Finding himself ready to plunge into that dreadful gulf with which he was so often threatened during life, he would feign seek aid from the grace of religion, and, like Saul, he sends for the minister of God whose admonitions he hitherto disregarded. On beholding the minister of the Gospel he may exclaim, with the same unfortunate king, "I am in mortal anguish, and I am straitened exceedingly on every side; therefore have I called thee to show me what I must do in the extremity in which I find myself."[1] And perhaps were the priest to give expression to his own fears he might say with Samuel: "Why hast thou disturbed me to come hither? Why dost thou ask me seeing the Lord has departed from thee." Not presuming, however, to limit the mercies of the Almighty, which he knows to be infinite, he administers to him the last sacraments, trembling at the same time lest they should be sacrilegious, and recalling to his mind the terrible language of Jesus Christ: "I go my way and you shall seek me, and you shall die in your sins."[2] He receives the sacraments, which, instead of being the sources of life, become to him perhaps the seal of his reprobation, the inward anguish of his soul betrays itself in every feature, and after struggling in the dreadful agonies of terror and despair, he breathes forth his impious soul in blasphemy, fearfully

---

[1] 1 Kings, xxviii. 28.     [2] St. John, viii. 21.

exemplifying the words of St. Paul: "Although with tears he had sought it he found no place of repentance."[1]

From the terror of this discourse, in which I have pressed upon your minds the danger of delaying your conversion, you may imagine that I wish to terrify you into despair. Far be from me such a thought. No; but I wish to guard you against the opposite and equally fatal danger of presumption. With the words of God Himself for my guide, I wish to inspire into your hearts a salutary terror of His judgments by showing you that those who abuse the patient mercies of heaven will feel in an evil hour all the vengeance of His justice. I wish to impress upon your minds the wholesome precepts of St. Peter, to endeavour by good works to make your election and vocation sure, and to work out your salvation with fear and trembling. The most obdurate and profligate sinner among you would feign die the death of the just. Let him after what he has heard interrogate his own conscience whether his hopes are not as fallacious as his conduct is impious. A virtuous life is the only security which men can have for the hope of a happy death, since, as St. Paul says, "their end shall be according to their works."[2] Are your works, then, good? If so, your end will be happy. Are they evil, they will lead you to an evil end. For Job says of the wicked: "His bones shall be filled with the vices of his youth, and they shall sleep with him in the dust."[3] Would to God I were able to convey my feelings of the deplorable state of that soul which refuses to comply with the inspirations of heaven, and daringly defers its conversion to a more seasonable time. Were there equal chances of mercy as of vengeance, would not the folly of him be inconceivable who would expose

[1] Heb. xii. 17   [2] 2 Cor. xi. 15.   [3] Job, xx. 11.

to doubtful hazard the only concern for which he was created? But when he discovers so much to fear on one side and such little ground for hope on the other, he must first extinguish in his soul the commonest principles of reason as well as of piety, who abandons his salvation to the treacherous plank of a death-bed repentance. Tell me not of the penitent thief or the sudden conversion of Magdalen. Who ever thought of abandoning a general rule and substituting the exception for this general rule of his conduct? Would anyone consider his confidence reasonable who would attempt a gulf where thousands had perished because one or two individuals miraculously escaped the danger? Similar would be the fatuity of him who would trust his soul to a death-bed conversion, because, though to millions it proved fatal, a few have been saved by the miraculous and mysterious grace of the Almighty. Let me, then, in conclusion exhort you to labour diligently in the work of your salvation before the night cometh, when nobody works. Although God may spurn his prayers who waits till the hour of death, yet He will not refuse His grace to those who, during life, sincerely resolve to be converted. Turn, then, to your God, who is still prolonging your life in the hope of your return, and who, like the father of the prodigal child, will stretch forth His arms to receive you. Too long have you abused His mercy. Beware, lest by your presumption you drive the Spirit of God from you so as never to visit you more.

You will not, I trust, allow this holy season to pass away without bringing forth fruit worthy of penance. Perhaps it is the last season that the judgment of Jesus Christ may be announced to you, and that ere its return again you should hear the tremendous reality of that judgment which awaits the impenitent sinner. You sleep on a precipice. Arise from the slumbers of death, lest you should awaken to the neverdying torments of hell. If you reject God when He now calls on you, He will reject you when you call on Him, and He will laugh at your destruction. But if at length you hear His voice, He will visit you with His grace, bind up your sins, restore peace to your soul, extinguish the fire of your passions by which you are tormented; and when the trouble of death and fear of His judgments shall encompass you, He shall send the angels of His mercy to liberate you from your afflictions, and conduct you to His own kingdom, where the possession of Himself shall constitute your eternal happiness. Amen.

## ON DEATH.

"Be you, then, ready; for at what hour you think not the Son of Man will come."—St. LUKE, xii. 40.

IN these few but emphatic words we are furnished with a salutary and seasonable warning of the uncertainty of our last hour. What? A seasonable warning—to mingle the thoughts of death with the celebration of thanksgiving, and sadden with the gloomy anticipations of the grave the cheerful season of festivity! While joy and gladness reign throughout the Church, and every assembly partakes of that feeling which the advent of redemption is calculated to inspire; while every tongue is gratitude, and every heart is rapture, and every ear is yet filled with the sweet and lofty anthems of glory to God and peace to man, which were pealed in every temple during this anniversary of love; whilst all who have passed through the last year accost their surviving friends in the warm and cordial language with which one greets his companions' escape from a shipwreck, and are entering on the next with much of that buoyancy of youth which looks but on the sunny side of life, promising to itself a lengthened series of enjoyments, unseasonable, no doubt, must appear the introduction of a topic calculated to disturb such dreams of happiness by casting the shadow of death over the brightness of the fancied prospect. Unseasonable, however, as the subject might appear to the votaries of the world, I should rather be guided by the selection of the Church, whose judgments, like those of God, are often different from those of men. The text which I have quoted is that with which on the festival of St. Sylvester, one of the most venerable of her Pontiffs, she closes the Liturgy of the year. Nay, as if to impress the same doctrine more strongly upon the faithful, St. Paul, in the epistle of this day, addresses Titus in similar language: "For the grace of God our Saviour hath appeared to all men, instructing us that, denying ungodliness and worldly desires, we should live soberly and justly and godly in this world, looking for the blessed hope and coming of the glory of the great God and our Saviour Jesus Christ."[1] Behold, then, how at the conclusion of the old and the commencement of the new year the Church labours to awaken our vigilance and our piety by warning us of the coming of Christ, and, what is still more awful, of the uncertainty of His coming. Nay, the very reluctance of the world to listen to such a theme is a reason why it is chosen to prevent its spiritual joy from running into those excesses of worldly merriment which, we are assured by the inspired writings, always terminate in mourning. Besides, the conclusion of the year is analogous to the conclusion of life, and must naturally remind us that we are rapidly advancing to that goal at which all its days are ended. As it is, then, of vast importance to make good use of the portion that yet remains, I shall endeavour to impress upon you that

---

[1] Titus, ii. 11-13.

the hour of death is not only uncertain, but comes when least expected; and then deduce the necessity of being constantly prepared for an event on which depends our eternal misery or happiness.

That death is the common doom of all mankind is a truth so clear and palpable that to dwell on it for a moment would be to engage your attention without adding to your knowledge, or, perhaps, awakening any serious reflections. God Himself has issued the warrant of our death in the judgment pronounced on the crime of our first parents, and the experience of six thousand years has witnessed its solemn and invariable execution. But surely it is not necessary for me to expatiate upon this truth after the solemn attestation of the inspired writings that He has "filled all things with death."[1] Yes; the dismal emblems of mortality meet us everywhere, and especially in this place, which, with better reason than the far-famed Necropolis of Egypt, might be called the city of the dead; where every stone is a sepulchral monument, and every letter is a fragment of a sepulchral inscription; where the loftiest columns that rise amidst the desolation of the past, serve but as the gnomons of time, by which you might count the fleeting generations that glided across their shadows into the vaults beneath, since, to use the fine language of Job, "the kings and consuls of the earth built to themselves those solitudes,"[2] which, apparently by accident, but to me it would appear by a superior providence, are now abandoned to the sports of wild beasts, that they who sought in life no higher happiness than the indulgence of their brutal desires should now be associated to them in the same ignominious end, thus realising the sentence of the inspired writings: "Man when he was in honour did not

[1] Wisd. xviii. 16. [2] Job, iii. 1

understand; he hath been compared to senseless beasts, and made like unto them." [1]

Yet, though the certainty of death is a truth too clear to require illustration, whence comes it that it is seldom or so superficially considered, as if it were one in which the interests of mankind had no share? Oh, my dear Christians, this is the strange inconsistency which I am anxious to combat. It is against this melancholy and general delusion, which has wrought the ruin of thousands, I wish to arm all your vigilance. Death is every day thinning society of its members, our friends, our relatives; nay, our inmates are snatched from around us, and yet, instead of trembling for the danger of an unprepared death, do not we generally live in a calm but treacherous security. This is the folly which every day excites our surprise, and yet is left uncorrected. What can be the reason of an infatuation of which all seem to be sensible, and yet continue to be the victims? It is that, however convinced we are of the necessity of dying, still each, by an interpretation favourable to himself, puts off that sad event to a remote period. Amidst the general conviction of the frailty of mortals, each one cherishes the confidence that he at least may live longer; and hence, by a kind of epidemic delusion, which seizes the old as well as the young, and the feeble as well as the healthy, there is scarce an individual living that does not promise himself another year of existence. Of this dangerous hope the fallacy is rendered evident by the testimonies of the inspired writings as well as your own experience. "Man," says the Wise-man, "knows not his own end; but as fishes are taken with the hook, and as birds are caught with a snare, so men are taken in the evil time,

[1] Ps. xlviii. 21.

when it shall suddenly come upon them."[1] And again: "Our life shall pass away as the trace of a cloud, and shall be dispersed as a mist that is driven away by the beams of the sun."[2] What, then, can equal the presumption of mortals, the fleetness of whose life is thus compared to the mist of the morning, and whose blind confidence is as suddenly surprised by death as the fishes that are caught while they thoughtlessly gambol in the waters? But we cannot omit on this occasion the language of Job on the shortness and uncertainty of life, which is consecrated by its frequent use in the Liturgy of the Church, and which is fraught with such a rich fund of pathetic feeling as never to be exhausted by repetition. "Man born of a woman, living for a short time, cometh forth like a flower, and is destroyed and fleeth as a shadow, and never continueth in the same state."[3] And in another place, talking of the wicked man, he concludes in words equally clear and emphatic: "Before his days be full he shall perish, and his hands shall wither away, and he shall be blasted as a vine whose grapes are in the first flower."[4] How deplorable, then, is the fatuity of those who, as if the tenure of their lives were secured by a covenant, persevere in their wicked courses, vainly calculating on the hour of their conversion! To convince, however, those people of their perverse folly, let us listen to the awful instructions which the Redeemer Himself conveys to us on this important subject in a simple and expressive parable. In the twenty-fifth chapter of St. Matthew He likens the kingdom of God to ten virgins, who took their lamps and went out to meet the bridegroom, of whom five were wise and five foolish. The five prudent ones furnished their lamps with oil; the five others, calculating on the

---

[1] Eccle. ix. 12.   [2] Wisd. ii. 3.   [3] Job, xiv. 1, 2.   [4] Job, xv. 32.

delay of the bridegroom, neglect the necessary caution. In the meantime the bridegroom arrives, and the foolish virgins having applied in vain to their companions for a share of their oil, are obliged to run in the hurry and confusion of the moment to buy it and furnish their empty lamps. In the critical and perilous interval of their absence the bridegroom enters; they, too, come and eagerly demand admittance, but, alas! they are repulsed with the terrible refusal: "I know you not," and the doors of the house are closed against them for ever. Such is the Redeemer's salutary lesson on the dangerous uncertainty of life, which he concludes with this profitable warning: "Watch you, therefore; because you know not the day nor the hour." Nay, He still goes farther, and tells us, in the language of my text, that the hour of death is not only uncertain, but will come when not expected: "Be you, then, ready; for at what hour you think not the Son of Man will come." Good God! what infatuation seizes the sinner to live on in a calm and careless confidence, fondly representing to himself at some distant and indefinite time the blessings of repentance, while the oracle of truth thunders in his ears that the approach of death will be as sudden and insidious as that of the midnight robber, who surprises the house when its inmates are plunged in a secure and profound repose! To follow up the illustration of our Divine Redeemer, were the most confident of you to be told that your house would surely be attacked by thieves, what precautions would you not resort to to avert the threatened danger? You would, doubtless, put a guard upon your house, and take your station among its sentinels; no expedient of defence would be left untried, nor would you suffer your vigilance to slumber until you were fully satisfied of the efficacy of the means resorted to for protection. And yet, inconceivable delusion! while man thus watches and labours against misfortunes which, at worst, can only be temporary, and which his future industry may repair, he is insensible to the eternal and irremediable danger to which he exposes himself by abandoning to the mercy of every accident the rich and invaluable inheritance, of which Christ says: "What profiteth it a man if he gain the whole world and lose his own soul."[1]

It is thus the Redeemer Himself, in forcible and familiar parables, inculcates the silent and unobserved approaches of death, and warns us to be continually watching lest we should be surprised by his covert hostility. Who, then, can presume on a length of life, or vainly count upon his conversion, especially when he reflects that the Saviour's words are verified by sad experience? Let the least experienced among you look around and meditate upon those deaths which you yourselves may have witnessed, and how many will present themselves to which you might give the name of sudden and premature. One swooning away to death in his chair; another at his meal; a third, in the bloom of life and spirits, sinking into the stream of the Tiber, to rise no more, at a moment, perhaps, when her fancy fondly turned to those dear salutations which should greet her on her return to a home which she never was to visit.[*] In fine, not to crowd the description with a detail which could not equal the varied but melancholy reality, others cited before the tribunal of their God amidst circumstances calculated to chill the soul with horror. Nay, have you not known the whiteness of the wedding

---

[1] St. Matt. xvi. 26.

[*] NOTE.—With the view of impressing his hearers with the terrible truth here announced to them, the Archbishop alludes to the recent melancholy death of a young English lady, who, walking on the banks of the Tiber, accidently fell in and was drowned, in the year 1825.—EDITOR.

garment to be often suddenly exchanged for the weeds of widowhood and mourning, and the song that was raised to gladden the marriage feast to die away in the funeral dirge over the bride or the bridegroom? Even of those who are said to die a natural death, how many are unexpectedly taken away, flattered by false friends with the assurance of recovery, and deluded by the hope with which they cling to life until that hope is suddenly snatched away for ever. Whence we come to the sad conclusion contained in the words of Christ, that the generality of mankind die when they do not expect it. If so, another important truth clearly follows, that the death of the generality of mankind is like their lives; and if their lives are not holy the hope of a happy death must be presumptuous. If then, on a serious self-examination, you find yourselves unprepared to die, what reasonable confidence of salvation can you entertain? The hope, or rather the presumption, that animates you at the opening of this year, will equally accompany you to the next, should you live to reach it; and, again, to the year after, it will thus be the companion of your entire lives, growing with your growth, and strengthening as you advance, until, betrayed by its treachery, you are summoned, laden with your iniquities, before the tribunal of that God whose threats and admonitions you so often disregarded! Such is the fatal end of that procrastination which is for ever deferring its conversion until to-morrow. But what, in truth, is this to-morrow which inspires sinners with such confidence? A wise man never calculates on resources not his own. But to-morrow, far from being in our possession, is in reality in another world, over which we have as little control as the eternity to which it belongs, especially in the case of those for whom it shall never arrive. But making the most favourable supposition that this to-morrow should come, mark the deceitfulness of its prospects and the shiftings of its positions. You depend now upon to-morrow. But this very day on which I address you, was it not the equally flattering to-morrow of yesterday? If so, and that you are not still prepared, will not to-morrow when it comes, assuming the place of to-day, become the fancied master of the day after, and like its past predecessors, exercise the same privilege of thoughtless indulgence entailing on another to-morrow the painful duty of conversion which is thus handed down as an unredeemed incumbrance running coeval with man's life, and convincing us of the truth of the observation of a contemplative writer, that this to-morrow is the thief of time, who silently filches away our lives while we remain unalarmed because this petty stealth of one day after another appears as trifling in the sum of our existence as the little atom of sand appears in the glass that measures its duration; when lo! we are startled with the conviction that, like the same subtle, silent, and insinuating mass, it has flown, never to be replaced, into the gulf of eternity. Were not many of those who have gone before us equally sanguine in their reliance on futurity? Engaged in the same pursuits, actuated by the same passions, panting for the same amusements, and victims of the same thoughtlessness, they, too, looked forward into life, until the darkness of death, and, perhaps, of unutterable despair, suddenly closed upon their prospects. Do not those who listen to me now fondly hope that their day will not soon be ended? The hope which one entertains, his neighbour cherishes with equal confidence, and thus all are equally sanguine though it may be certain that some ere a long time, will be consigned to the grave. Were any temporal misfortune impending over us, each one would, doubtless, tremble for his own safety, though the risk were divided among a great number of people; and when you are threatened with the chance of an event which involves your eternal happiness or misery, to feel no anxiety and to betray no alarm—Oh! call it not courage. No; it is a dire insensibility, and that insensibility is the most terrific presage of your danger.

Against the fatal consequences of an unexpected death there cannot be a more effectual security than its habitual meditation. "Think of your last end,"[1] is the solemn advice of the Wise-man, of which the efficacy has been proved by many saints in the preservation of their virtue, and by many sinners in awakening them to a sincere and fervent repentance. Were we to reflect in the morning that that day may be the last of our lives, the thought would act as a salutary check on the temptations to which we may be exposed. This reflection would moderate those schemes of ambition which frequently make its votaries forgetful of their God; it would regulate that thirst of gain which, when indulged, hurries on to dishonesty, and quench the fire of those passions to which the unfortunate libertine falls a premature and melancholy victim. In short, it would detach us from the world, making us feel, according to the lofty sentiments of St. Paul, "that we are pilgrims and strangers on the earth who have no permanent city here, and are looking for a city that hath foundations, and whose builder is God."[2] Reflect, therefore, frequently on your last end. There cannot be at the same time a more ennobling or a more consoling reflection. As God exhorted His chosen people to think on His commandments, I would exhort you to think upon death when you go in and when you go out, during your business and on your journeys, but principally on commencing

---

[1] Eccli. vii. 40.   [2] Heb. xi., xiii.

and concluding any important transaction. Ask yourselves, if I were immediately to die, would I do such an action, or whether it would bring consolation or remorse at that awful hour? If you thus meditate on death you will live according to God's commandments; and though your death should be apparently sudden, it will still be precious in the sight of the Lord.

Tell me not that such continual meditation upon death is incompatible with your duties; that it would interrupt the hours of business and embitter the moments of relaxation, and, in fine, that it would sadden your entire lives, and drive you from the intercourse of man into the solitude of the wilderness. Do not be frightened by such idle terrors. In advising you to prepare for death by its meditation, I do not advise you to quit the world, or neglect the important duties with which you may be entrusted; on the contrary, my object is to furnish stronger aid and incentives to sustain you in the discharge of its painful duties while you reflect that you are responsible beings who must, ere long, render an account of their neglect or performance. But should the consequence be an interruption of the world's enjoyments, better would it be that you should be gradually weaned from it in time, which would render the last separation easy, than be torn from it by death after a violent and painful struggle. Painful beyond description is that awful hour to those whose thoughts are entirely engrossed by the world, and who reflect not on death until it knocks at their doors. "O Death, how bitter is the remembrance of thee to a man that hath peace in his possessions, to a man that is at rest, and whose ways are prosperous in all things."[1] The pleasures in which they indulged, now stripped of their delusion, disappear like a dream leaving naught behind but the

[1] Eccli. xli. 1.

sting of their remembrance, and throwing their unhappy victim into the arms of death who summons him away. This is the hour that will reveal the vanity of the world, and induce the Christian to make a true estimate of things. It is the light that flashes in the soul in that awful moment that made, it is said, one of the greatest monarchs in Europe exclaim in an agony of affliction, "Would to God that I had spent my days in the desert instead of being on a throne." It was a serious reflection on that hour that peopled the desert with saints who, in spite of the scorn of the world, trampled on all its maxims, and endured every species of penance, however austere, to ensure their own salvation. Do then frequently meditate on death. Every day, in the toll of the funeral bell, or in the solemnity of the funeral procession, affords you an opportunity of cherishing its remembrance. When the stroke of death deprives you of a friend or an acquaintance, strive not in the dissipation of the world to drown the memory of his departure. Imitate not those who, when they inter the remains of a relative, labour to bury the thoughts of death in the same grave. The affliction that is felt on account of the death of a friend might, if regulated by sentiments of religion, become instrumental in our happiness. But, alas! such opportunities of grace are generally lost upon the votaries of the world. Instead of soothing their sorrow by the consolations of faith; instead of following their friend to the other world and communing with his departed spirit; instead of reflecting that but a short time will separate their condition, and that the brief interval ought to be put to the best account, do they not generally reverse this prudent conduct by flying back to that treacherous world by which they were recently wounded, and striving to forget in the tumult of its follies those seasonable warnings that were sent for their conversion. Again, they receive another and a severer shock, and again they rush like maniacs into the arms of that very world which murdered all their joys, and against the vanity of which they were heard, in the frenzy of their grief, to utter the most passionate execrations. Thus they drag on a life of the strangest inconsistency, wedded to a world whose arrows they often feel. Every messenger who announces in a neighbour's death the approach of their own is unheeded; every such impression is erased by the next tide of dissipation as easily as the letters scrawled by children on the sandy shore are blotted out by the returning waters, and when, at last, after having "wearied themselves in the way of iniquity, and walked through hard ways,"[1] the Angel of Death announces that their days are ended. The feelings of the royal drunkards of Babylon, on beholding that a mysterious hand had dashed their unholy revels, might convey some faint idea of their confusion, and of the horrors of their despair.

Let me then, in conclusion, adjure you to treasure up those instructions. Let me once more exhort you to watch; because the Son of Man will come like a thief in the night, when you do not expect Him. "Watch, because you know not the day nor the hour"[2]—that awful and inexorable hour which will make you eternally miserable or happy. Perhaps this is the last admonition with which some of you might be favoured. I would, therefore, address you in the language of Isaias to Ezechias: "Prepare thy house, for thou shalt die and not live."[3] Let your constant prayer be, "From a sudden and unprovided death deliver us, O Lord," and with a strong and affectionate reliance on the influence of the Holy Virgin, the Mother of Mercies, with her Divine Son, supplicate her in the tender language of the Church: "Holy Mary, Mother of God, pray for us,

[1] Wisd. v. 7.   [2] St. Matt. xxv. 13.   [3] Isai. xx. 1.

sinners, now and at the hour of our death." Should the thoughts of death afflict you, consider that it is the last act and final accomplishment of that sacrifice which we owe to the Almighty. Every sacrifice must be perfected by the death of the victim; and we, as God's creatures, owe to our Creator the sacrifice of ourselves, of which death is the consummation. Let us reflect, too, that Christ Himself has gone before us conquering the terrors of the tomb, and that the gate of death, which before was beset with darkness, has since His passage been converted into a triumphal arch, with the lamp of faith burning at its portals, which dissipates the horrors that hung around the grave, and reveals to the Christian soul the glory that is beyond it. By making the remembrance of death familiar during your lives the reality will bring with it joy and consolation, and in your last end will be exemplified the language of the inspired writer: "Blessed in the eyes of the Lord is the death of his saints." [1]

## ON PURGATORY.

"It is, therefore, a holy and wholesome thought to pray for the dead."—2 MACH. xii. 46.

SUCH is the holy reflection with which the inspired writer concludes the account of the offerings which were made by the piety of Judas for the repose of the soldiers who had fallen in his service: a reflection which is consecrated by the adoption of the Catholic Church, and embodied with her solemn service for the dead. This language proves to us the explicit belief of the Jewish Church in the doctrine of purgatory; for if there had been no hope of their release sacrifice had been useless. But as if to prevent the necessity of

[1] Ps. cxv. 15.

reasoning on the subject the inspired writer himself has thus anticipated the obvious conclusion. For if he had not hoped that they that were slain should rise again it would have seemed superfluous and vain to pray for the dead. This consoling doctrine, which formed a part of the Jewish creed, has been sanctioned by Jesus Christ, and transmitted to us with the sacred inheritance which He bequeathed to His Church. The book in which it is contained forms a portion of the inspired canon of Scripture. It is entitled to the same reverence as all the other books which the Church proffers to her children as the vehicles of the Divine Word. To her sacred authority the precious legacy has been confided. It is only through that authority that it is entitled to our veneration and that we can recognise its inspiration. Reject the book from which my text has been extracted, and the motive of your rejection will equally affect others that are acknowledged as inspired. Tear away this part from the chapter of Revelation and you loosen the very principle that keeps its different parts together. Encouraged by your rashness, another will make an attempt still more sacrilegious, by taking asunder some obnoxious portions; and thus the different parts of Christ's doctrine, bound together by no fixed principle, and guarded by no authority, will fall asunder. Thus every part of the Christian inheritance must be forfeited to any man who presumes to question the validity of its possession, and the sacred charter that contains it must be yielded to every critic who presumes to impeach its claims to inspiration. But no, my brethren, we encourage no such licence; we acknowledge the Church as the guardian of the Divine Word, and as the expounder of its spirit. The words with which God always promised the Israelites support and victory: "Behold, I am with you;" the words by which He assured the prophet, that should he walk through the fire it would not burn him: for "I will be with thee;"[1] the same He has addressed to His Church in the persons of the Apostles: "For behold I am with you until the end of time."[2] And under the protection of that promise we may securely repose, receiving with unhesitating assent the books which she offers for our acceptance.

I shall now, my dear Christians, briefly explain the arguments which the Scriptures and the Fathers of the Church furnish in support of the practice of praying for the dead, and then direct your attention to the moral obligations that spring from the nature of this doctrine. The belief of this doctrine is so consonant to reason, was so preserved in the traditions of the people of God, and was so blended with the religious rites of the Jews, that we find it in Scripture rather incidentally connected with some other subjects than solemnly proposed as a new and unheard-of revelation. Thus Christ, speaking of the guilt of blasphemy against the Holy Ghost, concludes by saying, "that he that shall speak against the Holy Ghost it shall not be forgiven either in this world or in the world to come."[3] Here we find one of the strongest proofs of the doctrine of purgatory incidentally introduced in confirmation of another doctrine. Our Redeemer, wishing to point out the grievous enormity of rejecting the graces of the Holy Ghost, to show its guilt in the clearest point of view, He declares that it is a sin which cannot be forgiven in this life or in the next: which latter expression was entirely unmeaning if there were not some sins expiated in the other world.

Thus the Apostle, reproving the vain teachers among the Corinthians, who were distracting the flock of Christ by the jealousies that prevailed among them, reminds

[1] Isai. xliii. 2.    [2] S. Matt. xxviii. 20    [3] S. Matt: xii. 32.

them that they shall be punished for all their motives of vanity which infected the purity of their doctrine. "The day of the Lord shall be revealed by fire, and the fire shall try every man's work of what sort it is. If any man's work abide, he shall receive his reward. If any man's work be burnt, he shall suffer loss; but he himself shall be saved, yet as by fire."[1] These two passages, while they prove sufficiently the doctrine of purgatory, confirm the observation already made, that it is adverted to as a doctrine with which the people were familiarly acquainted—a circumstance which sufficiently explains why it is not more frequently or forcibly insisted on by the inspired writers.

If, however, the testimonies of Scripture are sparing they are abundantly supplied by their living witnesses, to whom the Christian Revelation was entrusted by Christ and His Apostles. This method of handing down His doctrine through a regular and unbroken chain of witnesses is the plan that has been adopted by Jesus Christ to preserve and perpetuate it. Hence St. Paul, in his instructions to Timothy, exhorts him: "Hold the form of sound words which thou hast heard of me in faith and in the love which is in Christ Jesus."[2] . . . "And the things which thou hast heard of me before many witnesses, the same commit to faithful men, who shall be fit to teach others also."[3]

You see, then, that, according to the rule laid down by the apostle, the Christian religion is nothing else than a precious legacy, regularly transmitted through a series of witnesses who bequeath it unaltered to their authorised successors, and conveyed by them with similar fidelity to the rising generation. Of their authorised witnesses I could cite many; on the present occasion I shall however, content myself with two or three attesta-

[1] 1 Cor. iii. 13, 14, 15.    [2] 2 Tim. i. 13.    [3] 2 Tim. ii. 2.

tions. Tertullian, who lived in the second century, thus speaks of a faithful widow: "She both prays for the soul of her husband and begs refreshment for him in the meantime." And to show that this practice was conformable to the practice of his times, he concludes: "We make anniversary oblations for the dead."[1] To the words of Tertullian we can add the more copious testimony of St. Chrysostom, the light of the Eastern Church: "Oblations for the dead are not in vain, nor prayers, nor alms; the Holy Ghost ordered all these things that we might help one another. The Apostles did not command in vain that in the venerable and dreadful mysteries the dead should be remembered. They knew they would derive a considerable advantage from them. While all the people stand with open arms, as well as the priests, and the tremendous Sacrifice is present, how should we not appease God by prayer for them? But this I say of the faithful departed."[2] Not to prolong your attention with the testimonies of St. Cyril or St. Jerome, I shall conclude the tradition of the Fathers with the words of St. Augustine: "By the prayers of the Holy Church, and the wholesome sacrifice and alms, it is not to be doubted but the dead are assisted. These, however, are not beneficial to all the dead, but to those whose lives were such as that they might partake of the benefits."[3] The doctrine which St. Augustine here inculcates he illustrates by his own example in commemorating his mother Monica, who piously requested to be remembered by her son in the adorable Sacrifice of the Altar.

It is unnecessary to multiply further testimonies in confirmation of a tenet which derives the strongest support from reason. When a soul habitually employed in the service of her God is summoned before His tribunal,

---

[1] Tertul. lib. de Corona Militis, cap. iii.  [2] Homil 21, in Acta.
[3] Serm. 32 de Verbis Apost.

some venial transgressions, rarely separable from human nature, are found mixed with her virtues. As nothing defiled can enter into the kingdom of God, such a soul cannot be immediately associated with the assembly of the saints; and yet, as she is free from mortal guilt, a God of mercy and of justice will not consign her to eternal torments. What, then, are we to suppose to be the lot of such a soul? To reconcile God's justice with His sanctity, we must suppose her to be consigned to a place of temporary purgation, where, while she expiates her guilt, she is prepared for the assembly of the just. To imagine that such a soul is to share the fate of them that are defiled with mortal sin would be offering an injury to the justice of that God whose rewards and punishments will be regulated according to our works. Never will He judge by the same standard the faults of inadvertence and the malice of studied guilt, nor award the same measure of punishment to an officious untruth and the detestable crimes of sacrilege or murder. Such is the solid foundation of purgatory—a foundation that is laid on our knowledge of the perfections of the Divinity. Hence it is that of all the tenets of the Catholic Church the most widely diffused and the most generally adopted by her adversaries is this doctrine of piety. The knowledge of a God both just and holy has united the most hostile religions in the belief of a middle state of purgation, in which imperfect souls are detained before they are admitted into the mansions of eternal bliss. This doctrine has been found among all the religions of the earth: it is believed by the Greek churches, though long separated from the Church of Rome by an obstinate and protracted schism. Nay, it formed a part of the doctrine taught by the sages of ancient times—a circumstance which proves that it was first derived from the science of truth, though disfigured by many superstitions in the channels through which it passed. The superstitious practices by which the pagan nations encumbered its simplicity are no reproach to the doctrine itself; the doctrine remains true, notwithstanding the additions of error; and while the clumsy superstructure which, erected by superstition, has disappeared, the foundation that is laid on truth and nature shall ever remain unshaken.

Having thus laid before you the solid reasons upon which your belief of purgatory is grounded, let me now call your attention to the moral practical obligations which spring from this belief. From the testimonies of the Fathers we may collect not only that there is a purgatory, but likewise that the souls there detained are benefited by our prayers and the oblation of the Sacrifice of the Mass. What a consolation does the Catholic Church afford her children in the assurance that death destroys not those interchanges of kindness and of charity which endear men to each other while here on earth, but that they may extend their charitable solicitude beyond the grave. The Council of Trent, the solemn organ of the Catholic Church, defines that "the souls detained in purgatory are helped by the suffrages of the faithful and particularly by the acceptable sacrifice of the altar."[1] This much known, and it is sufficient to interest our sympathy for their sufferings, although we are not acquainted with the precise nature of their punishment. Charity and justice both concur in enforcing this obligation. If we are obliged to succour our neighbour in his temporal distress, can we be insensible to the acuteness of that pain which no human suffering can equal, while we are conscious that it is in our power to mitigate its intensity, and abridge its duration? Justice may also strengthen

[1] Concil. Trid. Sess. 25.

the obligation which charity suggests. May not it happen that some are now suffering in purgatory for sins to which they were prompted by an advice, or seduced by an example? When we reflect on the extent of our obligation on this head it is difficult to free us from the charge of the most unfeeling indifference. Few, perhaps, are found sufficiently pure to be immediately received into the presence of their God. Not only venial sin excludes from his enjoyment; but, though the eternal guilt of mortal sin is remitted, some temporal punishment remains due to the justice of the Almighty, which, if not paid in this life, must be inflicted in the other. Thus Moses and Aaron and David had sinned; and though their sins were forgiven, they were subjected to temporal punishment. This atonement which we must offer to the offended justice of heaven, so far from being incompatible with the merits of the Redeemer, derives its efficacy from those merits, and is enjoined as a condition to insure their application. Thus St. Paul, whose mind did not comprehend the vastness of God's charity; and whose eloquence sank under the attempt at describing it, hesitates not to say that he underwent corporal mortification in order to fill up what was wanting in the sufferings of Christ. Enter, then, my brethren into the tender spirit of the Church. Avail yourselves of the opportunity which she affords you of extending relief to your departed brethren. This capability of affording mutual aid to each other is founded on that article: "I believe in the communion of saints," which is recited by Christians of every denomination. Hence it follows that all the members of the Church enjoy a mutual spiritual communion, partaking of each other's prayers and works of penance; and hence they are justly likened by St. Paul to the members of the human body, of which the pleasure or the sufferings through the medium of a common head are felt through the entire frame. We have examples of this vicarious penance in Scripture. Although the friends of Job could not propitiate the anger of the Divinity, still, through his intercession, they found favour in his sight. Often was the threatened vengeance of the Almighty averted from the guilty Israelites on account of the virtues of His servants, David and Abraham. From the same principle St. Paul so often recommends himself to the prayers of the faithful; and when on a certain occasion he met with some great affliction, he says to the people of Philippi: " I know that this shall turn to my salvation through your prayers." [1] But to convince you that the prayers and penitential works of the servants of God are, through the merits of Christ, accepted for the benefit of all the members of the Church, let us listen to the language of the same apostle: " Out of their abundance our wants are supplied."[2] Here we have a solemn assurance from the pen of an inspired apostle that our good works may benefit each other, and, of course, may be profitable to the souls in purgatory, as they are living members of the mystic body of Christ. Good God! how sublime is this doctrine of the Catholic Church, which not only appeals to the convictions of the most gifted intellect, but likewise sympathises with the finest feelings of our nature, strengthening and refining our affections by the spiritual charity which springs from the communion of saints. This is the spiritual link that binds all its members together—a link that is not sundered by distance nor by death, but stretches to the other world, uniting heaven and earth and purgatory in the amplitude of its connection. The stroke of death inflicts a bitter pang and conveys a silent warning that everything this side the grave has an end. Yet for this very pang the doc-

[1] Phil. i. 19.   [2] 2 Cor. viii. 14.

trine of purgatory offers a consolation which is sought for in vain in the cold and cheerless teaching of a different religion. Of the religions which embrace or exclude this tenet, the one resembles the state of savage life where all live in sullen independence, neither assisted by the aid nor ministering to the wants of each other, and thus unconnected by any community of mutual interchanges of kindness; while the other resembles society in the fullest tide of civilisation, bringing together regions the most remote and people the most dissociated, diffusing the fruits of its connection to every tribe and nation, and pouring over the barrenness of one country the superfluous riches of another.

To conclude, let me exhort you to exercise towards the faithful departed the tender offices of charity. Listen to their poor souls supplicating your aid in the tender language of Scripture: "Have pity on me, have pity on me; you, at least, my friends, have pity on me; for the hand of the Lord hath touched me."[1] But, alas! their supplications are often unheeded; and though we embrace our friends in this world with the warmest attachment, when they are gone we often bury their remembrance in the same grave, and they are left to reproach our insensibility in the language of the prophet: "I am forgotten as one dead from the heart, and they who passed by said not, The blessing of the Lord be with you."[2] Be not, therefore, my dear Christians, insensible to their distress. A sense even of your own interest should quicken your compassion. Mercy to him that showeth mercy. If you are active in endeavouring to relieve by your prayers the suffering souls in purgatory, others may extend the same pious duty to yourself, and those whom you have assisted by your piety will not fail to intercede for your relief, and to hasten your arrival into heaven. Amen.

[1] Job. xix. 21.    [2] Ps. cxxviii. 8.

## ON PENANCE.

"Behold, now is the acceptable time; behold, now is the day of salvation."—2 COR. vi. 2.

WHAT is the rich source of grace and mercy to which the Church draws our attention through the preceding words of the apostle? What is there in the present period that it should be introduced with the important character of an acceptable time, and a day of salvation? Is not the fountain of God's mercy always accessible to sinners, or is there a time when His favours are poured forth upon the faithful with a more unsparing abundance? Yes, such is the assurance contained in the language of my text, and on this day the voice of St. Paul resounds throughout the Church of God, exhorting the people to avail themselves of this acceptable season. Nay, the warnings of the prophets are heard to mingle with the invitations of the apostle, in order to awaken the people to a feeling sense of the graces that are proffered them; and Joel ushers in this penitential time with the following exhortation: "Be converted to me, saith the Lord, with all your heart, in fasting, in weeping, and in mourning, and rend your hearts and not your garments, and turn to the Lord your God, . . . for He is patient and rich in mercy. . . . Who knoweth but He will return and forgive, and leave a blessing behind Him? Blow the trumpet in Sion, sanctify a fast, call a solemn assembly, gather together the people, sanctify the Church, assemble the ancients, gather together the little ones and them that suck at the breasts. . . . Between the porch and the altar the priests, the Lord's ministers, will weep and say: Spare, O Lord, spare Thy people, and give not Thy inheritance to reproach."[1]

[1] Joel, ii. 12, 13, 14, 15, 16, 17.

## ON PENANCE.

Such is the cogent and impressive adjuration with which Joel calls upon the people, the young as well as the old, the priest as well as the laity, to be converted to the Lord with all their hearts, and to give proofs of this heartfelt conversion in weeping, in fasting, and in mourning. Such, too, is the theme which I shall address to you this day, taking the prophet of the Old and the apostle of the New Testament for my guides, impressing on you, with the authority of both, the necessity of expiating your sins by fasting and mortification, and exhorting you not to let pass, without availing yourselves of it, this acceptable time of salvation.

Of all the palpable contradictions between profession and practice which so often excite our wonder there is none, perhaps, more striking or humiliating than the utter disregard of the holy discipline of fasting manifested by individuals who pretend to follow the inspired volume as their guide. That those whose enjoyments consist solely in the animal pleasures of life, and whose gross sensuality is incapable of aspiring to the pure happiness of another, who have made a covenant like Esau to resign the reversion of an eternal inheritance for a miserable mess of pottage, incapable of satisfying the thirst of an immortal soul; who by consequence give themselves up to their own corrupt desires, "glorying," as the apostle says, "in their shame, and making a God of their belly;"[1] who in short, like the voluptuaries mentioned by the Wise Man, crown themselves with garlands, and riot in unbounded licence, because, as their hope extends not beyond the present hour, they strive to avert their thoughts from any retribution beyond the grave; that they should laugh at Lent, or any other living monument of religion is natural, since they revive those thoughts of immortality which they labour

[1] Phil. iii. 19.

to extinguish. But that a person who professes to take his faith from the Holy Bible should deny the necessity of fasting, while he reads in that sacred volume the melancholy history of man's fall, the incentive that occasioned it, the corruption that followed, the punishments which were provoked by the excesses of concupiscence, the pardons that were obtained by mortification and repentance, the examples of the prophets and apostles that consecrated the practice, together with their forcible inculcations of its necessity, notwithstanding all the graces of redemption—that such a one should look upon the penitential austerities of Lent as a useless or unnecessary labour, is one of the strangest paradoxes that can be exhibited in the annals of the weakness and inconsistency of the human mind. What betrayed our first parents into that abyss of misfortune into which they plunged their posterity? Concupiscence; and if it proved immoderate in them is it to be supposed that it requires no corrective or control in their degenerate descendants?

What a strong contrast between the purity produced by fasting and the guilt which springs from intemperance do we discover in the example of Moses and the Hebrew people. While the one was admitted to a familiarity with his God, purified by a course of fasting, we find the other reproved by the Almighty for the sins of their sensuality. "The beloved grew fat and kicked . . . he grew fat and forsook God who made him, and departed from God his Saviour."[1] Thus was the bounty of the Almighty, which should have excited gratitude, converted into an instrument of sin; the wanton use of the favours which He bestowed on them became the first step towards the idolatry into which they had fallen; nor was the anger which they excited by their excess appeased but by a rigorous process of

[1] Deut. xxxii. 15.

humiliation and repentance. When the prophet denounced the just vengeance of God on David, we find that even after the assurance that his sin was forgiven him, still, from the sincerity of his sorrow, which kept his transgression continually in his sight, his knees became feeble from fasting, and his couch was constantly watered with the torrent of his tears. Elias menaced Achab for his oppression of Naboth; Achab, terrified by the impending judgment, "rent his garments, put hair-cloth upon his flesh, fasted and slept in sackcloth, and walked with his head cast down;"[1] by which humiliation the wrath of heaven was averted. Elias, too, fasted forty days. Nor shall I pass over the memorable example of the fast which saved from utter destruction the guilty city of Nineve. The awful prediction, "forty days and Nineve shall be destroyed," went forth among the frighted inhabitants. Their doom appeared already sealed, and the time for their utter ruin seemed to be marked by the positive denunciations of heaven; yet it entered into their hearts that the anger of God might be appeased by repentance. Accordingly they proclaimed a fast, "and the king rose from his throne, and cast away his robe from him, and was clothed with sackcloth, and sat in ashes, and he caused it to be proclaimed that neither men nor beasts, oxen or sheep, should taste anything."[2] The fasts and fervent supplications of the people found favour in the sight of God, and the direful prophecies of their destruction were changed into the merciful assurance of their pardon and their deliverance. But not only do we find the practice of fasting invariably to accompany an expiation for sin, but we find the favourites of heaven distinguished by this virtue who were chosen as the instruments of God's favours to His people. When Esther exposed her

[1] 3 Kings, xxi. 27.  [2] Jonas, iii. 4, 6, 7.

own life to plead the cause of an oppressed nation, far from relying on the aid of vanity, she covered her head with ashes instead of precious ointments, and humbled her body with fasting, and after a process which the world would deem so unsuited to win the favour of a monarch, she appears before Assuerus, whose will was suddenly subdued by Him in whose hands are the hearts of kings, to lend a gracious ear to her petitions. When Holofernes poured his myriads over Judea, who threatened to overturn every sacred monument of religion, the instrument selected by the Almighty for the salvation of his people was a virtuous widow, who made " a private chamber " in her house, and "wore hair-cloth upon her loins, and fasted all the days of her life," except the feasts of the House of Israel. "And all the people cried to the Lord with great earnestness, and they humbled their souls in fastings and prayers, both they and their wives. And the priests put on hair-cloths, and they caused the little children to lie prostrate before the temple of the Lord, and the altar of the Lord they covered with hair-cloth." [1] In short, not to repeat the numberless examples of the efficacy of fasting recorded in Scripture, such as the births of Samson, of Samuel, and St. John, the fruit of their mothers' fasting and prayers, we read in the annals of the last wars which the Hebrews waged for their country and their temple, that abstinence and prayer strung their courage to a higher pitch, and that fasting was the arms which were most instrumental in the achievement of their victories. Before they engaged, on one occasion, they craved mercy of the Lord with weeping and fasting, "lying prostrate on the ground for three days continually." [2] And on another their intrepid leader tells his followers, who were faint from fasting, " that the success of war is

[1] Judith viii. 5, 6, and iv. 7, 8, 9.     [2] 2 Mac. xiii. 12.

not in the multitude of the army,"[1] and, relying on the assurance of the divine favour, he discomfited his enemies.

But why thus loiter so long on the confines of the ancient covenant, and not approach the evidences of the same truth that are furnished by the new dispensation? Why confine myself to a religion which was confessedly one of many rites and expiatory ordinances, some of which have been abrogated by the plenitude of the great sacrifice of redemption which supplied their deficiency? Yes, many of the rites and ceremonies and mere external forms of the Jewish law have been abolished; but the human heart, with its impure desires, its passions, and its concupiscence still remains. The law, then, that requires to subdue its continual mutiny by fasting and by prayer, is neither limited nor temporary—no, it is coeval with the fall of our nature, and must descend to the latest period of time; and as long as man carries about one particle of that flesh through which the infection of original sin has spread its corruption, so long will stand the truth of the Redeemer's words that there are "certain devils which cannot be banished but by prayer and fasting."[2] Behold then the reason why I have directed your attention to the copious references in favour of fasting which are spread over the pages of the Old Testament. They are of that portion of the ancient law which remains still unrepealed; they extend their influence to the Christian as well as to the Jewish religion, and, like the commandments which are the common foundation of the morality of both, the practice of fasting and self-denial is equally necessary for their purity and perfection. Why the rigorous fasts and mortification of the great Precursor of our religion? or why the long fast of forty days, consecrated by the example of its Divine Founder, if the necessity of such

---

[1] 1 Mach. iii. 19.   [2] St. Matt. xvii. 20.

observances had entirely passed away? Why the prediction that when He should retire from the world His disciples should fast—a prediction which we find verified in the lives and writings of His apostles? Hence no weighty or important business undertaken, no solemn duties of religion discharged, without the favour of heaven being sought, or its wrath propitiated by prayer and fasting. When the Holy Ghost separated Saul and Barnabas unto the ministry, it was while people were "ministering to the Lord and fasting"[1] He made the communication; nor was their ordination accomplished until after a similar ceremony: "Then they, fasting and praying, and imposing hands on them, sent them away."[2] When the same apostles ordained priests in the churches which they erected, they took care to repeat, in order to perpetuate, the same holy example, as we are assured in the Acts of the Apostles, "And when they ordained to them priests in every church, and prayed with fasting, they commended them to the Lord in whom they believed."[3] Again, when St. Paul, on his journey to Rome, was overtaken by a violent tempest which wrapt the heavens for several days in darkness, the first gleam of hope which broke upon them was after a solemn fast, when the Apostle cheered them with the assurance of a speedy deliverance. After a train of evidences in favour of this holy practice, from the first dawn of religion until it was spread by the apostles over every region of the earth, am I not justified in expressing my astonishment how any institution for continuing it should be slighted by those who have a reverence for the holy ordinances of scripture? Is it that the repeated injunctions of this virtue should have lain a dead letter to amuse the readers of the inspired volume, without ever being enforced? Is it that fasting might have been

[1] Acts, xiii. 2.   [2] Ibid.   [3] Acts, xiv. 22.

good for the first fervent disciples of Christianity, but altogether superfluous for its more tepid followers of a remoter age?

The Acts of the Apostles and Epistles were written after Christ had offered the great sacrifice of atonement on the cross. Surely the apostles were as well convinced of its infinite efficacy, as any of the modern profligates who affect not to fast lest they should be undervaluing its merits, whence we must conclude that they have a clearer knowledge of the economy of our redemption than those to whom it was directly imparted from its source, and that they are less in need of any aids to virtue than those who came in contact with the very fountain of grace and mercy! With such strong and cogent recommendations in its favour it is natural that the practice of fasting should have accompanied the progress of Christianity; and, accordingly, we find it most intimately intertwined with its institutions. Thus the controversy which arose in the middle of the second century regarding the time of celebrating Easter informs us, at the same time, of the universal fast which preceded it; and Irenæus, who flourished at the end of the same century, attests that it was extended by many to the term of forty days. As we descend from that period the testimonies in its favour accumulate, all acquiescing in the sentiment of St. Jerome: "We fast one Lent by apostolic tradition, the whole world agreeing with us herein."[1] Nor was the observance of this holy season arbitrary, or left to the caprices of each individual. A strong line of demarcation was drawn between the austerities which each one was free to practise at other times, and those which were of precept in this penitential season. Hence St. Cæsarius of Arles emphatically says: "He who fasts at another time shall

[1] Ep. 27, ad Marcellam.

obtain pardon; but he who is able and does not fast on those days shall suffer punishment."[1] "To break the fast prescribed," says St. Ambrose, "is no slight offence; to transgress in part the fast of Lent is a sin, but to neglect it entirely a sacrilege."[2] The fervour of the faithful generally corresponded with the instructions of their pastors, and Lent was hailed with a particular devotion as a season that was fraught with a profusion of blessings. Then all the frivolities of the world were laid aside, the revels of mirth and intemperance gave way to a different spirit, the robes of vanity and dissipation were exchanged for sackcloth, and amidst the solitude to which this sudden interruption of worldly merriment gave rise, the accents of religion were heard with a more awful solemnity. Then piety was propagated with all the aid and influence of custom, the torrent of bad example was stemmed by the current of virtue, bringing thousands in an opposite direction; in short, each one was cheered on through the rugged way by the contemplation of the far more heroic austerity of others, and, to use the language of St. Bernard, "Kings, princes, clergy, laity, nobility, and the common people, rich and poor, entered with cheerfulness on the holy exercise of fasting,"[3] forgetful of every other distinction but what might arise from the disastrous pre-eminence of their sins, and competing only for a larger share of sufferings and humiliations. Some, it is true, might relapse into their former sins, and be again borne down by the tide of bad example; but then, are we to forget that while some may fall away thousands remain steady; or who, but the systematic friend of vice and immorality, will not praise the wisdom of an institution which brings thus the blessing of reflection amidst the children of the world, which stops the shifting scenes of folly which

[1] Hom. ii.    [2] Hom. vii.    [3] Serm. iii. de Quadrag.

hurried away their attention without giving them a moment's time for reflection, which enables them to pause and look round as from a fixed position, and remark from what place they wandered and whither they are fast hurrying; and, when at length, they hear the noise of the breakers, and startle at the dangers that are unperceived by those who are unconscious of their situation, enables them, even then, to abandon the thoughtless crew that are rushing on their fate, and grasp that only plank of penance which is left to man after the wreck of his innocence?

Look on Lent, then, in this point of view, not only illustrating the precepts and practice of all who, both in the Old and New Testament were distinguished for sanctity and wisdom, but also affording to fleeting generations of man a resting-place for reflection, and equalising its different ranks by a community of good works and an interchange of charity—and what institution can be dearer to the purest affections of the human heart? If you imagine that Lent is productive of no other advantages than the mere mortification of the flesh, you labour under a serious error. This is a necessary condition, and, when rightly performed, becomes the root of many other incalculable blessings. Yes, the mortification of our appetites by closing many of those vain and artificial wants that swallow up all our substance, becomes a rich source of benevolence to our distressed fellow-creatures. Such has been the mortification always recommended by the Church, and, lest avarice should feed upon the retrenchments of luxury, the faithful were commanded, while their own diet was more coarse and sparing, to divide their substance more abundantly with the poor. Nay, they were taught, in the language of the prophet, that the relief which it enabled them to afford to their afflicted brethren was one of the most acceptable conditions of their penance. "Is this such a fast as I have chosen," says Isaias, "for a man to afflict his soul for a day, and spread sackcloth and ashes? Is not this rather the fast that I have chosen? Loose the bonds of wickedness, undo the bundles that oppress, let them that are broken go free, and break asunder every burden; deal thy bread to the hungry, and bring the needy and harbourless into thy house. When thou shalt see one naked cover him, and despise not thy own flesh; then shall thy light break forth as the morning, and thy health shall speedily arise, and thy justice shall go before thy face, and the glory of the Lord shall gather thee up. Then thou shalt call and the Lord shall hear; thou shalt cry and He shall say, here I am. If thou wilt take away the chain out of the midst of thee, when thou shalt pour out thy soul to the hungry, and shalt satisfy the afflicted soul, then shall thy light rise up in darkness, and thy darkness shall be as the noonday, and the Lord will give thee rest continually, and will fill thy soul with brightness, and deliver thy house, and thou shalt be like a watered garden, and like a fountain of waters whose waters shall not fail."[1]

What a delightful prospect is here unfolded by the prophet; a prospect of which the Pagan nations never felt the charms, because they knew not the virtue of benevolence, nor the deeper root of individual privation from which it springs. Their doctrine was the doctrine of the voluptuaries of every age, so well described by the Wise-man, who thus represents them in the midst of their revels: "Come let us enjoy the good things that are present, and let us speedily use the creatures as in youth; let us fill ourselves with costly wines and ointments; let us crown ourselves with roses before they be withered; let no meadow escape our riot; let none of

[1] Isaia. lviii. 5, 6, 7, 8, 9, 10, 11.

us go without his part in luxury; let us everywhere leave tokens of joy."[1] Such is the enjoyment to which the world invites its votaries, exciting, no doubt, from the ingredients of which it is composed, but evanescent as the roses with which they are crowned. But who are they in reality whose lives appear thus enviable, encircled with so many enjoyments? It is only by listening to the language in which they conclude their eulogy of pleasure, we will be able to estimate their genuine character. "Let us oppress the poor just man, and not spare the widow, nor honour the ancient grey hairs of the aged, but let our strength be the law of justice; for that which is feeble is found to be worth nothing."[2] Behold, then, the genuine features of those amiable and eloquent assertors of an unrestricted use of all the bounties of creation. Behold the natural alliance between sensuality and cruelty. Do but close your ears for a moment against the song that may have lulled your senses; divert your eyes from the garlands with which they mask their features; and look at those sensualists when the atmosphere is freed from the vapours, which arose from their intemperance, that surrounded them; how clearly does the strong light reflected on them by the inspired writings reveal their hideous deformity, enabling you to recognise in those joyous revellers the habitual oppressors of the poor. Yes, the same lips that pronounce the treacherous language of pleasure are they which drop the withering resolutions of oppressing the widow; the same ears that are captivated by the sounds of the harp and timbrel are those which listen with most indifference to the cries of the orphan; and the youth, apparently all innocent gaiety, who intertwines the wreaths of roses round his temples, is the monster who blushes not to confess that he wil

[1] Wisd. ii. 6, 7, 8.  [2] Ibid. 10, 11.

scatter the grey hairs of the aged and infirm to the wind. Who, then, promote best the happiness of society—those who feast or who deny themselves no enjoyment—let the two passages I have put before you decide. In the one, we find those who are sparing to themselves and breaking their bread to the poor compared to rich fountains of water that are never exhausted, and spreading blessings where they pass. In the other, we find those who dream of nought but riot and ointments and rich wine, and whose short passage through life is strewn with the ruin of the cottage and the dishonoured hair of its aged and feeble inmates. These two examples of good and evil are to-day set before you—which will you choose for your adoption? Oh, you cannot hesitate between those of which one has been the practice of the libertines of every age, and which has uniformly brought misery in its train, and the other has been consecrated by all the saints of God, and fraught with such incalculable advantages to society. Need I dwell further on the illustration of this truth, or need I point to you by historical references that where no restraint is put upon the appetite the support of thousands is sacrificed to their rapacity. Hence it is that charity is not so much regulated by the means as by the inclinations of mankind. Without that virtue of abstinence which is the principle of fasting the largest fortunes vanish and are unproductive. This wish satisfied, another starts up; one vanity purchased, its votary becomes more craving for another; luxury succeeds luxury, while the appetite, instead of being satisfied becomes more and more ravenous by indulgence; at length the earth itself is ransacked for its voracity, and when all fail of filling those desires that are insatiable as the grave, even the precious metals must be dissolved, as in the case of the Roman Emperors, for those monstrous gratifications.

May not such be compared to bottomless gulfs eternally devouring and yielding nothing to the poor? But when, as we have been taught by the Christian religion, men deny themselves, this self-denial changes at once the human heart, and instead of being that insatiable gulf which luxury makes it, it becomes a living fountain, as it is described by the prophet, always pouring forth its abundance upon others, thus compensating by the diffusion of its charity for the inequality of fortune, and spreading joy and gladness over every tract which is marked by the current of its waters. Let us, then, embrace a discipline teeming with such blessings. But whilst we fast from food and bring the senses under subjection, let us recollect that fasting from sin is the chief end of Lent; and that without a mortification of the soul and all its appetites, we would be frustrating the great object of this holy season. Yes, it is in vain that you abstain from food which is lawful to eat at other seasons unless you curb those sinful appetites of lust, of pride, and of revenge, which are forbidden at all times, as they violate the laws of God. Let us, then, join the ranks of those holy penitents who are commencing at this season by making war upon themselves —the most arduous of all combats—resolved, to use the language of the Redeemer, to take heaven by storm. At other periods of the year we might be disheartened not only by the ruggedness but by the solitude of the way. Now, however, instead of any such apprehension, we are cheered by the number of intrepid companions of the mortification of the cross, who will not only share the fatigues of this toilsome exercise, but who will actually chide our pusillanimity by the generous ardour of their example. Behold, what a change in the habits of the people has been wrought by the blessed influence of fasting; and as St. Chrysostom remarked of Constantinople, instead of all the noise of revelry which rung through the streets, the city is become like a grave, sober, chaste matron of a family, and the hearts of all are subdued by the contagious influence of religion. Let us not, by a spirit of indifference or indolence, disentitle ourselves to the graces that God is ready to pour forth on His people. We have all sinned, we all stand in need of mercy, and you have seen by repeated proofs from the Old and the New Testament that fasting and humiliations are among the channels through which the mercies of the Redeemer's passion are conveyed. What apology, then, can you have for declining this exercise? Not any complaceny in your own virtue, for should you entertain it, St. James will inform you that there is no truth in the presumption, since we all are sinners.

Avail yourselves, then, of this acceptable time: let not the days of salvation pass over unprofitably. Christ is knocking for admittance to your souls; refuse Him not an entrance. Recollect and profit by the example of the blind man of Jericho, who loudly cried out and persevered in spite of the fastidious murmers of the profane: "Jesus, Son of David, have mercy on me."[1] Had he listened to their suggestions, he would not have received the graces, since it is remarked that Jesus never passed that way more. Awful reflection, and perhaps this is the last time that Jesus would favour us with such a merciful visitation. To conclude, then, in the words of Joel, with which I opened this discourse: "Be ye converted to the Lord with all your heart, in weeping, in fasting, and in mourning, rend your hearts and turn to the Lord, for He is rich in mercy. Between the porch and the altar let the priest weep and say: Spare, O Lord, spare thy people, and give not thy inheritance to reproach." Amen.

[1] St. Luke, xviii. 38.

## THE SACRAMENT OF PENANCE.

"Amen, I say unto you whatsoever you shall bind on earth shall be bound also in heaven; and whatsoever you shall loose upon earth shall be loosed also in heaven."—MATT. xviii. 18.

WHAT an extraordinary degree of power conferred upon man to become the depositary of an authority which belongs to God alone. It is no wonder that the assumption of such power on the part of our Redeemer should have scandalised the Jews, while they were yet ignorant of His divinity. Jesus Christ tells the man struck with the palsy: "Son, thy sins are forgiven thee;"[1] and immediately the reproaches of blasphemy assail him from every quarter. "Why doth this man speak thus: he blasphemeth. Who can forgive sins but God only?" The language with which the Scribes and Pharisees freely reproached our Saviour is the same which is frequently directed against the priests of the Catholic Church; as if they claimed to themselves an inherent power of forgiving sin, a power which is the prerogative of the Divinity alone. How often do you hear the invidious observation of the Pharisees repeated: "Why doth this man speak thus: he blasphemeth. Who can forgive sins but God alone?" It is true, my dear Christians, God alone has the power of forgiving sins, and if the priests of the New Law claim a participation of that power, it is not from the blasphemous arrogance of human pride, but because, in mercy to man, Christ has vested them with that authority. In vain, then, will the charge of blasphemy be preferred against

[1] S. Mark, ii. 5.

them. While they have the solemn words of Jesus Christ as the credentials of their authority, they will submit with patience to the imputation. Fully impressed, then, with the merciful view, on account of which this power has been imparted to them, I shall in the following discourse explain to you the sacrament of penance, and principally what regards confession and the dispositions with which it ought to be accompanied.

However extraordinary it might appear to the views of human wisdom, that a creature should be invested with the authority of loosing or binding the sins of a fellow mortal, still, when Christ has spoken in such explicit terms, the duty of man requires of him to resign his presumption. Nay, if we consider what was the object of our Redeemer in giving such a commission to His priests, our wonder at the vastness of the power will be lost in the vaster and more comprehensive mercy that conferred it. It was not for the purpose of ministering to human pride. It was not to make it an instrument of oppression. No; instead of making it an engine to scatter the ills of human life, it was intended as a medicine to heal its worst disorders. This one reflection may be sufficient to arrest the presumptuous speculation of those who would insinuate that the pride of man is flattered by this power. It is true, as St. Chrysostom remarks, that the priests of the New Law are invested with a power which far exceeds any other upon earth. They only can bind the body; the authority of the priest extends to the soul. But, alas! the awful responsibility that is annexed to the use of this power, instead of nourishing the suggestions of pride, is calculated to humble him to the earth.

If the duty of doing justice between man and man brings with it a weight of obligation, which ought to appal the most intrepid conscience, what ought not to be the apprehension of a man who is entrusted with the office of doing justice between man and his Creator. Yet such are the obligations that are involved in the words of my text: "Amen, I say to you, whatsoever you shall bind on earth shall be bound also in heaven, and whatsoever you shall loose on earth shall be loosed also in heaven." However, if these words import strict duties on the part of the priest, they are pregnant with instructions no less important to the faithful. They imply, on their part, the necessity of submitting the secrets of their hearts to the jurisdiction of his tribunal. Holding the place and fulfilling the duties of a judge, the priest cannot ascertain what sins he is to loose and what to bind, unless he becomes acquainted with the nature of the offences. Since many of these offences are secret transgressions, of which the penitent alone is conscious, he cannot arrive at their knowledge but through his communication. He is invested, however, with the power of binding or loosing their sins, as Christ Himself assures us; and hence the power of the priest involves the necessity of the penitent's confession. Such has been in every age the doctrine of the Catholic Church, as it is ascertained from the writings of the ancient Fathers and the practice of the faithful. Thus St. Gregory of Nyssa speaks in one of his discourses: "Reveal with confidence your secrets to the priest; open your hidden wounds to the physician of your soul, who will feel a tender regard both for your character and your health."[1] And St. Chrysostom: "The condemnation and confession of sin form the medicine of penance."[2] Finally, St. Augustine, comparing the disorders of the soul with those that destroy the health of the body, uses the strong but appropriate compari-

[1] Orat. in eos qui alios acerbe judicant.   [2] Homil. 9, in Epist. ad Heb.

sons: "Has your conscience been suppurated? have you been tormented by the collection of poisonous matter? Acknowledge the hand; submit to the operation of your physician; confess, and let the latent virus find vent in your confession."[1] Similar has been the language of the other Fathers of the Church.

But to show how they connected the practice of confession with the power of binding and loosing sins, which Christ transferred upon his Church, St. Leo expressly affirms "that Christ conferred upon the rulers of his Church the authority of conducting to the participation of the sacraments those who were purified by a wholesome confession, and had passed through the gate of reconciliation."[2] How, then, should not we venerate an institution which is derived from the divine source of Jesus Christ Himself, and consecrated by the practice of all ages of the Church? But it is not more venerable in its origin than it is wholesome in its consequences. These consequences are the health of the soul and its reconciliation with the Almighty, in which you are all interested. Adopting, then, the words of St. Chrysostom, that "the condemnation and confession of sin forms the medicine of penance," I shall endeavour to press upon your attention the dispositions that are required in order that you may reap the fruits of this holy institution. First, "the condemnation of sin forms the medicine of penance," an ingredient so necessary that without it our confession would be not only vain but sacrilegious, were the omission of it culpable. This condemnation of sin has in every age of the world formed a part of true repentance, and while God shall be invested with His justice, it shall not cease to enter into the conditions of reconciliation. It is by requiring this condition that the pastors of the Catholic Church

[1] Hom. 50.     [2] In Ep. ad Theodor.

repel the unjust imputations of blasphemy. They arrogate not the power of forgiving sin, unless when the heart pronounces its condemnation; and so necessary do they deem this self-condemnation of the soul, that without it their absolution would be without fruit or benefit. This conversion of heart was always necessary to disarm the justice and recover the favour of heaven.

Thus the Psalmist, speaking of a sinner: "Behold, he hath been in labour with injustice; he hath conceived sorrow and brought forth iniquity; he hath opened a pit and dug it, and he is fallen into the hole he made,"[1] shows that it is only by conversion that he can rise from his fallen state. "God is a just Judge, strong and patient. Except you will be converted, He will brandish his sword: He hath bent his bow and made it ready, and in it He hath prepared the instruments of death."[2]

And again the same Psalmist, deprecating the vengeance of God, thus offers up his humble supplication: "Convert us, O God, our Saviour, and turn off Thy anger from us. . . . Show us, O Lord, Thy mercy, and grant us Thy salvation." After which prayer he thus concludes: "God will speak peace unto His people and unto His saints, and unto them that are converted to the heart. Surely His salvation is near to them that fear Him, that glory may dwell in our land."[3] Numberless are the testimonies that might be collected out of those inspired effusions of a contrite heart to prove the necessity of that contrition of which the royal penitent gave, himself, the example. I shall, however, satisfy myself with one passage more, which begins and concludes with the necessity of this conversion: "Convert us, O Lord," he piously exclaims, "and show us Thy face, and we shall be saved. How long, O God of Hosts, wilt Thou feed us with the bread of tears, and give us for

[1] Ps. vii. 15, 16. [2] Ibid. 12, 13. [3] Ps. lxxxiv. 5, 6, 9, 10, 11.

our drink tears in measure? O God of Hosts, convert us, and show thy face, and we shall be saved."[1] But these exhortations to a condemnation of sin are not confined to the Psalmist. No; they are scattered over every portion of the inspired writings. "Delay not to be converted," says the Wise-man, "and defer it not from day to day; for His wrath shall come on a sudden, and in the time of vengeance He will destroy thee."[2]

And again: "To the penitent God hath given the way of justice, and He had strengthened them that were fainting in patience. Turn, then, to the Lord, and forsake thy sins. Make thy prayer before the face of the Lord, and offend less. Return to the Lord, and turn away from thy injustice, and greatly hate abomination. Tarry not in the error of the ungodly, and give glory before death."[3]

In fine, the prophet Zachary thus exhibits the mutual connection between the mercy of God and the conversion of sinners: "Turn ye to me, saith the Lord of Hosts, turn ye from your evils and from your wicked thoughts, and I will turn to you, saith the Lord of Hosts."[4] In short, whenever we find God holding out to His sinful people the consoling assurance of pardon, He always requires a detestation of sin and a conversion of the heart as a preliminary condition.

But why do I dwell on the testimonies of the Old Law when the Gospel furnishes us with the most perfect models of this conversion that is required? Cast your eyes on the penitent Magdalene throwing herself at the feet of the Redeemer, bathing them with her tears, and wiping them with her hair; and will you not recognise in her conduct an illustration of the doctrine which I preach? Christ pronounces that many sins are forgiven her: and why? because she loved much. Yes, moved

[1] Ps. lxxix. 4, 5, 8. [2] Eccl. v. 8, 9. [3] Eccl. xvii. 20. [4] Zach. i. 3, 4.

with the divine grace, which gave her a view of the hideous deformity of sin, she turned from her evil ways, and by ministering to Jesus Christ gave a proof of her conversion. It is, then, in vain that you will come to the tribunal of confession, and throw yourself at the feet of the priest unless you feel a similar detestation of sin and a sorrow for having offended Him who is entitled to all your affections. In the New Law, then, as well as the Old this conversion of the heart, this condemnation of sin, is equally necessary, with this difference only, that what might have been a most difficult task in the Old Law now becomes lightened by the sweetness of that grace that is dispensed through the sacrament of penance. Be not then deceived; you must come to this sacrament with humble and contrite heart, conscious of the evil you have done, and resolved to turn your back upon your iniquity, otherwise, you will have no share in its graces. Do you, then, wish to have a model laid before you for your imitation? If you do you have it in the picture of the prodigal child drawn by Christ Himself, and held up to all penitents as the pattern for them to follow. Having dissipated in luxury and riot the share of the substance which was given to him by his father, he was reduced to a state of misery too deplorable for description. He lived for awhile insensible to his state, but, awakened at length by the recollection of what he lost, contrasted with the wretchedness into which he had fallen, he thus expostulates with himself: "How many hired servants in my father's house have plenty of bread, and I here perish with hunger. I will rise and will go to my father, and say to him: Father, I have sinned against heaven and before thee; I am not worthy to be called thy son, make me as one of thy hired servants. And, rising up, he went to his father. And when he was yet a great way off, his father saw him, and was moved with compassion, and, running to him, fell upon his neck and kissed him. And the son said to him: Father, I have sinned against heaven and before thee; I am not now worthy to be called thy son. But the father said to his servants: Bring forth quickly the first robe and put it on him, and put a ring on his hand and shoes on his feet, and bring hither the fatted calf, and kill it, and let us eat and make merry, because this my son was dead and is come to life again; he was lost and is found."[1]

I have thus detailed to you the parable at length, unwilling to diminish that moving tenderness which is found in the simple language of the Gospel. Here you see a perfect model for your contemplation. Mark, my dear Christians, the progress of his conversion. After the first feeling of consciousness of the misery into which he had fallen, he immediately expresses the generous resolution, "I will rise." This resolution was an inspiration of grace. However, being unable to fulfil it by his natural strength, his father had compassion on him when he was afar off; to show us, as St. Jerome remarks, that the grace of God will come to assist the sinner's feeble but generous resolution. But what is particularly instructive in this parable is that, according to St. Augustine, the repentance of the prodigal child not only included a conversion of his heart from his sins, but likewise the generous resolution of confessing them. If you, then, are anxious for a reconciliation with your God, imitate this model of all true penitents. Let a feeling conviction of the misery into which you are sunk inspire you, like him, with the strong resolution of rising, and though you may be yet far from arriving at that perfect state in which you might be invested with your first robe, the grace of the Almighty will come to succour your advancement.

[1] S. Luke, xv. 17-24.

Thus disposed, come with an humble and penitent heart to the tribunal of penance, and you will profit of all its spiritual advantages. Thus you will realise St. Chrysostom's idea of penance, including at once "the condemnation and confession of sin:" "Go, then, and show yourself to the priests."[1] If our Redeemer required of the lepers whom He had perfectly cleansed from their leprosy to show themselves to the priests, how much more so is it necessary for the penitents of the New Law to show themselves to those of whom he pronounced, "Amen, I say unto you, whatsoever you shall bind on earth shall be bound also in heaven; and whatsoever you shall loose on earth shall be loosed also in heaven." Instead of feeling repugnance to submit to this salutary remedy, ought you not to be grateful for the mercy by which it was instituted. It is painful, you will say, and humiliating to confess our sins to a fellow-man. It is; and it is because it is painful and humiliating it may be justly deemed a portion of penance. To be cured of a temporal disease you refuse not to submit to a painful operation. And to be freed from the spiritual leprosy of the soul you deem the exposing of that leprosy to your spiritual physician painful beyond endurance. Alas! if you could estimate the extent of the evil you get rid of, and the graces which you obtain by such an humble confession, you would not hesitate an instant to submit to all its rigours. Hence, I shall not deny that the confession of our sins has in it something mortifying to human pride; but, like the operation which inflicts pain, while it opens the wound and discharges the latent venom, so confession, while it opens the spiritual wounds of our soul, heals at the same time that it irritates. How justly, therefore, is it called by Tertullian, "A discipline by which man is humbled."[2] If,

---

[1] S. Luke, xvii. 14.  [2] Fertull. de Pœnit.

however, he is humbled by confession, it is also a discipline by which he is afterwards exalted. If it brings with it a temporary confusion, it is a confusion which is succeeded by an unspeakable peace of mind. Should anyone, then, feel repugnance in disclosing his sins to the minister of Christ, under the most sacred seal, let him consider what would be his confusion when they should be published to the whole world. Who could balance between the alternative of a private confession, which is to be followed by pardon, and a public one in the face of the universe, followed by eternal torments. " Let no one be ashamed to exhibit his wounds," says St. Augustine, "which cannot be healed without disclosure."[1] It is therefore, I trust, almost unnecessary to press further on your attention the necessity of a full and circumstantial disclosure of all your sins. If anyone hitherto could have imagined it a slight offence to have concealed any sin from the physician of his soul let him reflect on the examples of Ananias and Sapphira, in order that he may escape the magnitude of their guilt and punishment. It might have seemed a trivial circumstance to have concealed a part of that property which they were at liberty to give or to withhold. But having pretended that they disposed of the entire, their hypocrisy irritated the Almighty, and they fell dead at the feet of St. Peter because they had lied to the Holy Ghost. This awful warning is justly applicable to those who, while they pretend to lay open their conscience in confession, lie not to man but to the Holy Ghost whose ministry he holds.

Do not, then, suffer yourselves to be betrayed into such a snare, and aggravate not your past guilt by an imperfect confession. Should not every individual rejoice, on the contrary, that he is to obtain, on such easy

---

[1] St. Aug. Serm. 171 de Pœnit.

terms, a reconciliation with his God. "Unheard of process of judgment!" exclaims a holy man, "in which the criminal is condemned if he conceals, and absolved if he confesses his delinquency." It is an unheard of process; since in human tribunals the judges punish what is discovered, and here the Almighty only punishes the guilt that is concealed, while He extends mercy to that which is openly and humbly unfolded. How applicable are the words of Scripture: "He that hideth his sins shall not prosper; but he that shall confess and forsake them shall obtain mercy."[1]

If you then wish to obtain mercy, come and confess your sins. Throw yourselves at the feet of the minister of Jesus Christ, who has power to loose them, oppressed with sorrow for having offended the Almighty, and you will obtain mercy from Him "who healeth the broken of heart, and bindeth up their bruises."[2] Imitate the prodigal child, saying, like him, with a courageous generosity, "I will rise and go to my father, and I will say, father, I have offended against heaven and before thee." If you do, your Heavenly Father will cast an eye of mercy on you, and assist your resolution. Yes, He will strengthen your feeble steps, nay, will advance to meet you. Forgetful of your past infidelity He will indulge only in the exercise of His mercy, and receiving you again into His household He will diffuse joy among the angels, and clothe you with the robe of justice which you shall wear to all eternity. Amen.

[1] Prov. xxviii. 13.  [2] Ps. cxlvi. 3.

## ON PRIDE.

### THE PHARISEE AND THE PUBLICAN.

"I say to you, this man went down into his house justified rather than the other, because every one that exalteth himself shall be humbled, and he that humbleth himself shall be exalted."—LUKE xviii. 14.

WHAT an admirable picture of humility does not the Gospel exhibit to our view in this parable of the Pharisee and the Publican—a picture rendered still more engaging by its striking contrast with the deformity of pride. Two men of opposite dispositions and habits of life repair to the temple of the Lord, there to offer the homage of their prayers. The one a Pharisee, the other a publican; the one a doctor of the law, whose sayings were revered for their wisdom, and whose conduct was a pattern of regularity; the other a character whose name was a term of reproach, and whose office was identified with fraud and injustice; the one almost idolised for his virtue, the other equally execrated for his guilt; in fine, the one a reputed saint, the other a notorious sinner. Such are the characters that present themselves in the temple of the Almighty. If, my dear Christians, human views were to be the criterion for forming a judgment of their merits, the balance would probably incline in favour of the Pharisee. But, God! how different are Thy judgments from those of men; the Pharisee is condemned, the publican is justified. And why? Because the Pharisee is proud of his pretended justice, and because the publican is humble and penitent for his crimes. Hence, we are taught to deplore the cruel and melancholy effects of pride in the one, and to appreciate the blessings of humility in the other—two essential and practical points of Christian morality which I shall attempt to develop in the following discourse:

I cannot more appropriately open this discourse than in the words of St. Gregory, which are most applicable to the subject. "I am generally employed," says this holy Pontiff, "in cautioning you against evil, but now I must caution you against the pride which may lurk in your good works and infect the purity of your intention." How arduous, then, is the passage of the Christian through life. He must not only not stray into the paths of profligacy and dissipation, but in pursuing the narrow way which Christ has commanded him to tread, he must guard himself against the approaches of any secret complacency that would rob him of the merit of his toils. This pride is the deadliest of all the foes that meditate our ruin; we are on our guard against other vices because then danger is apparent, but pride secretly insinuates itself into our virtuous actions, poisoning their best qualities, and hence its attacks are the more fatal because they are treacherous and unseen. Of an enemy so subtle and designing, it is necessary to point out the danger that you may not be betrayed by its seduction. If we are to estimate the enormity of any sin by the misery which it inflicts, or the punishment that is to await it, the sin of pride will be almost without a parallel. What is it that first dispeopled heaven of its inhabitants and consigned them to the bottomless abyss, there to roll in penal fire, and to sustain the wrath of an angry Deity? Pride. Yes, their arrogant leader, proud of the gifts for which he was indebted to the Almighty, said, in the presumption of his swollen heart, "I shall ascend into the throne of the most High, and I shall be like unto Him."[1] But the vengeance of heaven overtook him in his career of folly and ambition, and hurled him into endless torture. What is it that entailed on the human

[1] Isai. xiv. 14.

kind such an endless train of woes and misery? Pride. Yes, it was a perverse and unreasonable curiosity of knowledge that prompted our unhappy parents to hear and to follow the suggestions of the tempter in defiance of God's positive prohibition. Pride is, then, the prolific source of that large and complicated mass of misery, of ignorance, of passion, and of suffering, that are comprised in that word of vast and mysterious import—original sin. Waving, then, spiritual evils, what is it that has brought misfortune on families, ruin on cities, and desolation on empires? The whole history of the Old Testament will tell us, it was pride. "Therefore, as I live, saith the Lord of Hosts, the God of Israel, Moab shall be as Sodom, and the children of Ammon as Gomorrha, the dryness of thorns and heaps of salt, and a desert even for ever: the remnant of my people shall make a spoil of them, and the residue of my nation shall possess them. This shall befal them for their pride, because they have blasphemed and have been magnified against the people of the Lord of Hosts."[1] The prophetic books are full of awful denunciations against those who provoked by their pride the vengeance of the Almighty. Of this vengeance we have a terrible example in Antiochus, King of Syria, who, while he breathed destruction on the religion of the Almighty, was suddenly arrested in his impious career. "Moreover, being filled with pride, breathing out fire in his rage against the Jews, it happened, as he was going with violence, that he fell from his chariot, so that his limbs were much pained by a grievous bruising of the body. Thus, he that seemed to himself to command even the waves of the sea, being proud above the condition of man, and to weigh the heights of the mountains in a

[1] Soph. ii. 9, 10.

balance, now being cast down to the ground, was carried in a litter, bearing witness to the manifest power of God in himself. So that worms swarmed out of the body of this man, and whilst he lived in sorrow and pain, his flesh fell off. . . . And the man that thought a little before he could reach to the stars of heaven, no man could endure to carry. . . . And by this means, being brought from his great pride, he began to come to the knowledge of himself, being admonished by the scourge of God, his pains increasing every moment."[1] Such is one of the visible monuments by which God has attested to the world His horror of this sin—a monument which ought to guard us against the indulgence of a passion which was punished even in this life with a disease too loathsome for utterance, and which even shut the ears of heaven against the prayers of the unfortunate man's repentance. " Then this wicked man prayed to the Lord, of whom he was not to obtain mercy."[2]

In fine, my dear Christians—and remark that what I am going to observe, is not a forced but a most natural consequence of pride—what is it that has engendered those fantastic errors that have sprung up in every age, disfiguring the purity of the Christian doctrine, rending the seamless garment of Christ, and converting, by the wild variety of their dialects, the temple of God into a theatre of fanaticism and discord? Pride. If I were to exhibit the series of heretics that disturbed the peace of the Church, pride would be the most striking feature in their character. Thus, the Arian heresy, which of all others carried on the most violent warfare against the Catholic Church, sprung from the source of disappointed pride. Its author, a restless, turbulent priest, aspires to the Episcopacy of Alexandria, while the promotion of

[1] 2 Mach. ix. 7, 8, 9, 10, 11.   [2] Ibid. 13.

another candidate disappoints his expectations. His impatient spirit first vents itself in anger against the bishop, and next against the Church, until at length, in the rage of disappointed hope, he aims his blasphemous hostility against the Son of God Himself by denying His divinity. Such was the small spark which quickly spread over the Church and engaged it in a fierce contest during the space of three centuries. To illustrate still more the dismal effects of pride in the Church, I will only mention another example in the person of Tertullian, a man almost unequalled for the extent of his erudition and the acuteness of his intellect. Yet this man, than whom the Church could not once boast a greater ornament, was so blinded by pride as afterwards to plunge into errors which would have disgraced not only an humble but a disordered understanding. Without, however, fatiguing your patience with further examples, you may rest assured that pride, in some shape, however disguised under other motives, is the principle that actuates the authors of novelty and error. Disappointed in a favourite hope, or writhing under the recollection of, perhaps, an imagined injury, or impelled by the example and success of others who have become notorious for their errors, they, too, are eager to follow in their footsteps, and to plunge the Church in all the evils of error and discord in order to indulge an inordinate ambition.

You see, then, my dear Christians, from this short but comprehensive view of the evils that afflicted the fallen angels in heaven, and our first parents in paradise, as well as from those which we read in the histories of the Jews and the Christian Church, how fatal are the effects of pride and how extensive is its mischief. How truly, then, is it said in Ecclesiasticus : " For pride is the beginning of all sins."[1] Yes, it is the root of all mis-

[1] Eccles. x. 15.

chief, and its branches are so extensive as to spread its baleful influence over the nations of the earth. Now, you may naturally inquire why is this sin of pride so particularly hateful to the Almighty. I will tell you the reason. Because it more directly assails Him than any other, stripping Him of His prerogatives, and arrogating as its own merit what is the pure gift of His mercy. The proud man forgets the language of St. Paul and of reason itself; what have you that you have not received, and why glory in it as if you had not received it? The proud man, then, who feels a vain complacency in what he possesses, and renders not thanks to God, is guilty of an act of injustice, and as far as depends on him, violates the Supreme Majesty of heaven. Hence, the awful threats which are so pointedly denounced against the proud man in Scripture: "Behold, I am come against thee, proud one, saith the Lord of Hosts, for thy day is come, and the time of thy visitation. And the proud one shall fall; he shall fall down, and there shall be none to lift him up."[1] And again, Abdias, after personifying a proud soul in these words, "Who shall bring me down to the ground?" replies: "Though thou be exalted as an eagle, and though thou set thy nest among the stars, thence will I bring thee down, saith the Lord."[2] There are few who will deny the enormity of pride, but there are fewer who will put up with its imputation. Hence, all the arguments brought from Scripture against it may be deemed by some as pointed against a vice from which they are exempt, while they fail not to apply them to their neighbour. But however offensive the conduct of the Pharisee may appear, it is certain that numbers are secretly infected with the pride which sullied his actions.

[1] Jerem. l. 31, &c.     [2] Abdias i. 3, 4.

There are but few, indeed, so lost to modesty as to break out into such an indecent parade of their merits, because, if not awed by a consciousness of their defects, they are at least restrained by a sense of propriety. So true are the words of Ecclesiasticus that pride is hateful to God and to man. But consult your own hearts and see if there are any among you who carry into the temple that arrogant and imperious demeanour that disgraced the conduct of the Pharisee. Are there any who look upon their humble brother with a contemptuous disdain and carry their levity, nay, their profaneness to the temple of God, where every earthly passion should be hushed, and the distinctions of society lost in the immeasurable distance between man and the Divinity? But, above all, are there any among you who have to charge themselves with having made invidious comparisons between themselves and their neighbours, saying, like the Pharisee, in the pride of their hearts, "I am not a drunkard nor a libertine, nor an extortioner, like this or that individual?" Yes, this is a vice more common than many of you are aware of. In the comparison between our own life and that of others, self-love will devise some motive to extenuate our guilt, while we condemn our neighbour with unfeeling severity. The man who scruples not to quench his reason by excess, will perhaps say, "Thank God, I am not an extortioner like my neighbour;" another may say, "Thank God, I am not stained with a neighbour's blood," while perhaps he inflicts a deadly wound on his reputation; and another, in fine, who may lead the tranquil life of a pagan, regardless of the precepts of the Christian religion, may still thank God that he is free from those outrages against decorum that stain the reputation of his neighbour. Thus, everyone leans towards his own defects, so true are the words of our Redeemer: "We see the mote in our brother's eye, while we behold not the beam in our own."[1]

However, of all Christians there are none more apt to be misled by this vice of complacency towards themselves and severity towards others than the devout and regular. The view of the lives which they have led is continually recurring to their minds, the prayers which they have repeated, the alms which they have distributed, the pilgrimages which they performed, and the Masses at which they assisted; these are objects on which a mind, disgusted with the dark picture of the lives of worldlings, reposes with some delight. The more singular and extraordinary the practices of devotion may be, the more danger there is of delusion. God forbid that I should ever discourage any practice of piety that may have for its object the mortification of the flesh and the expiation of sin. No; but I am cautioning the pious against the secret pleasure they may feel, which would poison the fruit of a life spent in the utmost regularity. I wish to guard them against that piety which exhibits itself for the purpose of being seen and admired, and which frequently destroyed the merit of the austerest penances of the Anchorets, and betrayed them into melancholy falls. I want to secure you against the presumptuous spirit of the Pharisee, which made him refer his actions to his own merit rather than to God's glory, which presumption, the Gospel tells us, was the cause of his condemnation. To guard you still more effectually against the dangers of pride, let us briefly state the advantages of humility which distinguished the Publican. As vices are cured by the habits of opposite virtues, to guard against the danger of pride you must practise the virtue of humility. Alas! I fear that this is a virtue to which, however necessary

[1] St. Mat. vii. 3.

it may seem, many may be strangers. It is a virtue so frequently recommended and strongly enforced in Scripture, that I should transgress the ordinary limits of a discourse were I to adduce the many passages that prove its advantages and necessity. Without it we cannot possess the grace of God; for God resisteth the proud and giveth His grace to the humble. "And He shall save the humble in spirit,"[1] says the Psalmist. Nay, Christ closes the parable from which my text is taken by the awful sentence: "Every man that exalteth himself shall be humbled, and every man that humbleth himself shall be exalted." Can you, then, require further reasons to convince you of the importance of this virtue? But perhaps you will say, must a person feel no complacency in those gifts of fortune, of nature, or of grace, which he finds himself possessed of? Ah, my brethren, these are reflections in which I fear you too often indulge, and which are the rocks on which your virtue suffers or is endangered. But to suppress that pride which may thus betray you, reflect on this single consideration: what have you that you have not received, and why glory in it as if you had not received it? Are not your riches, your talents, and every advantage of mind or person you possess, the free gifts of God, which He may dispose of at His pleasure. Besides, the proudest will be humbled if he reflects what he was, what he is, and what he may be.

What were we? Nothing; nay, worse than nothing. For we came into the world children of wrath, with sin as our inheritance, until we were justified gratis by the grace of God through the redemption that is in Jesus Christ. "Where is, then, thy boasting,"[2] as the Apostle saith. What are we? Are we in the state of grace or in sin, objects of God's hatred or affection? Oh! no one knows whether he is worthy of love or hatred.

[1] Ps. xxxiii. 19.  [2] Rom. iii. 27.

And what will we be? In possession of eternal happiness or consigned to eternal torture? These, my dearly beloved, are questions capable of moving the firmest heart and making it tremble at the state of its uncertainty. This sole reflection shook the greatest saints with terror and alarm, and made St. Paul exclaim: "I chastise my body and reduce it under subjection; lest whilst I preach to others, I myself become a reprobate."[1] What, my brethren, St. Paul, the Apostle of the Gentiles, whose love of Jesus no dangers could subdue, and whose preaching overthrew the pagan divinities, whose sanctity raised him to the privilege of conversing with God Himself, and diving into mysteries which it is not given to human tongue to utter! Yes, St. Paul so dreaded that a secret vanity might eat up the fruit of his labours, that he trembled, lest whilst he preached to others, himself should become a reprobate.

If you are proud of the gifts of fortune, recollect that they are fleeting and perishable. How truly could the happiest among you say with Job, "My days have passed more swiftly than the web that is cut by the weaver."[2] If you are proud of your beauty, recollect that it is frail as the flower that blossoms and withers under the same sun. If you are vain of your riches, think that they often disappear like the "vapour of the morning."[3] And if you fancy that your talents may command admiration, call to mind the salutary words of Solomon: "Our life shall pass away as a trace of a cloud, and our name in time shall be forgotten, and no man shall have any remembrance of our work."[4] Why, then, should creatures of a day, and children of the dust, be filled with vanity? Oh, no, rather acknowledge, in the sincerity of your souls, your nothingness and unworthiness. Refer all your actions to the honour and glory of God, saying, "Not to us, O Lord, not to us, but to Thy

[1] Cor. ix. 27.    [2] Job. vii. 6.    [3] Osee vi. 4.    [4] Wisd. ii. 3, 4.

name give glory."[1] You must always entertain an humble opinion of yourselves. If you wish, says St. Augustine, to raise high the edifice of perfection, you must sink deep the foundation of humility.

Such was the sentiment expressed by the Apostle in these words: "I will glory in my infirmities that the grace of God may dwell in me."[2] Yes, my dear Christians, our infirmities are the only things we have to glory in; and from a feeling consciousness of these infirmities, we ought to say with the Publican: "Lord, have mercy on me a sinner;" and God will not despise a contrite and humble heart. "The prayer of the humble shall pierce the clouds," says the Wise-man, "and he will not depart until the Most High behold."[3] Let me, then, in conclusion, exhort you to the practice of the virtue of humility. "Learn of me," says Jesus Christ, "because I am meek and humble of heart."[4] If you approach the throne of heaven like the Publican, with an humble, heartfelt sorrow, disposed to follow the impulse of divine grace, you may be confident that if you should be in error, God will enlighten you, and if you be in sin, He will forgive you. I will therefore, my dear Christians, conclude with the tender expressions of St. Paul to the Philippians. "If there be, therefore, any consolation in Christ, if any comfort of charity, if any society of the spirit, if any bowels of commiseration, fulfil ye my joy, that you be of one mind, having the same charity, being of one accord, agreeing in sentiment. Let nothing be done through contention or vain glory, but in humility let each esteem others better than themselves."[5] Follow, then, the advice of the Apostle, and you have Christ's assurance that if you humble yourselves here, you shall be exalted hereafter—a blessing which I pray He may grant you in the name of the Father, &c. Amen.

[1] Ps. cxiii. 1. [2] 2 Cor. xii. 9. [3] Eccl. xxxv. 21. [4] St. Mat. xi. 29. [5] Philip. ii. 1, 2, 3.

## PROSPERITY: ITS DANGERS.

"Blessed are the poor in spirit: for theirs is the kingdom of heaven."—
MATT. v. 3.

OF all the subjects that have long engaged the study and inquiries of man none has been so warmly controverted as this simple question—in what consists human happiness. Long had this question baffled the researches of the curious and the wisdom of the philosopher. By some it was held to consist in the possession of that power that is gratified by dependence, and by others in the indulgence of sensuality. Thus, the opinions of those who sought happiness, varied with the different dispositions of its votaries, until human reason, mocked by fruitless investigation, owned the mysterious question to be beyond the reach of its capacity. It is to the divine Author of Christianity alone, who dispelled the darkness of human ignorance, that we are indebted for the solution of this perplexing difficulty. Were human reason to range the wide sphere of all the situations in life, that would be the last it would select to which Christ annexes happiness. Who are they whom Christ pronounces happy? The poor, and they that suffer persecution. This is a doctrine which has no charms for the passions. Worldly pride recoils at the preference thus given to the condition of the poor. That happiness could be found amidst the privations of poverty, or the rigours of persecution is a doctrine which the world cannot understand. However harsh this doctrine may appear, and seeing that it is the duty of the Christian preacher to enforce the precepts of his Divine Master, I shall briefly illustrate the truth of my text by showing the dangers of those who are in the uninterrupted enjoyment of prosperity and the advantages attendant on that state of life which is exposed to all the rigours of the world.

To prove the dangers attendant on a state of ease and affluence we have only to consider what is the just destination of man. Created to enjoy God for all eternity, he cannot consider the present life as his end, but only a preparation for the enjoyment of the other. Whatever, therefore, tends to attach him to this life, to make him forgetful of the next, or to risk his eternal salvation, so far from being a blessing, ought to be deemed the deepest misfortune. Now of all the obstacles which through the course of life are opposed to our salvation, none can be greater than the enjoyment of riches. An unbroken series of prosperity rivets our affections to the world, creates an indifference to the most necessary duties of religion, and is often the source of the most serious disorders. We might adduce from the inspired writings the examples of many who are warning monuments of the dangers of a life never embittered with affliction. The truth of this doctrine was unhappily verified in Saul, the King of Israel. While Saul lived in the obscurity of a private station, we may presume, from the sacred text, that he was devoted to the service of God. Happy, had he remained in the same humble condition. But he was called to the throne of Israel, and the virtue which was the handmaid of his obscurity fled from the sinful contagion of a court. His heart was intoxicated with the pleasures of regal power, and the height to which he was raised soon made him forget his former humility. Peace disappeared from his habitation, his breast was torn with the cruelest jealousy, which prompted him to persecute the innocent David and despise the authority of religion in the person of Samuel, its minister. At length God, in punishment of his crimes, transferred the kingdom of Israel to the persecuted David, while Saul, in despair, had recourse to the aid of sorcery, and to crown his abandonment, terminated his own life. Unhappy Saul! how dearly purchased was his dignity! Who would wish to purchase the honours of royalty at the expense of his immortal soul?

We have another instance of the dangers of riches in the life of the glutton mentioned in the Gospel. Forgetful of his elevated end, he indulged in all the luxuries of life, feasting on the rarest delicacies, and clothed with purple and fine linen. But how did these pleasures terminate, which so often excite the envy of men? They all passed away like a shadow. Soon do we behold this unfortunate man plunged in the bottom of hell, writhing in unutterable torture, and crying out to Abraham, in the agony of pain, "To send him Lazarus to dip the tip of his finger in water and to cool his tongue, for he was tormented in the flame." Abraham's answer is very remarkable: "Son," he says, "remember thou didst receive good things in thy lifetime."[1] He reminds him not of any grievous crimes he might have committed. He speaks not of the oppression of the poor, or the affliction of the widow. No; but he merely tells him "Son, thou didst receive good things in thy lifetime, and Lazarus evil things. Wherefore thou art tormented." Whence we may draw this awful conclusion, that seldom are the blessings of this life unattended with those disorders which expose us to the imminent danger of forfeiting eternity. Judge, then, how little worthy our attention are those perishable riches which so frequently terminate in endless misery. But, alas! so great is the prevalence of our senses over our judgment, that we are impressed with an idea of the happiness of those who are constantly running the round of pleasure, and dazzling the multitude by the splendour of

---

[1] St. Luke, xvi. 23, 24.

their appearance. Were we able to sound their hearts, we might behold, in spite of the mask of gaiety which they assume, that they are a prey to envy, to jealousy, to sensuality, and other foul passions which rob them of their repose. The greatest favourites of fortune are convinced of this truth by melancholy experience. But since it is not given to the greater part of mankind to be acquainted with this truth, I will confirm it by a striking example recorded in Holy Writ. In the splendid court of the King of Persia lived a certain courtier named Aman, who shared in all the confidence of his Sovereign, and enjoyed the highest dignity of the Empire. Having thus attained the first rank, all his wishes were gratified, since there was no other degree of eminence which his ambition could desire, or his Sovereign's liberality could bestow. Who could imagine that this highly-honoured favourite, on whom fortune had exhausted all her treasures, could still be unhappy? Yet, envy preyed upon his mind and deprived him of his repose. All the splendour of the court, all the magnificence of his Sovereign, could not satisfy his ambitious soul while he saw a certain Jew named Mardochai, who stood at the palace-gate, refuse him the ceremonious honour of a salute. Hear what the unhappy man says, after recounting the ample honours he possessed: "And while I possess all these things, I imagine I possess nothing while I see Mardochai before the palace-gate."[1] You see, my dear Christians, what a trifling circumstance prevented Aman from enjoying his good fortune. The neglect of a mere ceremony wounded his pride, gnawed his very heart, and damped in a moment all his former felicity. It is an illusion, then, to imagine that the rich are happy, and exempt from those cares that are the usual lot of mortals.

[1] Esther, v. 13.

Who ever enjoyed a greater temporal prosperity than Solomon? Blessed with the gifts of fortune, the possession of a throne, and a greater share of wisdom than ever fell to the portion of man, his name filled the world with admiration. And yet what does he say: "Vanity of vanities, and all is vanity,"[1] except loving God and fearing Him alone. And with justice did Solomon make use of this language. For such was the influence of riches over his heart that, notwithstanding all his wisdom, he fell into idolatry and plunged into such excesses of licentiousness, that the sacred text leaves us in doubt concerning his salvation. And truly the lives of the rich are nothing but a series of vanity and vexation of spirit. They spend their whole time in forming schemes for their advancement, thinking that each increase of fortune will be an accession to their happiness. Their views still extend as they advance; still some favourite object is unattained, which, if secured, would complete their felicity. Thus do they live in all the torment and anxiety of inordinate desires; and if at last we allow that their every wish is gratified, how often do they share the fate of the man recorded in the Gospel, who, on finding his storehouses full, while he said to himself, "Soul, thou hast much goods laid up for many years; take thy rest, eat, drink, and make good cheer." Hear the Almighty thus rebuking his presumption: "Thou fool, this night do they require thy soul of thee; and whose shall those things be which thou hast provided?"[2] Thus, it frequently happens with many, who, while they think to enjoy the fruit of their past labours, and suffer their fancy to revel in the enjoyment of anticipated happiness, are arrested by the hand of death and summoned before the tribunal of the Almighty, to account for the manner in which they accumulated

---

[1] Eccli. i. 2.   [2] St. Luke xii., 19, 20.

their riches. If any ever felt his heart torn with envy at the opulence of the great, let him contemplate for a moment the truly tragic scene of a man wedded to the world, torn from its embraces, and hurried into eternity. How deplorable his condition leaving the world which he made the sole idol of his heart, and looking into a cheerless region for which he made no preparation! Does the remembrance of the former scenes of festivity allay the anguish of his feelings? Does the reflection that he repaired a ruined fortune and enriched his family render his separation more tolerable? Alas! all these reflections serve, perhaps, but to aggravate his distress by recalling the various acts of iniquity by which he accomplished his prospects. His ears, that were hitherto deaf to the calls of wretchedness, are now assailed with the cries of the widow and the orphan, appealing to heaven for vengeance against his hard-heartedness. Unhappy man! should he look on his past life, not a ray of consolation does it furnish, and all his future prospects are darkened by despair, while he imagines he beholds an angry God armed with all His terrors and plunging him into hell for a miserable eternity. Such is often the fate of the man who, perhaps but a few days before, said in the pride of his abundance, "I will not be moved for ever."[1] Blind, presumptuous man, how justly might we apply to him the words of Scripture, "I have seen the wicked exalted and lifted up like the cedars of Lebanon, and I passed by, and lo, he was not, and I sought him, and his place was not found."[2] How frequently within the remembrance of the youngest amongst us are those words verified? How often do we behold the wicked suddenly elevated? Yet, in the lapse of a few years, their prosperity is flown; no vestige of their greatness can be traced, nay, their very names and

[1] Ps. xxix. 7.   [2] Ps. xxxvi. 35, 36.

honours are forgotten. We ought, therefore, to profit of the admonition of the Psalmist: "Trust not in iniquity. If riches abound, set not your heart upon them."[1] It is this attachment to riches that renders their possession so dangerous. By the facility they afford of indulging every passion, they corrupt man's heart, who centres all his happiness in this life, and then suddenly passes away into a miserable eternity. How applicable to such persons are the words of Job: "They rejoice at the sound of the organ, they spend their days in wealth, and in a moment they go down to hell."[2] How transient, then, are the pleasures of the wicked and how unworthy the ambition of an immortal soul!

Will anyone, then, still say with the prophet: "Why doth the way of the wicked prosper?"[3] Should anyone seem surprised that their prosperity is without alloy, I will answer, with St. Augustine, that God in His justice rewards everyone according to his deserts. Now, as even the most abandoned sometimes perform actions which are worthy of some reward, though not deserving of an eternal one; hence the Almighty bestows on them in this life those rewards that are proportioned to their virtues. Let not discontent, then, murmur blasphemy against heaven, or impiously arraign its just dispensations. Should you presume to charge God with injustice for bestowing such blessings as riches on the wicked, I will argue, on the contrary, that riches must oftentimes be a curse, when we behold them so profusely lavished on the enemies of God. If riches are not really the source of much misfortune to their votaries, why the repeated language of Christ: "Woe to you rich; for you have your consolation!"[4] And the still more terrific words: "It is easier for a camel to pass through the eye of a needle than for a rich man to enter

[1] Ps. lxi. 11. [2] Job, xxi. 12, 13. [3] Jerm. xii. 1. [4] S. Luke, vi. 24.

into the kingdom of God."[1] Why such repeated blessings on the poor and persecuted? Why say that He was sent by His Father to preach the Gospel to the poor, as if the rest of mankind were incapable of profiting by His precepts, or of being reformed by His admonitions?

But, my dear Christians, imagine not that I am arraigning the bounty of Providence, or that I number riches among the necessary evils of the world. No; they are the fruit of God's beneficence, and only become evil by being converted into instruments of sin. Hence the admonition of the Psalmist: "If riches abound, do not place your heart in them." It is, therefore, the attachment to wealth, and not its possession that is really injurious to our eternal salvation. Among the saints who are enrolled in the calendar, there were many who possessed extensive wealth and honours. But, remark, they were poor in spirit amidst riches, and humble in heart in the enjoyment of the highest dignities. Such were St. Gregory and St. Leo, whom the first dignity in the Christian world could not prevent retaining the humility of the Gospel amidst the splendours of a palace. Such were St. Louis, St. Margaret, St. Matilda, and other illustrious saints of either sex, who proved that virtue was not incompatible with the possession of a crown. Such, in fine, were the numberless saints who filled the highest stations in the Church, and who made no other use of their immense wealth than to secure for themselves a title to the kingdom of heaven. Do you imitate their example, and your possessions, instead of being instrumental in your ruin, will become the means of your justification. Our Saviour, it is true, has pronounced woes against the rich; yet He entered the house of the wealthy Zaccheus, and applauded his virtue. We

[1] S. Matt. xix. 24.

see by these examples that grace and innocence may still reside amidst riches without being infected by the vices with which they are generally connected. It is, then, that inordinate attachment to wealth which separates the creature from his God that is condemned: that covetousness which is never satisfied with money, but still thirsts for more, according to the words of Ecclesiastes: "A covetous man shall not be satisfied with money, and he that loveth riches shall reap no fruit from them; so this also is vanity."[1] Yes, it is worse than vanity, for its end is eternal reprobation. Such is the declaration of inspired wisdom itself which thus depicts the despair of those who in their life boasted of their riches, reputing poverty a reproach: "These are they (meaning the poor) whom we had sometimes in derision and for a parable of reproach; we fools esteemed their life madness and their end without honour. Behold how they are numbered among the children of God, and their lot is among the saints. Therefore we have erred from the way of truth, and the light of justice hath not shined on us, and the sun of understanding hath not risen upon us. We wearied ourselves in the way of iniquity and destruction, and have walked through hard ways; but the way of the Lord we have not known. What hath pride profited us, or what advantage hath the boasting of riches brought us? All these things are passed away like a shadow and like a post that runneth on. . . . So we also being born, forthwith ceased to be, and have been able to show no marks of virtue, but are consumed in our wickedness. Such things as these the sinners said in hell: For the hope of the wicked is as dust, or as a thin froth which is dispersed by the storm."[2] After such a terrific picture of the punishment of the wicked, should we not tremble lest we also should share

---

[1] Eccles. v. 9.  [2] Wisd. v. 3-15.

their unhappy fate. Remark that those sinners who are thus introduced were wealthy men who despised the poor and made a mockery of their condition. They do not say that they were condemned, merely because they possessed riches, but because they held the poor in contempt, boasted vainly of their riches, and left no trace of virtue behind them. Such are the causes which the inspired writer assigns for their reprobation. Do you, then, who possess the wealth of the world, if you wish to avoid their fate, compassionate the poor; be humble in your elevation, and strive to overcome the dangers of riches by employing them in acts of virtue. In the language of St. Paul to Timothy, I charge the rich of this world not to be high-minded, nor to hope in uncertain riches, but in the living God, who giveth us abundantly all things to enjoy. I exhort you, in this holy season, to redeem your sins, not only by fasting, but by alms-deeds, and other acts of mercy, that you may obtain the grace of the Almighty. Your riches are not given you for the purpose of indulging your vanity or your profligacy, but for the purpose of exercising works of charity towards the afflicted. Make to yourselves, then, friends of the mammon of iniquity, that when you quit this world you may be received into the eternal tabernacle of the just. Despise not now the poverty of Lazarus, if you wish not to be excluded from a share in the bosom of Abraham. Recollect that we are but pilgrims here below. Convert not, then, into a perpetual mansion that which is intended only for a place of exile and sojournment. Like the patriarchs of old, look to your eternal country, and forget not, in the sordid enjoyments of this world, that noble destiny for which you were created.

To conclude, in the words of St. Paul: "This, therefore, I say, the time is short. It remaineth, then, that they who buy be as if they were not possessing anything ; and they who rejoice as they who are not rejoicing ; and they who use this world as if they used it not ; for the figure of this world passeth away."[1] As the figure of the world, then, so quickly passeth, let me exhort you not to forfeit for its transient pleasures the possession of your God. If you are rich, study also to be rich in good works, and then those very riches which otherwise might rivet you to this world will become the powerful means of securing for you the prayers of the poor and the possession of the kingdom of heaven. Amen.

## ON THE LOVE OF GOD.

"And one of the Pharisees, a doctor of the law, asked Him, tempting Him: Master, which is the great commandment in the law. Jesus said to him : Thou shalt love the Lord thy God with thy whole heart, and with thy whole soul, and with thy whole mind."—MATT. xxii. 35, 36, 37.

WE are informed by the Evangelist St. Matthew that some of the Pharisees came to our Redeemer to inquire and ascertain from Him which was the great commandment of the law. It will, doubtless, excite your surprise that any of those among whom God displayed such stupendous wonders, could have been ignorant of this precept. For them the sea opened a passage when flying from the wrath of Pharaoh ; for them the heavens rained manna to support them during forty years in the wilderness ; for them the law was promulgated on Sinai while the Almighty spoke in thunders from its summit ; for them Solomon wrote the inspired effusions of his

[1] 1 Cor. vii. 29, 30, 31.

wisdom which breathe, through every page, this heavenly precept. In short, Judea exhibited the most signal monuments of God's love for His chosen people. And yet amidst this profusion of divine favours they are ignorant of the first and greatest precept of the law. Though we may wonder at such ingratitude, we ought to forbear lest the reproach we made to the Jews should come with increased force upon ourselves. Are there none among the Christians of the present day living in similar ignorance of their duty? Are there none whose ignorance of the law is still more criminal than that recorded in the Gospel? It is in vain that Christ Himself has promulgated this doctrine. It is in vain that the Apostles preached it through the world. It is in vain that the Church, by the unwearied efforts of her ministers, still proclaims the precept which Christ and his Apostles so solemnly sanctioned. Notwithstanding the blaze of evidence by which it is supported, there are still among Christians many who are ignorant of the obligations of this commandment. But let us reflect that it was not ignorance alone that prompted the Pharisees to catechise our Redeemer. No, my brethren, it was not for the purpose of instruction, but rather to ensnare Him in His replies that they proposed their insidious interrogatories. Jealous of the ascendant which Christ had gained among the people, they were resolved to undermine His authority. They were provoked at the freedom with which He exposed their vices, and unmasked their hypocrisy. Thus, alarmed at the decline of their own influence, they seized every opportunity of perplexing our Lord by the subtlety of their questions, in order to expose Him to the resentment of the people. Vain and foolish presumption! Every attempt that was made to embarrass our Redeemer served only to place

His wisdom in a more conspicuous light, and the Pharisees were obliged to retire, confounded by His wisdom, and abashed by His authority.

Are there, however, no similar characters among Christians of the present day? Men who would feign reconcile the profession of Christians with the practice of infidels, and whose curiosity might prompt them to inquire about the Commandments rather with the hope that the weakness of the explanations might be an apology for their guilt, than that its force should be a motive for its correction. If such there be here—and I trust there are none—let them reflect on the fate of the Jews, whose prejudices blinded them against the miracles of Christ; and profit of the awful warning which is held out in their punishment. For to such persons, unless moved by that powerful grace which subdues the hearts of the most stubborn, instruction would be superfluous, and preaching unprofitable.

To love God above all things is a duty which flows from the relation that connects the Almighty with His creatures. If there be a propensity in man to love what is excellent, the higher that excellence the more worthy the object must be of his affections. And hence, as God is the Supreme Good of which every other is but a borrowed reflection, it is only He that can be worthy of our unbounded attachment. The precept, then, of loving God with our whole heart and with our whole soul, is one that must be as grateful to the feelings of the one as it is conformable to the lights of the other. Nay, he who refuses to submit to this precept by suffering his affections to repose on any lesser object must be agitated by the violence of an intestine warfare. Destined for the enjoyment of supreme happiness which is found in God alone, yet transferring his love to creatures in which it ought not to centre, he feels the struggle arising from the activity of that affection which he in vain endeavours to check, and which will not be satisfied but by the possession of the Almighty. Like the great St. Augustine, who suffered his early attachments to stray through a variety of unworthy objects in quest of that happiness which he sought in vain; the man, who fixes not his heart on God alone, is obliged to exclaim in all the bitterness of his disappointment: "For thee I have been created, O my God, and my soul cannot rest until it rest in Thee."[1]

To enforce, then, this obligation of the love of God, it would be sufficient to refer you to the suggestion of your own heart, in order to examine that craving after some mysterious good which no object in nature can appease. But since few are found to give the subject that deep reflection which would enable them to penetrate to the secret spring of their desires; and since many are found to settle their hearts upon objects which were only intended by the Almighty as mediums to elevate them higher, I shall lay before you now striking motives to impress this obligation on your minds. These motives to love God are: 1st, because He has commanded it; 2nd, because He has loved us; and 3rd, because it is only by fulfilling this command we can fulfil the end of our creation, and be crowned with eternal happiness.

Were we influenced by no other motive to love God than the conviction that such is His command, that motive alone should be sufficient to ensure its observance. In the most solemn manner that the will of God could be communicated to man, while Mount Sinai blazed with the light, and shook with the thunder of His presence, this precept was announced: "Thou shalt love the Lord thy God with thy whole heart, and with thy whole soul, and with all thy strength."[2] And lest it

---

[1] S. August. Conf. lib. 1 c. 1.     [2] Deut. vi. 5.

should be imagined that this was a precept which expired with the Old Law, Christ gives it in the New all the weight and sanction of His authority. Now, we are entirely dependent on Almighy God. We have been not only created by His power, but are still preserved by His providence. As His power, then, over us is absolute and unlimited, hence our obligation of yielding to whatever law He promulgates, and whatever precepts He imposes. This jurisdiction of the Almighty extends over creation, embracing every order of beings, the most sublime in heaven as well as the humblest upon earth, the king on his throne as well as the lowliest of his subjects. But while He enforces His commands He threatens their infraction with punishment, in the infliction of which His wisdom is His sole rule, and mercy is the only control on His omnipotence. "Who shall say to Thee, O God, what hast Thou done? . . . or who shall come before Thee to be a revenger of wicked men? For there is no other God but Thee. . . . Neither shall king nor tyrant in Thy sight inquire about them whom Thou hast destroyed."[1] Now, my dear Christians, what obligation can there be on us of obeying our superiors equal to that by which we are bound to God, or what claim have they upon our services or attachment compared to that which arises from the unlimited dominion of the Almighty over those who are only the work of His own hands? Yet, do we not behold men exerting all their powers to serve their worldly masters, cheerfully encountering thirst and hunger, and not only enduring labour by day, but even denying themselves by night the comforts of repose. We see men not only zealously discharging their duties towards them, but not unfrequently abandoning the law of God at the beck of their worldly masters, ready to incur the hatred of others and

[1] Wisd. xii. 12, 13, 14.

the reproach of their own consciences. And for what such a sacrifice? To serve a master frail and feeble like themselves, whose bounty is at best but slender, and who may dismiss them in his caprices. And shall we refuse obedience to the commands of the Almighty, whose rewards shall be imperishable, and whose vengeance in punishing the wicked is thus described in the inspired writing?—"See ye," says God Himself, "that I alone am, and there is no other God besides Me: I will kill and I will make alive, and there is none that can deliver out of My hands. . . . If I shall whet my sword as the lightning, and my hand shall take hold on judgment, I will render vengeance to my enemies, and repay them that hate Me."[1] Hear, again, how one of the prophets describes the terrors of His wrath: "The Lord is a jealous God, and a revenger. . . . The Lord's ways are in a tempest, and whirlwind, and clouds are the dust of His feet. He rebuketh the sea, and drieth it up. . . . Who shall resist in the fierceness of His anger? His indignation is poured out like fire, and the rocks are melted away."[2] If any of you, then, has been hitherto so forgetful of your God as to violate that great commandment of the law which requires of you to love Him with your whole heart, and if you have done so from a timid compliance with the will of the proud man who would require any sacrifices inconsistent with duty, let him recollect that the Scripture says of the proud man that "He disappears like a vision of the night,"[3] and meditate on the awful admonition of our Redeemer: "Fear not those that kill the body, and cannot kill the soul; but rather fear Him that can destroy both soul and body in hell."[4]

But, my dear Christians, this motive suggested by the consideration of God's power may be calculated

Deut. xxxii. 39, 40, 41.  [2] Nahum, i. 2, 3, &c.  [3] Job, xx., 8.  [4] S. Matt. x. 28.

rather to inspire you with fear than to kindle your affections. Would to God that it were attended even with that effect of awakening a salutary terror. For, according to the Wise Man the beginning of wisdom is the fear of the Lord, and, according to St. Augustine, that salutary fear may, by the operation of divine grace, ripen into charity. But as the soul of man is generous by nature, and as gratitude is one of the finest feelings of the human heart, I shall next point out a motive of gratitude to animate us to the love of God, namely, because God has first loved us.

The love of God towards us is a theme so vast and extensive as to surpass not only the description of language, but the comprehension of the human mind. It is boundless as the Divinity from which it proceeds. The inspired Apostle himself seems to labour with the difficulty of his subject when treating of the mystery of divine love he expresses himself in the following manner: "For this cause I bow my knees to the Father of our Lord Jesus Christ . . . that Christ may dwell by faith in your hearts, that being rooted and founded in charity, you may be able to comprehend with all the saints what is the breadth and length, and height and depth; to know also the charity of Christ, which surpasseth all knowledge that you may be filled unto all the fulness of God."[1] I will not now dwell upon God's having created us in preference to others whom He might have called into existence. I will not dwell on the beauties which He has scattered over creation, and which He has destined for the rational and temperate enjoyment of man. I will not dwell on the natural endowments with which He has enriched us at our creation, though all are so many proofs of His love, and

[1] Ephes. iii. 14-19.

should be so many pledges of our gratitude. I shall not speak of that charity which, according to St. Paul, surpasseth all knowledge. After the disobedience of our first parents, the misfortune of the unhappy father became the inheritance of his children. Born children of malediction, the whole race of Adam would have been doomed to drag out a life of sin and sorrow, helpless in this world and hopeless in the next. Such was the malice of original sin, that not the tears and penance of the whole world could appease the anger of the Deity. And hence, after the dreary sojournment of this world we would have been fated to sustain the eternal weight of God's anger in the other. In such a distressing crisis Christ interposes, offering Himself a propitiation to His Eternal Father to redeem a guilty world. For this purpose He descends from heaven; and clothes His divinity in the form of sinful man. He lives in obscurity and privation; He diffuses blessings around Him, and His return is ingratitude; He heals the sick, the lame, and the blind, and calumny is still His reward; He loosens the bond of sinners, and He is accused of blasphemy; He selects His apostles, and they desert Him in the hour of distress; He gives them His Body and Blood for their food, and one of them requites Him with the foulest treachery; He sinks in the garden under the load of His agony, and there is none to comfort Him; and, at length, to close the recital of His sufferings, He is nailed to an ignominious cross amidst the scoffs of an insulting populace, and at length resigns His life with a prayer of forgiveness for His enemies.

Let, then, those whose feelings cannot endure the exhibition of ingratitude come and see whether there can be love like that of Jesus, or ingratitude like that of the soul, purchased by His Blood from the tyranny of hell to the right of the kingdom of heaven, still refusing to love that God who gave life itself for her salvation, and saying, perhaps, with Lucifer, I shall not obey His commands. O astonishing prodigy of love, which made the psalmist exclaim with prophetic rapture: "What is man that Thou are mindful of him, or the son of man that Thou visitest him. Thou hast made him a little less than the angels; Thou hast crowned him with glory and honour."[1] He spared not the rebel angels, and He has extended His mercy to fallen man! Incomprehensible charity of God, and eqally incomprehensible insensibility of man! Christ has not only suffered for us, but left us also the fruits of His sufferings—His Body and Blood, which are offered up for us in the Eucharist, as a permanent memorial of His affection. After such prodigies of grace, how justly could He not reproach Christians in the language of the prophet to the hardened Jews: "What could I have done to my vine that I have not done, and yet it has not produced grapes, but thistles and thorns."[2] And to you who have been often refreshed with the bread of angels in the Eucharist, how applicable the tender and reproachful language: "If my enemy had reviled me I would verily have borne with it; but thou, a man of one mind, my guide and my familiar, who dost take sweetmeats together with me."[3] Surely whoever seriously reflects on the goodness of God and the ingratitude of man, will not be surprised at the tenderness of a great saint who constantly wept, and on being asked the cause of his tears, replied: "How can I refrain from tears while I meditate on the prodigy of love manifested in Christ's sufferings, and yet so little regarded by the ingratitude of mankind." But if you are moved neither by fear nor generosity, be moved at least

---

[1] Ps. viii. 5, 6.   [2] Isai. v. 4, 6.   [3] Ps. liv. 13, 14, 15.

by a regard for your own interest. Our observance of this great precept of the law will be requited with eternal happiness; eternal misery will be the punishment of its violation. For Jesus tells us: "If anyone love Me he will keep My word, and My Father will love him, and We will come to him and make our abode with him."[1] But, besides eternal happiness, the man who fulfils this great precept of love enjoys, even in this life, a cheerfulness of mind, to which the sinner is utterly a stranger. We have Christ's word in pledge, that to him who for His sake leaveth father or mother, or brother or sister, shall be given an hundredfold in this world, and life everlasting in the next. Hence that calm tranquillity which is the lot of the pious man through life, equally undisturbed by pride in his prosperity as he is by dejection under misfortune. His is not the transient joy of the libertine, which is soon succeeded by the gloom of despondency; but his is the heartfelt peace of which St. Paul says that it exceedeth every sense, and which made himself exclaim in the midst of worldly affliction: "I am filled with comfort; I exceedingly abound with joy in all our tribulations."[2] Our blessed Saviour Himself invites us to His service from the consideration of that sweet peace of mind which will be our reward. "Come to me," He says, "all you that labour and are burthened, and I will refresh you; take up My yoke upon you, and you shall find rest to your souls."[3] Yes, it is only in bearing the yoke of Christ and fulfilling His commandments that you can find repose. So true is it that we have been created only to love God on earth and afterwards to enjoy Him in heaven. While you have, then, wandered in pursuit of pleasure, have you found the peace or happiness which you sought? If

---

[1] S. John, xiv. 23.   [2] 2 Cor. vii. 4.   [3] S. Matt. xi. 29.

you have obeyed the impulse of ambition, has it purchased for you that good for which you had been panting? Have you found in the accumulation of riches that tranquillity for which you were sighing? No; so true are the words of St. Augustine that our hearts are formed for God, and that they cannot rest until they rest in Him. Return, then, at length to the only true source of happiness from which you have strayed so long. Do not suffer yourselves to be still deluded by the vain promises of the world, whose emptiness you may experience only when it is too late to cure your infatuation. Divide not your hearts between God and the world. He shall not be content with half; He requires that we love Him with our whole hearts and with our whole souls, and with our whole strength, for He is a jealous God, and will have no rival. But since human resolution is vain, unless aided by the grace of the Almighty, let us beseech the Author of all good so to purify our affections that they may be entirely centred in Him. Come, then, O Holy Spirit, which inflamed the hearts of the apostles, and kindle in us the fire of divine love. Spirit of Charity, which proceedest from the mutual affection of the Father and Son, take possession of our souls, that we may feel at length Thy heavenly influence. Too late have I known Thee; too late have I loved Thee. Draw at length, by Thy secret inspirations, our erring affections towards Thee, that, after having found peace in fulfilling Thy commandments here, we may have eternal repose in Thy love and enjoyment hereafter. Amen.

## CHRISTMAS DAY.

*"Behold, I bring you good tidings of great joy, that shall be to all the people. For this day is born to you a Saviour, who is Christ the Lord in the City of David. And this shall be a sign unto you: You shall find the Infant wrapped in swaddling clothes and laid in a manger."*—S. LUKE, ii. 10, 11, 12.

YES, I bring you good tidings. I am the messenger of joy, which shall not be confined to the bosom of one individual, nor to the inmates of one family, but which is sufficiently great to spread to all the people. And what are these joyful tidings which shall thus gladden the hearts of mankind? The birth of the Infant Saviour who was to accomplish their redemption. This day is born to you a Saviour in the city of David. This day is born to you the mysterious Child who was to tread on the serpent's head and achieve the deliverance of the seed of her who was deceived by his artifices. This day you celebrate the birth of that Messiah for whom the Patriarchs sighed, and whom the Prophets so often predicted. On this auspicious morning we hail the rising of the star of Jacob, which dispersed the darkness which hitherto overspread the earth, and ushered in upon mankind the light of grace and salvation. Like children who are grateful for a precious inheritance, we are assembled this day to pour forth the feelings of our souls to Him whose birth was the first signal of our deliverance from the bondage that enslaved us. In short, we are celebrating the most splendid, as well as the most joyous event that ever yet was offered to human contemplation. Light substituted for darkness, grace for sin, and truth for error, the worship of God purified from idolatry, and peace established among mankind; in fine, man redeemed from the tyranny of sin, and the world regenerated from error. These are the triumphs which this day records, and which shall ever render its anniversary an object of joyous veneration. It is too solemn a theme for human tongue to touch on; it is too spiritual a one for carnal hearts to conceive. And it is only in the stillness of the night, when the mind is at rest from the agitation of the world, that it is fit to hear the heavenly anthem which angels sung while shepherds listened to the first announcement of the glad tidings of this day. To form an adequate idea of the greatness of our redemption we must seriously reflect on the state of servitude and degradation to which mankind was sunk. For more than four thousand years was this Saviour of the world expected and delayed. During that disastrous interval of sin and error, the knowledge of the true God had almost departed from the earth, and the human heart became a victim to the most deplorable corruption. For a short time there were some feeble traces of man's origin, and some faint notions of that end for which he was created. But those traces were soon swept away in the tide of idolatry that overran the earth, and the faint notions which had been preserved among the patriarchs were dissipated, as their children were spreading among the nations. Thus, like an hereditary property which is considerable when kept together, but diminished as it is divided, the original stock of hereditary truth was broken by its partition among the nations of the earth until its fragments were entirely almost lost in the mass of errors with which they mingled. The Psalmist beautifully expresses this thought: "Truths were gradually diminished among the sons of men,"[1] and in proportion as they lost a view of that light which guided their steps their way became entangled; nor were they able to disengage themselves from the dangers that beset them. The homage which was hitherto peculiarly appropriated to the Divinity was now transferred to the creature. The heavenly bodies, which are only the mirrors

[1] Ps. xi. 2.

that reflect the benevolence and majesty of the Godhead, became objects of adoration. Nay, the impurest vices that ever sprung from the corruption of the human heart had their votaries and altars. And man, degraded man, whose eyes, whose mien, whose erect attitude, and, above all, whose features still breathe the intelligence and life with which God animated his earthly substance at creation, man, with all those attestations of immortality about him, still lowered in shameful homage to the reptiles of the field, or the more degrading adoration of his own passions, realising the words of the Psalmist: "And man, when he was in honour, did not understand; he is compared to senseless beasts and is become like to them."[1]

Amidst this universal reign of sin virtue languished and became almost extinct; and all flesh, as the Scripture says, had corrupted its way. Vice, which is the early and spontaneous fruit of human nature, diseased as it is by the infection of original sin, grew and spread with a fruitful rapidity. Without a single obstacle to check, nay, with every incentive to aid its growth, its baleful progress was such as to infect to the very marrow of the bones the entire mass of mankind. It was encouraged by example, favoured by education, nay, authorised by the corrupted worship of the times, and if now, when it is checked by the restraints of religion and education, the current of vice is so impetuous, you may conceive how it must have swept away every vestige of innocence and virtue when it was swelled by the aid of custom and education which ran in the same direction. Some few might have attempted to stem the torrent, but they were unable to attempt it long, and, like persons rowing against the tide, when they were wearied by exertion they were borne down by its force.

[1] Ps. xlviii. 13.

You all can conceive what the world was when men were impelled by such incentives to vice and immorality. It was, as might be expected, a hideous mass of sin and corruption: no peace, no mercy, no chastity, no love, no charity. All the elements of society were in strife and confusion, and the world was in the last stage of infirmity, out of which the spirit and virtue had almost departed. There were some men, and virtuous men, who were conscious of this disorder, yet unable to apply a remedy. They knew it was too inveterate and too widely spread to be healed by human skill, and on that account they stretched forth their suppliant hands to heaven, imploring divine succour. Amidst this darkness of infidelity, was there no science to guide the people. Yes, but it was a feeble light which was quite insufficient to direct them. Some guides, who pretended to superior wisdom, pointed to one way; others, of equal pretension, directed to another. Amidst these opposite paths, in which they were desired to tread, the people were distracted, and it frequently happened that the precepts of their guides were entirely weakened by the profligacy of their examples. There were some schools, it is true, but they were schools which revealed to their disciples the immorality from which they could not save. Nay, they only increased the horrors of that period, and might be compared to those fires that are lit on some dangerous coasts, which, without being sufficiently strong to enable the vessels to escape shipwreck, reveal, however, the rocks on which they are doomed to perish, and thus throw a more frightful glare over the horrors of their situation. But since human language is incapable of conveying an adequate description of that period, it will be furnished by the picture of an inspired Apostle. "Because, that when they knew God, they have not glorified Him as God or given thanks, but became vain in their thoughts, and their foolish heart was darkened; for, professing themselves to be wise, they became fools, and they changed the glory of the incorruptible God into the likeness of the image of a corruptible man, and of birds, and of fourfooted beasts, and of creeping things; wherefore, God gave them up to the desires of their heart."[1]

Amidst this universal and inveterate disease which afflicted mankind, without the hope of any remedy, Jesus Christ descends upon earth, and assumes human nature to heal all its disorders. And what are the signs that shall point out this Redeemer? What are the emblems of royalty by which the King of Heaven was surrounded? If His ideas of grandeur were to be estimated by ours, He would descend with all the pomp of the most powerful monarch, surrounded with a retinue, glittering in splendour, and reposing in a palace, such as the princes of the earth never inhabited. But, O God! how different are Thy judgments from those of men. And do you know that these much-valued acquisitions are evidences of lowliness rather than of greatness? Man, conscious of his insignificance, labours to exalt it by something beyond himself. Aware of his own littleness, he strives to hide it in the splendour of his office, and imagines he is exalted by the honours with which he is invested. Conscious what a little place he occupies in society, he labours to supply it by the largeness of his retinue, fancying that he extends and multiplies himself in proportion to the extent or number of his dependents. It is on this account that wealth, and pomp, and splendour are so much valued, because they dazzle the world, and throw a transient lustre about an object which would be insignificant without their assistance. Knowing, then, that pomp, and retinue, and robes of office are the

[1] Rom. i. 20-24.

draperies that conceal the infirmities of man, can you be surprised that God appeared without them? Did the Son of God require that splendid covering which is the evidence of man's poverty? No; instead of their being scandalised at the lowliness of His condition, they should rather be surprised if He sought honour from any created thing. And though creatures may borrow consequence from splendour of equipage or rank, what could they add to His dignity, by whom they were created, and who, in the noble language of a holy father, long before their existence, had filled all space with the solitude of His own magnificence? Away, then, with these vain emblems of worldly royalty. Well may they be sought by those who want them. They might well direct you to the abode of a prince who would require to conceal his own weakness by their aid; but they were not the fit signs to point out the mansion in which a God was born. No artificial splendour should be suffered to divert the eye or distract the heart from the one immense object of adoration that should engage all his faculties. No; though the foolish votary of the world may think it unworthy of the majesty of the Godhead, yet, for me, I find in the words "you shall find the Infant wrapped in swaddling clothes and laid in a manger;" I find in them more evidence of His Divinity than all the pomp the world could bestow on Him. Yes; and such was the idea of the angels who directed the shepherds to the manger in which the Lord of glory was laid; "And this shall be a sign unto you: you shall find the Infant wrapped in swaddling clothes and laid in a manger."

What an extraordinary sign to mark the birth of the Redeemer. Be not surprised it was the only one befitting His character. He was our Saviour, you will recollect, and it was therefore expedient that He should heal those wounds which sin had inflicted on human nature.

Pride and sensuality were the chief sources of man's disorders. If Christ, then, had displayed them at His coming, He would have increased rather than cured his infirmities. Nothing, then, but the opposite virtues should have marked the coming of Him who was to be the Saviour of the world. Man had sinned by pride, humility was its remedy; he trangressed by sensuality, it was expedient that it should be corrected by mortification; and, therefore, Christ appearing in an humble and suffering condition was invested with those qualities that became the nature of His office.

I know that this lowly appearance is not one that is flattering to opulence or pride. It is one under which the children of the world are unwilling to recognise their Redeemer. I am not surprised it was one that was not pleasing to His own contemporaries; and many who would have gladly confessed Him, had He come in all the pomp of a worldly king, rejected Him because He was born in a stable in Bethlehem. There were numbers among the Jews who expected that He would be a powerful prince, who would reward His followers with the spoils of His temporal conquests. Having witnessed the lowliness of His birth, they turned with disdain from one who deceived all their expectations; and though He afterwards wrought miracles in support of His mission they would have still preferred a Messiah who would have flattered all their carnal hopes.

You may be surprised at their blindness; but do not Christians furnish many similar characters, who make of religion a matter of temporal policy, and who, like the Jews who expected a worldly Messiah, would rather follow him who would flatter their passions, than the other who would dash all their hopes by telling them that the God whom they adored recommended suffering and mortification. They may look for religion under a more pleasing form than it is exhibited by the ministers of Christ; but if they do, let me tell them they will share the fate of the voluptuous Jews, who, plunged in sensuality and vice, knew nothing of the birth of the Redeemer, while it was announced by angels to the humble shepherds who were tending their flock, and keeping the watches of the night. Imitate, then, those holy men, saying, with them, " Let us go over to Bethlehem, and let us see this word that is come to pass, which the Lord hath shown to us."[1] If you do, you will find your infant Saviour lying in a manger, and return home, like them, glorifying God for the things you have seen and heard. Yes, you will see realised there the words of the prophet : " A Child is born to us, and a Son is given to us. And His name shall be called Wonderful, God the Mighty, the Father of the world to come, the Prince of peace."[2] Such is the Redeemer whose birth you celebrate this day, and who is also adored by all the nations of the earth.

Yet it is not these titles which awaken on this occasion our liveliest feelings of gratitude and veneration. No; were He to remain for ever in the enjoyment of His own solitary happiness, without approaching nearer to His creatures, He would, it is true, command our respect, but it would be a respect which terror would inspire; whereas, by humbling Himself, and assuming our nature, He becomes at once the partner of our sufferings, and therefore entitled to the warmest affections of the human heart. This is the circumstance that gives the mystery of this day its greatest charm, reminding us that our Saviour, as God, is able, and, as man, is willing to heal our infirmities. Were He only God, the fear of His power might repulse us from approaching Him.

[1] S. Luke, ii. 15.     [2] Isaias, ix. 6.

Were He only man, we might approach Him in vain, since the feelings of pity are not always joined to the power of giving relief. But being God and man, have we not the strongest grounds of confidence; and how consoling is the mystery of this day, which represents the Divinity clothed with our nature and sharing in all its tenderness, thus engaging all our love without diminishing our veneration. But you may like to hear on this subject the inspired language of St. Paul: "Having therefore, a great High Priest, who hath penetrated the heavens, Jesus the Son of God: let us hold fast our confession. For we have not a High Priest who cannot have compassion on our infirmities: but One tempted in all things like as we are, without sin. Let us go therefore with confidence to the throne of grace: that we may obtain mercy, and find grace in seasonable aid."[1] These words of the Apostle unfold to us one of the strongest motives of confidence that ever swayed the human heart. He exhorts us to approach with confidence the throne of grace. And why? Because our High Priest is not one "who cannot have compassion on our infirmities; but One tempted in all things, except sin, like as we are." Let a poor man tell his distress to him who never knew what misery was. His tale cannot reach his heart, because it is a stranger to such feeling. Let him talk to the luxurious, who revel in enjoyment, of sorrow and privation: he talks to him of a subject he cannot understand, because it never came home to his own bosom; he therefore talks to one who has no sympathy with his sorrow, and who therefore may fling his petition to the wind. But let him tell the same story to one of a generous nature, who himself endured the same afflictions which he hears; his heart is

[1] Heb. iv. 14, 15, 16.

immediately touched with the feelings of pity which instantly mingle with those of the supplicant; and thus, by sharing in his woe, he lightens the load of his afflictions. Such is precisely the reasoning of St. Paul. Let us go, therefore, with confidence to the throne of grace, because we have a High Priest who was tempted in all things like as we are. He will lend an ear to the tale of your distress, because He Himself has felt it. If you are in poverty, Jesus Christ, your High Priest, has felt it too; for what poverty could have been greater than to have been born in a cave, without any other canopy to shelter Him than that which covered the oxen of the field? If you are exposed to cold by the inclemency of the weather, your High Priest has experienced it, too, since His infant limbs were exposed to the most chilling cold in the depth of the severest season. In short, you cannot suffer anything that He did not endure before you. And hence St. Paul remarks: "Wherefore it behoved Him in all things to be made like to His brethren that He might become a merciful and faithful High Priest before God, that He might be a propitiation for the sins of the people. For in that wherein He Himself hath suffered and been tempted, He is able to succour those also who are tempted."[1] Hence our very misery is a motive of our confidence, and our weakness is converted into a source of joy, according to the language of the Psalmist: "According to the multitude of my sorrows in my heart thy comforts have given joy to my soul."[2]

Approach, then, with confidence to your Redeemer, who teaches you from His cradle in Bethlehem with more efficacy than any language could teach you. Listen to the doctrine which He enforces by His example, and learn the spirit of compassion and tenderness

[1] Heb. ii. 17, 18.   [2] Ps. xciii. 19.

from Him whose pity for the human race brought Him down from heaven to alleviate their sufferings. Having reconciled in His own person God and man, who were hitherto at such awful distance from each other, He becomes a link of love and affection to the remotest members of mankind. He is our head, we are His members; and if He has made those members unequal, it is only to attach them more and more to each other by the mutual interchanges of kindness and of charity. Let, then, those with whom God has shared the goods of this world prove their gratitude to Him by sharing it with their poorer members. "Blessed is he," says the Psalmist, "who understandeth concerning the poor and the needy. The Lord will deliver him in the evil day, and make him blessed upon the earth, and will help him on his bed of sorrow."[1] If ever there was a season for exercising this tender compassion to the poor it is in this holy time, when we celebrate the deliverance of mankind. The anniversary of any great benefit is always a day of joy, when the human heart is expanded in benevolence to the poor beyond its usual dimensions. And what benefit can be like unto that which this day recalls to our minds? Not the deliverance of our country, or the discomfiture of our temporal foes, but the deliverance of the world from the slavery of sin and the victory of that Redeemer who conquered death and hell, and raised us from the eternal bondage in which we lay, to the confident hope of sharing in the rewards of His triumphs. Well, then, may it be deemed a season of joy which stirs within us all the kinder emotions, which were chilled by the cold anxieties of the world. It is a period of lofty sentiment and regenerated feeling, calculated to knit again those ties of charity and friendship which the cares of life are gradually loosening. It is a

[1] Ps. xl. 2, 3, 4.

season in which the spirit of jubilee that emanates from the Head, Jesus Christ, vibrates through every member of the Church, until it is communicated through the entire of His mystical Body. Yes; there is a contagious joy about the solemn festivals of the Christian religion which silently steals upon every individual, and which you look for in vain in the artificial pomp of the world. And why do not the feasts of the world impart the same pleasure? Because they are only counterfeit exhibitions, where everyone wears a mask, and enjoyment must become vapid, because the true soul of joy is not there. No; it is only religion that gives it; and hence the quickness with which its impulse is communicated instinctively, because the heart, the source from which it issues, is sincere. This was the grand spirit that swayed the Catholic Church in the institution of her festivals: not for the suspension of labour, or the indulgence of sensuality. No; she was guided by loftier motives. But she instituted them for the suspension of the passions and for the indulgence of charity. It is enough, it is too much, that the rest of our time should be devoted to the more sordid cares of making a provision for the few days of our pilgrimage here below, while this has been appointed to lead the heart to its native home, and fix its affections upon heaven. This is the festival on which pledges of mutual love are interchanged among families to seal a covenant of alliance during the remainder of life; on which ancient friendships are revived, and ancient enmities forgotten, fostering that peace which Jesus Christ brought from heaven to earth, and proclaiming a truce to the passions of mankind. Like the genial season which wakens vegetation through all nature, these festivals have the effect of quickening a moral spring of good qualities, and even the evergreens with which you adorn your homes on Christmas Day are but the emblems of that newness with which the virtues are renovated in the breast of every Christian. Go, then, this day and adore your Redeemer in Bethlehem, and lay at His feet the homage of your affections. Burn upon the altar your enmities, your resentments, and all the other passions. Bring home, as the companion of your way and the inmate of your houses that peace which the Infant Jesus offers to all mankind. It is by cultivating that peace you will be enabled to promote the glory of God on earth, and afterwards to enjoy His peace and glory in heaven. Amen.

## ON THE PASSION OF OUR LORD.

"Daughters of Jerusalem, weep not over me, but weep for yourselves and for your children."—LUKE, xxiii. 28.

WE are told by the Evangelist that when Jesus was led to be crucified He was followed by a great multitude of people of either sex, who lamented His fate, and wept over the severity of His sufferings. Struck with the innocence of the Redeemer's life, they generously expressed their sorrow that He was made the victim of the rulers of the Jewish Synagogue. Yet, my dear Christians, this was still but a compassion merely human, a pity such as one feels for the misfortunes of a fellow-creature, and which regarded not the cause of the suffering of Jesus. It was this tender but blind compassion of the Jewish women that awakened feelings of genuine and sincere pity in the breast of the Redeemer. Seeing how they felt for His misfortunes while they were insensible to their own, He seems to reproach their unseasonable tenderness by telling them, "Weep not over Me, ye daughters of Jerusalem, but weep for yourselves and for your children." Thus He checks the indulgence of their grief, or rather directs it to its legitimate object. He wishes to signify to them that for Him they might spare their tears, but that there were other evils far more deserving of their compassion. He labours to impress on them the enormity of their guilt in rejecting all the graces, and extinguishing all the lights with which they had been hitherto favoured. And, touched with a deep and generous sensibility, He strives to divert the current of their grief from Him who was the victim to the consideration of that cause which had inflicted His sufferings. It is true there never was a victim more deserving of compassion than our suffering Redeemer. If innocence the most immaculate, condemned by a tribunal the most iniquitous, and subjected to the cruelest torments that patience could endure, can possess any claims to the sympathy of a generous heart, never was there an individual who possessed so many claims to it as the Sufferer whom we commemorate this day. There was, however, another object, in the contemplation of which Christ forgot His own sorrows; and that object was sin. In imitation therefore, of our Redeemer, I propose this day to make you turn your attention to your own transgressions. I mean not by any high-wrought picture of our Saviour's Passion to wind up your feelings to a transient and unproductive sensibility. But I mean, through the sufferings of Christ, to show you the hideous deformity of that sin which inflicted them. Following, therefore, the narrative of the Passion, in the order in which it is told by the inspired historians, I shall exhibit to you those lessons of compunction which it teaches, after saluting the cross, that sacred symbol of our faith and pledge of our salvation, *Ave Crux*, &c.

To enable you to conceive a true horror for sin, only reflect that it is the cause of that bloody tragedy which this festival commemorates over all the Christian world. The majesty of God was outraged by the disobedience of our first parents, and nothing less than infinite satisfaction could atone for the infinite enormity of the insult. Accordingly, God in His mercy promised that from the woman's seed should spring one who would crush the head of the serpent. During the long period that elapsed from the fall to the redemption, a series of prophets appeared, foretelling the time and circumstances of His coming. At length He descends on earth, preaches His Gospel, and establishes His divinity by miracles the most incontestable, restoring the sight to the blind, hearing to the deaf, speech to the dumb, and health to those who were oppressed with infirmities. He preached penance unto the remission of sins, and those who were burdened with the weight of iniquity He dismissed after comforting them by His merciful consolations. Yet those acts of kindness and compassion which should have awakened the gratitude of the Jews, stirred up their envy, and the miracles by which He established His power only exasperated their desire of revenge. Such was the purity of His doctrine, exemplified in the unimpeachable integrity of His life, that multitudes became His disciples. But after the stupendous miracle of raising Lazarus from the tomb, the priests and princes of the people were so stung with rage that without further provocation they resolved upon His death. The time fixed by the decrees of the Almighty was now fast approaching. On the eve before His Passion Christ calls His Apostles together, He celebrates the Jewish Passover, and bequeaths to them the last legacy of His affection in the Blessed Sacrament of the Eucharist, in which He refreshed them with His own Body and Blood. After supper was concluded He returned, with some of His Apostles, to the garden of Gethsemani, beyond the torrent of Cedron, where He was often wont to retire during the still solitude of the night, to converse with His Father on the stupendous plan of man's redemption, which had been meditated from all eternity. Here commences the first scene of that bloody tragedy which was consummated on Calvary. The Son of God, who had displayed through life a calmness and tranquillity which nothing could disturb, becomes on a sudden violently agitated. His soul is sorrowful even unto death; a dreadful terror seizes His entire frame; the intense acuteness of His agony forces drops of bloody sweat to come over His Body, until, unable to sustain the overwhelming pressure of His sorrows, He falls prostrate on the ground, uttering the melancholy prayer: "O my Father, if it be possible, let this chalice pass from Me. Nevertheless, not as I will but as Thou wilt." What, it may be asked, could have thus subdued our Redeemer, invested with the strength of the Godhead, or saddened with such unutterable grief a soul that was in the constant contemplation and possession of supreme happiness? Was it the fear of His approaching death, or the desertion of the Apostles, or the ignominy of the cross, which could have thus troubled the peace of Jesus and stirred up such an intestine war within His breast? No; to ascribe His agony to any of those causes would not be conceiving a just idea of the sufferings of the Man-God. He could not have been frightened by the shame of that cross which was afterwards to become the badge and instrument of His triumphs, nor was He appalled by the terrors of approaching death, which He rather courted than feared: "And I have a baptism wherewith I am to be baptised, and how am I straitened until it be accomplished."[1] No; all this was incapable of afflicting the Son of God. It was the weight of the load of the sins of mankind that thus prostrated Him on the earth.

Whilst the priests and rulers of the nation, assembled in the house of Caiphas, were devising their iniquitous purpose of putting Him to death, Jesus, without any prejudice to His own innocence, considered Himself charged with the accumulated iniquities of the world, and destined to sustain in His own Person the collected weight of the divine vengeance that was due to them all. For God, according to the language of the prophet, "hath laid on Him all our iniquities."[2] In consequence of this transfer made by the Almighty, the just One, who knew not sin, became an imputed sinner; and in the language of St. Paul, "Him who knew no sin He hath made sin for us, that we might be made the justice of God in Him."[3] Now, only represent to yourselves a God gifted with the clearest knowledge of all that was to happen, as well as all that was passed, who alone could conceive the majesty of the Divinity and the deformity of sin by which He was insulted; imagine to yourselves a frame endued with the liveliest and most exquisite sensibility that ever was bestowed upon man, and you will still form only an imperfect notion of the horror that seized the soul of the Man-God when the hideous catalogue of the sins of the world rose in dreadful review before His unclouded mind—its frauds, its injustices, its murders, its blasphemies, its impurities, its calumnies, and its sacrileges, the heresies by which His own seamless garment was to be rent asunder, and the Blood of His covenant to be made void; in short, the collected mass of all the sins of every age and country and condi-

---

[1] St. Luke, xii. 50.  [2] Isai. liii. 6.  [3] 2 Cor. v. 21.

tion in life, but principally those shameful scenes of darkness, which even the profligate is studious to conceal. What wonder if Christ should have been borne to the earth under the overwhelming tide of such a sea of iniquity realising the words of the psalmist: " The sorrows of death have surrounded me, and the torrents of iniquity troubled me?"[1]

After this dreadful agony had subsided into calm resignation to His Father's will, He rose to meet His disciples, whom He found in profound sleep, as if careless of His sufferings. He gently reproves their drowsiness, saying: "Could you not watch one hour with me?" And then He adds: "Sleep ye now and take your rest: behold the hour is at hand, and the Son of Man shall be betrayed into the hands of his enemies: Rise, let us go: behold he is at hand who will betray Me. And he that betrayed Him, forthwith coming to Jesus, said: Hail, Rabbi. And he kissed Him. And Jesus said to him: Friend, whereto art thou come?" As we advance in the history of His Passion, every circumstance is calculated to unfold more fully the poignant afflictions of our Redeemer. One would imagine that, after the painful agony which He had just endured, He could have found some repose in the kindness and fellow-feeling of the chosen friends of His bosom. One would have imagined that the cruel stroke which was to fall upon Him would have been lightened by the reflection that there were still some few to share His afflictions. But Jesus was destined not only to suffer from His enemies, but, what inflicts a deeper wound on a confiding heart, He suffered from the treachery of His apostate friends. The traitor Judas, under the influence of one sordid passion, which, like a viper, had coiled and wound itself round his heart, binding up every noble feeling,

[1] Ps. xvii. 5.

thinks of no other object but the gratification of his avarice, and for thirty pieces of silver betrays his Master to His inveterate foes. Perfidious traitor, thus to sell the Master who ranked you among His Apostles, and confided to you the most precious treasures of His Church!!! The tenderness of the Redeemer who had given him at His Last Supper the most loving pledge of His attachment, could not soften his relentless passion; and with the most deliberate treachery he converts into an instrument of his wicked purpose a sign which the world had consecrated to friendship and affection. Although Jesus knew the dark designs which he meditated, yet, with a look breathing sweetness, He accosts him in the endearing language of "friend." But no language could soften the obdurate soul of Judas; and regardless of the feelings of pity or of friendship, he rushes on his victim, abusing the grace of mercy which was offered, until the unfortunate man closed a train of sacrilege and perfidy by the horrid deed of putting an end to his own life. You are doubtless shocked at the treachery of Judas; a generous resentment burns within you at the recollection of his crime. But pause, and examine whether you have not been guilty of the same crime which kindles your indignation. As often as you approach the sacrament of the Eucharist, reeking in your crimes, and covered with iniquities unexpiated by repentance, are not you imitators of the sacrilege of Judas? As often as you prefer your avarice, your ambition, or your pleasure to the sweet dominion of Jesus, do not you, like Judas, betray Him into the hands of His enemies? If, therefore, you feel a just resentment against Judas, turn, I beseech you, its direction against yourselves, that while you weep for the perfidy to which Christ fell a victim, you may also shed a tear over your own transgressions.

Jesus was now arrested, and bound by the soldiers, who dragged him to the court of Caiphas, where His disciples, with the exception of Peter, fled, fulfilling the words of the prophet: "Strike the shepherd and the sheep shall be scattered."[1] Peter, however, followed at a distance to the hall of the court, where the most iniquitous expedients were resorted to, to procure the condemnation of Jesus. Witnesses were seduced to give false testimony against Him, the malicious ingenuity of the priests was put on the rack in conjuring up imaginary crimes; but the inconsistency of the witnesses defeated their malignity, and the innocence of the Redeemer, who confidently appealed to the publicity of His life and doctrine, triumphed over the shameless injustice of His accusers. "I have," He said, "spoken openly in the world; I have always taught in the synagogues, and in the Temple, whither all the Jews resort; and in private I have spoken nothing." Abashed and confounded by so triumphant an appeal, they accuse Him of sedition by stirring up the people against the authority of Cæsar, and in the morning bring him before Pilate, the Roman governor.

While these proceedings were going on in the hall, Peter was accosted by a servant maid, saying: "Art not thou also one of this Man's disciples?" He answered, "I am not." And three times, accompanying it at last by the awful solemnity of an oath, he repeated this denial. This denial on the part of the man on whom He had bestowed His choicest favours, was one of the heaviest strokes that smote the tender heart of our Redeemer. Surrounded by His enemies, who struck and buffeted Him on every side, treating Him with every insult, and covering Him with indignities too loathsome to utter, judge what could have equalled

[1] Zach. xiii. 7.

the desolation of His heart who was betrayed by one of His apostles, denied by another, and deserted and abandoned by all. From the denial of Peter we ought, however, to take a salutary warning against the danger of presumption. When Christ had foretold that in the hour of His distress all would be scandalised in Him, Peter, relying on the generosity of his attachment, and the confidence of his strength, declared that though all should be scandalised in Him he would not be scandalised. But the hour of temptation came, and the breath of a female voice shook his resolution, who imagined himself above the fear of denial or desertion. Jesus, however, cast on Peter a look of compassion, which penetrated his very soul, and melting it into tenderness he went and wept and washed away his sins in the abundance of his sorrow. It is true, then, that the pillar of the Church has fallen. Yes, but let us recollect that it was while its Divine Architect was on earth to raise it. After the presumption of Peter was cured by his fall he was strengthened by Jesus Christ thus assuring him: "I have prayed for thee that thy faith fail not; and thou, being once converted, confirm thy brethren."[1] Do I mention this for the purpose of controversy? No; but to confirm the belief of those who might be scandalised by the denial of Peter, by seeing in the very passage that attests the fall of its chief the divine assurance of the Church's indefectibility: "And then, being once converted, confirm thy brethren." After his conversion then, sustained by the prayer of Christ, who never prayed in vain, he was not only established in his place, but destined to support all the parts of the edifice. And accordingly we find that while the churches of Asia and Africa have fallen, that of Rome, the seat of Peter,

[1] St. Luke, xxii. 32.

has remained firm against the tempest; and that while the other columns have been gradually torn from their places, and the Church of God has been strewn with their ruins, that of St. Peter has stood unmoved amidst the revolutions of time, like one of the Egyptian pyramids, while the fleeting sectary who meditates its fall reminds me of the wandering Arabs, who strive to detach some fragment from the massy monument, and pitches his shifting tent under the shelter of its greatness; but, mocked by his fruitless efforts, he quickly disappears, and is heard of no more amidst the solitude of the desert. You may be scandalised at the fall of Peter, but let me observe to you that he has many imitators of his fall, but few of his repentance. All, then, who abjure their religion through fear or pusillanimity like Peter deny Jesus Christ. All who are ashamed of the maxims and practices of that religion which they profess only in name, like Peter, deny Jesus. All who would willingly follow Christ to Thabor and deny Him on Calvary, that is, all, who would willingly profess a religion surrounded with pomp and affluence, which they would desert when assailed with persecution, like Peter, deny Jesus; but would to God that they who are scandalised at his weakness would reflect that they have been often imitators of his sin without having imitated the fervour and sincerity of his repentance.

From Caiphas He was led to Pilate, amidst the scoffs and insults of a brutal soldiery. Pilate inquires what accusation they had against this Man. They, in order to find the way to the prejudices of the governor, accused Christ of sedition, saying that He forbade to give tribute to Cæsar, calling Himself Christ the King. Pilate immediately saw through their dark designs, and struck with the calm and dignified air of conscious innocence which the Redeemer exhibited, he was resolved on His acquittal. Hearing, however, that He was of Galilee, he sends Him to Herod, who was Tetrarch of that province, to be tried by his jurisdiction. "And Herod seeing Jesus was very glad, for he was desirous for a long time to see Him, because he had heard many things of Him, and he hoped to see some miracles wrought by Him. And he questioned Him with many words, but He answered him nothing. And the chief priests and scribes stood by earnestly accusing Him. And Herod, with his soldiers, despised Him and mocked Him, putting on Him a white garment, and sent Him back to Pilate. And Herod and Pilate were made friends together that same day, for before they were enemies one to the other." Good God! what a lesson, to behold two individuals who before were enemies, become reconciled by the oppression of an innocent Man. Herod and Pilate had hitherto been enemies, and their injustice to Christ became the bond of their union. What was the pleasure felt by Herod on seeing the wonderful Man whose fame had gone far among the people? Was it, do you think, a desire of either instruction or conversion that prompted him to question Jesus, or to expect the exhibition of a miracle? No, my brethren, it was a perverse and presumptuous curiosity that would feign controvert the wisdom to which he should listen with reverence. He was one of those characters who would feign erect himself into a judge of religion, fancying that heaven itself should bend to his caprices, though more anxious to gratify his pride by disputation than to surrender his conviction to the majesty of truth. But Jesus confounded his vain curiosity. He that often discoursed at length to instruct the meek and humble of heart opens not His lips to the idle curiosity of Herod. And He that often wrought wonders to cure the blind, the lame, and the insane abstains from the exhibition of His power to gratify the pride and presumption of a court. Had Herod sought instruction, and manifested a zeal for truth, enough had been already done to achieve his conversion. But Herod was one of those characters who are eternally looking for further manifestations of the divine power, whose understandings no arguments can enlighten, and whose obstinacy no authority can subdue. But Jesus really wrought a miracle before him in forbearing from any idle display of power, which would have had no other effect than that of gratifying a profane curiosity. Herod, stung with rage at his disappointment, sends Him back to Pilate, clothed with a white garment, in token of derision; and thus the Son of God, the wisdom of His Father, is sent back and forward the scorn of two haughty great ones, who imagined themselves privileged to sport with the infirmities of man as if they were destined to minister to their savage and unfeeling merriment. Pilate, conscious of the innocence of Jesus, and terrified by the dreams of his wife, attempted His release; but the Jews were still urgent and clamorous in demanding His condemnation. The crafty politician has recourse to as savage and iniquitous an expedient as history records in the annals of legal cruelty to assuage the fury of the multitude. He orders Him to be whipped and scourged, the order is instantly obeyed by the thirsty vengeance of His executioners. A hundred lashes instantly resound from every spot of His virginal flesh until His bones are laid bare, and in this mangled state He was presented by Pilate to the people, saying : " Behold the man." But the sight of His suffering instead of appeasing their lust of blood, only ministered fresh fuel to their vengeance, and with horrid and tumultuous uproar they repeatedly cried: "Crucify Him, crucify Him." Pilate pressed, by their furious importunity, had recourse to another expedient for His liberation. There happened to be then in prison a notorious robber and murderer of the name of Barabbas. The Jews had an ancient custom of having a criminal released on the day of the Passover. Pilate, imagining that all would demand the instant death of him whose crimes and infamy deserved the last vengeance of the law, asks them: "Whom will you that I release to you, Barabbas or Jesus, who is called the Christ?" They cried out, "Barabbas." Pilate said, "What shall I do with Jesus?" They exclaimed: "Let Him be crucified." The governor still pressed, saying: "What evil hath He done?" But they only replied with louder and more savage importunity, "Let Him be crucified."

Be astonished, O ye heavens, at the perverse judgment of men. What! Jesus Christ, the public benefactor compared to Barabbas, a notorious transgressor of the laws; the worst and most infamous of culprits preferred to Jesus Christ, in whom the cruel vigilance of His enemies could not discover the shadow of a crime, and a monster whose blood should have atoned for the injured justice of the law to be released, while the Author of life, who knew no sin, is loudly demanded for instant execution. You are, doubtless, astonished at the horrible ingratitude of the Jews, who preferred Barabbas to Jesus. And are you not daily guilty of a similar enormity, as often as you prefer the indulgence of your passions to the authority of God? While your lawless appetites, like the Jewish rabble, clamour for their gratification, as often as you yield to their importunity, you are guilty of preferring Barabbas to Jesus. While you are ready to indulge the brutal vices of drunkenness and impurity, do not you sacrifice your Redeemer, not only saying with the Jews: "Crucify Him, crucify Him," but actually, as St. Paul assures us, "crucifying unto yourselves again the Son of God, and making a mockery of Him."[1] Pilate, in whose breast the voice of conscience and humanity was not utterly extinguished, makes one more faint appeal to their reason by asking them, "Would they put to death the King of the Jews?" Attend, now, and witness how a jealousy and hatred of the person of our Saviour extinguishes every other feeling in the hearts of that hardened people. They who were hitherto so jealous of their laws as to spurn any foreign jurisdiction, now sacrifice every regard for their country, exclaiming, with one accord, "We have no king but Cæsar; if thou dost dismiss this Man, thou art not a friend to Cæsar." At the sound of these last words the resolution of the governor was completely subdued. Hitherto he wavered between the opposite dictates of duty and worldly prudence, like many of those timid characters who strive to reconcile their consciences and their interests. But as soon as he was threatened with the displeasure of Cæsar, conscience, which hitherto made a feeble stand, entirely gave way, and this crafty and cruel statesman, lest he should incur the displeasure of man, gave up to the merciless fury of the Jews Him whom his conscience pronounced innocent. And how often is the weak and crooked policy of Pilate imitated in the world by those irresolute characters who, rather than displease a powerful man, scruple not to sacrifice their duty. Complying with the dictates of conscience as far as they do not interfere with their worldly views, ashamed to renounce their religion, yet equally ashamed to fulfil all its precepts, struggling like Pilate between the fear of violating their duty and offending the great ones of the world, until, like him, they sacrifice Christ Himself at the shrine of a worldly and interested policy.

[1] Heb. vi. 6.

Yet this cruel governor would fain preserve some appearance of integrity at the same time that he was committing the grossest injustice. He asks water, as if to wash his hands out of the guilt of Christ's Blood, and the Jews exclaim, "His Blood be upon us and our children." Unfortunate people! They demand that the Blood of the Just One should be visited on them and their posterity. Their unhallowed prayer has had its effect: their crime has been transmitted, their city has been destroyed, their temple burnt; and their seed scattered over the nations of the earth, still attests the melancholy curse which they have inherited from their fathers.

Now that Jesus is delivered up to their rage, they instantly discharge on the devoted Victim their hitherto restrained vengeance. After scourging Him until, in the language of the Prophet, "there was not a sound spot left in Him,"[1] they embitter cruelty with insult by putting a scarlet cloak upon Him, as an emblem of mock royalty. Then placing a crown of thorns on His head, which pierced His sacred temples, they gave Him a reed in His right hand, and bowed the knee in derision, saying, "Hail, King of the Jews." In this disguise, calculated no less to excite the horror than the pity of the spectators, Pilate presented Him to the Jews, hoping to arouse their obdurate hearts to mercy; but with redoubled eagerness they cried, "Crucify Him, crucify Him." Vainly should we endeavour to describe the pealing laughter, the scornful shouts, the frantic execrations which assailed Him in His transition from one tribunal to another, and on His way to Calvary. . . .

Thus the Victim of the sins of the world mounts with tottering steps the painful ascent of Calvary. Oh! how truly might He say now in the words of the prophet, "Oh, all you that pass by, attend and see if there is

[1] Isai. i. 6.

sorrow like to my sorrow."[1] "I looked for one that would grieve together with Me, but there was none, and for one that would comfort Me, and I found none."[2] Having reached the hill of Calvary, they suspended Him on the cross, and in their efforts to strain His members to their allotted places, His whole frame was almost disjointed and subjected to the most agonising torture. Here their cruelty was again redoubled, and again they renewed their savage and insulting mockeries, while the Mother of our Redeemer stood at the foot of the cross, witnessing the tragic scene. Oh! how every stroke that was inflicted upon Jesus fell upon the tender heart of His Mother; and if there be here the mother of an only child, she can have still but a faint idea of the sharpness of the sword, which pierced the soul of Mary on witnessing the agonies of her dying Son. At length He thirsts, and His unrelenting executioners fulfil the prophecy of the Psalmist by giving Him for a drink gall mixed with vinegar. While His persecutors were discharging on Him the utmost efforts of their rage, Jesus, as if insensible to His own sufferings, feels only for their blindness, and incapable of harbouring any other feeling but charity, He thus pours forth His last dying supplication: "Father, forgive them, for they know not what they do." Such was the mercy He prayed for His enemies, and that mercy He exhibited towards one of the thieves who expired with Him on the cross. Struck with the meekness and dignity with which Christ supported His torments, He confessed the divinity of the Redeemer. . . .

But while we admire the mercy of Jesus to the penitent thief, we must pause to reprobate the presumptuous impiety of those who abuse the example of the penitent thief to expect the grace of a death-bed repentance. I

---

[1] Lam. i. 12.   [2] Ps. lxviii. 21.

know not what to wonder at most, the folly or the impiety of those people. If a solitary instance of such a conversion occur in the sacred writings, amidst circumstances without example, what grounds have we to expect a similar mercy? Did the penitent thief abuse the same graces which are daily rejected by Christians? Did he repeatedly relapse into sin after having been favoured with a reconciliation? It is true, however, that the dying thief was converted. Yes; but let it be recollected that it was in the midst of the most awful and unheard of prodigies. Let, then, those, who calculate on the miraculous grace of a death-bed conversion expect that the sun will be again veiled in darkness, that the rocks will be rent asunder, and the earth tremble to its centre, that the dead will awaken, and their frightful apparitions stalk abroad in noonday. Let them, in fine, expect the same prodigies that attested that the Author of nature was expiring, and then may they expect the more supernatural prodigy of a death-bed repentance. . . . The types and figures of the Old Law were now abolished, the ancient prophecies were fulfilled, the expiation of sin was perfected, and in the infinite ransom which was now paid to the Divine Justice, man was finally liberated from the dominion of sin and Satan.

What, now, is the conclusion which we should draw from our Redeemer's passion? While you were pursuing with me the tragic history of His sufferings, what was the train of feeling which it awakened in your minds? Doubtless, your bosoms glowed with a noble resentment against the savage executioners who were insensible to pity, while the sun veiled in darkness, the earth shaken to its centre, rocks rent asunder, and, in fine, the agitation of nature, more feeling than man, seemed to sympathise with the agonies of its God. And who were those executioners whose cruelty thus excited the revolt of the elements? Your sins; yes, your sins were the executioners; nor is there any among you who could say that he was innocent of His blood. How applicable, then, to you are the words of my text, and how justly may I tell you, while you weep over the sufferings of Jesus, to weep for yourselves and your children. Do; weep, lest He should have suffered for you in vain, and lest, by an obstinate resistance to His grace, you make void the blood of His covenant. Recollect that though He has paid our ransom, He still expects our co-operation. You are redeemed by a great price, says St Peter; learn, therefore, the importance of your salvation, and from the greatness of the price do not fail to estimate the value of the purchase. If you do, Christ will assist you by His powerful grace. "For if," as the Apostle says, "while we were enemies we were reconciled to God by the death of His Son, much more being reconciled shall we be saved by His life."[1] What grace can He refuse us after having given already the treasure of His blood for our redemption? "Let us go therefore with confidence to the throne of grace,"[2] and beseech our High Priest, by His agony in the garden, by the thorns which pierced His temples, and by the spear which opened His sacred side; in short, by the torrents of mercy that flowed from His passion, to make us partakers in His merits and be numbered the last day amongst the trophies of His redemption. Amen.

[1] Rom. v. 10.   [2] Heb. iv. 16.

## ST. PATRICK'S DAY.

*"We are the children of the saints, and look for that life which God will give to those who change not their faith from Him."*—TOBIAS, ii. 18.

AMONG the various trials through which Ireland has passed, and may be still fated to endure, it has, in the recollection of the past, and in the hope of the future, one of the richest sources of human enjoyment. The records of an honourable lineage must console the humblest descendant who is conscious of not tarnishing the lustre of his name, and when there is hope it is capable of lighting up the horrors of a dungeon. Between those two lights it was the consolation of Ireland to walk in the darkest days of her adversity. By the past I mean not the glories of a profane and remote antiquity, on which the world dwells with rapture, but I mean the more valuable claims of a sainted heraldry, by which our people have been so signally distinguished. Whilst they contemplated the illustrious models, which their Church in every age held out to them, they were endued with courage to brave every persecution; and when, like the old Tobias, their devotion to their God was made a subject of bitter raillery, their piety rose superior to every provocation, and, like him, they exclaimed, "We are the children of saints, and look for that life which God will give to those who change not their faith from Him." Happy people, who have preserved with such fidelity the precious legacy bequeathed to them by our great national Apostle! I purpose, then, in this discourse to give a brief outline of his life and labours, and then to take a rapid glance at the various fortunes of the Irish Church, still so steadfast in the faith which he planted.

It has been the fate of St. Patrick, like that of other eminent men, to have rival nations contending for the honour of being the place of his nativity. It is no wonder the steps of boyhood, light and bounding as the spirits that guide them, seldom leave a sufficiently deep impression for the historian to track them by; and few there are, like St. John of God, over whose birth a heavenly light is seen to play, to direct the biographer through the earlier stages of his life. Our best guides in this question are his own confessions, and a metrical life of the Apostle by Fiech, one of his episcopal disciples. He tells us himself, in clear and distinct terms, where he was born; but, to a modern ear, more accustomed to the Saxon tongue than to the venerable language in which those confessions were written, the simple expression of the words would not decide the controversy. Much ingenuity has been resorted to in giving them interpretations of which they are not naturally susceptible, in order to confirm the opinions of the respective advocates of Scotland and of Gaul.

But notwithstanding the process of refinement to which they have been subjected, enough of their ancient form still remains to determine every intelligent and unprejudiced antiquarian in favour of the opinion that assigns the birth of St. Patrick to the northern provinces of France. But why occupy your time or patience upon a point which can have but little influence on the object for which you are assembled? It matters little where the Saint was born, since he is one of those extraordinary individuals that are sent by Providence to bless mankind at distant intervals, and who, on that account, may be claimed as the common property of the human race. Nor shall I stop to refute an opinion of which the malignity is neutralised by its folly, that because of this discrepancy of opinion regarding the place of his birth, St. Patrick was a phantom.[1] Were such sophistry to have any weight, it would, assuredly, strip history of some of its most illustrious ornaments. What? must the inhabitants of Egypt doubt the existence of the source of their great river because European travellers cannot agree about the spot from which it springs? Let others, then, expend their darkling labours in exploring the small and distant fountain of the faith of Ireland, we shall be content with the incontestable proofs that are furnished of its existence, whilst we contemplate the majesty of the flood that has already filled the nations with the noise, and spread over a large country the fertility of its waters.

Scarce had Patrick attained his sixteenth year when he was seized by a band of freebooters, who infested the coast of Gaul, and carried him captive into Ireland. From a mind, less disciplined to piety, and a conformity with the will of God, such a disaster would have called forth murmurs against Providence. Far, however, from turning his misfortune into a theme of vexatious complaints, it became to him a rich source of spiritual consolation. It was his painful duty to tend his master's flock on the mountains of Antrim, in the province of Ultonia. His solicitude always anticipated the morning sun; the cold of winter could not chill the ardour of his devotions. From the rough elements which surrounded him he drew canticles of praise, commanding the frost and the snows, in the sublime apostrophe of the Hebrew

[1] Here the extravagant opinions of Drs. Reeves and Ledwich are alluded to, the former of whom doubted, and the latter denied the existence of St. Patrick (ED.).

youths, to praise the Lord; and in the canopy of heaven, which was spread over him, he beheld a faint image of the glory of its Creator. "When I came to Ireland," says the saint (for there is a simple unction in his own words, which evaporates in any other language) "I fed my master's flocks, and prayed frequently in the day. The fear and love of God were gradually increasing in me, and His faith and spirit gaining such ground, that each day I said a hundred prayers, and as many by night, so that I stayed in the woods and on the mountains, and rose to prayer before the light, through the frost, and the snow, and the rain; and yet I felt no inconvenience, nor was there any sloth about me, because the spirit was then fervent within my breast." What an interesting spectacle do we here contemplate in the early life of our Apostle; and how well adapted such a severe discipline to the lofty destiny to which he was afterwards to be raised. Yes; for those who are destined for the ordinary situations of life, an ordinary training may be well suited; but for him who was intended to be the Apostle of a nation, and the conqueror of its vices, the Almighty had prepared a discipline analagous to the arduous nature of his future labours. Hence he was early transplanted to that solitude without which no growth in the moral and intellectual, as well as the physical world, can ever attain strength or majesty. Far from the contagion of the world, his virtue was here pure as the atmosphere which he breathed; and his thoughts were simple and elevated as the lofty scenery around him. Such was the school in which St. Patrick's virtue was formed. The commands of a hard master exercised his obedience; his patience was tried by this man's capricious disposition. In the solicitude with which he watched his flock, he was inured to that vigilance which he was afterwards to exercise over a portion of Christ's fold; and if, according to the admonition of St. Peter, it be the perfection of a Christian pastor to become "a pattern of the flock from the heart,"[1] nothing could be more worthy of God's providence than thus to enable the future Church of Ireland to contemplate, in its great Apostle, the model which was shown it on the mount—being thus the most appropriate—and, as if the prophetic type of a priesthood, which, like him, was doomed to look for shelter from the cruelty of man, amidst the severity of frosts and snows, and to offer the pure sacrifice of the Lord in the caverns of the rocks and the solitude of the mountains.

After six years of servitude he was at length released under circumstances which impress a conviction that his life was under the immediate guidance of heaven. On landing in his own country, he had to traverse a vast and dreary wilderness, in which he and his companions were exposed to perish from hunger. The Saint sustained their desponding spirits by his reliance on his God; when lo! a herd of swine, like the quails that relieved the Hebrews of old, seasonably appeared and convinced them of the justness of his confidence. A few years elapsed, and he was again carried into a similar captivity, and after the short interval of six months again restored to the embraces of his affectionate parents. When absent, they deplored his loss, and now that he was returned, they adjured him not to quit them more, in hope that, like the young Tobias after his escape from a strange country, he would become "the light of our eyes, the staff of our old age, the comfort of our life, the hope of our posterity."[2] But St. Patrick was destined to be the father of a different and a holier offspring. It was not for the improve-

---

[1] 1 Pet. v. 3.    [2] Tob. x. 4.

ment of his family fortune he was exercised in his early warfare. The Almighty had destined another sphere for his exertions, and whilst, perhaps, the secret whispers of grace calling him to a holier state were in danger of yielding to the louder importunity which repeated the subduing language of father and mother and of home, he was favoured with a vision of the night, in which he beheld an old man of the name of Victor, standing on the western shore of Ireland, in the barony of Tyrawley, handing him one of many letters which he held in his hand, inscribed with these words: "The voice of the Irish," on perusing which he fancied to have heard the collected voices of numbers of children, who, with outstretched arms, adjured him in the following earnest supplication: "We entreat thee, holy young man, to come and walk among us;" and thus were the entreaties of parents and of friends drowned amidst the more imperative and importuning cries of a people who were perishing for want of religious instruction. The Saint hesitated not, but, like Samuel, who was only anxious to know the divine will, immediately obeyed the call of heaven. Far, however, from imitating those who mistake their own presumption for the impulse of the Spirit, he had recourse to the regular channel through which God has ordained the conveyance of His high commission, and accordingly sought, like the Apostle, another Ananias in the person of St. Germanus, the holy Bishop of Auxerre, into whose hands he resigned himself, in order to become duly qualified for the ministry. Under the advice of this eminent prelate, he spent, as we are informed by the Bishop who wrote his life, a portion of his time in the islands of the Tuscan Sea, and most probably in the Island of Lerins, then famed for a learned seminary, in which the monastic discipline of St. Martin of Tours was associated with the successful cultivation of ecclesiastical learning. Thirteen years are said to have been employed by the Saint in the alternate exercise of solitary study and of active duties in the ministry, under the immediate direction of St. Germanus, by which long and laborious preparation he became admirably fitted for the great work to which he was called by the Almighty. Thus prepared and furnished with ample testimonials of his merits, he sets out for Rome, the centre of Christian unity, to obtain, ere he embarked on his intended mission, the benediction and approval of the Sovereign Pontiff. St. Celestine then sat on the chair of St. Peter, who, having already invested Palladius, with episcopal powers for the mission of Ireland, now gives his sanction to St. Patrick, as a subordinate associate in the same holy work. Palladius' stay in Ireland was but short, the success of his mission partial; in less than a year he quitted Ireland, and before St. Patrick had time to reach that country he was informed that Palladius died in Great Britain. This recent death of one who had been sent to convert Ireland, together with his own early captivity there, as well as the mysterious vision which he saw upon its shores, must have impressed upon his mind that to him was reserved the spiritual conquest of that country. He therefore receives without delay the episcopal consecration, and, accompanied by a few select associates, burns with a holy impatience to impart to that benighted land the glad tidings of salvation. Accordingly, he lands on its shores in the year of our Lord 432, in the neighbourhood of Dublin, and soon shapes his course to the northern province, which had been the early scene of his captivity. There he gained a few converts; but it was only from the festival of Easter the following year we may date the glorious era of Ireland's liberation from spiritual bondage. Instead of wasting his time in obscure and unprofitable labours along the extremities, he meditates at once his attack upon the centre, and directs his spiritual thunders against the very citadel of paganism. On Holy Saturday, the day set apart by the Church for the blessing of the fire, a large mass of flame, kindled by the saint on an opposite eminence, is seen from the royal residence at Tara, and the jealousy of the Druidical priests trembled for the reigning superstition. The monarch, who was taught by those artful ministers to connect the safety of his throne with the Druidical worship, was alarmed at the sight of those flames, which were to spread nought but sedition through the land. He, therefore, sets out, accompanied by those who were most skilled in the devices of his craft, in order to extinguish those forbidden fires. They were met by the Saint, with no other arms than the crucifix, who soon convinced them that theirs were the lurid and murky fires, lit by a dire and sanguinary superstition, whilst his was but an emblem of that mild light which came from heaven to dissipate the darkness of sin and death; and in the universal tradition of the country, that when the fire of St. Patrick was kindled, those of Baal went out, we may recognise another truth, that the feeble light of the Magi was eclipsed by the overpowering splendour of his religion. On the following day he was summoned to give an account of the faith that was in him before the assembly of Pagan sages who crowded the monarch's court. Like Moses, he spoke before kings, and was not confounded: all the arts with which the Druids were gifted were put in requisition to rival the wonders which he wrought; but the wisdom of the world was subdued by the folly of the cross; all the powers of superstition gave way before the virtue that went forth from the man of God, and though, like Festus or Pharaoh, the heart of the monarch remained unsubdued, the conversion of numbers on that memorable day, among whom are ranked some of the King's children, attested the triumph of St. Patrick and the discomfiture of his enemies.

Henceforth the progress of the Gospel was rapid and irresistible. In the county of Meath, which was the cradle of the Christian religion, he remained for some time propagating his infant Church, and fortifying it by the establishment of piety and learning. From hence he directed his way to the West of Ireland, spreading the blessings of the Gospel over the country which he traversed. Wherever he went he was received as the messenger of heaven. By his preaching the people were reclaimed from turbulence and immorality; at his interposition rival chieftains forgot their feuds, and left their resentments as a sacrifice at his feet; females in the full enjoyment of youth and fortune were glad to exchange the fleeting prospects of life for the happiness of virginity; and princes gladly resigned their crowns to purchase the promised blessings of religion. From a lofty mountain on the shores of the Atlantic, which still bears his name from being the scene of his penitential exercises, he turns his steps towards the people of the district, now the Diocese of Killala, who were the first to invite him in the vision to come to Ireland. There his spiritual succours were commensurate with the wants of the inhabitants. After appeasing the deadly feuds that raged between the children of the chief, he baptised them, together with twelve thousand people in a running fountain, which still remains as a monument of their immersion; and in the language of the Psalmist, "We will adore in the place where his feet stood."[1] I am aware that, like

[1] Ps. cxxxi. 7.

other practices of Catholic piety, this feeling of reverence for the footsteps of the saints has been much misrepresented. But surely it is not necessary to dwell, especially here, on its vindication, surrounded as I must be by generous individuals who have resigned all the solace of their domestic circle to come and meditate among the monuments of those ancient masters whose lofty deeds and ardent language first kindled in their own hearts the like aspirations. Those who would loiter an entire day along the fabled fountain where a benevolent monarch studied those lessons of wisdom by which he subdued a turbulent race to the arts of civilised life; or gladly forego their morning's repast to look for those spots, on which the violation of female virtue was avenged, and utterance was given to those burning appeals to a nation's justice and a nation's freedom, of which the warmth has not been chilled through the transit of ages—men who would cheerfully risk all the perils of distant voyages to visit those fields in which their fancy might behold the spirits of the heroes of Marathon thronging round them, invoked by the Athenian orator, and awakened by the magic of that invocation—yes; those at least who have a heart can understand (and for those who have not, preaching is useless), what must be the feelings which burn within the breast of a Catholic when he touches those hallowed spots that streamed with the Redeemer's blood, or were sanctified by His baptismal immersion; or what must be the similar sentiments, though fainter in degree, that must fill his mind as often as he treads over ground which bears the monuments of the benevolent power of Christ's Saints and Apostles? Do we not view with admiration every trophy which a country has erected to those warriors who conquered its enemies and protected its freedom? And are we to evince no gratitude towards those who conquered vice and error, the deadliest of man's foes? Nay, they are deserving of a more heartfelt homage, since such is the vicissitude of war that the glory and the greatness of one country cannot be purchased without a corresponding depression and misery in another, whereas the saints of God are the only heroes whose laurels were never soiled with a single tear, and whose success has not cost mankind one solitary execration.

The northern coast, from Killala to Down, through the intermediate county of Donegal, was the next theatre of his labours. Those who hitherto sat in darkness saw now a great light, and the joyous sounds of mercy and salvation were heard amidst those remote solitudes which were hitherto involved in all the darkness of paganism. Again, from the north, the Apostle turns his steps to Meath, the first scene of his mission, and labours, in the province of Leinster, to enlarge the boundaries of the Church. The trophies which everywhere marked his progress, and the fame that was gathering round him as he went, rendered obedience prompt and resistance fruitless, so that on his arrival in Cashel, the centre of Munster, the monarch of that province, surrounded by his nobles, came forth to greet a conqueror, who, instead of leaving desolation in his path, filled the land with gladness, and was cheered with the blessings of its inhabitants. Not Cashel alone, but various other places in the south, were favoured for some years with the enlivening presence of the Apostle. In short, there was scarcely a portion of Ireland which felt not his joyous influence. Like the Saviour of the world, he went round doing good unto all; monuments of mercy and beneficence long attested the footsteps of the man of God, and the passage of St. Patrick through the land, like the broad and lucid zone which is seen to cross the heavens, could be tracked by the superior brilliancy that streamed along the path which the Apostle had traversed.

Now that the vineyard which was let out to this faithful labourer was reclaimed and cultivated, his solicitude was naturally turned to the means by which it might be protected. For the purpose, then, of modelling the Church of Ireland to the rest of the Catholic Church, which is beautifully compared to an army in battle-array, in the ascending gradation of its hierarchy, from the humblest levite who ministers in the temple to the Supreme Pontiff, he appointed bishops in the different Sees which he established, leaving to his successors in Armagh the authority of Primate, with which he himself was invested, and bequeathing to them all, as a most valuable inheritance, obedience to that See from which his own mission was derived. Never was bequest preserved with more devout reverence; and the tenacity with which the Irish Church has clung to the faith of Peter has been only equalled by the enlightened docility with which it was first adopted. I have passed over the numberless miracles of the Saint, content to observe, with St. Augustine, on the propagation of Christianity, that such an astonishing submission to the yoke of the Gospel, unaccompanied by miracles, would have been more miraculous than the signs and wonders in which St. Patrick was so powerful. Content with the proofs of those miracles, and the piety of its first preachers, the Irish people readily embraced the Christian religion. Its martyrs were reserved for a remoter period; and the cheerfulness with which those martyrs died for the faith showed how strong and indelible were its first proofs, which the interval of centuries could not weaken. Besides, they kept a steady eye on the source from which that faith was first imparted. There is no example of a national church, having sundered its connection with the chair of Peter, that can resist the storm by which the Church is continually assailed. Firm, therefore, in its indissoluble connection with Rome, the Irish Church resisted every innovation; and if it has risen triumphant over the tide which deluged the faith of other countries, it is because its anchorage was never torn from that rock on which the Church of Christ was erected.

After thus providing for the safety of that Church, which he planted with so much care, the Saint went to rest from his labours in the enjoyment of that reward which his virtues had merited. His obsequies were celebrated with peculiar veneration. From the remotest parts of Ireland the clergy assembled to pay the last rites to his remains. The people mourned for him twelve successive days; and, in the simple tradition, that during that period there was a continual day without any interval of darkness, we may perceive how brilliant and continuous was the light of the funeral-tapers which dispelled the gloom of the night during the melancholy solemnity.

However, the hopes of religion were far from being buried in his grave. The seeds which he had scattered fell on a grateful soil; and not many years elapsed from the death of St. Patrick when the Church of Ireland became one of the fairest and most flourishing portions of the extensive vineyard of Christ. Every province had its colleges and its cloisters, in which the youth of Ireland might spend their time in perpetual vigils round the sacred fire of the temple, or go forth to cast its light and heat into the midst of a corrupt world. Besides Clonard and other schools which arose in the centre of the kingdom, Armagh and Bangor in the north, Cashel and Lismore in the south, Clonfert and Mayo in the west, at once became seminaries of learning, which not only educated the natives of Ireland, but soon attracted by their fame the youth of the Continent who panted for science. Not only were these colleges gratuitously opened to strangers, they were likewise furnished with books and other necessaries for instruction; and, far from relying on legendary lore, or the high-wrought praises of national minstrelsy in this picture of the hospitality and learning of the Irish Church, I am only translating the sober testimony of Bede, who tells us, that such was the confluence of strangers into Ireland, that Mayo was denominated, from the number of its Saxon monks, Mayo of the Saxons. No; it is not to Ireland I shall turn, lest it should become abashed by repeating the echo of its own eulogy. I shall appeal to the people of the Continent, who have been too grateful for the benefits of the faith to conceal the source from which it was derived. To commence with the north. No scholar is ignorant of the labours of Columba, the Apostle of the Picts,[1] who, from his zeal to multiply the temples of God, has been known by the name of Columbkill, or Columba of the Churches; and though many of the monuments of his piety have been since defaced, his fame still sheds its grateful odour round the hallowed tombs of Iona. From this island, likewise, came forth some of the principal missionaries of Great Britain; and to the zeal of Aidanus[2] and the Irish Monks,

---

[1] Venit de Hibernia Presbyter et Abbas, habitu et vita Monachi insignis, nomine Columba, Brittaniam, prædicaturus verbum Dei provinciis septentrionalibus Pictorum.—BEDA Hist. Ecc. lib. 3, c. iv.

[2] Sitôt que le Roi Oswald fut établi dans son Royaume, il songea à rendre chrétien tout son peuple; et pour cet effet, il envoya aux anciens des Ecossais, c'est à dire des Irlandais, chez lesquels 'il avait reçu le Baptême, demandant un evêque pour instruire ses sujets.—FLEURY Hist. Ecc. liv. 38. §§ xviii.(ED.)

the companions of his labours, was the kingdom of Northumberland indebted for the Christian religion. The memory of St. Livinus, who shed his blood for their conversion, is still revered by the devout gratitude of the Belgians. Colman, an Irish saint, is honoured as the Patron of Austria. The episcopal throne of Strasbourg was twice filled by Irish ecclesiastics; nor need I allude to Virgilius,[1] the Bishop of Salzburg, famed for his piety, but still more famed for his persecutions, because his mind had outstripped, in its pursuit of astronomical knowledge, the slow progress of the age. Luxeuil is still associated with the historic monuments of the Island of Saints. Amidst the recesses of the Alps, the memory of St. Gallus is inscribed on the grateful hearts of the Swiss peasantry; and while the confines of France and Germany were preoccupied by more of his countrymen, such was the zeal of St. Fridolinus that he sought fresh ground for his labours by building a monastery in one of the hitherto uninhabited islands of the Rhine. Even Italy herself, the mistress of the world in religion and in arts, as once in arms, did not disdain to participate in the blessings which the Irish Church poured forth with such profusion. The name of Frigidianus is enrolled in the catalogue of the bishops of Lucca. Florence felt the holy influence of the neighbourhood of Donatus; and when I recollect the position of his episcopal seat, I am only transcribing the Scriptural allusion in saying, that he shone like a burning light from the lofty eminence of Fiesole. Far, however, from imitating those systematic absentees, who are forever arraigning the crimes which they inflict, and calum-

---

[1] Sublato e vivis Joanne Episcopo Salsiburgensi creatus est Virgilius Episcopus . . . . Hunc ex Hibernia natum testis est Alcuinus in epigrammate in quo ejus sanctitatem ac integritatem celebrat.—Ann. Benedic. tom. 2, lib. xxiii. §§ xxi. (ED.)

niating the country which they plunder, Donatus never forgot his duties to his country, which distance had only endeared to him; and in lines which a fastidious critic would not find unworthy of a more classic period, the Arno was heard to resound with the just praise of the land of his nativity. Bobio preserves the fame of Columbanus [1] in the depths of the Apennines; and such was the veneration of the natives of the north of Italy for this illustrious saint, that they have associated his name with the topography of their soil. Naples, too, exhibits traces of the holy heroism of our Church; and without dwelling on the circumstance that an Irish ecclesiastic was one of the masters of the illustrious doctor who has filled the world with his fame, the name of Cataldus appears conspicuous among the Bishops of Tarentum. I have thus only glanced at some of the most conspicuous theatres of the labours and the learning of the Irish Saints, since, to dwell on them with more minuteness would require to transcribe a large portion of the ecclesiastical history of the Continent. In short, from the most southern point of Europe to the Wall of Adrian, and from the shores of the Atlantic to the banks of the Vistula there is not one solitary district over which the massive fragments of Irish genius and of Irish sanctity are not profusely scattered; and though a stone should not be left upon a stone in that ill-starred land to tell of the holy men by whom it was once trodden, still, through the luminous and faithful pages of a Bede, a Bernard, a Muratori, a Mabillon, a Tillemont, and a Fleury, the learned scholar may yet view, as

---

[1] Ed appunto a questo Re dei Lombardi ricorse circa i correnti tempi San Colombano Abbate celebratissimo, nato in Irlanda, fundatore del monastero di Luxeuil e di altri monasteri. . . . vi andò (a Bobio) San Colombano, e quivi diede principio ad uno dei piu celebri monasteri d'Italia che tuttora fiorisce.—Muratori Ann. d'Italia, tom. 4, p. 1; anno 612. (ED.)

in so many mirrors, a strong though imperfect image of the ancient splendours of the Irish Hierarchy.

But no; the Church of Ireland will not, I trust, be obliged to seek among foreign nations alone, the title-deeds of its fame, nor be doomed to taste that bitter solace which springs from the consciousness that the source which supplies it is no more. It is deserving of a better destiny, and it is a pleasing reflection that amidst all its calamities its religion promises to be lasting and immortal. Yes, there is something providential in the relation which this insular Church, embosomed in the Western Ocean, has maintained with the nations of the Continent. When the Roman empire, which was destined for the easier propagation of the Gospel, had, on the fulfilment of its end, been consigned to destruction, and law and order threatened to retire from the world, scared by the savage conflicts of the tribes who fought for the fragments of the mighty ruin; when the holy men who survived the shock of one revolution were swept away by another, and the asylums of religion, which stood after one storm, were buried under a more disastrous hurricane; when, in short, amidst the strife of fierce and contending passions, the materials of God's temple were sometimes seen adrift upon the tide, and the few that attempted to arrest its fury were almost ready to sink in the common ruin, exhausted by their unremitting labours: then comes forth a body of men full of all the life and energy with which a youthful faith inspired them, having had just sufficient time to be trained to that discipline which, by detaching man from the cares of life, braces his spirit to that lofty tension of virtue which worldlings cannot understand; at such a critical and perilous juncture are the exertions of the Irish Church called forth to succour the labouring virtue of the Continent; and from the West the dove-like spirit of religion was felt to come across the deep, passing over the dark and troubled mass of a falling empire, and calming, as it passed, the mutinous elements of society.

Think you that I speak those things in the spirit of national vaunting? What! shall the earthen or more polished vessels presume to interrogate the craftsman who fashioned them of different materials? No, I allude to those topics rather to teach us humility by showing how the exaltation or depression of Churches, like those of kingdoms, are only instruments in achieving the higher purposes of Providence. I instance them to show how the Churches, like the members of which they are composed, are all knitted together by the spirit of unity; and how, as the Apostle says, they ought to sympathise in each other's sufferings, or rejoice in each other's glory. It was thus the Irish Church, in the days of its prosperity, extended its relief to its distressed brethren of the Continent, little, perhaps, imagining that in the revolution of human affairs it should stand in need of a reciprocal assistance. I do not allude to the ravages of the Danes. Though their fury was violent it was not artful or systematic, and, like the fiery eruptions of Vesuvius, its traces disappeared in the labour and industry of a few years. Not so with the hostility of heresy; it is more dangerous because more enduring; and when the attempts of violence and storm become frustrated, it has recourse to the slow and insidious process of the mine. Thus it was with the Irish Church. The fury of the Danes passed over it without tarnishing a faith that resembles in its freshness the verdure of the national symbol, the shamrock, that clothes its soil. It was destined to pass through a severer ordeal. Ireland gave the Continent aid against the destructive rage of pagan idolatry. It now sought its assistance against a foe which is always more deadly in its hostility to the Church, because it springs from its own bosom. Never was call more faithfully responded to; and the nations that might have felt the sense of former favours have since nobly cancelled the obligation. I shall not detail, for the detail would be harrowing, all the violence that was offered to the piety and tenderness of the human heart by a code of laws which have had no parallel in the annals of the most sanguinary legislation. Suffice it to say of the Church of Ireland, that "her sanctuary was desolate like a wilderness, her festival days were turned into mourning, her Sabbaths into reproach, her honours were brought to nothing,"[1] "and the vessels of her glory were carried away captive." Then her priests, who returned from a far country fraught with that knowledge which was made penal in their own land, snatched the fire from the altars of the falling temples and hid it in a valley; and like the tabernacle which was rescued by the prophet from the ruins of Jerusalem, the ark of our religion has been preserved amidst the solitude of our mountains. Do I allude to those scenes in order to stir up any angry recollections? God forbid! From the lips of a minister of the Saviour of the world no accents but those of charity should fall, and the Church should be always an asylum in which a truce should be given to the passions of mankind. I allude to them in the instructive spirit of the historian of Rome, in order that from the experience of the past, people should draw a lesson for the future, and that those who are still anxious for the pure perpetuity of the faith, should imitate the holy disinterestedness of their fathers. The whole secret of the fortitude of the Irish people lay in the deep-rooted sen-

---

[1] I Mac. i. 41.

timent so well expressed in the language of my text:
"We are the children of saints, and look for that life
which God shall give to those who never change their
faith from Him." Yes, they looked forward to that life
which their faith clearly revealed to them, and in the
brightness of that vision every other object disappeared.
No courtly arts, no crooked intrigues, no cunning schemes
of a wily and tortuous diplomacy were suffered to insinuate themselves into their councils. Their purpose
was single and straightforward—the preservation of their
faith; and compared to this one object every other consideration was valueless. Hence no compromise with
a hostile government in the nomination of their chief
pastors.[1] For they knew from the history of Alcimus,
the unprincipled high priest of Judea, as well as from the
present melancholy experience of other countries, that
those whose sins should exclude them from the sanctuary
would be the most unremitting and successful in their
canvass for an appointment to the high places of God's
temple. Hence no compromise in the education of their
children by suffering them to drink out of those impure
fountains formed by the experiments of a chemical theology combining the various ingredients of error in stated
proportions. Hence, in fine, no compromise on the
part of the priesthood in bartering the affections of their
flocks for the gold of the Government, well knowing
that the measure was fraught with the Macedonian policy
of purchasing by bribes that unconquerable attachment
to the country's faith which open warfare was not able
to subdue. But like the virtuous Fabricius, they have
hitherto rejected the bribe; and like him, they might

[1] Here allusion is made to the fidelity of the Irish Hierarchy, in condemning the insidious project of the VETO, and to their constancy in rejecting any terms of state endowment which the British Government might be disposed to propose for their acceptance. (ED.)

conduct the diplomatists of corruption into their humble cots to show whether those who could be content with the most homely fare were likely to be seduced into the betrayal of their country's faith or freedom. It was this virtuous poverty and ascetic independence which, like the similar early virtues of Rome, achieved all the triumphs of the Irish Church; and if ever the lust of money succeeds such pious disinterestedness—a curse which may heaven avert—it is then, and only then, like the same Roman state, it shall be seen to verge to its decline. It was by keeping aloof from the contagious atmosphere of kings and courts that the faith of Ireland burned with so much brilliancy, and whoever looks on the contrast between two lamps, the one scarcely winking its dark and flickering flame in the midst of halls laden with the effects of intemperance, and the other streaming its bright and unbroken blaze in the pure air of heaven, will not be surprised at the incessant splendour that has played around the Catholic hierarchy of Ireland. If we wish to transmit to after ages the purity of the faith of our fathers, we must labour to imitate their virtues, and, in order to cultivate those virtues, to follow the same process under which they had thriven. Yes, by keeping aloof from those occasions that are often fatal to its influence, not only will the faith of Ireland be preserved, but likewise those virtues that invariably follow in its train, but principally that virtue of chastity which has exclusively grown out of Christianity, and which may be called the touchstone by the practice or neglect of which you may ascertain its progress or decline: a virtue which has always distinguished in a peculiar manner not only the priesthood of Ireland, but likewise inspired its laity with an instinctive horror for vices to which, alas! a profligate world labours to give currency by opening its fashionable saloons for their admission, but which, like its other noxious reptiles, found death in the atmosphere of Ireland, or were obliged to creep away, shunned and detested, from its soil. Knowing, however, that it is in vain that we plant or water unless God give the increase, we should fervently implore the Almighty that He pour his blessing upon our labours. Let us also implore the intercession of St. Patrick that he continue to watch over that nation to which he has been an Apostle, and to protect the faith which he planted. For, if the friends of Job were required to have recourse to him as a condition of their acceptance with Heaven while as yet he struggled with the temptations of life, it surely cannot be imagined that the friends of God have less influence with Him when their spirits are freed from every earthly dross; or that they have less charity when in contact with the source of charity itself. But recollecting that all the apostles were only the ministers of Him who came to throw down the wall of separation, and to gather into one fold the scattered children of mankind let us endeavour to promote the great object for which they all laboured, by endeavouring to inspire all with the same faith, and animate them with the same charity; that after having enjoyed the happiness of living as children of the same family on earth, we may be associated in the enjoyment of the plenitude of that happiness which we hope to possess in the kingdom of our Heavenly Father. Amen.

## THE FEAST OF PENTECOST.

"And when the days of Pentecost were accomplished, they were all together in one place, and suddenly there came a sound from heaven as if of a mighty wind coming, and it filled the whole house where they were sitting. . . . And there appeared to them parted tongues as if it were of fire, and it sat upon every one of them; and they were all filled with the Holy Ghost, and they began to speak with divers tongues."—ACTS, ii. 1, 2, 3, 4.

To nourish the faith and inflame the devotion of her children, the Church has interspersed through the different seasons of the year the solemn commemoration of the principal mysteries of our religion. From the birth to the final triumph of our Redeemer, every interval is filled up by some festival which recalls the memory and celebrates the fruits of the different stages of His life. Nay, she extends her gratitude to the celebration of the other mysteries which are connected with the Incarnation, and among those, the descent of the Holy Ghost on the day of Pentecost has been particularly honoured by the institution of this holy anniversary. In the other festivals which we have commemorated we have contemplated the gradual development of the treasures of redemption; in this we behold as if the consummation of that great work. In the other mysteries we participate in the fruits of our justification; in this we ascend to its source and trace it to that divine fountain from which it is derived. I shall, therefore, in the following discourse attempt to impress upon your minds some idea of this mystery by dwelling on the effects which were wrought by the first descent of the Holy Spirit, effects which are still renewed in the minds of the faithful who labour to dispose themselves for a participation in His graces.

Of the effects produced by the Holy Spirit, one of the most stupendous is that which was wrought in the Apostles. Nursed in the bosom of a religion whose charity was cold, and whose prospects were carnal, their prejudices could not yield to the spiritual instructions of our Redeemer. During the latter years of His life the Apostles were His companions, to whom He imparted, in frequent and familiar conversation, the choicest treasures of His wisdom. Yet, notwithstanding such access to the source of inspiration itself, they retained all the prejudices of their nation concerning the restoration of their earthly kingdom. The hope of sharing in its principal honours animated the Apostles until the last moment of the Redeemer's life. Like the Pharisees, they contended for the first places, and the mother of the sons of Zebedee sought in their behalf the most honourable seats near the throne of the Messiah. Nor was this illusion removed by Christ's resurrection. Though He had conversed with them forty days, during which interval He unveiled the shadows of ancient prophecy; yet we find that they clung to the hope of worldly conquest and dominion to the day of His ascension. While they were assembled together, previous to that glorious event, they thus addressed Him in language which fully betrayed the leaven of their earthly views: "Lord, wilt Thou at this time restore again the kingdom to Israel? But He said to them: It is not for you to know the times or moments which the Father hath put in His own power. But you shall receive the power of the Holy Ghost coming upon you, and you shall be witnesses unto Me in Jerusalem, and in all Judea, and Samaria, and even to the uttermost part of the earth."[1] You behold, then, that as yet the Apostles breathed a carnal spirit, and though witnesses of the glory of the resurrection, their minds could not comprehend the nature of Christ's kingdom. But when the days of Pentecost were accomplished, and the Holy Ghost, with the "sound of a mighty wind," and in the "form of cloven tongues of fire sat upon each of them," they then went forward, manifesting the transformation their hearts had undergone. No longer restrained by apprehension from the Jews, whose fury they had before dreaded, they intrepidly announced the divinity of Christ, and the wonders of which they themselves were witnesses. But a few days before, they deserted their Master, and consulting for their own safety by an ignominious flight, cruelly abandoned Him to the vengeance of His enemies. Yet now, with an undaunted firmness, they brave all their menaces, and Peter, whose faltering voice trembled to acknowledge his Master, now proclaims to the assembled people : " Ye men of Israel, hear these words : Jesus of Nazareth, a man approved of God among you by miracles and wonders and signs, which God did by Him in the midst of you, as you also know; this same, being delivered up by the determinate counsel and foreknowledge of God, you, by the hands of wicked men, have crucified and slain, whom God had raised up, having loosed the sorrows of hell, as it was impossible that He should be holden by it. . . . This Jesus hath God raised again, whereof all we are witnesses. Being exalted, therefore, by the right hand of God, and having received of the Father the promise of the Holy Ghost, He hath poured forth this which you see and hear."[2] Astonished by the inspiration that burned in every expression, the multitude saw and felt the mighty

---

[1] Acts, i. 6, 7, 8.   [2] Acts, ii. 22, &c.

effects of the Holy Spirit. But while the impiety of some would fain mock the divine mystery, by ascribing to the effects of wine the inspiration that was manifest, St. Peter, in a still more astonishing effusion of the Holy Spirit, converting their blasphemy into evidence of its influence, "lifted up his voice and spoke to them: Ye men of Judea, and all you that dwell in Jerusalem, be this known to you, and with your ears receive my words; for these are not drunk as you suppose. . . . But this is that which was spoken of by the Prophet Joel: And it shall come to pass in the last days (saith the Lord) I will pour out of my Spirit upon all flesh, and your sons and your daughters shall prophesy. . . . And upon my servants, indeed, and upon my handmaids will I pour out in those days, of my Spirit, and they shall prophesy. And I will show wonders in the heaven above, and signs on the earth beneath."[1] Yes, the Apostles now amply realised this prediction, in the words which they spoke, and the wonders which they accomplished. No matter what might have been the country or the dialect of each individual, the language of the Apostles reached the hearts of all: "Now there were dwelling at Jerusalem Jews, devout men, out of every nation under heaven, and when this was noised abroad, the multitude came together, and were confounded in mind, because that every man heard them speak in his own tongue. Parthians, and Medes, and Elamites, and inhabitants of Mesopotamia . . . and strangers of Rome . . . and Arabians," and they were all astonished, because they heard them speak in their own tongues "the wonderful works of God."[2] The fruits of the Holy Spirit corresponded with its vigour, seizing the hearts of those on whom it descended, it extinguished all their passions

---

[1] Acts, ii. 14, &c.    [2] Acts, ii. 5, &c.

and purified their affections. Henceforward no timidity could check the ardour of their zeal; no worldly views to divide their hearts or weaken their holy energies; no compromise with error; no capitulation with self-interest; no wavering indecision between God and the world. No; that jealous God, who endures no rival, so covered their hearts by the effusion of His ample Spirit as to leave no room for any other interest. Inflamed by its devouring fire, and impelled by its omnipotent action, they feel no obstacles, and resistance vanishes before them. In vain did the priests and princes of the people endeavour to arrest their career, and extinguish their religion in its birth. In vain did they cite them before their tribunals, and endeavour to intimidate them by the infliction of torture. In vain they "charged them not to speak at all nor teach in the name of Jesus." For Peter and John said to them: "If it be just in the sight of God to hear you rather than God, judge ye: for we cannot but speak the things which we have seen and heard."[1] In vain were they cast into prison, since the Spirit which spoke by their mouth unlocked their dungeon, and sent them forth again to give fresh attestations of the power that inspired them. The obstacles which they combated only gave new impulse to their zeal, and the ease with which they conquered them renewed their confidence of victory. Disdaining any longer the narrow limits of Judea, they rubbed the dust off their feet against the ungrateful cities which spurned their proffered favours, resolved to carry the glad tidings of salvation to the remotest regions of the earth. In this glorious enterprise of rescuing mankind from the bondage of sin, they gave the most signal evidence of the Divine Spirit which sustained them. Like the unfortunate age which preceded the flood, mankind had become a mass of depravity, and in the language of the inspired

---

[1] Acts, iv. 18, 19.

writer, "all flesh had corrupted its way."[1] In the midst of the darkness which overspread the understanding, and the corruption which made its way to the heart, you could scarce discern a feeble light scattered here and there in the schools of philosophy, or find a solitary virtue which escaped the taint of the general corruption; yet such was the world which the Apostles undertook to reform and to fill with the Spirit of the Lord. Regardless of suffering, and unappalled by danger, they appear before the king and the potentates, and wherever they appeared, error retired at their approach. Now before the chief governors of Rome, and again before the assembled sages of Greece, they shook, by the terrors of their eloquence, the powers of the one, and confounded, by the folly of the cross, the wisdom of the other. Nations, which hitherto sat in darkness, beheld the sun of justice now rising upon them and animating into life the virtues which had withered among them. The influence of the Holy Spirit now visited the most distant people, taking from them the "stony heart out of their flesh, and will give them a heart of flesh."[2] In the language of the inspired writer, "their sound hath gone forth into all the earth,"[3] and in the blessings which followed in their train we behold the literal accomplishment of the prophetic words: "Thou shalt send forth Thy spirit, and they shall be created, and Thou shalt renew the face of the earth."[4] Who can contemplate such a wonderful revolution in the belief and morals of mankind, produced by such humble instruments, without recognising "the finger of God," and admiring His omnipotence? A few humble individuals, "the reproach of men and the outcast of the people,"[5] without power to subdue, or eloquence to persuade, or wealth to seduce, triumphantly announced a doctrine

[1] Gen. vi. 12. [2] Ezech. xi. 19. [3] Ps. xviii. 5. [4] Ps. ciii. 30. [5] Ps. xxi. 7.

which warred against the licentiousness of the heart and the pride of the understanding, and though combated by the combined opposition which the power of kings or the pride of philosophers, or the fury of the people could excite, they went on glorying in their sufferings, until they planted the banner of the cross in the very centre of the pagan world. The humbler the instruments appeared in our eyes, the more striking the evidence which they furnish of the Spirit by which they were strengthened. It only shows how different are the counsels of God from those of men, and that while they ascribe everything to their own power or their own wisdom, God, on the contrary, chooses "the weak things of the world that He may confound the strong, that no flesh should glory in His sight,"[1] or rob Him of the homage which is His exclusive prerogative.

Such were the fruits of the mystery we celebrate this day, a mystery which is renewed on the return of this anniversary since the first promulgation of the Christian religion. It is true that the Holy Ghost does not now descend in the visible form of fiery tongues, or with the noise of a rushing wind, as when He descended on the Apostles; nor does He communicate the extraordinary gift of miracles and prophecy which then accompanied His descent and announced His living influence through the world. No; these were rare manifestations, which the exigencies of the times then required to sustain the combats with which the infant faith of Christianity had yet to struggle. But although the Holy Spirit now but rarely imparts those extraordinary gifts, He communicates Himself in an invisible manner to the souls of the faithful. To us, and to all Christians, Jesus has said, in the person of the Apostles: "I will not leave you orphans, I will come to you."[2] And the

---

[1] 1 Cor. i. 27-29.   [2] John, xiv. 18.

exhaustless fountain of grace, which was then so amply poured upon the Apostles, has not since ceased to flow through the Church, to enrich the souls of her children according to their spiritual necessities. Hence, speaking of them who should receive the Holy Spirit which He was to send, Christ says, "that out of their bosoms rivers of living water shall issue."[1] And the Royal Prophet, alluding to the same Spirit, declares that "the stream of the river maketh the city of God joyful."[2] In short, my dear Christians, this Spirit of God is the prolific source of every virtue, without which our souls are a dark and dreary void, barren and unproductive; but when visited by its influence, they are clothed with light and quickened into animation, producing "charity, joy, peace, patience, benignity, goodness, longanimity, mildness, faith, modesty, continency, and chastity," which are called by the Apostle "the fruits of the Spirit."[3] As you, then, value those precious gifts, it is your duty to invoke the descent and cherish the presence of the Spirit that produces them. Nay, without this sanctifying Spirit we are completely dead, since the Apostle assures us "that if by the Spirit you shall mortify the deeds of the flesh, you shall live; but if you shall not mortify them, you shall die."[4] Have you, then, this Holy Spirit, without which you are dead? Although invisible to our eyes, it is still discernible by its fruits, which I have just recounted, and which are still rendered more striking by contrasting them with the fruits of the flesh, which are thus enumerated by the same Apostle: "Now, the works of the flesh are manifest, which are fornication, emulation, wraths, quarrels, dissensions, sects, envy, murders, drunkenness, revilings, and such like."[5] Behold the works of the flesh, in which the

---

[1] S. John, vii. 38. [2] Ps. xlv. 5. [3] Gal v. 22, 23. [4] Rom. viii. 13. [5] Gal. v. 19.

Spirit has no share. Which of those works do you produce? and then you may form a judgment whether the Holy Ghost has descended on your souls and invested them with sanctifying grace. Alas! from the frequency of your quarrels, the envy of your neighbour's prosperity, at which you are accustomed to repine; the habits of intemperance, in which you so often indulge; and that spirit of uncleanness which, like a leprosy, infects so great a number of mankind, it is to be feared that the Spirit of God resides only among a few in this world. From this frequency and inveteracy of such scenes of anger and drunkenness, would not one conclude that there are many in those days like the disciples whom the Apostle found at Ephesus, "who had not so much as heard whether there be a Holy Ghost?"[1] If, then, you have been hitherto negligent in setting a sufficient value upon His graces, now, at least, on this anniversary you ought to send up your prayers that the Spirit of truth may take possession of your souls. If He shall once fill your hearts, He will dissipate your spiritual darkness, purify your affections, and extinguish the rage of your enemies. The fire under the form of which He descended is emblematic of all those effects which are produced by the Holy Ghost, at once the Spirit of truth, of sanctity, and of strength. This holy fire dissipates our ignorance by its light, purifies and inflames our affections by its heat, and strengthens by its power the weakness of our nature; unlike that human knowledge, which is but partial and imperfect, the knowledge which is communicated by the Holy Ghost, is a full manifestation of all the truths which are necessary for salvation. Hence Christ says of Him, "when He shall come He shall teach you all truth."[2] It is not more efficacious in

[1] Acts, xix. 2.     [2] S. John, xvi. 13.

enlightening our intellect than it is in purifying our affections—an effect which is ascribed to it by Christ in those words: "But you shall be baptised by the Holy Ghost not many days hence."[1] Such is the profusion of the Holy Spirit which comes upon the faithful that Christ compares it to the waters of baptism, in which the Christians are immersed and purged from their sins. To receive the Holy Ghost, then, is to be cleansed from our iniquities, and, in the strong language of Tertullian, to be immersed in the Holy Spirit. If you are, therefore, desirous that this Holy Spirit would take possesion of your hearts, you must turn away from your sins, and renounce every carnal attachment. "My spirit shall not abide in man," says the Almighty, "because he is flesh."[2] Hence Jesus Christ tells the Apostles: "For if I go not, the Paraclete will not come unto you."[3] What? And was the presence of Jesus an obstacle to the descent of the Holy Ghost? Yes; it was necessary that the hearts of the Apostles should be first detached from the carnal affections which the sensible presence of the Redeemer inspired before they could become the fit abode for the pure and heavenly love of the Holy Spirit. How much more necessary is it for us, then, to wean our affections from sin, if we wish that the Holy Ghost would take up His residence in our hearts! Be not deceived; light and darkness are not more opposed than the Spirit of grace and the spirit of iniquity. The Apostles retired from the world, spent their days in devotion in the Temple, to prepare themselves for the descent of the Holy Spirit. Let us, like them, put up our fervent prayers to the Almighty, that He may send down upon us the same Comforter to cheer us in our pilgrimage, and cry out: "Come, O Holy

---

[1] Acts, i. 5.    [2] Gen. vi. 3.    [3] S. John, xvi. 7.

Spirit: enlighten our hearts by Thy grace, and inflame them with the Spirit of charity. Be to us a strengthener in our weakness, and a comforter in our afflictions. We recollect the promises of Jesus to send us the Paraclete. Relying on His promise, we invoke Thee, our light and our comfort, to console us in the land of sorrow, until we arrive at that kingdom, of which He is gone to take possession, and where He promised to prepare a place for us for ever and ever. Amen.

## THE ASSUMPTION OF THE BLESSED VIRGIN.

"Who is this that cometh up from the desert, flowing with delights, leaning upon her beloved?—CANT. viii. 5.

Such is the rapturous exclamation with which the Virgin is saluted by the choirs of heaven on her Assumption to the kingdom of her Son. Aware of the curse that was long since pronounced upon the earth, and which had converted its beauty into a desert, the angels are struck with astonishment that the desert could produce a plant breathing such fragrance, and "flowing with such delights." Beholding her "leaning upon her beloved," they hail her approach into His eternal mansions, and pour forth their gratulations that her humility has been rewarded by a share in the splendour of His triumphs. It is this glorious Assumption of the Blessed Virgin which the Church celebrates on the festival of this day, inviting us to participate in the joyous solemnity. Contemplating the happiness with which she is crowned, and the virtue by which it was acquired, the Church animates us to aspire after the one by a faithful practice of the other. Such is the subject which I mean to propose to your consideration in this day's discourse. After speaking of that glory to which Mary has been raised above the most exalted of God's creatures, I shall next direct your attention to those virtues by which she earned this reward, and conclude by recommending a particular devotion to her whom God has honoured with such signal marks of His favour and predilection.

The glory to which the Blessed Virgin has been exalted by our Redeemer is sufficiently attested in those festivals that have been consecrated to her memory. Although splendid marks of reverence have been exhibited to other saints who have triumphed by their virtues over the vices of the world, yet it is the singular prerogative of the Mother of God to have a number of festivals dedicated to her merits and her name. Of these festivals which the piety of the Church has instituted that of her Assumption, which we commemorate this day, is the most splendid; and though the spirit of ancient piety has been relaxed in the retrenchment of some, yet that of the Assumption remains still dedicated to the honour of the Blessed Virgin. On the other occasions which have been consecrated to her memory we celebrate those mysteries which were fulfilled in her while she yet remained on earth; but on this day we contemplate her glorious Assumption into heaven—a mystery which strikes us more forcibly than all the others, and which may be considered the consummation of them all;—for, in the other festivals we follow her through the stages of her pilgrimage, and in this we are conducted to the goal of her triumphs. Here we pause to contemplate the Queen of Heaven raised from the most humble condition, and seated so far above the most exalted spirits that minister before the throne of the Almighty. "Leaning on her beloved" she is seated next that glorified humanity of Jesus Christ, which was formed out of her chaste womb, and beholds the entire host of heaven doing homage to their Queen. Such is the doctrine of the Church founded on her ancient and most venerable traditions. It has been a pious belief, derived from the purest sources, that not only the soul but likewise the body of the Blessed Virgin has been raised to share in the glory which Jesus Christ has prepared for His Beloved Mother. And what can appear more conformable to her immaculate purity, and the omnipotence of Jesus Christ, than to have rescued from corruption that chaste body out of which His own was formed, and to have preserved from the common punishment of sin that only individual of the human race whom sin had never infected. The resurrection of Jesus Christ is thus announced by the Royal Prophet: "Thou shalt not suffer thy holy one to see corruption."[1] She, therefore, whom the angel of the Lord had not only pronounced holy but "full of grace,"[2] was not "suffered to see corruption." Since corruption has been the effect and punishment of that first transgression that has been since propagated through all mankind, she who was freed from the least stain of sin became entitled to an exemption from its consequences; nor is it to be wondered that she whose blessed womb was so long the abode of the Divinity would have been preserved from the effects of death, and translated to share in the immortality of her Son. Such are the strong and satisfactory reasons on which, independent of the sources through which it has been conveyed, this pious belief of all the faithful reposes. Accordingly, it has spread throughout the entire

[1] Ps. xv. 10.     [2] Luke, i. 28.

Church, and though not constituting one of those dogmas which we cannot disbelieve without the guilt of heresy, it is yet entitled to our highest veneration. It is one of those ancient and pious traditions of which the origin is lost in the remoteness of time, and of which the progress was universal. And since we cannot explore the date of its introduction we may deservedly rank it among those traditions that are intertwined with the progress of the Church which St. Augustine deems to be coeval with its origin. Hence, from the earliest ages the festival of the Assumption has been celebrated both in the Western and Oriental Churches, embodying the general belief that, after her death at Ephesus or Jerusalem, not only the soul of the Blessed Virgin but likewise her immaculate body was taken up to share in that glory with which the human nature of Jesus Christ was invested. Having abode nine months in her chaste womb until His humanity was formed out of her sacred flesh, He now takes her into His eternal abode; and in raising her humanity above the cherubim and seraphim and the whole hierarchy of heaven, Jesus Christ was only displaying the immense weight of glory which He purchased for His own. It is no wonder, then, if on account of her holding the place next to Jesus Christ she would, in the language of my text, be said " to be leaning upon her beloved." It is no wonder that Moses, in the spirit of prophecy contemplating the future glories of this august Queen, should have broken forth into this rapturous language: "A star shall rise out of Jacob, and a branch shall spring up from Israel."[1] Under the influence of the like inspiration, Ezechiel sets forth her virginity and divine conception under the image of a sanctuary always shut, and through which the Lord

[1] Num. xxiv. 17.

alone had a passage: "This gate shall be shut: it shall not be opened, and no man shall pass through it: because the Lord, the God of Israel hath entered in by it."[1] And the Royal prophet, in a strain of loftier ecstasy, thus describes the majesty that encircled her: "The Queen stood on Thy right hand, in gilded clothing; surrounded with variety. . . . All the glory of the King's daughter is within in golden borders, clothed around with varieties. After her shall virgins be brought to the King. . . . They shall be brought with gladness and rejoicing. . . . They shall be brought into the temple of the King."[2] Such was the glory in which the Royal Prophet beheld the Virgin arrayed; and such was the jubilee which was diffused through heaven on her triumphal entrance, while she still meditated the sentiments of humility, which she thus expressed on the salutation of the angel: "My soul doth magnify the Lord: and my spirit hath rejoiced in God, my Saviour, because He hath regarded the humility of His handmaid, for behold from henceforth all nations shall call me blessed."[3]

Behold the sentiments which naturally close this august and magnificent ceremony of the Assumption. While the angels of heaven pour out their anthems of praise before her throne whom their King had exalted, she converts the praise into the glory of the Most High, and imposes a respectful silence on the heavenly host by the solemn anthem of that humility which entitled her to that elevation. What! was it her humility that raised her to the highest throne of heaven, next to the Divinity itself? Yes. You may imagine that it was because she was Mother of God. From her character of Mother of God she was entitled, it is true, to

---

[1] Ezech. xliv. 2.  [2] Ps. xliv. 10-16.  [3] S. Luke, i. 46.

extraordinary honour. But this very dignity of being chosen the Mother of God was the reward of her humility. "For behold all nations shall call me blessed, because God hath regarded the humility of his handmaid." This truth is further illustrated by the words of the Redeemer, who, in reply to the woman who said: "Blessed is the womb that bore thee," answered: "Yea, rather blessed are they who hear the word of God and keep it:"[1] words which are pregnant with consolation as well as instruction, since they show us that the glory with which Mary is crowned is not so much on account of the dignity of Mother of God, which was peculiar to her alone, as for her extraordinary advancement in those virtues which it is in the power of all to practise. If, therefore, we wish to come to the source of Mary's greatness we must find it in those virtues in which she has excelled all others no less than in her elevation. Destined from all eternity to be the Mother of Jesus Christ, the Virgin was preserved pure from the stain of original sin, and adorned with the richest treasures of God's grace. This inestimable treasure was guarded by her with the holiest caution, and improved by her faithful correspondence, until she was saluted "full of grace" by the ambassador of heaven. Instead of feeling any complacency in the gifts with which she was adorned she referred them to that Being from whom they were derived, reflecting, with the Apostle, that she "possessed nothing which she did not receive,"[2] and for which she would not be accountable to the Almighty. She, therefore, treasured up in her heart the divine graces, and listened with docility to the secret inspirations of heaven, thus guarding the divine word, and meriting the benediction which Christ pronounces on those "who hear the word and keep it."

[1] S. Luke, xi. 28.     [2] 1 Cor. iv. 7.

This was the first source of the sanctification of the Blessed Virgin, the preventing grace of the Almighty, seconded by her own co-operation. From this divine charity which burned in her bosom, kindling as she grew, sprung the other virtues of humility and chastity for which she was conspicuous, and which contributed so much to procure for her the singular dignity with which she has been crowned.

The grace with which the Virgin was first invested by her Creator, acting on a docile mind which obeyed its suggestions, threw a continual light around her which pointed out the path of her duty. In the splendour of the graces with which she was invested, she contemplated the immeasurable distance between herself and her Creator, and far from arrogating to herself that beauty with which she was clothed, she humbly recognised it as the gratuitous gift of the Almighty. Here we behold the first cause of her extraordinary humility. If a gratuitous gift, to which we are not entitled, has a claim upon our humble and grateful acknowledgment, the more valuable the gift the livelier ought to be our gratitude; and since the soul of Mary was adorned with graces such as never fell to the lot of mortal to possess, hence her acknowledgments became more fervent and intense, until, oppressed as if under the weight of divine favour, every feeling was lost in the magnitude of her obligations. Thus the more she felt and acknowledged her unworthiness, the more she became deserving of God's predilection; the more she retired into the abyss of her own nothingness, the more was the Almighty glorified in exalting her. And since pride robbed not the divinity of any portion of His gifts, He felt complacency in pouring fresh graces on a creature who reflected all His blessings. In her was, therefore, fully realised the truth of the words: "God resisteth the proud, and giveth grace to the humble;"[1] and if Mary became of all God's creatures the most exalted in rank, it is only because she was the profoundest in her sentiments of humility. Admirable virtue! but little known, and much less practised among the children of the world. How precious is that humility which makes one of the lowliest of God's creatures an object of complacency in His sight, which renders her the abode of the Holy Spirit, and the temple of the Son of God, until she was exalted above the purest spirits in heaven, in proportion to the depth of her humility upon earth. While we meditate on the humility from which she rose to the dignity to which she has been elevated, how justly may we apply to her the words of the inspired writer: "I was exalted like a cedar in Libanus, and as a cypress-tree on Mount Sion. I was exalted like a palm-tree in Cades, and as a rose-plant in Jericho: as a fair olive-tree in the plains, and as a plane-tree by the water in the streets, was I exalted. . . . I took root in an honourable people, and in the portion of my God is my inheritance, and my abode is in the full assembly of saints."[2] If the humility of the Blessed Virgin rendered her acceptable to Almighty God, her immaculate purity still heightened the lustre of her graces. To form an adequate notion of this purity of the Virgin, let us only reflect on the intimate union which the Divine Word had formed with her by deriving from her womb the human nature with which He was clothed. In this union Jesus sought a corresponding purity. What, then, must have been the chastity of her in whose womb the Author of purity itself condescended to repose? According to the strong language of St. Thomas, the grace of the Almighty had been so abundantly

---

[1] S. James, iv. 6.    [2] Eccles. xxiv. 17-19.

poured upon her soul as not only to allay the heat and quench the flame of concupiscence, but even to extinguish, or rather suppress, its very seed. It is, therefore, impossible to comprehend the purity of the Blessed Virgin without comprehending likewise that infinite purity with which she was allied. In comparison with her brightness, the most splendid objects in nature lose their lustre; and it is only to accommodate themselves to our feeble conceptions that the inspired writings characterise her under the most agreeable images. "I gave a sweet smell like cinnamon; I yielded a sweet odour like the best myrrh. . . . I perfumed my dwelling as the frankincense, and my odour is the purest balm. I have stretched out my branches as the turpentine-tree; and my branches are of honour and grace. As the vine I have brought forth a pleasant odour; and my flowers are the fruit of honour and riches. . . . In me is all grace of the way and of truth; in me is all hope of life and of virtue."[1] While her humility, then, became the source of her greatness, her chastity was a vesture of brightness, before which the splendour of the heavenly bodies faded away. Hence the inspired Apostle of Patmos, finding the energy of language to sink beneath an adequate description of her glory, compares her to "a woman clothed with the sun, and the moon under her feet, and on her head a crown of twelve stars."[2] Besides her charity, her humility, and her extraordinary purity, there was another feature in the life of Mary which, in the order of God's providence, entitled her to an extraordinary elevation—I mean her suffering. If our reward in the other life is to be proportioned to the severity of the combat we sustain, and to the magnitude of our sufferings, unparalleled ought to have been the

---

[1] Eccles. xxiv. 20-25.  [2] Apoc. xii. 1.

glory of Mary, whose sufferings exceeded those of any other mortal. I shall not speak of the hardships of her journey to Egypt, when she fled from the persecuting fury of Herod; nor of the affliction she endured in having lost Him in the Temple. I shall not speak of her continual anxiety to guard His infancy from the vengeance of the royal family of Judea; nor of the more poignant sorrow which she felt on seeing him assailed by the implacable and unrelenting malice of the Pharisees. No; I shall pass over those scenes of suffering, and solely direct your attention to this Virgin Mother standing on Calvary at the foot of the cross, on which her Divine Son hung in torture, and then conceive, if you can, the sharpness of that sword of grief which, in the language of Simeon, pierced the tender heart of this most affectionate of mothers. No; nature has no feeling equivalent to the affection which Mary bore to Jesus Christ. It arose from a cause peculiar to herself—the conception of a God of infinite love, in which she partook, as far as human nature could share such a feeling; and hence, in proportion to the ardour and extent of her affection, her anguish was the more piercing and acute on beholding the object of her affection the victim of contumely the most insulting, and sufferings the most excruciating. What, again, must have been the suffering of this Blessed Mother on finding herself, after the Ascension of her Son, doomed to sojourn longer upon earth! Nothing but the patient meekness which distinguished her through life could enable her to support this trying separation. How weary must she have been in her pilgrimage on earth, who had so long enjoyed such intimate and affectionate conversation with the King of Heaven! If St. Paul, from having caught a glimpse of the joyous sights of heaven, longed to be dissolved and be with Christ, how intense must have been the flame of her aspirations to be united again to her Divine Son! Yes, Blessed Virgin, thy pilgrimage on earth was an uninterrupted scene of suffering since the Ascension, and thy desires to be again united with the object of thy affections would be but feebly conveyed in the language of the spouse in the Canticles: "I sought Him whom my soul loveth, and found Him not; I will rise and I will seek Him whom my soul loveth. . . . I adjure you, O daughters of Jerusalem, if you find my beloved, that you tell Him that I languish with love."[1] Thus languished the Virgin upon earth, longing to be united to Him whom she bore in her chaste womb. Any other love less ardent than that of Mary might have been extinguished in her afflictions. "But many waters cannot quench charity, neither can the floods drown it;"[2] and hence the flame of her charity continually ascended, growing stronger with age, until at length, impatient as if of longer separation from that centre to which it tended and from which it was derived, it gently dissolved her earthly tabernacle, bearing aloft her soul on the pure cloud of her own aspirations. "Who is it that goeth up by the desert, as a pillar of smoke of aromatical spices, of myrrh, and frankincense, and of all the powders of the perfumer."[3] Thus was the Blessed Virgin raised to heaven by the mysterious force of her own impatient desire to be dissolved and be with Jesus Christ.

Such is the consummation of that mystery which we celebrate this day—a mystery in which we contemplate the most heroic virtues struggling with the sharpest trials, until they are crowned with ineffable glory. What a lesson to you, my dear Christians. What an incentive to practise the same virtues. What a pattern will not every female find in the life of the Blessed Virgin. If you wish to

---

[1] Canti. iii. 1, 2, v. 8.   [2] Canti. viii. 7.   [3] Canti. iii. 6.

preserve that pure and delicate virtue which is the chief ornament of your sex, study the life of Mary—her modesty, her retirement, her humility. It was this latter virtue that shadowed the purity of the Virgin, and guarded it against the danger to which it is exposed from vanity and ostentation. If, therefore, you wish to aspire to the imitation, you must begin by imitating her humility. What a lesson, too, to the children of sorrow! Can they complain that suffering is their portion, when the Mother of Jesus Christ herself was not exempt from affliction? Nay, her afflictions were more trying, because she was to receive a greater reward. But we must not be content with the study of her virtues; we must likewise implore her intercession. It was at her request that Jesus Christ is recorded to have wrought the first miracle, and surely her prayers will not now be less efficacious that He has crowned her with glory. "Go to Job, my servant," says the Scripture, "and he shall pray for you." [1] Here we find the interposition of a sinful mortal recommended by God Himself, an interposition which was efficacious. And shall we hesitate to implore the intercession of her who knew not sin; who was always an object of complacency in the sight of heaven, and who now exceeds in rank and dignity angels and archangels and thrones and principalities, who all do homage to the Mother of their God. Jesus Christ forgets not the tender affection she bore Him while in her womb, the assiduity with which she watched over His infancy, and the sword of grief that pierced her heart while He suffered on Calvary. What is more consonant to nature and to reason than that the best of Mothers would have powerful influence with the best of Sons? Hence the pious of all ages have invoked her

---

[1] Job, xlii. 8.

intercession; her own prophetic Canticle has been fulfilled; all the nations of the earth have called her blessed, and in the language of the Royal Psalmist: "and all the rich among the people shall entreat thy countenance."[1] Let us, therefore, entreat her countenance; let us invoke her intercession this day whom her Son has exalted, and endeavour to deserve her intercession by an imitation of her virtues. Obtain for us, O Holy Virgin, purity of heart, that we may love God above all things, and have patience under our trials; obtain for us the grace of humility, that after having been humbled in this life we may be exalted in the next. Amen.

## ALL SAINTS.

*"After this I saw a great multitude which no man could number, of all nations, and tribes, and peoples, and tongues: standing before the throne, and in sight of the Lamb clothed with white robes, and palms in their hands."—* Apoc. vii. 9.

Such is the splendid vision which presented itself to the prophetic sight of St. John, the beloved disciple of Jesus. While he sojourned in the lonely island of Patmos, to which he was banished for the faith, the secrets of futurity were unfolded to his view, and mysteries which were hitherto sealed in darkness were partially revealed to the eye of the Apostle. The wonders which he saw are rapidly sketched in the inspired writings of the prophet. The various fortunes of the Church pass in quick review before him, the combats which it sustained, the triumphs which it achieved, the melancholy fate of its persecutors, the sufferings and final reward of its champions, over

[1] Ps. xliv. 13.

which scenes a veil of mystery still hangs, and which it would be presumptuous to attempt to remove until the fulness of time. The Almighty has purposely involved these mysteries in darkness in order to awe our minds into a respectful submission. But though enough is hidden to excite our reverence, enough is also revealed for our instruction: and among the sublime truths with which the vision of St. John is fraught, there is none which touches so nearly our interests and our affections as that recorded in my text: " After this I saw a great multitude, which no man could number, of all nations and tribes, and peoples and tongues, standing before the throne, and in sight of the Lamb, clothed with white robes, and palms in their hands." What a wonderful vision, as consoling as it is magnificent, which dispels the horrors which hitherto hung over the grave, and reveals to us another world beyond its confines peopled with a host of the blessed, who carry palms in their hands as the emblem of their victory, and enjoy in presence of the Lamb the rewards of their labours. This is not one of those vain spectacles in which you can feel no interest. No, it comes home to your bosoms, since the happiness of the saints whom the Apostle saw encircling the throne of the Lamb is a scene in which you all hope to participate. This, then, is the subject which shall form this day's discourse, the happiness with which God has crowned the saints, together with the advantages to be derived from their intercession.

Of all the incentives that sway the conduct of man there is none more powerful and active than the prospect of an adequate reward. Place before him a recompense worthy of his toils his courage overcomes every obstacle, and the most formidable dangers vanish before his view. Neither fatigued by labour, nor discouraged by disappointment, he cheerfully submits to all his sufferings, while his eye is steadily on the palm that shall crown them. It is by the influence of this vigorous motive of human actions that God wishes to engage us in His service. To draw us to the observance of His commandments He directs our attention to the most animating rewards, thus mercifully uniting His own glory with the happiness of His creatures. This is the reason why the Church has instituted this festival, in order to raise our thoughts from earth, and fix them on that heavenly assembly of every "tongue, and tribe, and nation," who, after having passed through the ordeal of this world, are now in the enjoyment of eternal repose. Such is the motive by which our Divine Redeemer wished to sustain the courage of His followers under the various afflictions they were destined to endure. "Blessed are ye when they shall revile you, and persecute you, and speak all that is evil against you, untruly, for my sake. Be glad and rejoice, for your reward is very great in heaven."[1] Yes, in order to enable them to vanquish all the obstacles they had to contend with, He lays before their eyes the recompense with which they were to be crowned. Nay, instead of sinking under the pressure of their suffering He desires them to rejoice, and to contemplate the crown that awaited them. "Behold," He says, "your reward is exceeding great in heaven." "Behold"—to impress upon their minds that it was neither a doubtful nor a distant recompense, but one which the eye of faith placed within their immediate grasp, while, like St. Stephen, the first martyr, they might see the heavens opening, and unfolding the glory of that God of which they were to be put in possession. This,

[1] St. Matt. v. 11, 12.

however, is not the only quality in this reward which is entitled to our consideration. "Behold, your reward is exceeding great." Yes, like the God from whom it proceeds, this reward shall be immeasurable, far exceeding our conceptions, limited only by the capacity of the human heart, and the omnipotence of the Almighty. Nay, to fit it for the reception of so much happiness, the heart shall be enlarged beyond the measure of its present enjoyment. Seated at the very fountain of life, the blessed shall drink of the torrent of pleasure which it unceasingly supplies, until, in the strong language of the Psalmist: "they shall be inebriated with the plenty of Thy house."[1] And, finally, the reward will not be less copious in its measure than permanent in its enjoyment. "Behold, your reward is exceeding great in heaven." "In heaven"—to contrast it with the perishable rewards of the world, which are uncertain in their possession and transient in their duration, while those reserved for the saints, unbounded by any period of time, are coeval with the Divinity itself. What is there, then, that can divert the human heart from aspiring with all its energy to the happiness of the saints? Is it because it is uncertain? Provided we comply with the conditions required it is as sure as that God cannot deceive us, or that man is to die. Is it because it is not of sufficient value? A reward which is to be the last effort of God's omnipotence and bounty, and of which an inspired Apostle was incapable of conveying any other idea, than that "Eye hath not seen, nor ear heard, neither hath it entered into the heart of man what things God hath prepared for them that love Him."[2] Or is it, in fine, because it may not be lasting? No. "To him that shall overcome," says Christ,

---

[1] Ps. xxxv. 9.     [2] 1 Cor. ii. 9.

"I will give to sit with me in my throne."[1] Far, then, from being exposed to the vicissitudes of time or the caprices of fortune, the reward of the saints shall be as fixed and secure as the throne on which our Redeemer shall be seated. What, then, shall be their infatuation who toil through life in the service of the world, which cannot requite their labours, while they turn their backs upon the only object to which they should aspire? And why this incessant anxiety and fatigue with which the days of man are wasted in the service of the world if not to purchase its rewards? And now, to address myself to that very self-interest which guides every thought and action of the votaries of the world, have its rewards those qualities of certainty, of richness, and permanence that are found in that which is proffered by our Redeemer to His followers? Put, then, the question; take a survey of society; consult the records of their lives; and they will tell you if the world is faithful to its engagements. Notwithstanding the assiduity with which its favours are sought, what does it present to our contemplation but a wreck of disappointments? Listen to those who hung upon its promises, and what do you hear but the melancholy tale of its deceits and of its falsehood? Yes, look abroad upon the scenes that are every day passing, and will not promises broken, engagements violated, services forgotten, favourites discarded, fidelity rewarded with treachery, and all the series of disappointments that sicken the human heart proclaim if the world is worthy of that competition with which its honours have been sought? Every day brings new instances of its treachery; time is only swelling the number of those who bear fresh attestations to its falsehood, and instead of reposing in peace and quiet after their labours the words of the Wise Man are those

[1] Apoc. iii. 21.

which are found most frequently to drop from the lips of the worldlings: "We wearied ourselves in the way of iniquity and destruction, and have walked through hard ways, but the way of the Lord we have not known."[1]

What wonder, then, if the saints, conscious of the world's vanity, and knowing that disappointment and remorse were the last legacies it bequeathed to its admirers, should turn with disdain from that which was unworthy of their homage, and fix their hearts upon Him who alone was deserving of their affections. Strong in faith, and relying on the promises of the Almighty, they considered themselves strangers upon earth, and sighed for that heavenly country which was to terminate their happiness. With this one grand object in view, no other could arrest their attention; in vain were they tempted to repose until they had arrived at the end of their journey. Instead of relaxing at the close of life, their ardour was quickened as they were approaching nearer the goal of their labours. In the intensity of their desire to grasp the crown for which they panted, every other object was heedlessly passed by; and the brightest honours which might dazzle him who saw no other light, faded away before the fulness of that eternal glory which they kept constantly in view. The more they meditated on this happiness the more they were lost in its contemplation. No earthly object could convey even a resemblance of the joys for which they sighed. Though heaven is compared by St. John to the most beautiful images in nature, yet it is only to accommodate himself to the weakness of our conceptions; "And He took me up in spirit," says the Apostle, "and He showed me the holy city Jerusalem coming down out of heaven from God; having the glory of God

[1] Wisd. v. 7.

and the light thereof was like to a precious stone. . . . and the twelve gates are twelve pearls. . . . and the city hath no need of the sun nor of the moon to shine in it: for the glory of God hath enlightened it, and the Lamb is the lamp thereof, and the nations shall walk in the light of it, and the kings of the earth shall bring their glory and honour into it: and the gates thereof shall not be shut by day, for there shall be no night there. And there shall be no curse any more, but the throne of God and of the Lamb shall be in it: and night shall be no more: and they shall not need the light of a lamp nor the light of the sun: because the Lord God shall enlighten them, and they shall reign for ever and ever. And God shall wipe away all tears from their eyes; and death shall be no more, nor mourning, nor crying, nor sorrow shall be any more, for the former things are passed away."[1] St. Paul, too, who was rapt to the third heaven, and caught a glimpse of the mysterious things which it is not given to human tongue to utter, knew not by what language to convey an idea of its bliss. It is only of the most general nature without marking a single quality of which it was composed, "that you may be able," he says, "to comprehend with all the saints what is the length and breadth and height and depth."[2] Who would not imagine that he hears the language of one transported into one of those palaces found in oriental description, and who could talk only of the loftiness of its roofs, the depth of its foundations, and the boundless extent of its scenery, so oppressed was he by the idea of its immensity and magnificence. But ask St. Paul to give you any distinct notion of that happiness, tell him to illustrate it by any image in nature. Though creation, with all its splendour, lay before him, he sought

---

[1] Apoc. xxi.-xxii.  [2] Ephes. iii. 18.

one in vain, until at length, impatient of any comparison, he breaks forth: "I count them but as dung, that I may gain Christ."[1] It was this strong and lively comprehension of eternal bliss that taught the Apostle to disregard all the afflictions of life, and to exclaim, in the midst of his sufferings: "I reckon that the sufferings of this time are not worthy to be compared with the glory to come that shall be revealed in us."[2] It was the same indifference for the world that made him consider that "to die was gain," and to express an ardent desire "to be dissolved and to be with Christ."[3] In short, it was the prospect of the glory that awaited him that cheered him in all his labours; and amidst all the tempests by which he was assailed, hope, to use his own language, was a sure and firm anchor on which he laid hold, and which joined him fast to the throne of our Redeemer. It was the same strong faith and firm assurance of eternal bliss that sustained the courage of the martyrs amidst the most painful torments which their persecutors could inflict. It enabled the virgins to forget the weakness of their sex, and to triumph with a heroic fortitude over all the trials with which they were assailed, rather than be robbed of the precious treasure of their virtue. In fine, it was the animating hope of eternal glory which was held out to them that raised up in every age hosts of pious men, who, enlisting under the banner of Jesus Christ, spread through the world the trophies of His conquests. In vain were they opposed by the world, the devil, and the flesh. Their fortitude and perseverance vanquished all their temptations. Though the devil went round like a roaring lion, seeking whom he might devour, still they eluded all his fury. Though the flesh, that constant enemy of

---

[1] Phil. iii. 8.   [2] Rom. viii. 18.   [3] Philip. i. 23.

man, which he carries about him, sought to seduce them by its desires, its ardour, however, yielded to the stronger flame of the love of God. And though the world had set itself up against them, arraying all the host of its impiety, its profane maxims, and even its ridicule, against their virtue, with a lofty disdain of its emptiness, they were even proud of its condemnation, and saying with St. Paul, "it is a thing of the least account to be judged by human judgment,"[1] they appealed from its iniquitous sentence to the unerring tribunal of the Almighty. Triumphant champions of the cross! who now sit round the throne of the Lamb, the trials which proved your virtue are passed away. The crown to which they have conducted you shall last for ever. Yes, blessed Spirits! no more shall you endure the afflictions of life, since God "shall wipe away all tears from their eyes, and death shall be no more: nor mourning, nor crying, nor sorrow shall be any more; for the former things are passed away."[2]

And who are they whose triumphs we celebrate this day, and by what means did they earn them? Who are they that compose that multitude seen by the Apostle, which no man could number, standing in sight of the Lamb, with white robes and palms in their hands? Are they blessed spirits of a nature different from ours, or who never were subject to our infirmities? Are they angels who were never clothed with the weakness of man, or vested with his infirmity? If so, we might contemplate their happiness at an awful distance, and revere them as a superior order of beings placed in a station far above our reach, whose bliss we might admire without presuming to aspire to its attainment. No, my dear Christians, but those glorious spirits who

---

[1] 1 Cor. iv. 3.   [2] Apoc. xxi. 4.

are now sitting on the throne of heaven were men such as you are now, invested with the same nature, subject to the same infirmities, assailed by the same passions, and encompassed by the same temptations. And how did they conquer all the dangers that surrounded them, and gain possession of that glory which they shall eternally enjoy? This is the reflection that shall naturally be made by all who set a value on their bliss. Just as if one were to secure a kingdom or a prize of great value, the first thing he would inquire, what arts were made use of by those distinguished men who had achieved similar conquests? Not a single action of their life he would not study, not a record connected with their history would escape his notice; and in his anxiety to attain the same eminence which they had reached, their characters would become models of study, by which he would endeavour to regulate his own. Are you, then, anxious to obtain the rewards of the saints? Do you feel an emulation to bear the same palms in presence of the Lamb with which their hands are now decorated? or do you pant after that heavenly kingdom for which they fought and suffered, and which many of them literally purchased with their blood? If you do, it may be of use to point out the road which they have travelled. But if, on the contrary, you are men who never felt a single aspiration after eternal happiness; if you are those animal men mentioned by St. Paul, who understand not the things that are of the Spirit of God, whose soul, almost as carnal as the flesh which it animates, never could be purified into a heavenly desire, all whose care and agitation and anxiety are only bounded by the world, and whose best consolation would be the melancholy hope that the grave which shall entomb their remains would be the dark and dreary goal of all their labours, to talk to such men of the virtues of the saints would be to introduce a subject which they could not understand, to whom the mortification of the Cross would appear folly, and who, rather than encounter its hardships, would gladly resign the reversion of their heavenly kingdom, like the degenerate son of some great conqueror, sunk in voluptuousness and ease, would be terrified by the very sound of war, and would suffer the inheritance which was dearly purchased to be gradually torn from him, while he, shut up in his palace, would not suffer his indolent repose to be disturbed by any alarm, until, like Balthasar, he should be seized by the enemy in the midst of his drunken feast, and cast for ever out of his kingdom. Yes; if you are men of soft or indolent habits, who cannot endure the idea of labour, or who cannot refuse yourselves any gratification which the flesh solicits, you cannot follow the saints, and you must, therefore, forfeit the kingdom which they inhabit. "The kingdom of heaven," says Jesus Christ, "suffereth violence, and the violent bear it away."[1] Without offering ourselves violence, then, and struggling with our enemies, we shall not possess the kingdom of God. What! The smallest reward with which the world can tempt you cannot be obtained without hardship, without anxiety, without labour; and is it the kingdom of God, that highest reward for which man was destined, that alone is unworthy of exertion! For every other prize he shall contend manfully, though at the risk of a failure. Nay, he will endure hunger and thirst, and fatigue and want of rest; and yet to purchase heaven, for which God Himself is pledged if we are faithful, he should think it painful to mortify his passions, those enemies of his salvation, by a single fast, or to interrupt his repose by one half hour's prayer! Thus the champions at the

---

[1] S. Matt. xi. 12.

Olympic games, as St Paul remarks, fasted, in order to possess more suppleness for the contest. And for what, after all? To have their temples crowned with a branch of laurels, and to be saluted victors by the applause of their assembled countrymen. To gain this empty honour, thousands started as candidates, at the risk of evident disappointment, since, as the Apostle remarks, only one was to be crowned. Yet, the hope of being that one, inspired emulation into all: and shall we feel no emulation to grasp a crown whose splendour shall never fade away; do we feel no throb at the thought that our victory shall be cheered, not by thousands of men, whose judgments are false, but by the acclamations of the whole host of heaven, especially as it is one which all may attain, and where one man's reward shall not be purchased by another's disappointment. Deceive not, then, yourselves: the kingdom of God is like every other kingdom—to be possessed only by those who think it worth a contest. Such is the declaration of St. John. Hear his own words: "To him that shall overcome, I will give to sit with Me in My throne, as I also have overcome and am set down with My Father in His throne."[1] It is, then, to him alone that overcometh, Christ promises a share in His throne. Nay, He tells us it is only because he overcame, that he has been associated to the throne of His Father. This is the case with all the saints. Of the immense number whom St. John saw, not one is crowned but one who overcame his spiritual enemies. Who are the saints whom he saw in his vision? "These are," said the Lord, "they who came out of great tribulation, and washed their robes and made them white in the Blood of the Lamb."[2] They were men, then, who came out of great tribulation;

[1] Apoc. iii. 21.     [2] Apoc. vii. 14.

who washed their robes in the Blood of the Lamb; who walked in the narrow way that leadeth to life; who bore the Redeemer's Cross with patience; who confessed Him on earth by fulfilling His commandments; in fine, those who overcame the world and its concupiscences, the flesh and all its softness, and triumphed over all the ridicule and the malignity which have been arrayed against them; and whom, in exchange for all the ignominy they endured, the Father has confessed and glorified before the angels in heaven. And cannot you do what they have done? It was thus the great St. Agustine rebuked his own tepidity. Tell me not that the virtues of the saints are too exalted for you to imitate. I tell you in return, that if you do not imitate them you shall not obtain their rewards. But in reality is it reverence altogether that prohibits the tepid Christian from imitating the saints? Now that they are the friends of God, the most profane must honour those whom Jesus Christ placed on His own throne. Is it an oppresive feeling of their superior sanctity that prevents you from complying with the duty of prayer? Is it because you are awed with a reverence for the friends of God that you dare not imitate the rigour of their fasting? Is it for fear of approaching too near their excellence by a presumptuous imitation that you refuse to forgive your offending brother? Is it because their virtue is too far beyond your reach that you cannot frequent the sacraments of penance and the Eucharist, which they frequented? These are actions which come down to the level of the humblest Christian, and by which the saints sanctified themselves. What, then, becomes of that veneration which throws us back, we pretend, from approaching such excessive sanctity? The fact is, and conceal it not from yourselves, it is shame and indolence, rather than respect, deters you from their imitation. It is shame, I say, the world attaches no honour to these actions. Thus by a strange inconsistency people would fain obtain the rewards of the saints, while they are ashamed of their actions; yet, such is the homage that religion extorts, that they attempt to conceal their shame under an affectation of veneration.

This secret shame of the practices of religion which, however, you dare not proclaim, you must overcome among your other enemies, if you wish to be crowned. For Christ says: "For he that shall be ashamed of Me, and of My words, of him shall the Son of Man be ashamed when He shall come in His majesty, and that of His Father and of the holy angels."[1] Far from being ashamed of any part of Christ's doctrine, the saints gloried in proclaiming it, and by overcoming that contempt and scorn in which the world indulges against its humility, its patience, and its self-denial, they have become the friends of Jesus Christ and the partakers of His glory.

There is still another consideration of this subject well worthy of your attention. Now that they are in the enjoyment of eternal bliss, have they entirely forgotten their connections upon earth? Do they feel no interest for those they have left behind, or do they possess no power of intercession with the Redeemer who has honoured them with His friendship? If all connection between them and us is severed, what becomes of the article of the communion of saints, which all Christians profess in reciting their common creed? Is "I believe in the communion of saints" an empty and unmeaning sound, or does it not mean that all the members of Christ's Body are connected through Him, their common Head, by mutual interchanges of benefits and

---

[1] S. Luke, ix. 26.

of suffering? If so, then the connection between them and us is not broken, but rather brought closer together. No; I cannot believe that the charity which warmed their hearts upon earth has grown cold as they approached its source; nay, has been utterly extinguished in the bosom of charity itself. But their charity may be warm, yet their power of succouring us ineffectual. I cannot forget, however, that they are the friends of God, nor shall I easily believe that those, whose prayers were heard from earth, while they were yet in danger of forfeiting God's friendship, should be now disregarded in heaven, when that friendship is firm and secure. What! The Israelites were spared the infliction of God's vengeance on account of the interposition of Moses, who yet, in punishment for his sins, was not permitted to enter the Land of Promise. And can I think that every saint in heaven, who is more honoured than Moses was then, does not possess a similar influence? God accepted the penance of Job for his friends; nay, they were required by God Himself as a condition of pardon, to offer up their prayers through his interposition. And is it to be imagined that the prayer of the afflicted man was more acceptable to the Almighty while his spirit, yet joined with the impurity of earth, was going through the process of its purgation in the furnace of affliction, than when the same spirit, purified from every stain, was united to its Maker? St. Paul sought the intercession of the faithful who needed assistance themselves; and can I believe that it was more precious than the odours of the prayers of the saints which St. John assures us are deposited in golden phials, and which the four and twenty ancients presented to the Lamb? No; God values the intercession of the saints, and the more because it is the fruit of the Redemption of His Son. Can the merit, then, of the Redemption suffer from that which only proves the more its richness and its magnificence? Who ever conceived a less idea of the immensity of the ocean from the grandeur of the floods which it is pouring from its bosom? Did you ever conceive the stem of the tree less majestic from the profusion of its fruit or the variety of its branches? In applying, therefore, to the merits of the saints we are only recognising the infinite source of the Redemption from which they flow. What, then, should prevent us from soliciting the aid of their prayers since they still feel a holy solicitude for our misfortunes? They are not like the companions of Joseph's prison, who forgot him in their prosperity. No; they rather resemble Joseph himself, who remembered and relieved the distress of his nation. And when the king ordered a robe to be put round his neck, and that he should be made the organ of his bounty, were they thought to forget the respect due to Pharaoh, who sought fame through his own representative? . . .

---

## THE GENERAL JUDGMENT.

"And I saw the dead, great and small, standing in the presence of the throne, and the books were opened: and another book was opened: which is the Book of Life, and the dead were judged by those things which were written in the books, according to their works.—APOC. XX. 12.

BEHOLD, as described by the prophetic Apostle, the awful scene which shall close the long, and dark, and complicated series of events which have continued to perplex the reason of mankind. Behold the scene which will put an end to the afflictions of the just and the triumphs of the wicked, and develop to an assembled world the strict and impartial justice of the Almighty. Without this last and general judgment, which will award to the virtuous and the wicked their respective retributions, their career through life would be an irreconcilable problem, and the world would deservedly be considered as a place where men were cast at hazard to be the victims of a blind and capricious fatality. Such was the impression made on the Wise Man, from the contemplation of those events of which he was the witness. Beholding the confusion with which health, and riches, and honours, and all the gifts of fortune were indiscriminately scattered among the worthless and the deserving; finding that the wicked had often seized on the rewards which virtue had earned, and should have obtained, he breaks forth into the following language: "I turned me to another thing, and I saw that under the sun, the race is not to the swift, nor the battle to the strong, nor bread to the wise, nor riches to the learned, nor favour to the skilful: but time and chance in all."[1] Such would be the impression made on every mind that seriously reflects on the unequal lot of God's creatures, if the injustice of this world were not to be corrected by a final arrangement that will reconcile the mysterious counsels of the Divinity. In the striking words with which I have commenced this discourse, the prophet of Patmos has partially removed the veil in which God's justice was involved, and unfolded a terrific scene, where all must participate in the rewards or the punishments of an eternal retribution. However distant this scene may be, the moment of our death shall decide the sentence by which our doom shall be fixed for ever. Since, then, the last judgment involves consequences so awful, that on it our eternal happiness or misery is

[1] Eccles. ix. 11.

suspended, I shall endeavour in the following discourse to lay before you the nature and consequences of this extraordinary judgment, in order that by exciting in your minds a salutary terror of God's justice, you may stand unmoved in the presence of your Judge.

What shall be the signs which will announce the grand and solemn sitting, in which God shall be the Judge, and all mankind the clients? They shall be worthy of the majesty of the scene that is to follow. The sun, the moon, the stars, the earth, the ocean, will be precursors of this tremendous event. In short, all nature, which hitherto attested by the steady regularity of its movements its obedience to the will of heaven, shall now, in obedience to the same will, be dissolved and proclaim with all the terrors of its dissolution that the hour of judgment is at hand. But since the mind of man is unable to conceive or tongue to utter the horrors that shall usher in the last assizes, I shall tell them, in the language of that Redeemer who has mercifully revealed to us this mystery, in order to guard us against its terrors: "And there shall be signs in the sun, and in the moon, and in the stars, and upon the earth, distress of nations, by reason of the confusion of the roaring of the sea and of the waves: men withering away for fear and expectation of what shall come upon the whole world; for the powers of heaven shall be moved."[1] Such is the simple and sublime description with which Christ announces His second coming, to judge the living and the dead. Amidst this "great tribulation, such as hath not been from the beginning of the world until now,"[2] while "the sun shall be darkened, and the moon shall not give her light, and the stars shall fall from heaven."[3]

[1] S. Luke, xxi. 25, 26.   [2] S. Matt. xxiv. 21.   [3] S. Matt. xxiv. 29.

"Then shall appear the sign of the Son of Man in heaven: and they shall see the Son of Man coming in the clouds of heaven with much power and majesty."[1] Yes, Jesus Christ, once the Man of sorrows and the Victim of persecution, whose doctrine was reproached with blasphemy, and whose person was loaded with insults, who amidst the sufferings of Calvary was treated as the outcast of mankind, comes now refulgent with all the majesty of the Godhead; His human nature not only associated with the Divinity, but partaking of all its splendour, whilst the cross, then the emblem of shame, now floats through the heavens, the brightest symbol of His glory, and the assembled nations of the earth behold the scandal of His passion entirely effaced by the glory of His triumphs.

Surrounded by the hosts of heaven, the messengers of His will, the Son of Man shall descend into the valley of Josaphat, and will plead for His people and for His inheritance.[2] "And then shall He send His angels, and shall gather together His elect from the four winds, from the uttermost part of the earth to the uttermost part of heaven,"[3] commanding them, in the words of the prophet: "Let them arise, and let all the nations come up into the valley of Josaphat: for there I will sit to judge all nations round about."[4] Prompt to the Divine command, the angels, "with a trumpet, and a great voice,"[5] shall send the dread summons over the most distant regions of the earth. "Break forth, and come, all ye nations from round about, and gather yourselves together."[6] Struck with the tremendous peal, which will penetrate the remotest recesses of the earth and sea, all mankind shall suddenly start from the slumber of ages, and, reinvested

---

[1] S. Matt. xxiv. 30.  [2] Joel, iii. 2.  [3] S. Mark, xiii. 27.
[4] Joel, iii. 12.  [5] S. Matt. xxiv. 31.  [6] Joel, iii. 11.

with the bodies which so long lay scattered in ashes through the tombs, shall stand in an instant of time in the awful presence of their Judge. "Amen, amen, I say unto you that the hour cometh . . . when the dead shall hear the voice of the Son of God, . . . and they that have done good shall come forth unto the resurrection of life; but they that have done evil unto the resurrection of judgment."[1] What a terrible alternative—eternal life or eternal death—which, according to the unerring oracle of truth itself, is to be the certain lot of all the children of Adam. It is, therefore, of the last importance to ascertain what is to be the standard by which this twofold division is to be regulated. Is this last and general gathering of the human race in presence of their King to be like those human assemblies where one's station may be determined by his rank or his wealth, or his talents or worldly influence? No; these artificial distinctions, as often the rewards of injustice as of virtue, shall then be of no avail to secure admission into life, since Christ Himself assures us that "He will render to every man according to his works."[2] Yes, to every man, without distinction of rank, or station, according to his works: to the poor as well as to the rich, to the king as well as to the lowliest of his subjects; not to any particular tribe or family or generation, indiscriminately grouped together, but to every individul of the human race, according to his works. It is not according to his station in society that his election will then be determined, or according to the office which he filled, or the dignity with which he was invested, not according to the extent of power which he enjoyed, or fame which he acquired; not, in fine, according to the delusive standard of human opinion, by which the judg-

---

[1] S. John, v. 25, 29.  [2] S. Matt. xvi. 27.

ment is so often betrayed, but according to his works. For we are assured by the Apostle St. Paul, "that we must all be manifest before the judgment seat of Christ, that everyone may receive the proper things of the body, according as he hath done, whether it be good or evil."[1] His works alone, then, his own individual words, thoughts, and actions laid open, without guise or palliation, before an assembled world, shall be the rule by which his place shall be eternally determined. Without respect of persons—for kings and potentates are as dust in His sight—He shall not only judge public and glaring guilt, but shall likewise expose to open view those secret and shameful scenes at which the most hardened profligacy would blush; nay, He shall unmask those hidden springs of vanity or ambition which might have prompted some of those actions which wore the exterior of virtue. Thus, in the language of Scripture, He will "judge justices,"[2] and discover in the fairest actions the latent motives by which they were infected. In the language of Sophonias, He will "search Jerusalem with lamps,"[3] and in the glare of their searching light no crimes, however hitherto concealed, shall escape exposure. This awful truth of the discrimination which shall then be made between the closest relatives on account of their guilt or virtue is thus confirmed by our Divine Redeemer: "Then two shall be in the field: one shall be taken, and one shall be left. Two women shall be grinding at the mill: one shall be taken, and one shall be left."[4] Not only shall the artificial links of society be dissolved on that occasion, but the closest bonds of kindred and of nature shall be forcibly rent asunder, in order to separate into opposite ranks those whom their good or bad works alone can discri-

[1] 2 Cor. v. 10.   [2] Ps. ix. 5.   [3] Soph. i. 12.   [4] S. Matt. xxiv. 40, 41.

minate. Nor shall this separation be tedious or difficult. With much more ease than a shepherd distinguishes and directs his flock, Christ shall recognise and place at His right hand those who through life followed the guidance of His precepts. Instead of attempting to counteract the Omnipotent will, all shall in a moment of time assume that place which has been assigned them by the previous verdict of their own conscience. "Think not," says Christ, "that I will accuse you to the Father. There is one that accuses you, Moses, in whom you trust,"[1] intimating that the religion of Moses, to the profession and practice of which they were bound, should stand in judgment against them. Thus the Gospel which has been preached to mankind shall on that day bear testimony to their actions, and the Word of God which was announced to them, quickened with the living energy which St. Paul ascribes to it shall be "more piercing than any two-edged sword: and reaching unto the division of the soul and the spirit, of the joints also, and the marrow, and is a discerner of the thoughts and intents of the heart."[2] Smitten with this shining sword, whose brightness will reveal the darkest recesses, and whose sharpness shall cut through the closest folds of the human heart, conscience, notwithstanding all its secret struggles, must yield and anticipate the decision of its Judge. It might have slumbered through life, oppressed by habits of guilt; but then, it shall be fearfully awakened to all the terrors it disregarded, and all shall feel the justness of the words of the Apostle who thus describes the force of that self-accuser: "Their conscience bearing witness to them, and their thoughts between themselves accusing or else defending one another."[3] The Gospel shall lay before the sinner

---

[1] S. John, v. 45.  [2] Heb. iv. 12.  [3] Rom. ii. 15.

the code of his belief; his conscience shall bear testimony to his practice; and in the conflict between those testimonies the sinner shall discover the melancholy justice of his doom. In vain shall conscience endeavour to stand against the majesty of the Gospel; its searching and overpowering splendour shall reveal all its vain subterfuges, and its vengeance pursue it through all the windings of self-love in which it looks for shelter, until at length subdued in the conflict, conscience sinks under the confusion and the agony of self-condemnation.

Oppressed by the splendour of the "lamps with which the Judge will search Jerusalem," and which will attest each one's crimes to the world, the guilty will shrink with horror from the sight, and "shall go into the holes of rocks and into the caves of the earth from the face of the fear of the Lord and the glory of His Majesty."[1] Pursued, however, and dragged from hence by the searching vengeance of heaven which it is no longer possible to elude, "They shall say to the mountains: Fall upon us; and to the hills: Cover us."[2] But the hills and mountains shall be deaf to their prayers, and though they should gladly shelter themselves in the lowest abyss of hell, they must abide the burning reproaches of His presence. Now, alas! they believe the prophetic prediction, and find that the "Great day of the Lord is a day of wrath, a day of tribulation and distress; a day of calamity and misery; a day of darkness and obscurity; a day of clouds and whirlwinds; a day of trumpet and alarm ... in which men will walk like blind men because they have sinned against the Lord." Seated on His august tribunal, the angels of heaven ministering at His feet, and all the nations of

---

[1] Isa. ii. 19.　[2] S. Luke, xxiii. 30.　[3] Soph. i. 15, 16, &c.

the earth struck with silent terror in His presence, the Judge shall pronounce the twofold sentence, in which each one of us will be included, and which will decide our happiness or misery for all eternity. Turning to the wicked, with a countenance which will convey to each individual the reproaches of his own conscience, He shall utter the dreadful sentence in a "voice as the sound of many waters:"[1] "Depart from Me, ye cursed, into everlasting fire, which was prepared for the devil and his angels. For I was hungry, and you gave Me not to eat: I was thirsty, and you gave Me not to drink: I was a stranger, and you took Me not in: naked, and you covered Me not: sick and in prison, and you did not visit Me. Then they also shall answer Him, saying: Lord, when did we see Thee hungry, or thirsty, or a stranger, or naked, or sick, or in prison, and did not minister to Thee? Then He shall answer them, saying: Amen, I say to you, as long as you did it not to one of these little ones, neither did you do it to Me; and these shall go into everlasting punishment."[2] Everlasting punishment! Tremendous doom, of which the very idea shakes the strongest nerve, and makes the very flesh creep with horror; of which the meditation filled the mind of the holy Teresa with such awful feelings as to be almost overwhelmed by its terrors. And the reason which the Redeemer assigns for this sentence of unutterable woe which associates the reprobate to the punishment of the fallen spirits, is because they refused to perform the offices of mercy towards the poorer members of the body of Christ. Hear this dreadful sentence you, if there be any such, who have set your hearts upon the wealth of this world, adoring it as the only idol of your affections, closing your hearts against the supplications of your brother in distress, while, perhaps,

---

[1] Apoc. i. 15.   [2] Matt. xxv. 41-46.

you were revelling in luxury, and striving to drown the cries of misery amidst the louder clamour of intemperance and dissipation. Would to God that this sentence were now to strike with the terrors of the thunder the flinty hearts of those cruel oppressors of God's people, who under every shape and denomination are to be found in the country "grinding the face of the poor,"[1] as if they envied them the comeliness of the human form, and wringing from them the very bread which was watered with the sweat of their brow, fleecing them of the raiment with which the Almighty wished to clothe their nakedness, and for this purpose wielding the worse than screw-like engine, which laws passed by tigers in the shape of men put into their hands as if in defiance of God and His judgment, to force the very vitals out of those dear members of Christ's body. It is no wonder, as love, and mercy, and compassion are the virtues that breathe through the entire of the Christian law that it is the vices of cruelty, and hard-heartedness, and oppression which should be most signally denounced by the vengeance of its Divine Founder. Meditate, then, upon this sentence all you, whose hearts were hitherto steeled against the appeals of your suffering brother; and if you find it now painful to your bodies, pampered by intemperance, to sustain the salutary severity which the Church would inflict for your sins, accompany in spirit the reprobate on that day, and ask with the prophet: "Which of you can dwell with devouring fire? which of you shall dwell with everlasting burnings?"[2]

Imagine not that it is the unmerciful alone who on that awful day must sustain the wrath of their offended God. No, heaven and earth shall pass away, but not one iota of His law shall pass away. All the crimes,

---

[1] Isa. iii. 15.   [2] Isa. xxxiii. 14.

then, that are condemned in the Gospel, and which have not been washed away in the waters of penance, shall provoke the same sentence of eternal reprobation. " Do not err," says St. Paul, " neither fornicators, nor idolaters, nor adulterers, nor the effeminate, nor thieves, nor the covetous, nor drunkards, nor railers, nor extortioners, shall possess the kingdom of God."[1] If so, how dreadful shall be the confusion of all those classes when Christ shall accost them in the same withering language: "Depart from Me, ye cursed, into everlasting fire prepared for the devil and his angels." How dreadful that sentence to the licentious and the profligate, whose immoral conversation "spreads like a cancer,"[2] and whose days and nights are spent in plotting the destruction of innocence and virtue. You have heard that "he that defileth the temple of God him shall God destroy,"[3] since, then, you have converted the temple of the living God into the abode of impure spirits, you shall be associated with the companions of your choice, and share in their punishment. "Go into everlasting fire prepared for the devil and his angels." To the uncharitable who pursue their brother with hatred, and refuse every overture of reconciliation for an imaginary offence, it is written: " He that hateth his brother is a murderer."[4] Life and death were placed before you; since, then, you have made choice of death, eternal death shall be your inheritance. "Go into everlasting fire prepared for the devil and his angels." In fine, to those tepid and indiffent Catholics, who are Christians in name but infidels in practice, who mix the profligacy of the world with some external but superficial observances of religion; who, though they profess to be followers of the cross of Christ, know naught of its humility, its patience, its mortification of the flesh, which

[1] 1 Cor. vi. 9, 10. [2] 2 Tim. ii. 17. [3] 1 Cor. iii. 17. [4] 1 S. John, iii. 15.

alone breathe its spirit—practices which, in common with the infidel, they neglect or deride, thus dishonouring their religion by the omission of what it inculcates, and the practice of what it condemns. You have heard it said: "If anyone wishes to be My disciple let him take up his cross and follow Me."[1] "No man can serve two masters."[2] "Whosoever shall be ashamed of Me and of My words, of him the Son of Man shall be ashamed when He shall come in His majesty."[3] Since, then, you have divided your services between two masters whose interests were irreconcilable, since you have been ashamed of Me and of My words, I shall now be ashamed of you; since you have been ashamed of the cross in its humiliation, nor shall you mix in the glorious train that shall to-day grace its triumphs: go into everlasting fire prepared for the devil and his angels.

"Then shall the King say to them that shall be on his right hand: Come ye blessed of My Father, possess the kingdom prepared for you from the foundation of the world." What a consoling termination of all the labours and sorrows of this life. Among the train whom Christ shall thus pronounce blessed will be seen the poor in spirit, the meek, the merciful, the clean of heart, the peacemakers, those that mourned and were reviled for Christ's sake, those that hungered and thirsted and suffered persecution for justice' sake.[4] Theirs shall be for ever more the kingdom of God. The trials and afflictions by which they purchased it have passed away: the reward with which they are crowned shall last for ever. In life they were often treated with ignominy and insult, objects of derision to the proud and of persecution to the oppressors; sometimes driven into exile, and not unfrequently the victims of death. But now when

[1] S. Matt. xvi. 24. [2] S. Matt. vi. 24. [3] S. Luke, ix. 26. [4] S. Matt. v. 3, &c.

they shall stand with great constancy against those that have afflicted them, and taken away their labours; "These seeing it shall be troubled with terrible fear, and shall be amazed at the suddenness of their unexpected salvation, saying within themselves repenting and groaning for anguish of spirit: These are they whom we had sometimes in derision, and for a parable of reproach. We fools esteemed their life madness, and their end without honour. Behold how they are numbered among the children of God, and their lot is among the saints."[1] Such shall be the final arrangement that will put an end to the strange confusion of good and evil that are mingled together in this world, and shall vindicate before the assembled world the long-blasphemed counsels of the Almighty. It is comprehended in these few words: "And these shall go into everlasting punishment: but the just, into life everlasting."[2]

Which of those sentences, then, do you expect? for which of those dooms have you been hitherto labouring—for that of eternal life or eternal punishment? I put you this solemn and interesting interrogatory as to rational and intelligent beings invested with full liberty of good or evil, and thus having the choice of your eternal destiny in your own hands. Yes, and you can draw this consoling truth from the words of the Redeemer Himself, since, as St. John Chrysostom remarks: "The eternal fire into which the reprobate shall be rolled was prepared, not for them, but for the devil and his angels. If, therefore, they are to be cast into its unquenchable flames, it is owing to the obdurate malice of their own wills rather than to the foredoom of God; whereas the rewards that are to crown the just were prepared for them from the foundation of the world."[3] Ask yourselves

---

[1] Wisd. v. 2, &c.   [2] Matt. xxv. 46.   [3] Homilies, 79.

seriously, then, what retribution do you deserve? Were the last trumpet now to strike upon your ears, and the Son of Man to descend in great power and majesty, would you stand with great constancy before the face of the fear of the Lord, or would you not strive to go into the caverns of the rocks to hide your confusion from His presence, and invoke in vain the mountains to fall upon you? Let your conscience answer this moment: not such a conscience as is found in the midst of the world, feeble, irresolute, compromising, sacrificing its convictions to a temporary self-interest, bending to the force of bad example, and fancying to find an apology for its own guilt in the delinquency of others. No, but a conscience looking its God in the face, and awed only by His presence; detached from every tie of friends, of connections, of interest, of fashion—in fine, of the world— as it will then be found, solitary, helpless, resting only on itself in the presence of its Creator and its Judge. Let such a conscience now pronounce its verdict, and if that verdict be your condemnation, in the name of heaven what grounds have you for expecting a different judgment on the last day? Hopes of repentance. Treacherous hopes, to which many, to their utter ruin, have rashly confided their salvation. Often before have you heard the awful description of the terrors of the last day. Often, perhaps, have you formed resolutions of repentance. When your terror subsided did not those resolutions vanish? Did you not return, not only to your ordinary occupations, but also to your follies and to your sins, resembling "those who, in the days before the flood, were eating and drinking, marrying and giving in marriage, until the day that Noe entered into the Ark. And they knew not until the flood came and took them all away: so also shall the coming of the Son of

Man be."[1] Good God, and notwithstanding this threat of the sudden and unexpected arrival of the great Judge, men live with as much security as if they had calculated the time of His coming, and obviated all its consequences. What means, then, must we adopt in order to stand secure against the danger? Unremitting vigilance and fervent prayer. Unremitting vigilance! It is the admonition of Christ Himself; "And take heed to yourselves lest, perhaps, your hearts be overcharged with surfeiting, and drunkenness, and the cares of this life, and that day come upon you suddenly. For as a snare shall it come upon all that sit upon the face of the earth."[2] Watch ye, therefore, praying at all times, that you may be accounted worthy to escape all those things that are to come, and to stand before the Son of Man. Watch, then, and pray. Imitate St. Jerome, who often imagined to Himself the last trumpet striking on his ear and awakening him to judgment. Offer up your fervent prayers to Jesus, who now comes in sweetness and in mercy to purify your hearts by His grace, and to attach them to Him by the influence of His love that at His second coming you may stand unmoved before His judgment-seat, and share in the eternal rewards of the blessed. Amen.

[1] S. Matt. xxiv. 38, 39.   [2] S. Luke, xxi. 34, &c.

## PREACHING OF ST. JOHN THE BAPTIST.

*"This is He of whom it is written: behold I send my angel before thy face, who shall prepare thy way before thee.—S. MATT. XI. 10.*

SUCH is the language in which the Redeemer of the world bore testimony to the merits of John the Baptist. Such, too, is the language in which Malachy, the last of the prophets, announced his coming, and to which our Saviour refers as a proof that the Baptist realised in his character the truth of the prophetic prediction. We read in the Gospel that John sent a respectful embassy to our Saviour to inquire into the leading characters of His mission, and that the Redeemer availed Himself of this circumstance to point the attention of the people to the life and precepts of the Baptist. In a strain of the most pointed and significant interrogation, He asks them: What had they gone out into the desert to see? Was it a reed shaken by the wind? Was it a man clothed in soft garments? No; for they that are clothed in soft garments are in the palaces of kings.[1] The soft and flexible life of the voluptuous relaxed with the luxurious indolence of a palace, and bending to every whim of a capricious master, but ill suited the simple solitary who was sent to teach an austere and unchangeable morality. What, then, did they go out into the desert to see? A prophet; and the Redeemer emphatically adds: "I tell you, and more than a prophet, for this is he of whom it is written: Behold, I send my angel before thy face who shall prepare thy way before thee." Yes, standing on the confines of the Jewish and the Christian covenant, John

[1] S. Matt. xi. 7, &c.

was the prophet of the one and the apostle of the other in proclaiming the coming of the Lamb who was to take away the sins of the world, as well as in exhorting the people "to prepare the way of the Lord, and make straight His paths." Unlike the vain philosophers, so well described by St. Augustine, who dispense lofty lectures on virtue, but leave to others the burden of their fulfilment, the Baptist was the living model of the doctrine which he preached. His food was locusts and wild honey, his drink the running fountain, his couch the mossy rock, and his roof the canopy of heaven. His garments were of camel's hair, and thus attired the man of God walked along the banks of the Jordan, filling the wilderness with an awful voice, that awakened the surrounding people to repentance and conversion. Such was the preparation with which the first advent of the Redeemer of this world was ushered in by His faithful precursor. It is the same voice and the same doctrine that have been since re-echoed throughout the Church of God on the recurrence of every other advent of redemption. It is the same important precept of preparing the way of the Lord, and making straight His paths that I purpose to impress on you on this solemn occasion, in order to enable you to participate in the abundant graces that are diffused among the faithful at the approaching festival.

You are all, no doubt, anxious to be of the number of those who shall hail the Redeemer of the World on the coming feast of His nativity. You are likewise solicitous to receive on that solemn occasion some token of His favour. But above all, you burn with a holy desire to be enrolled among those who shall swell His last and most glorious triumph when He shall come to judge the living and the dead. This is a truth which cannot be combated. It is attested by the conscience of every individual; and there is none, however careless or indifferent about the means of purchasing it, that does not cherish the wish, and if his heart allowed it, even the hope of participating in the rewards of religion. The Saviour for whom the patriarchs sighed, whom the prophets foretold, and whom all the saints of the Old Law, to use the inspired language, saluted from afar, is on the eve of descending among us with all the spiritual treasures expressed in the words: "Let the clouds rain down the just One,"[1] and we are invited to "prepare His ways, and make straight His paths."[2] All, then, who desire to welcome the Son of God—and surely there is not one who could bear to be overlooked as He passes—must be anxious to learn how His ways are to be prepared, and by what means His paths are to be so smoothed and made straight, as may enable the sinner, without the fear of stumbling or going astray, to meet the Divine Dispenser of grace and mercy. Those who aspire to perfection in the arts, and are anxious to learn how that perfection is attainable, seldom trust to the caprices of their own mind, or to the suggestions of those who are strangers to such a study. No; they instantly ascend to the purest sources of information. The correctest models are carefully examined, the precepts of the first masters are listened to with attention; and thus the mind is trained to a conviction, which the shallow and superficial remarks of the unpractised in such subjects are unable to shake. Applying this obvious principle we may briefly ascertain the most effectual means of preparing a suitable reception for our Saviour, and the finding acceptance in His sight. What were the means promulgated by His precursor? Repentance. He came preaching penance unto the remission of sins.

[1] Isa. xlv. 8.   [2] S Luke, iii. 4.

What were the means which he practised? An austere and penitential life. But lest it should be imagined that such austerity and mortification were only a relic of the Old Law, which was on the point of being abrogated, let us turn to our Divine Master, and listen to His instructions. In the same warning spirit that dictated the strong denunciations of the Baptist, the Redeemer says: "I say to you: but unless you shall do penance you shall all likewise perish"[1]—a sentence which He repeats with a solemn emphasis, in order that it might sink deeply into the hearts of His hearers. The penance of which the Redeemer speaks, far from being the transient affection of the heart, which may pass away without leaving any impression behind, must be a deep and settled sorrow for sin, manifesting itself in habitual mortification. "If any man will come after Me, let him deny himself, and take up his cross and follow Me."[2] Here, then, is the unequivocal badge which Christ requires of us to wear if we wish to be recognised among His followers. We must carry our cross; and lest it should be thought that this signifies only a vague profession of the Christian name, we are told that we must deny ourselves, and thus encounter all the rigorous trials that are incidental to a real warfare. Yes, we must participate in the sufferings if we hope to share in the triumphs of the Redeemer. Though His sufferings are the rich source of our justification, we are not on that account released from the necessity of penitential austerity. Such an opinion would be to make void the cross of Christ, and prevent the fountains of His mercy from flowing into our souls. Hence the Apostle says that Christ suffered, leaving us an example that we might follow in His footsteps.[3] If, then, we wish to

---

[1] S. Luke, xiii. 3.   [2] S. Matt. xvi. 24.   [3] 1 S. Pet. Epist. ii. 21.

arrive at the happiness to which the Cross has conducted, it is on condition that we walk in the same rough way which the Redeemer has trodden. "If we be dead with Him," says St. Paul, "we shall also live with Him; if we suffer we shall also reign with Him."[1] Who would, then, imagine that any could have laboured under the melancholy delusion that because Christ has suffered man was released from the necessity of self-denial; as if the merits of the Passion, instead of being an incentive to holiness of life, were to become a patent for sensuality. How different is the doctrine of the great Apostle, whose mind, beyond that of any other mortal, sounded the inexhaustible depths of the great mystery of redemption! Though he strives to unfold the infinite mercies of God by talking of "the height and depth and length and breadth" of God's love to us,[2] yet he says that "those who are Christ's have crucified their flesh with its vices and concupiscences."[3] Nay, he illustrates the same doctrine in his own example by assuring us that he chastised his own body, and brought it under subjection lest, whilst he preached to others, he himself should become a reprobate. And again the same Apostle declares: "I rejoice in my sufferings, and fill up those things that are wanting of the sufferings of Christ in my flesh."[4] What! to fill up in his flesh the things that are wanting of the sufferings of Christ! Who is he that has given expression to this language? The great St. Paul himself, who might be called, by way of pre-eminence, the oracle of gratuitous justification; who struggled with the weakness of human language in giving adequate expression to his thoughts of the infinity of Christ's atonement, whom he represents as blotting out the handwriting of the decree that was against us, and

---

[1] 2 Tim. ii. 11-12.  [2] Eph. iii. 18.  [3] Gal. v. 24.  [4] Col. i. 24.

fastening it as a trophy on the cross on which He suffered.'¹ And has he forgotten that our Saviour has reconciled all things unto Himself: did he imagine that His sufferings required any supplement from the paltry labours of man, or that the mortification of any individual could of itself, when merged in the ocean of His mercy, increase its value or enlarge its immensity? No; but the Apostle himself explains the reason in these words: "Bearing about in our body the mortification of Jesus, that the life also of Jesus may be made manifest in our bodies."² Yes; there ought to be a correspondence between the parts of the same body. "Unmortified members," says St. Bernard, "but ill accord with a crucified head; and veins swelling with the tumult of passion are not the fittest conductors of grace." Hence it is, that as the disposition of the members reveals at once whether they are animated by the life-blood that circulates from the heart, so the crucified flesh and concupiscences of those who are Christ's are a sign that the life of Jesus, which quickens their souls, is manifest in extending its influence to their bodies.

I beseech you, therefore, brethren, in the language of the same Apostle, to whom I have so often referred, "that you present your bodies a living sacrifice, holy and pleasing unto God."³ It is only on such condition that they can be animated with the life of Jesus, and become the temple of the Holy Ghost. It is only thus you can effectually prepare the way of the Lord, and make straight His paths. But, you must remark, it is in vain to mortify the flesh without crucifying its concupiscences. This would be only to cut off the branches and leaving untouched the deadly root from which they spring. Hence the heart, the seat of evil desires, must be regu-

---

¹ Col. ii. 14.   ² 2 Cor. iv. 10.   ³ Rom. xii. 1.

lated; those affections which are productive of sin must be corrected, and the penance which will work unto salvation must reach the inmost recesses of the heart, and eradicate its vices. Without this mortification of the soul, your external devotions would not only be unprofitable, but expose you to the just reproach contained in the prophetic language: "I hate and have rejected your festivities: And I will not receive the odour of your assemblies. And if you offer Me holocausts and gifts, I will not receive them. Take away from Me the tumult of thy songs, and I will not hear the canticles of thy harp."[1] Without this internal disposition of the heart, in harmony with the Divine Will, canticles would be as grating as tumultuous discord, and the effusions of a heart, boiling with passion, could never go forth with an agreeable odour in His sight.

You are now on the eve of the great festival, when the world is preparing to welcome the coming of the Redeemer; and I have endeavoured to arouse your attention to the most effectual means of preparing for His reception. There are none who would not cheerfully join in celebrating the joy of the festivity; but there are many who would shrink from the toil and difficulties of the preparation. Is it, then, the blessings of religion alone that are not worth contending for? There is not on earth an acquisition in the shape of arts, of wealth, or honours of any value, which can be procured without a systematic process, combining attention, industry, and toil. And is it to be imagined that our salvation alone, which, according to our Redeemer, the world's possession would not outweigh, is a patrimony into which we can stumble without efforts to secure? No; the laws of nature will not be reversed because you are

[1] Amos. v. 21.

indolent; upwards is not the natural tendency of things which make no effort to rise; and you might as well hope to be found, without any effort to ascend, on a lofty elevation, as to fall, in your career of thoughtlessness, into the kingdom of heaven. What, do you imagine, would be the feeling of a soldier who would desert his standard when he fancied the victory was too distant, or because he was disheartened by the toils of the campaign? Scarcely does he quit the service when he is awakened by the shouts of victory, his ears are saluted by the coming song of exultation, and his eye glances over the gorgeous vista of a lengthening procession, such as often passed under the triumphal arches of this city, whilst all hearts are ecstasy and all tongues are eager to testify, by the loudness of their shouts, the liveliness of their public exultation. In the elation of such a moment, all fatigues are forgotten: the past and the present seem to touch, without scarcely leaving an interval between them, and the faint recollection of the toils that were endured only sweetens the relish of the triumph to which they conducted. Who is it that could be justly entitled to be associated in such a celebration? Surely those alone who earned it by their labours. What, then, should be the mortification of him who shrunk from the struggle which was to terminate in such glory? And were he anxious to share in the spoils, he should be deterred by the consciousness of meeting the reproof:—you declined the labours of the campaign: you have, therefore, no right to share in the rewards of victory.

The folly and the anguish of such an individual are but a faint representation of the folly of the Christian who hopes for heaven without any contest, and of the despair which shall succeed the conviction of his folly. We are told in the very Gospel from which my text is taken, that from the days of John the Baptist until now the kingdom of heaven suffereth violence, and the violent bear it away. Here eternal happiness is represented under the lively image of a citadel, and the saints by valiant and laborious soldiers, who can get possession only by violence and storm; and yet the world seems to look upon it as a voyage of pleasure, in which one gently glides down the current of life, and labours to be supplied with every soft accompaniment that can enchant the heart and soothe the senses during the voluptuous passage. In vain are the woes which the Redeemer denounced against Corozain and Bethsaida pronounced against such criminal thoughtlessness; in vain are they reminded of the holy wonders of ancient times, wonders which, if wrought among pagan nations, would have awakened them to penance. No! such denunciations are listened to with indifference; the awful fate of those by whom such warnings were unheeded are set before them in vain, until their own melancholy fate is again set before others, who are resolved, as if by an hereditary fatuity, to be equally obdurate and insensible. O God! when shall this unaccountable stupidity of Thy creatures to their best interests be at an end? When shall they open their eyes to the light that is spread around them, and their ears to these secret admonitions which, as they walk the streets, must pursue them the entire way? Yes, how appropriate is the language of the Scripture? The words of the Wise Man cease to be metaphorical when applied to Rome: "Wisdom preacheth abroad, she uttereth her voice in the streets; at the head of multitudes she crieth out, in the entrance of the gates of the city she uttereth her words.... Turn ye at my reproof: behold, I will utter my spirit to you, and will show you my words."[1] Yes, under every form in which she was ever exhibited, and under every variety of costume which wisdom ever wore, she presents herself here to the admiration of her votaries. "She uttereth her voice in the streets," and he who in the solitude of his heart can listen to her accents must feel, like Moses, a secret warning that the ground on which he walks is holy, while he treads over sainted sepulchres, and feels a holy fire springing up from the ashes that are spread over the vast mausoleums of martyred heroes, from whom heaven suffered violence, and by whom its trophies were torn away. She uttereth her voice, while she represents the lives, the labours, the conflicts, and the triumphs of the followers of the cross, surrounded with all those historical accompaniments that give reality to the portraits, and call forth their spirits, as if to animate our zeal or rebuke our tepidity. Nay, to pursue further the analogy, "Wisdom crieth in the entrance of the gates of the city;" and is it not a singular coincidence that two of the most magnificent arches which have survived its ruins—the one of Constantine, and the other of Titus—should be placed next each other, as enduring monuments of the fall of one religion and the rise and glories of another, commanding us as if to pause at the threshold, and enabling those who run to read the fulfilment of the prophecies, that not a stone should be left upon a stone in the temple of Jerusalem, and that the nations should flow into the more splendid and magnificent church by which it was succeeded? Here Wisdom preaches still from the true cross of which the sight, like that of the serpent in the wilderness, produces miraculous effects in animating with fresh vigour the slumbering faith of its followers. In fine, it

[1] Proverbs, i. 20-24.

preaches with a living energy from the shrines and relics of St. Peter and St. Paul—those deep and refreshing springs of Christian faith which, pure and unfailing as the two fountains that play round the temple of their Chief, are continually flowing from that holy and happy sea, into which, to use the fine language of an ancient father, those two Apostles poured the commingled treasures of their doctrine and their blood. But though the enemy of mankind labours to weaken the effect of such lofty recollections, though a mist should be raised from the vices or the follies of a few, to intercept or to obscure those holy visions, still the pilgrims who come from afar will not fail to recognise the ancient spirit lingering in her institutions. Even this day, "Wisdom crieth out at the head of the multitude." Not the multitude of fashion, where folly reigns, which is often sought by foreigners, but the multitude of those religious, who are shunned because the appearance alone of such antique habits is revolting to their fastidiousness. They are practical disciples of St. John, whilst faithful to their rule, and living illustrations that the penance and the poverty of the cross are not yet extinct among mankind. Blessed are they who will not be scandalised in them. Our feelings regarding the living disciples who exemplify the Spirit of the cross is the best test of our veneration for that symbol of redemption. We may venerate the Baptist, since he has long since retired from the world; nor is there now any danger that his cutting reproaches could reach, as they once did, Herodias, the adulteress of the age. We can venerate the founders of the religious orders, because we are no longer offended with the exhibition of their austerities and their poverty, and because their sufferings have become now the shadowings by which painters set off the blaze of their glory. But if, with this veneration for departed virtue, we feel nought but contempt or disgust for the living disciples of penance, our veneration is but hypocrisy, we would fain share in the splendours of Thabor without treading the thorny path of Calvary. In fine, if we respect the cross when embroidered with gold and emblazoned with jewels, and despise it when seamed into the coarse vesture of penance, we mistake our vanity for devotion, and our reverence for the cross is only directed towards the splendour of its associations. Let us, therefore, endeavour to prepare the ways of the Lord by that sincere penance which His great precursor preached and practised. The time is short; the day which is allotted for toil is rapidly passing away, and the night is coming, when there shall be no opportunity for labour. Let not the voice crying out in the wilderness be addressed to you in vain, lest, like that of St. Paul to Festus, you should not be favoured with it again. Arise from sleep, and if the warnings of the Baptist are not sufficient to awaken you, you cannot be insensible to the trumpet of an Apostle and the terrors of an expiring world, which combine in the opening of this holy season to rouse man from his insensibility. Shake off the slumbers that have steeped your souls in forgetfulness of your duty, and take not counsel from that drowsy indolence which bereaves the soul of its powers. Look forward to those who still run the race of penance; be not disheartened by its difficulties, it shall be run over with the speed of a courser, and its goal shall be the possession of a never-ending glory. The road of the cross is not difficult, as you may fancy. Its difficulties are only found in the imagination or in the exaggerated reports of unfaithful explorers, who, like the lying spies of the Hebrew people, would fain divert others from trying the path of salvation, and, like other untried terrors, vanish when they are seriously grappled with. It has charms too, which can only be felt by those who tried it: it has its lively hope, which keeps the mind steadily on the one thing for which it is panting; and should the darkness of passion cross her path, faith, like the vision of St. Stephen, throws open the portals of heaven, and sustains her struggles by a glimpse of the near and certain prospect of her award.

Let me therefore conclude in the consoling language of St. Peter: "Dearly beloved, think not strange the burning heat which is to try you, as if some new thing happened to you; but if you partake of the sufferings of Christ, rejoice, that when His glory shall be revealed, you may also be glad with exceeding joy."[1]

## THE REPROBATION OF THE JEWS AND THE VOCATION OF THE GENTILES.

"And I say to you that many shall come from the East and the West, and shall sit down with Abraham and Isaac and Jacob in the kingdom of heaven. But the children of the kingdom shall be cast into exterior darkness."—S. MATT. viii. 11, 12.

WHAT a noble and comprehensive view of the future fortunes of His Church is contained in the foregoing words of our Redeemer! But whilst they elevate our thoughts, they are calculated at the same time to strike us with a salutary terror. At a time, when our Saviour had but just come forth from the solitude of His early life, little known to the world, and without any reliance on its favours, when the established religion of Judea seemed so firmly rooted that its supporters would look upon any attempt to overthrow it to be as impious as a war upon heaven; when, in short, the idols of the earth had formed an alliance to keep the people enslaved to their errors, and the people themselves seemed to rejoice

[1] 1 S. Peter, iv. 12-13.

in their ignominious bondage; at this juncture, when not one ray of hope derived from any earthly source could animate His future prospects, Jesus confidently predicts the wide extension of His reign, and, with one prophetic glance, lays before us the gradual rise and progress of His religion as well as the melancholy defection of some of its members. Yes, with that calm and noble confidence which the consciousness of His own Divinity inspired, He tells us that many shall come from the East and the West to sit down with Abraham and his children in the kingdom of heaven, whilst the children of the kingdom shall be cast into exterior darkness. The subject suggested by this Gospel is pregnant with much practical instruction. It embraces two of the most sublime and awful mysteries of religion—the gratuitous vocation of God's people to the faith—as well as their rejection from any share in such a boon when they prove themselves unworthy of such a favour. These, then, are the topics which I purpose to unfold to you as analogous to the Gospel of the day, which declares that the first shall be last and the last first; and while I endeavour to impress upon you the inestimable value of being called to the faith, I wish to warn you against the dangers of its forfeiture, as well as to advert to the means which may secure to you the continuance of such a blessing.

So limited is man's reason, notwithstanding its boasted powers, that it is incapable of comprehending at one view any vast and magnificent object. Every such production of nature or of art must be studied in detail and contemplated in its minute relations, and it is then, and only then, the mind can form, from the vastness of the plan, the variety of the materials and the toil and time expended in the execution, some idea of the value and grandeur of the work which makes but a faint and vague impression on the ignorant and the unthinking. It is with much more reason that a similar study is required regarding the great work of man's redemption, though confessedly the masterpiece, not of a creature, but of the Creator, and which is emphatically called by St. Paul, "the wisdom and the power of God."[1] Yet, as if it were the privilege of man to be presumptuous in proportion to his ignorance, this is the subject on which all affect to be most profound, and on which they are most flippant, who never gave one serious thought to its consideration. The Church of Christ is often designated in the Scripture under the familiar but expressive images of a house, a city, and, as you may have perceived by the text, a kingdom, to show us that, like every other house, city, kingdom, or well-regulated community, it has its founder, its boundaries, its laws, its governors, its subjects, and, in fine, its punishments, as well as its rewards. To enable us to form an accurate idea of the most inconsiderable state or government, we should form some acquaintance with its history and fundamental maxims. If so, it must be obvious that it requires much serious attention to discuss a subject of such importance as that kingdom which has Christ for its founder, the limits of the earth for its boundaries, time as the measure of its trials upon earth, and eternity the duration of its triumphs in heaven.

Of the establishment of this kingdom we find the announcement as early as the world itself, and scarcely was man seduced by the serpent when he was consoled by the merciful promise of a deliverer that would crush the author of his fall. This consoling assurance of a future deliverer was handed down like a sacred inheritance among a chosen race, who were kept apart from the surrounding corruption. Unfortunately, the fatal effects of the frailty of our first parents were spreading

[1] 1 Cor. i. 24.

and becoming more inveterate as they descended, and
would have overspread the earth had not God, by a code
of laws which forbade any intercourse with the nations,
raised, as it were, a wall around His people for their protection. The whole history of this people was merely prepa
ratory to Christ's kingdom, and their captivity in Egypt,
their deliverance from its bondage, their wars with the
neighbouring kingdoms, and the various fortunes of those
kingdoms themselves were so many events which, under
the guiding counsels of the Almighty, were intended for
its establishment. Who would imagine, while he peruses
the alternate rising and decline of the ancient empires
of the world, and passes from the history of one conqueror to that of another, and thus pursues the lengthened
and complicated annals of remote kingdoms through the
varied space over which they are spread, that he is at
the same time but contemplating the parts of one great
picture, and that the gorgeous magnificence of the Assyrians and Persians, the polished power of the Greeks,
and the more massive and solid strength of the Romans
were nought but the components of the one vast image:
its head of gold, its breast of silver, its thighs of brass,
and its feet of iron, mixed with potter's clay, which rose
before the prophetic sight of Daniel, and which, fleet as
the dream in which it first appeared, passed away as
soon as it was struck and broken by the stone from the
mountain to make room for that kingdom which shall
last for ever? Yet such was the case, and all the schemes
of legislators and the projects of conquerors were but as
so many instruments wielded by the Almighty to accomplish His own decrees in the fulness of time. While the
pagan nations, thus instigated by ambitious views, were
silently working as the agents of a Providence, of which
they were unconscious, the prophets of Judea were occasionally employed in reviving the promises that were

made to their fathers, and proclaiming that the Gentiles should be called into His Church. "Arise, and be enlightened, O Jerusalem," exclaims Isaias, "for thy light is come and the glory of the Lord is risen upon thee . . . . . and the Gentiles shall walk in thy light and kings in the brightness of thy rising. . . . Thy sons shall come from afar, and thy daughters shall rise up at thy side. Then shalt thou see and abound, and thy heart shall wonder and be enlarged, when the multitude of the sea shall be converted to thee, and the strength of the Gentiles shall come to thee. . . . And the children of strangers shall build up thy walls and their kings shall minister to thee . . . . and the glory of Libanus shall come to thee to beautify the place of My sanctuary."[1] And, again, the same Prophet thus repeats the same joyous prediction: "Fear not, for I am with thee. I will bring thy seed from the East and gather thee from the West. I will say to the North, give up, and to the South, keep not back, bring my sons from afar and my daughters from the ends of the earth. Bring forth the people that are blind and have eyes; that are deaf and have ears. All the nations are assembled together, and the tribes are gathered."[2] Similar are the announcements of this great event with which the holy messengers, whom the Almighty sent among them, excited the attention of His chosen people. In short, this coming of the Messiah was the one solitary hope which solaced them in their pilgrimage; it was the one great event for which they exclusively panted; it was the only object to which the whole economy of their religion had reference, and through the dark and tangled history of mankind the hope of the Messiah can be traced as a luminous path from the creation to the redemption, and becoming

[1] Isai. lx. 1-13.  [2] Isai. xliii. 5-9.

gradually more expansive in its brilliancy from the fresh prophetic light which it received as it descended. At length the Redeemer arrives, preaches His Gospel, proves His mission by miracles, the most incontestible, calls His Apostles, whom He establishes, the expounders of His doctrine and the depositaries of His authority; and after having selected Peter as the rock on which He firmly fixed the foundation of His kingdom, He lays down His life as the last pledge of His love to mankind, and seals the covenant, which He had made with them, with the effusion of His blood.

As yet we have no vestige of the extension of that kingdom which the prophets foretold; but scarcely is He laid in the tomb, when He rises with renovated energy from its slumbers. The grave, which is naturally the goal of mortals and the end of their power, becomes to Jesus the richest source of His glory; and His enemies, by placing a guard of soldiers round His tomb, become the reluctant witnesses of the triumphs of His resurrection. During the few days of His sojourn upon earth He gathers together the Apostles, who fled when the Shepherd was stricken, strengthens their faith, fortifies their courage, unfolds the mysteries of the Scriptures, which they were hitherto too weak and carnal to understand; and ere He takes His final leave of that world which He had loved unto the last, and as if to enable it to read in characters of light a brief epitome of all the precepts and instructions of His life regarding the great kingdom which He founded, He breathed upon His Apostles, and thus accosted them: " All power is given to Me in heaven and in earth. Going, therefore, teach ye all nations, baptising them in the name of the Father, and of the Son, and of the Holy Ghost, teaching them to observe all things whatsoever I have commanded you: and behold I am with you all days, even to the consummation of the world."[1] Not many days had elapsed after Christ's ascension when the Holy Ghost descended upon the Apostles, sitting upon each in the form of tongues of fire, confirming them in the truths they had been taught, and inflaming them with courage to carry the glad tidings to the uttermost ends of the earth. Now began to be realised the parable of the grain of mustard-seed, the smallest of all seeds, but which quickly grew to a tree, under the shades of which the nations of the world might rejoice. Yes; scarce were the Apostles endued with virtue from above, when they went forth impatient to impart the spirit that inflamed them. In vain were they scourged, in vain were they imprisoned, undaunted by dangers, unappalled by menaces; sufferings could not subdue nor chains confine those Apostles of a faith whose hopes were not of this world. The Gospel spread with the rapidity of lightning; the tracks of the feet of those messengers of peace, to use the Scripture thought, were visible on every mountain, their voice went over the earth, and wherever it went the temples of idolatry, like those of Jericho, shook and fell at the thunder of its denunciations. The enemy of mankind, now trembling for his long-established reign, arms all the powers of the world, which, unfortunately, since, as well as then, has been always his best ally, in opposing the progress of Christ's Church. But the Spirit of the Redeemer triumphed over both. The cross was ridiculed as folly, yet its spirit soon refuted all the learned wisdom of philosophy. Engines of torture were multiplied to an endless diversity, until invention was exhausted. In the hands of Providence they became engines for accelerating the progress of religion. The pagan spectators often wondered at the courage that sustained the

---

[1] S. Matt. xxviii. 18, 19, 20.

champions of the faith, and often, as in the case of Martina, an illustrious virgin and martyr of Rome, fell down and worshipped the God whose spirit was seen to walk with His servants amidst the flames that played innocuously round them. Thus the executioners themselves became martyrs in their turn, and the blood of those holy witnesses of the faith became, in the strong language of Tertullian, the prolific seed of Christianity. But it was not in the number of Christians alone that the influence of this blood was felt. It sanctified the soil on which it fell; at its hallowed touch the curse with which the earth was stricken disappeared, and instead of the lust, the avarice, the revenge, the ambition, and the cruelty which spread with such fearful growth over the waste of paganism, charity, humility, chastity, and mercy were the quick and spontaneous productions of the garden, which, to use his own metaphor, the Redeemer had planted, and which was watered with His own Blood as well as that of the martyrs. In short, the East and West, the North and South, were now invited into one fold under the guidance of a common pastor, and thus taught to exercise all the affections of mutual brotherhood from the conviction of a common redemption. The distraction and dismemberment of the Roman Empire, over which that of the Church was gradually rising, showed that it received that prophetic shock which doomed it to fall; nor did that stone, by which it was overturned, cease its motion until every fragment of the mighty mass crumbled into ruins, and until the cross of the Master and the keys of the disciple, placed over the fallen temples of its emperors and its gods, attracted the willing homage of nations who never bowed to the imperial dominion of Rome.

From this sketch of the formation and final establishment of Christ's Church, which from the nature of a discourse like this must have been necessarily brief and rapid, it must appear of what vast importance it is to belong to that kingdom. You have seen with what slow solemnity it was ushered into the world, what labour and wisdom have been expended in its erection, and how, in fine, before and during the progress of the great work, all the events of the world calculated to minister to its accomplishment. In fine, the earth, the sea, all the splendour of the firmament, and man himself, were called into existence by the word of the Almighty. But to erect this kingdom, which was to redeem him from slavery, cost not only the preparation of four thousand years, but what is more—the humiliation, the labour, and the death of the Son of God. How magnificent, then, must be this master-work, which surpasses all the conceptions of man, and how deservedly termed "the power and wisdom of God!" Would to God that in unfolding the splendour of this heavenly kingdom, I were free from the necessity of exhibiting any darksome contrast, and that our joy in contemplating the redemption wrought by Jesus were not saddened by the conviction of the reprobation of any portion of mankind. Is it, then, true that some will be shut out of this glorious kingdom, which cost the Redeemer the effusion of His Blood? Yes; Jesus Christ Himself has pronounced the awful truth in language too clear for misconception: "But the children of the kingdom shall be cast into exterior darkness, where there shall be weeping and gnashing of teeth."[1] Let now the advocates of the indiscriminate salvation of all, by virtue of Christ's Passion, seriously ponder on these words: those whose sensibilities are hurt by the exclusion of any from Christ's Church or kingdom; those who, like the deluded Jews of old, would fain tell their teachers,

[1] S. Matt. viii. 12.

"Prophesy unto us pleasing things,"[1] as if the doctrine of Christ were to bend to the caprices of the human heart, instead of the human heart bending its pride and its sensuality to the stubborn and inflexible standard of the Gospel; those enemies of the cross of Christ, as St. Paul calls them, who by soft and insinuating speeches strive to corrupt the human heart and lull every creature into a false security, as if their power over the Church of God were greater than that of its Founder, as if they could alter the terms which He requires for its possession, or as if their breasts burned with more fervent affection for their fellow-men than He who gave the last drop of His Blood for their salvation. O my brethren! be not deceived by fancies no less dangerous than delusive. If a human legislator is to be obeyed, is it to be supposed that it is God alone whose laws are to be trampled on with impunity? If the subject of every other realm must conform to the regulations of a state in order to be entitled to its honours and its privileges, is it to be supposed that Christ will heap the rewards of His kingdom upon those who may insult its ordinances, as well as those who are observant of its regulations? If, notwithstanding the general similarity of mankind, it has been found easy, by means of a particular badge or form of government, to distinguish the subjects of every state, are we to suppose that this kingdom of Christ alone was left without any external means by which one could easily be associated among its subjects? If, in fine, the lot of those who are excluded from His kingdom—and, mark, they are the words of Christ—is weeping and gnashing of teeth, must it not be conformable with a sense of His mercy that, in order to enable His creatures to escape such a dreadful doom, that characters as brilliant as the noonday sun should

[1] Isai. xxx. 10.

guide the entrance to His kingdom? Yes; and this is a position which none can contradict. For if some, in the fulness of a humanity, deem it incompatible with the mercy of Christ that any should be excluded from His kingdom, they cannot deny but it would be doubly cruel, if I may use the word, to condemn them if the path which leads to that kingdom were intricate or obscure.

But on the awful question of reprobation our business is not with those false sensibilities of the human heart which deceive while they flatter, but with the unerring words of Christ, who cannot lead astray: "The children of the kingdom shall be cast into exterior darkness, where there shall be weeping and gnashing of teeth." How sadly has this prophecy been fulfilled in the fate of those who were once the chosen people of God! And how simply is that event told in the following parable: "A certain man planted a vineyard and made a hedge about it, and built a tower and let it to husbandmen, and went into a far country. And at the season he sent to the husbandmen a servant to receive of the husbandmen of the fruit of the vineyard, who having laid hands on him, beat him and sent him away empty. And again he sent to them another, and him they wounded and used reproachfully. And again he sent another, and him they killed; and many others, of whom some they beat and others they killed. Therefore having yet one son, most dear to him, he also sent him unto them, last of all, saying: They will reverence my son. But the husbandmen said one to another: This is the heir; come, let us kill him, and the inheritance shall be ours. And having laid hold of him, they killed him and cast him out of the vineyard. What, therefore, will the lord of the vineyard do? He will come and destroy those husbandmen, and will give the vineyard to others."[1]

[1] S. Mark, xii. 1-9.

In this short parable we have an affecting epitome of the reprobation of the Jewish people. The Almighty in His mercy chose them for His inheritance; in the desert He cherished them, as the hen that spreads its wings over the young ones; when they forgot their God, He sent prophets to reclaim them; and when they killed them, He still continued to send others in their stead. At length, as the last and greatest proof of His mercy, He sends His Son, whose life was but one continued chain of mercy and benevolence. The benevolence, which ought to have awakened gratitude, but exasperated the hate of His enemies, who, impatient of virtue so transcendant, resolved to extinguish His influence in His Blood. Hardened and perverse people! thus continuing to close their eyes against every ray of light, and their hearts against every appeal that could move them. They execute their murderous projects, and the blood of all the prophets, to that of the Holy One whom they recently condemned, was avenged on their guilty heads. By a ruthless and sanguinary fanaticism they provoke the anger of the Romans, who resolve upon their destruction. Titus captures their city, its walls are levelled to the ground, the voice of howling is heard in the streets, the glory of Lebanon is laid low, and its people—the unfortunate people—are scattered by the breath of the divine wrath to the different quarters of the world, the alternate objects of its commiseration or its scorn; incapable, even in their most prosperous fortunes, of forming a lasting establishment; more generally doomed to linger out a despised existence, in preference to which they might sometimes sigh for an extinction, which, like the unfortunate reprobate in the Apocalypse, they never can find, because fated to carry with them the melancholy evidence that the curse which was invoked upon them by their fathers continues to be the descending inheritance of their posterity. But as if to leave, before their utter dispersion, an everlasting monument of their awful punishment, behold the huge pile, deservedly called a Coliseum, which has survived the wreck of human greatness, and which strikes strangers with an astonishment in which there is a sentiment more mysterious than that inspired by its vastness, and of which they are unconscious. Who were the architects of this structure? The captive thousands of this hapless people, who, when their own temple was levelled to the ground and their priesthood shorn of its honours, were, like their ancestors in Egypt, doomed to make bricks for the erection of a theatre, in which the tragedy commenced in the hall of Pilate should be continued, and which, after having served the disciples for the repetition of the same scenes of savage and ignominious torture which were already passed through by their Divine Master, should remain, in despite of the barbarism of one age or the vanity of another, an enduring monument of the triumph of the martyrs and of the ruin and reprobation of Abraham's unfortunate race.

The calamitous lot of the chosen people of God is an awful example to us, especially when we reflect that it is held up by the Apostle as a warning instruction to Christians. "If some of the branches be broken, and thou being a wild olive-tree art ingrafted in them, and art made partaker of the root and fatness of the olive-tree, boast not against the branches . . . Thou wilt say then: The branches were broken off that I might be grafted in, Well: because of unbelief they were broken. But thou standest by faith: be not high-minded, but fear; for if God had not spared the natural branches, lest perhaps He also spare not thee. See, then, the goodness of God: towards them, indeed, that are fallen, the severity; but towards thee the goodness of God, if thou abide in goodness, otherwise thou also shall be cut off."[1] If the words of the Redeemer, regarding the exclusion of some from His kingdom, required any commentary, we are furnished with one that is awfully clear in this passage of the Apostle. Let us not imagine that this reprobation was confined to the Jews. It is not natural, as St. Paul says, that the grafted branches should be preferred to the root, or that the adopted children should receive a preference over the first son, who possessed the inheritance. Hence he cautions us to fear and to abide in goodness, lest we also be cast off. Behold, then, the only condition on which we can hope to remain within the pale of God's kingdom, abiding in goodness and observing all things, which the Redeemer commanded His Apostles ere His ascension into heaven. If we fail to observe these things, which have been handed down to us, and, trusting to our own delusive guidance, stray from the beaten path in which the ancients have walked, then we have reason to tremble lest we be cast off, like other nations, in punishment of their incredulity. Yes; as St. Chrysostom remarks, the kingdom of God is not fixed or stationary. First, the Jews were chosen, to the exclusion of the Gentiles; again, the latter were called and the former forsaken, and still some of the Gentiles were abandoned, and the remnant of the Jews will be called again, the Almighty thus shifting His favours, as if to provoke people to a rivalry in His service. Distressing reflection! Little, perhaps, did this eloquent Father imagine that his own church should become a melancholy illustration of his doctrine. Could he have foreseen that the temple which resounded with the voice of his eloquence, and was

---

[1] Rom. xi. 17, &c.

filled with the odour of his virtue, would one day, like that of Solomon, be profaned by the worship of the unholy one seated in the sanctuary, how he should have fallen prostrate to adore the mysterious dispensations of the Almighty. But not only has Constantinople fallen, but Smyrna, Carthage, and a great portion of the East, once the cradle of Christianity, have shared the same fate. The oracles of St. Chrysostom, of St. Athanasius, of St. Augustine, or St. Cyprian, are heard no more. The solitudes, out of which gushed fountains of living water, clothing the desert with freshness and with verdure, are again parched up with a burning sand, where every virtue sickens, and the sun of heaven has gone down on the regions where it first arose.

Let us, too, fear and abide in goodness, lest because of our unbelief we also be cast off. Remark the words of the Apostle, to show that it was in punishment of that hardened unbelief, which wilfully resisted evidence the most convincing, that they were cast out from the kingdom of God. Let us, therefore, strive to stand fast in the faith, and profit of the sad example of others. Amidst all the wreck which Christianity has suffered, and the partial dismemberment of the once flourishing kingdom of Christ, there is still left enough to console and animate the Christian. Some of the extremities, it is true, have fallen, but the head remains sound and the centre remains unshaken. Antioch, Jerusalem, and Alexandria, where Apostles and Evangelists wrote and preached, have passed under the dominion of the Coran; but Rome, which was selected as its chief citadel by the vicegerent, to whom He gave the first authority in His kingdom, remains still the city on the mountain-top which was to diffuse its light among the nations of the world. In its connection with the prince of the Apostles, whose ashes repose here, it still inherits the triple prerogative which he received—of being the Rock, on which the Church was erected; the Pastor, who was to feed the sheep and lambs of the fold; and the Prince, who had received the keys of His kingdom. What an accumulation of prerogatives! and what more can a Christian require to guard him from the unbelief which may expose him to be cast away? Yes; Rome—that one word that has connected, from the infancy of Christianity, all the nations of the world—remains still a guide to fix those that remain, or to help those that are anxious to return. If they are driven to and fro by every wind of doctrine, here is the rock to which they may fasten a secure anchorage; if they should be annoyed by the wolf tempting the flock, in Rome resides the supreme pastor, to whom the entire fold was committed; and should they be distracted by the rival pretensions of different authorities, Rome still exercises the keys which it received for the government of God's kingdom. It requires no enthusiasm to see how, in the preservation of this city and the uninterrupted authority of its Pontiffs, the Almighty has meant to preserve all those tender and sensitive chords which have connected all the Christians of the world with this heart of their religion. Has there been in the world a country so exposed as Italy, or which was swept by so many revolutions? Exposed by its beauty to aggressions which it had not strength to repel, it has been the constant theatre of wars and battles since its first invasion by the barbarians to the late eventful contest that so long agitated the repose of Europe. Yet though other dynasties were crushed by those calamities, never again to recover, the successors of St. Peter were seen to rise triumphant after every storm; and Rome, the seat of their pontificate, when it appeared forever fallen, again lifted its head with renovated glory from the dust. This is not fancy, but the cool and impartial testimony of history. Alaric left the city a desert, and from the contemplation of the evils that followed, St. Jerome was enabled to illustrate more forcibly those prophetic pictures of woe which were drawn by Ezechiel. It was re-peopled, however, by the groups who sought and found shelter in the sanctuaries of the Apostles.

Attila next threatens it with a similar fate. It was saved, however, by the seasonable mediation of St. Leo, whose meek and majestic eloquence subdued the savage soul of the northern chief and arrested his destructive career. Again it was pillaged by Genseric, who spared neither the temples nor the sacred vessels which were revered by the fury of his predecessor. At length Totila, the fiercest and most inexorable of its foes, doomed it, in the next century, to utter destruction, and during forty days the historian might write, in the words of the Prophet, "Wild beasts rested there, and owls answered each other in the palaces of pleasure."[1] Without dwelling on the particulars of the varied and heroic events of their early history, its Pontiffs were exiled for seventy years beyond the Alps, while the city of the Seven Hills deplored its solitude, and its factious leaders, like what is fabled of the fallen spirits, were tearing from their foundations the massive monuments of former times and flinging their fragments with hostile fury against each other. The Turkish chief who rolled the tide of conquest over Europe, boasted, when flushed with triumph, that he would convert the Vatican into a stable. But, like Antiochus, he was stopped in his sacrilegious attempt upon the temple of the Lord. Nor need I but just allude to more recent events, which are yet fresh in the recollection of all, when the venerable Pius was torn from the centre of his fold, only to diffuse more exten-

[1] Isai. xiii. 21, 22.

sively the conviction of the "Virtue from above"[1] which always sustained the faith of Rome and the fortitude of its Pontiffs, and his imperial keeper was in continual awe from the light which cheered the dreariness of his dungeon. Or, when, again, after his courage was sufficiently proved, Rome witnessed a spectacle more splendid than any of its ancient triumphs in the multitudes of the old and the young, whom it poured forth to hail to his own home the return of their Father who honoured the faith, of which he was the head, by the glories of his captivity. In short, there was not one of the proud princes of the earth, whom a hatred of Christ's religion stirred up to falsify His promises of protection to His Church who did not become, like Julian, instrumental in strengthening the faith which they meditated to overthrow.

Such are the views which all who are anxious to retain or to recover the precious inheritance of faith ought to take—views which are worthy of the dignity of the human intellect as well as of the majesty of religion, and not the wretched and narrow views which may be suggested by the vices or follies of any of its members. Scandal, we are assured by the Divine Redeemer, is one of those evils from which His Church will not cease to suffer. To look for any society exempt from any personal reproach is to look, by anticipation, upon earth for what is to be only found in the regions of the blessed. The woes pronounced against those who may have the misfortune to be a stumbling-block to others, should make every individual tremble for himself. But where there is neither the will nor the power to correct it, vague insinuations against vice are anything but a proof of zeal for virtue, since they may rather betray more of the insect that loves to flutter around congenial

[1] S. Luke, xxiv. 49.

turpitude, than of that bird which soars to a purer atmosphere and wings his flight against the sun with eyes that wink not at its effulgence. Such are the views which inspire the good in their pilgrimage to the shrines of the Apostles, and which must continue to exalt their devotion in despite of all the cynicism of the profane who frequent churches but to criticise ceremonies which they have neither hearts to feel nor heads to understand, and who may justly talk of irreverence, since the worst of it may be traced to their own profanation. Even now, after the lapse of so many centuries, how must not the Catholic feel himself in communion with the nations and connected with the remotest time when on the great festivals of the birth, but more particularly of the resurrection of the Redeemer, he beholds that great sacrifice which was the last pledge of His love and memorial of His passion celebrated by a Pontiff who not only expresses the rite but the person of the royal patriarch, whose name it bears, in the singular coincidence of being at once a king and Pontiff, over the sacred spot in which the relics of that Apostle repose, whose spirit still speaks to his successors the confident assurance of the continuance of the power with which he was invested, and under a dome whose lofty roof was made to bear the soul to heaven, whilst the names of Syriac, Greek, Latin, and Spanish which he perceives written on the tribunals of mercy, still reminding him of the mysterious continuance of the miracle of one faith through such a variety of tongues by which Peter still, through the Roman Pontiffs, as formerly in his own person on the days of Pentecost, spoke to Parthians, and Medes, and Elamites, and the men of Mesopotamia the wonderful works of God; while the vastness of the edifice itself in which these dear and authentic memorials of his faith are accumulated, remind him that this is not the little conventicle of any one sect or country, but as he finds it like an unrolled volume continually stretching out its folded immensity to his view, when, borne along with the procession that encircles his Holiness to the lofty balcony from which the prostrate representatives of every nation are mingled with the immense multitude beneath to receive, with fervent affection, the blessing of the Common Father of the Faithful, he is obliged to exclaim that this is no other but the common temple of that one continuous and Catholic Church into which the nations are always to flow from the four winds of heaven.

To conclude, let us reflect that the Jews have been cut off, some of the Eastern churches have fallen, and the Catholic religion, like the sun of heaven, is spreading joy and gladness among the inhabitants of another hemisphere. Already has it withdrawn its light from some of the nations of Europe, and may now be threatening to go down upon the iniquity of others. We are still in a state of warfare, beset by spiritual foes, who are anxious for our ruin. Let us, therefore, fervently implore the Almighty that we may not be consigned to darkness, but that He may cause that luminary of faith, which is verging to the West, to loiter still over our horizon, in order that, having conquered by its aid all our enemies, we may arrive at the secure possession of that kingdom which Christ has promised to those who prove their fidelity by standing fast in the faith and fulfilling His commandments. Amen.

## ON THE FALSE PROPHETS.

"Beware of false prophets, who come to you in the clothing of sheep, but inwardly they are ravening wolves. By their fruits you shall know them."—S. Matt. vii. 15, 16.

Of the various tenets which the spirit of error has attempted to circulate, there is none more industriously or triumphantly asserted, than that mere difference of belief is no obstacle to salvation. The moment the authority of the Church is discarded, such a doctrine is substituted by an easy and necessary consequence. After the memorable revolt which in the sixteenth century severed so many churches from a union with the parent stock, each particular church—nay, every individual—claimed the same privilege by which this independence was originally established. The spirit of discord was kept alive, because the principle of unity was not acknowledged; and the rival sects proscribed each other with the same rancour which they first exhibited towards the Catholic Church. Weary at length of a warfare in which they wasted their mutual strength without being comforted by the hopes of victory, the counsels of peace were at length adopted, the contending parties stretched the hand of fellowship to each other, and charitably extended to their dissenting neighbour the hope of salvation which they claimed for themselves. Such mutual kindness is quite natural; for why should anyone attempt to impose his belief on another, whose right to interpret the Scripture is equally independent? From this principle another is deduced, that the Scripture is reduced to precepts of morality, and that points of doctrine are matters of little or no importance, which may safely be abandoned to each one's reason or discretion. To show you, my brethren, the inconsistency of those who insist upon this point, I need only to open and read to you the chapter of the Gospel from which my text is taken. There you see Christ cautioning His disciples against those impostors who would come in sheep's clothing to corrupt His doctrine. For what purpose, then, did He so diligently strive to guard us against the delusion of those impostors, if He did not consider the purity of our faith of the utmost importance to our salvation? If, then, I dwell to-day on this unpalatable subject, I only repeat and enforce the admonition of our Redeemer. I do not wantonly introduce it, but avail myself of a subject suggested by the Gospel; and if I were, through a timid compliance with the reigning indifference of the day, to neglect to convey the instruction with which it is pregnant, I should incur the reproach made in these words of St. Paul: "If I yet pleased men, I should not be the servant of Christ."[1] I should, therefore, first point out the dangers of listening to these false prophets or seducers, and then exhibit the features by which they may be distinguished.

If we weigh well the nature of man and the nature of the Christian religion, we will not be surprised that all the powers of the one have been constantly levelled against the authority of the other. Christ Himself has predicted there should be heresies. St. Paul says, in the Acts of the Apostles: "I know that after my departure ravenous wolves will enter in among you, not sparing the flock; and of your own selves will rise up men speaking perverse things to draw away disciples after them."[2] It is clear, then, from the authorities of St. Paul and Christ Himself, that the Christian religion will be attacked by many, who will endeavour to substitute for its precepts the fruits of their own invention.

[1] Gal. i. 10.   [2] Acts, xx. 29, 30.

And indeed, my brethren, we cannot doubt the truth of this prediction. The sum of the Christian doctrine consists of mysteries, that is, truths above the reach of reason, and precepts of morality that are at war with the corruption of the heart. Hence the pride of the understanding has been engaged in constant hostility against the apparent repugnance of its doctrines; and the corruption of the heart has inveighed with equal acrimony against the austerity of its moral maxims. Behold, then, my brethren, the two prolific sources of error in every age: the presumption of human reason, and the corruption of the human heart. We all know how far pride may lead one in defending a favourite maxim; and, if you but consult your own hearts, you will there discover how the indulgence of its corrupt desires makes you cling with a desperate attachment to a criminal passion, which in the cool and sober moments of reflection you would condemn. Hence impostors have arisen in every age to impugn the doctrine and oppose the authority of the Church, and not one of their heresies that has not sprung from one of the principles I have mentioned. There is not a mystery of Christianity that has not been combated by their pride, nor a maxim of morality that has not been arraigned by their profligacy. The austerity of the Gospel has been laid aside, and a milder standard of life has been substituted; and man's opposition to control has been flattered by invectives against authority. While men will be fond of doctrines that are flattering to their passions, designing men will not be wanting to minister to their depraved appetites; and hence the continual succession of the ministers of imposture in every age. To recite the long story of human errors, and the misfortunes that sprung from them, would exceed the limits I proposed to myself in this discourse: I will only remark that history records of the different sectaries, scenes at which decency would blush and humanity would shudder. But as what has been once done may be again and again repeated, as these impostors may yet appear as they appeared in past times, and as men may be equally desirous to drink the poison of their errors, I will point out to you the means to distinguish them and to guard against their errors.

My dear Christians, as we are commanded to preserve unaltered the doctrine which Christ has bequeathed to us, and cautioned against the false prophets who would fain deprive us of so valuable an inheritance, it must be supposed that God has left within the reach of every individual the means of ascertaining who are these apostles of delusion. These means, my brethren, cannot be such as to require much learning to understand them. No; they must be plain and simple, and brought down to the capacity of the lowliest individual that listens to me this day; otherwise the end of Christ would have been defeated, who came to preach His Gospel to the poor as well as to the rich, to the illiterate as well as to the learned; for, according to Himself: "To preach the Gospel to the poor He sent Me."[1] Now, my brethren, what is the first mark by which you will distinguish them? Here it is: If they come to you not sent, not appointed, not commissioned by that authority in which the fulness of Christ's power resides, by virtue of the unbroken succession, which can be traced back to the time of the Apostles. This is an obvious mark; for it is not to be supposed that one ever can claim to himself any power, unless granted by Him who alone can withhold or impart it. Thus St. Paul, speaking of the ministry of the Word, says: "Neither doth any man take the honour to himself but he who is called by God, as

[1] S. Luke, iv. 18.

Aaron was."[1] That is, no one can intrude himself into the ministry but he who, like Aaron, is publicly and solemnly invested with the priesthood. Now, my brethren, Christ has jealously reserved this honour for his Apostles and their successors, saying: "He that heareth you, heareth Me: and he that despiseth you, despiseth Me:"[2] "he that will not hear the Church, let him be to thee as a heathen and a publican."[3] And again: "Whose sins you shall forgive, they are forgiven; and whose sins you shall retain, they are retained."[4] "All power is given to me in heaven and on earth: go teach all nations, and behold I am with you until the end of time." Can any commission be more solemn, vesting in the Apostles and their successors, to the end of time, the plenitude of Christ's power? And can temerity be more impious than when one dares to grasp at a ministry which Christ has reserved for His own special appointment. Again, St. Paul, speaking to the Bishops whom he assembled together at Miletus thus addresses them: "Take heed to yourselves and to the whole flock wherein the Holy Ghost hath placed you, Bishops, to rule the Church of God, which He hath purchased with His Blood."[6] According, then, to the inspired Apostle, the Bishops are the supreme rulers of the Church of God, a commission which they have not assumed to themselves, nor derived from any earthly power, but which, according to St. Paul, has been immediately received from the Most High. Consequently they, and they alone, are empowered to delegate any portion of that power with which they have been invested. Whosoever, then, comes to you not deputed by them you are not to receive him; nay, you are to treat him as a thief or a robber, according to the words of Christ, unless he is able to

[1] Heb. v. 4. [2] S. Luke, x. 16. [3] S. Matt. xviii. 17.
[4] S. John, xx. 23. [5] S. Matt. xxviii. 18, 19, 20. [6] Acts, xx. 28.

produce the authentic seal of his commission. Those, then, impressed with this character you will hear; but those who are self-appointed God reproaches in these words of Jeremias: "The prophets prophesy falsely in My name: I sent them not, neither have I commanded them, nor have I spoken to them: they prophesy unto you a lying vision, and divination and deceit, and the seduction of their own heart."[1] And again he says: "I did not send prophets, yet they ran: I have not spoken to them, yet they prophesied.... How long shall this be in the heart of the prophets that prophesy lies, and that prophesy the delusion of their own hearts?"[2] Finally, the Prophet Jeremias closes a long invective against those deceitful enthusiasts by the following denunciations: "Therefore, behold I am against the prophets, saith the Lord: who steal my words every one from his neighbour. Behold I am against the prophets, saith the Lord: who use their tongues, and say: The Lord saith it. Behold I am against the prophets that have lying dreams, saith the Lord: and tell them, and cause my people to err, by their lying and by their wonders: when I sent them not, nor commanded them."[3] Here, then, my brethren, is a mark by which you may know these false teachers—a mark that is obvious to the humblest capacity among you, that is, that they come of themselves; for, according to St. Paul, "how can they preach unless they are sent?"[4]

But, my brethren, it may be said, and it has been said; why not hear the Word from anyone who dispenses it: the doctrine of their preaching is sound, and calculated to promote the interests of morality, and is generally drawn from the Scripture itself? The moment you would listen to suggestions like these, that moment you would expose yourselves to

[1] Jerm. xiv. 14.  [2] Jerm. xxiii. 21, 26.  [3] Jerm. xxiii. 30, 31, 32.  [4] Rom. x. 15.

the most imminent danger. A few words only will be sufficient to expose their fallacy. You know, my dear Christians, from your incapacity to learn the first elements of Christianity in the Catholic Church, how unequal you would be to the task of deciding on the soundness or the danger of any doctrine which might be addressed to you. If, then, you were the judges of the purity of doctrines, you would be left at the mercy of every knave or enthusiast, and after attaching yourself to one leader you would be still solicited by another more bold or artful to join his standard; and in the strong and emphatic language of St. Paul, you would be "carried about with every wind of doctrine."[1] You would be in the perplexity in which Tertullian, one of the Fathers, represents a man importuned by the adverse heretics of his day. Marcian says: "Seek with me, and you shall find." Basilides says: "Seek with me, and you shall find." Carponates assails me with a similar demand: "Seek with me, and you shall find." And thus I shall be always seeking, and never finding. But no, my brethren, such a state of continual insecurity cannot be reconciled to Christ's plan of imparting his religion to the little ones. You have a more sure and summary answer for them in the words of the same Tertullian: "Why do you invade my possession; why do you fell my wood; why do you cross my waters. I am the heir of the Apostles; you they have disinherited." Besides the mark of self-appointment, which is sufficient to defeat the claims of the false prophets, the Scripture gives us another in these words: "By their fruits you shall know them."

It must be confessed, my brethren, that these words require some explanation, because they have been abused ever by the false teachers to discredit the

---

[1] Ephes. iv. 14.

authority of the lawful pastors of the Church. Often do they come with language smooth and insinuating, with a demeanour wearing the appearance of devotion, contrasting their own piety with the profligacy of others. But, my brethren, beware of their insidious disguise; for Christ Himself says that the mildness of the sheep will cover the rapacity of the wolves. You will know them by their fruit, not, perhaps, by the sanctity of every individual, because their sanctity might lead us into as intricate an examination as the purity of their doctrine. But the fruit by which you will know them is their obedience or disobedience to their pastors, from whom they received their mission, and by whom they should be guided in conveying their instruction. This is the true touchstone by which their mission must be tried. Often does a meek and humble exterior conceal a proud, presumptuous spirit, which at length breaks out into open mutiny against a superior. If, then, such preachers should be visited with the censure of the Church, no matter how sound their doctrine or soothing their address, they are ranked among those against whom we are cautioned by our Redeemer. In vain, my brethren, will they represent to you the disorders of your own clergy, to withdraw you from their obedience; in vain will they tell you a bad tree cannot produce good fruit, and, therefore, a bad clergyman cannot be productive of good. Often, my brethren, has the Church wept over the vices of her pastors, and laboured with a pious solicitude to reclaim them. But, behold the difference between their disorders and those of the false pastors. The ministry of the lawful pastor is not necessarily dependent on his good or bad life; the prayers which he offers, the sacraments which he administers, borrow their efficacy not from him, but from the sacred office to which he has been appointed; and hence, though we may deplore the scandal of his life, we are still obliged to acknowledge the validity of his ministry. The priest may be a sinner; nay, his sins may be deeper than those of the penitent that falls prostrate at his feet; yet still, because he acts by virtue of his divine commission, the graces of which he is the minister are not infected by the impurity of the channel. Not so is the false prophet who is stripped of his power, or who steals into the fold: he receives no divine commission; God has promised no graces to his ministry; therefore, his sacraments are null, and his preaching is a mockery. Who is there that does not bow to the decision of a judge, though he may be a bad man, and that does not obey the authority of a magistrate, though an indifferent member of society? And why? Because they are the representatives of the supreme power of the State. I know not whether the man would excite your pity or indignation more who would attempt to despise the judge because he was a bad private character, and attempt by force or fraud to intrude himself into the seat of judgment. And if the jurisdiction of the judge is withdrawn by the power that conferred it, you no longer revere him as the representative of majesty. Equally presumptuous, then, would be the man who would force himself into the office of a pastor when not appointed by the Supreme Shepherd, and equally so is the priest divested of his jurisdiction, though his character cannot be blotted out, when that jurisdiction is withdrawn by his legitimate superior. Be not, then, dear Christians, seduced by such people. With St. Paul "I beseech you, brethren, to mark them who make dissensions and offences contrary to the doctrines which you have learned, and avoid them; for, by pleasing speeches and good words, they seduce the hearts of the innocent."[1] You see, then, from the words, or rather the predictions of St. Paul, that their teaching will be distinguished by pleasing speeches, nay, sometimes by good words. But should you be in danger of being betrayed by their flattery, the same Apostle furnishes you with a sovereign antidote in the following admonition: "Though we, or an angel from heaven, preach a Gospel to you besides that which we have preached to you, let him be anathema."[2] What language could be stronger? Were a man's eloquence almost divine; did his austerities seem to exceed the measure of human weakness; yet still, if he departs from the inherited doctrine delivered by the saints, let him be accursed. Such was the doctrine of the Holy Fathers in the primitive times, which are acknowledged by all to have been the brightest period of Christianity. In the time of St. Cyprian, a proud priest, separated from the Church, had, by an insinuating eloquence and a semblance of sanctity, seduced a number of unsuspecting people into an espousal of his cause. On the saint being asked by one of his abettors, what heresy had Novatian introduced, he replies, and his reply was sanctioned by the Church : "No matter what he teaches, who teaches out of the fold." Let, then, this be your reply to all: no matter how sanctimonious their airs, no matter how mortified their appearance; for, my brethren, such false apostles are deceitful labourers, transforming themselves into the Apostles of Christ: for Satan himself transformeth himself into an angel of light, therefore it is no great thing if his ministers be transformed as the ministers of justice: let your reply be; no matter what his doctrine is, who teacheth out of the fold. From what has been said, you must be convinced how false and pernicious must be the accom-

[1] Rom. xvi. 17, 18.  [2] Gal. i. 8.

modating principle of hearing the Word of God, wherever it may be preached. Independent of a lawful authority, experience tells us that preachers are found to flatter the follies of the hearers: men who would call good evil, and evil good; who mistake the illusions of their fancy for the inspirations of heaven. In a word, if such a tenet were once admitted, as there is no doctrine, however vile that has not been preached, it would follow that one could hear the Word of God in one of those obscure conventicles, where the language of Scripture is blasphemously perverted to the hope of a new Messiah.

Now, my brethren, that you are aware of the danger of false teachers, I trust you will guard against the delusion of their doctrines. But I must caution you, at the same time, not to force from the instruction of this day consequences of which it is not susceptible. He that would leave this church to indulge the insolence of triumph, would, indeed, derive but little benefit from this discourse. If you are blessed with the true faith, labour diligently to preserve it; but treat with indulgence the prejudices of others. You may rest assured that your religion alone will not save you; on the contrary, unless you fulfil its practical precepts, it will aggravate your condemnation. If God has been so merciful to you as to transmit to you from your father the Catholic religion, show by your pious observance of its duties that you are worthy of the sacred inheritance. Study to bequeath the same legacy to your children. The name of Catholic is the most valuable possession you can leave—it is a name inscribed in the creed of the Apostles—a name which attached St. Augustine to his religion—a name which has survived the vicissitudes of time, and has been never lost by the true believers, nor adopted by the sectaries. But let it be a substantial, significant name, not retained merely because it was a family distinction, preserved, like the empty pageants of heraldry, of which the spirit is gone and the memory is forgotten. Know that the barren tree that beareth no fruit will be cut down and cast into the fire. Know that it is not everyone that will say: Lord! Lord, shall enter into the kingdom of Christ, but he that doeth the will of His father. And with regard to your conduct towards your dissenting neighbour, it may be comprised in the strict but comprehensive admonition of St. Augustine: "Love the men, destroy their errors." Do, my brethren, love them; they deserve your pity and your prayers. But let not your compassion for them fill you with presumption. He to whom much is given of him much shall be required. Your judgment will be severe in proportion to your lights.

To conclude, my brethren, I exhort you with the Apostle to walk worthy of the vocation in which you are called, with all humility and mildness, with patience, supporting one another in charity; careful to keep the unity of spirit in the bond of peace, that you may enjoy hereafter that eternal peace which Christ has promised to those who fulfil His commandments. Amen.

## ON EDUCATION.

"Suffer the little children to come unto Me, and forbid them not, for of such is the kingdom of God."—S. MARK. x. 14.

WHAT a consolatory view is here given by our Divine Redeemer of the elevated destiny of children, who, until His merciful advent, were generally consigned to treatment the most careless and most cruel. Often the offspring of a licentiousness, in which a feeling of parental duty but little mingled, or, at best, of a union of which the bond was but loose and arbitrary, the little children of the pagan world were looked on with coldness bordering on aversion, many cut off in the very blossom of life, the victims of unnatural neglect, whilst those who survived found themselves strangers to every domestic endearment, and ignorant of the relations of fathers, save in the despotic and absolute control which they exercised over their very lives. The domestic hearth, instead of being a secure seat of joy and innocence, was converted into a gloomy prison, where the parent was often seen a cruel executioner taking away the lives of his children whom he should have protected; and the State, far from interfering to check the revolting cruelty, gave it a full sanction, becoming a participator in this legal slaughter of thousands of helpless innocents. Such was the melancholy lot of the young portion of human kind even among the nations most abounding in wealth as well as in the arts and refinements of civilisation—a lot which made the world unto them more than a vale of tears and sufferings, when the merciful sentence of our Divine Redeemer was uttered, which thenceforward achieved in their regard the most astonishing revolution. The young and helpless have become since the most interesting portion of society; instead of being abandoned to capricious cruelty, they are embraced with tender and respectful regard, and all seem anxious to rival each other in doing becoming honour to young citizens whose august prerogatives were so long hidden, but who now appear revealed to the world as the royal and first-born heirs of that kingdom which our Divine Redeemer has purchased, nay, whom we must imitate in their innocence and simplicity before we can aspire to a share in their blessed inheritance. It is for the purpose of your earning the favour of those young heirs of

God's eternal kingdom I address you on this occasion, for by aiding in the great work of their education you will be promoting the best interests of society here, and co-operating in the great work of their and your own salvation.

On the importance of early education as the most powerful agent in the advancement of society, it is unnecessary to occupy your attention long. It is a truth grounded on the evidence of those intellectual faculties with which man has been so profusely endowed by his Maker, and which is fully attested by the vast advantages of which their cultivation has been productive. It is a truth which is indelibly written in the records of the human race, and which fails not to strike every reader in those marked contrasts between savage and civilised life, that stand out so prominently in the history of ancient and modern times. To controvert the social advantages of what intellectual training has been productive, would be to controvert the judgment and experience of mankind, and to deny to the most powerful and polished nations of antiquity the social pre-eminence which their successful cultivation of the arts conferred on them. As well might you compare the rude and unshapen block, yet sleeping in the quarry, to the beautiful statue breathing the life and energy with which the cunning of the artist had formed it, as to compare man, emerging from the rudeness of savage life, with his compeer improved and adorned with those accumulated acquirements which belong to an intellectual state of society. Were you paradoxical enough to deny the benefits of education, you should, in all consistency, get rid of the social improvements that have followed in its train, again consigning your city* to comparative darkness, by burying its brilliant lights in those mines from

* Preached in Liverpool, in the month of November, 1869.—ED.

which they were evolved, restoring the primitive canoe for piratical excursions along your coasts, and discarding those magnificent creations of your hands and intellects that are seen careering through the western waters, freighted with the produce that lay so long useless on the trees of another hemisphere, and converted by your skill into raiment of the richest dye and texture for millions whom the scanty fleeces of their own flocks could never have supplied. We are not, then, disposed to controvert or undervalue the advantages of the most enlarged scientific education. Far from wishing to arrest or retard its progress, the Catholic Church encourages its fullest development, and lends its powerful aid in leading the human mind to explore the hidden laws of creation. Yes, but a mere scientific education, however full and extensive, can never satisfy her loftier requirements nor the aspirations of an immortal soul. It is not, then, to the Catholic Church that labours to exalt education by associating with it religion, any narrowness of views should be imputed. It is to its adversaries such a reproach more appropriately belongs. Numbers who are loudest in the praise of education confine it to its influence on society alone, we extend it to the interests of an imperishable soul; they limit it to the fleeting existence of time, we connect it with eternity; they look only to man's brief course on earth, and we to the same earthly career as exercising the most favourable or disastrous influence on his prospects of gaining heaven. What, then, is the fullest and most comprehensive system of education—the mere secular one of the modern materialists, or the moral and religious as well as scientific one of the Catholic Church—we leave to the decision of the dispassionate and impartial. Far from finding in the development of the laws of the material world any reason for deviating from the path which she has hitherto pursued in the education of her children, the Catholic Church beholds but fresh manifestations of the triumphs of the spiritual principle, and fresh arguments for the necessity of providing for man's spiritual destination. Who could seriously contemplate those modern prodigies of art, of which the realities surpass the boldest imaginings of fiction, could ever bring himself to believe that those who mastered obstacles, hitherto deemed unconquerable, could perish with the material elements which they so entirely subdued? Who could seriously believe that the vigorous spirit which hung without substructions those vaulted roads more ponderous in their materials than the roads of the ancient Romans, and through which vehicles more huge and lengthy than the caravans of old are projected with the velocity of the spirits of the air, could be other than immortal? The religious element alone is wanting to complete and perfect the education of such men, to guide them, as well as the more lowly masses, to the attainment of the goal for which they were created. To all such who are exclusively occupied in the investigations of nature, and but little solicitous about their salvation, the Church addresses herself. As you have explored with such diligence and applied with such success the laws that have been framed for the preservation of the natural being, why not, with a consistent perseverance, ascertain and reduce to practice those higher and holier laws of the same Creator by which He has ordained to save your immortal soul? As you contribute to smooth man's brief passage through life by removing the obstacles that lie in the way through the means of stupendous contrivances hitherto unknown, why not exhibit similar solicitude in determining the path that leads to heaven, and, in the language of the Prophet, level the mountains and fill up the valleys that have rendered it so uneven and so difficult to be trodden? Why make such ample and superfluous provision for the pilgrim of an hour—I am only transcribing the striking comparisons of the inspired writings—and discard all solicitude for the citizens of an eternal kingdom, or why fit up, with such sumptuous and elaborate embellishments, the shepherd's tent that is pitched to-day only to be shifted tomorrow on the moving sand of the desert, and forget the permanent city, not built with mortal hands, and lighted by the glory of the Lamb that was slain for our redemption? How applicable to those noble minds, the deluded worshippers of a mere material world, the words with which the holy founder of the Society of Jesus directed to its proper object the erring ambition of the young and generous Xavier! Having long sought to enlist the youth in the service of religion, he found him full of those dreams of horrors of worldly eminence and of fame with which high family claims and higher personal endowments had dazzled him. Instead of warping the goodly shoot, the saint only laboured to direct its aspiring tendency, and sympathising in the magnificent anticipations of a mind that vaguely sought distinction and renown, he asked: "Why waste your fancy and your energies on transient trifles which may never be realised, and not at once aspire to the conquest of that heavenly kingdom which Christ has prepared for His followers, unutterable in its happiness, and eternal in its duration?

Of this eternal kingdom, which, as our Saviour mentions in my text, the Catholic Church never loses sight in the education of her children; she never ceases to inculcate, and particularly while their young minds are yet soft and impressible; "What profiteth a man if he gain the whole world and lose his own soul."[1] They

---

[1] S. Matt. xvi. 26.

are destined for different occupations in life: some for mercantile pursuits, and others for the learned professions of which it is their duty to learn the qualifications in order that they may competently fill the post that is assigned them. But though called to fill the offices of the State, this is not their ultimate destination; and its functions, however important, must ever be subordinate to the attainment of that eternal happiness for which they were created; whence it follows, that it becomes the paramount duty of those who are entrusted with their education to furnish them amply with the means best fitted to enable them to secure the great end of their existence. From this incontestible position of salvation being the end—the sole necessary end of man—it must be an obvious consequence that religion becomes not only a co-ordinate, but the principal element in his education. This is a conclusion which reason cannot refuse to draw. It is founded on the eternal and necessary subordination of the lesser to the greater interests, of the lighter to the weightier obligations. Now, to devote almost the entire time of youth, from the beginning to the end of a week or month, to qualify one for offices or interests of which there will be no trace in a few years, and to snatch only a stealthy hour or two to give them to those interests which will endure for ever in the awful alternative of supreme blessedness or supreme misery, is a total subversion of the laws of just proportions. Behold, then, the active principle which renders education in the Catholic Church necessarily religious, without being divested of any of those attributes that are necessary for the secular and subordinate relations of man. But since it happens, by a strange reversal in the moral order, that the social or secular education is placed in a paramount position which it should not occupy by those who are outside the pale of the Catholic

Church, hence the necessity of always choosing the mental culture that is regulated by religion on the same principle by which we are guided in preferring the interests of eternity before those of the world and of time. By this supremacy of the religious principle over the various departments of knowledge, it will not be imagined that I am advocating the employment of the young in the continual recital of the Christian doctrine, or, valuable as it may be, in the perpetual perusal of the inspired volume. No; it was not thus the principle of religious education was understood in those times exclusively Catholic, when from the schools and universities of the Catholic Church went forth men, the lights not only of their own, but also of after times, to whom, every useful art was indebted for its cultivation and every science for the enlargement of its boundaries: men whose skill and enterprise conquered opposing oceans in exploring the opposite hemispheres, letting in the light of science, of civilisation, and of religion on nations that lay buried in darkness and the shadow of death, and enriching other countries, to the end of time, with the fruits of their discoveries. Whilst engaged in their scientific achievements, religion was the guide of their steps and the goal for which they panted, and the humble monks who first taught mankind to cement the sands of the sea and to fashion them into polished and flaming mirrors, by which not only the distant and hidden planets were brought within the range of the human eye, but even their interior thrown open to the gaze of mortals, those benefactors of the human race, so far from aiming at fame as their reward, tell us that the greatest incentive to their labour was that they might enable eccclesiastics, whose sight was dim and feeble from old age, to recite the divine office, and continue to intone with their living voice the divine praise, of which the stars themselves are but the mute heralds, proclaiming His glory through the splendour of the firmament. When, therefore, we insist on a religious education, we mean that it should still continue to hold in every school and college that sacred influence to which it is entitled from its divine origin. Far from permitting it to be cast aside, or doomed to some obscure hiding-place in the background, to which its worshipper may be allowed to pay, as if, stealthy visits, religion is to be seen enthroned in every place of education, and all the subordinate sciences doing homage to her whose mission is from heaven; whilst the halls are to be hung with the portraits of those eminent men who illustrated the laws of the land by their commentaries, the young student is not to look in vain for the portraits of those who exemplified by their precepts and practice the laws which our Divine Redeemer promulgated from the mountain. Whilst the young candidate for eloquence fixes his attention on the bust of the Athenian orator, meditating on the energy with which he surmounted every obstacle to eminence and to fame, he must have equal access to the contemplation of the still sublimer orator addressing the auditory of the same Athenian city, persuading them by his inspired eloquence to give to Christ the honour which they gave to " their unknown God." [1] And whilst he learns his military exercises, fired with the bust or portrait of some Roman or British conqueror, the former spreading devastation through your ancient province, and the latter making the distant regions of India to mourn through his rapacity, should not the student have the opportunity of contemplating at the same time, and in the same hall, the busts of other conquerors of a different type, those, for

[1] Acts, xvii. 23.

example, of a St. Augustine, planting the cross in Canterbury, where the altars streamed with the blood of human victims; or of a St. Xavier, stretching the conquest of the Gospel to the regions of India, without sullying his trophies with the blood, or the tears, of the native population. Let it not be imagined that the peculiar refinements of any country, or its extraordinary advances in civilisation, render it less necessary to insist on the predominance of religion in its colleges and schools. In no state of society should education be placed beyond its tutelage; but where its vigilance is more particularly required is when wealth increases the violence of the passions, and when luxury spreads around the contagion of depraved example. An artificial refinement of manners is no index whatever of innocence, and the examples of the ancient Egyptians, Greeks, and Romans unquestionably show how frequent is the alliance between vice and science, between a high state of civilisation and the most humiliating corruption. The intellects of the former, now soaring to the heavens, and measuring the celestial bodies in their orbits, were the next moment bowed down in shameful adoration to the vilest weeds of their gardens, or the most loathsome and noxious reptiles of their rivers. Of the Greeks, some of the maxims of their profoundest sages were such as St. Paul forbids us to utter, and the corruption of the most enlightened I cannot better describe than in the terrible picture which the same Apostle draws of them in his Epistle to the Romans: "Wherefore God gave them up to the desires of their heart, to uncleanness, to dishonour their bodies among themselves . . . to shameful affections, delivering them up to a reprobate sense, to do the things which are not convenient, being filled with all iniquity, malice, fornication, covetousness, wickedness, full of envy, murder, contention, deceit, malignity, whisperers, and without mercy."[1] It were well if this appalling picture were only applicable to those polished nations of antiquity, on which the light of the Gospel had not yet shone. A similar corruption keeps pace in modern times with the progress of arts and sciences, among all people, whose morals are not controlled by strong religious convictions and protected by the fences of a strict religious discipline. Man is prone to evil from his youth, says the inspired writer, and to curb the growing propensity to vice by training him to the discipline of virtue, becomes, no less than the infusion of knowledge, an essential part of his education. Where virtue, then, is not inculcated by precept and enforced by example, when the early buddings of vice are not nipped as soon as they appear, there the young cannot be placed with safety to society or to themselves, much less should they be suffered to be trained where the shoots of vice grow and spread with a rank luxuriance. But where there are unsound notions of faith there must be a corresponding decay of morality, and hence, for the protection of the one and the other, the young heirs of God's kingdom should be kept aloof from all schools where, by contact with error and bad practices, their faith might be tainted and their innocence destroyed. Our Redeemer assures us that "a bad tree does not produce good fruit, nor do men gather grapes from thorns."[2] Now, as faith is the vigorous principle that produces the abundant fruit of virtue and good works, it must be expected that if this prolific root is once decayed, instead of the produce of good works, meritorious of eternal life, nought is to be found but barrenness and corruption. In guarding, therefore, against the dangers of a mixed education, Catholics are only following up the principle of maintaining in all their

---

[1] Rom. i. 24-31.   [2] S. Matt. vii. 16, 17.

soundness the faith and innocence of their children. Though destined for a heavenly kingdom, its young heirs have certain laws to comply with, and certain obstacles to encounter and subdue, before they can attain the end of their creation. Those laws are the commandments of God, fully revealed, and more fixed and infallible for the moral guidance of the soul than are the physical laws of nature for regulating material bodies; and those laws of the commandments are again obstructed by sinful passions, thus described by St. Paul: "Now, the works of the flesh are manifest, which are fornication, uncleanness, immodesty, luxury, . . . enmities. contentions, emulations, wrath, quarrels, dissensions, sects, envy, murders, drunkenness, revellings, and the like."[1] Behold, then, the position of the child when first taken out of the domestic temple in which his innocence was enshrined. He is fully impressed with his high but arduous destiny, and while he has the laws of God for his shield in the spiritual combat in which he is about to engage, he finds himself encompassed by a host of sinful passions and desires, mutinying against those laws, and threatening to deprive him of the heavenly kingdom for which he is destined. Could it be said that parents would sufficiently discharge their duty towards this helpless child who should weaken his protection and strengthen the furious enemies by which he is to be assailed? Yet, such would be their conduct were they to abandon him to one of those mixed or promiscuous schools, where the laws of God are generally unheeded, and the worst propensities and passions are strengthened by indulgence. You believe your child was destined for a heavenly kingdom; you are well acquainted with the laws, of which the observance is to secure his safe passage, as well as

[1] Gal. v. 19-21.

with the dangers that threaten to engulf him beneath, and yet, with this knowledge, you place him in a position where the ordinary means of safety are rendered powerless by the overwhelming force of the dangers. You send him to a college from which the majestic form of religion is systematically excluded, and where immodesty, uncleanness, dissensions, quarrels, sects, and the other deeds of the flesh recorded by St. Paul, unawed by the reproving authority of faith, riot in unbounded lawlessness, deriving strength, like material forces from numbers gathered together, and worked into a fermented state from the leaven of the most impure errors. The cruelty of the parents who would thus treat their offspring, as yet but helpless to guard against the danger of their position, would be aptly typified by those parents who sacrificed their children to sanguinary deities, and looked on unmoved or rejoicing at their torments. Is it thus you would educate your son for military service, destined to be continually engaged against the enemies of his country? Who ever heard of faithful and valiant soldiers being sent to be associated with the very enemies they would have afterwards to subdue? Now, we are told by Job that " the life of man is a warfare upon earth,"[1] and of this warfare unquestionably the hottest stage is that of youth, when he is assailed by a tumultuous confederacy of lawless passions and desires; and yet it is in that awful crisis, that period on which, like a pivot, may hang his triumph or defeat, you withdraw from him all the aids of religion, and abandon him to the fury of his enemies. It is high time to discard this gross illusion regarding the education of youth, which makes paternal cruelty or neglect to be mistaken for paternal care. It is not mere science the Catholic youth is to learn at

[1] Job, vii. 1.

school: he is also to learn to practise virtue. It is in vain, as we are told by the pious author of the Imitation of Christ, that he should discourse learnedly about the Trinity, whilst he should be indifferent about offending the Trinity by his transgressions. His education is not a mere lesson to be retained by memory: it is likewise a discipline, a work, a labour, a succession of acts of self-denial, by which a stubborn and headstrong will is to be mastered and subdued. Such is the idea of true education cherished by the Catholic Church, and to which the fashionable votaries of the world are perfect strangers—an education which, like the wrestling in the ancient games, requires self-denial as the first requisite in the combatants, and sustains them in the contest, not with the hope of a laurel chaplet, liable to wither, but with the prospect of a magnificent kingdom, to be won, not by ease and indolence, but by toil and valour, our Saviour Himself saying that "the kingdom of heaven suffereth violence, and the violent bear it away."[1]

That any surprise should be felt at the inflexibility of the Catholic Church on this important point, of a purely religious and Catholic education, is an evident proof of a decay and degeneracy of faith in the present age, below the standard of former times. No matter, be they Catholics or be they Protestants, who advocate this principle or practice of a mixed education, destructive alike of faith and morality, they advocate an experiment which the Catholics and sectaries of former ages would have repudiated. Whilst those sectaries were cut off from the Catholic Church, on the ground of errors on some few points of faith or discipline, they held, at the same time, sound opinions on other points of doctrine. As long as they held those sound opinions they were generally as tenacious of their peculiar systems as the

[1] S. Matt. xi. 12.

Catholics themselves; nor did they ever dream of the anomalous junction of discordant bodies attempted to be formed under the specious name of a common Christianity. No; it was only when every tenet of the Catholic Church was assailed by the fresh succession of insurgents whom the spirit of error had sent forth, and the most sacred mysteries were not spared by their audacious blasphemy, that they bethought themselves of the unhallowed league of all errors combined together under the banners of a mixed and promiscuous education. That those who set no value on any Christian doctrine should adopt this system is not surprising; but it is melancholy that some, to whom religion is still dear, do not tremble at the consequences to which such promiscuous training inevitably leads. But, above all, Protestants, in order to be consistent, should not be parties to this system of a confused teaching. If the distinctions of faith be of so little importance that the amalgamation of all creeds be desirable, why trouble the peace of Europe in the sixteenth century, and break the most sacred ties of domestic affection in separating from the Catholic Church, in which they were reared? Then all were of one fold, as members of the same family, lisping the same faith, and animated by the same spirit of charity, when this harmonious body was rent asunder from a pretended zeal for the purity of sound doctrine. How, then, can it be that the descendants of those, who advocated this great schism, would now be parties to the perverse principle of blending truth and error, and thus throw discredit on the first authors of this separation? If, then, they rushed out of the Church in such eagerness, on account of its fancied or pretended errors, is it not strange that any rigorous Protestants should not now dread a contact with those schools and universities in which errors are nursed and propagated subversive of the very foundations of Christianity? It only shows how far the best and most religious and conscientious have been drifted away by the tide of error since that period. Better far, for the interests of society and religion, that separate training, however erroneous some might be, should be kept up, preserving at the same time a religious sincerity, a hopeful symptom of returning to the truth, than that, by a deadly alliance between error of every kind, truth and virtue and discipline, and, in a word, the Church of God, should be laid prostrate under the ruthless dominion of mere secular and material instruction generally exercised by those to whom any dogmatical creed is obnoxious.

Leave, then, to the professors of infidelity and licentiousness, as well as to mistaken statesmen, who know not what they are doing, the advocacy of so fatal a practice. Let them, under the specious name of a hollow liberality, extinguish in the hearts of youth the principle of charity, which true religion alone inspires; let them, under the pretence of smoothing the asperities of religious prejudice, as it is called, rub off every prominence of religious distinction, until society presents one smooth, and cold, and polished surface, out of which all heat is gone, and in which you look in vain for any religious landmark that would distinguish it from paganism; and when this process of assimilation shall have been effected, to the ruin of all dogma and sense of responsibility, then they may exhibit the triumph of their unhallowed labours in such frightful convulsions as recently prostrated society and order in various parts of Europe. Nor shall such disastrous effects be arrested until religion is restored to that supremacy from which it has been unseated in the important concerns of education. It is not enough that she should address her lessons to the matured but, perhaps, hardened and inaccessible intellect of the man, in the Church: she must have access to the more flexible mind of youth, in the schoolroom, whilst it can be easily moulded to the fairest form through the early infusion of sound doctrine, and imbued with the sweet odour of piety, which it will retain through life. Too long has society suffered from those experiments that would analyse and divide the departments of education, assigning the larger portion to mere material influences, and leaving an inconsiderable part under spiritual control. Too long has the best interest of mankind been suffering from the persevering importunity of the secular power to subject the young ones to this educational dissection, and in its inexorable demands to carry out this cruel operation, we may see realised the beautiful and instructive lesson of the Scripture story regarding the contest between the real and pretended mother of the infant, the State, like the unnatural and cruel claimant of another's offspring, loudly clamouring for the execution of the sentence of Solomon, for the partition of the child, whilst the Church, with the bowels of an affection that reveals the genuine mother, rushes in, entreating to suspend the execution of the murderous decree, and thus convincing the world that it is to her, by whom he was regenerated in baptism unto eternal life, the care of the education, by which eternal life was to be secured, should be particularly entrusted. Too long, however, have her tender entreaties in favour of her offspring been disregarded, and often has she been doomed to the affliction of witnessing their spiritual death through this process of political dissection—an affliction resembling the sorrow celebrated in this day's festival, by which the Mother of God was overwhelmed whilst contemplating the sufferings of her Divine Son expiring on the cross. The sword of grief by which the soul of the Blessed Virgin was then transpierced on witnessing the tragedy of our Redeemer's death, might be deemed an appropriate emblem of the grief of His chaste spouse on seeing her children regenerated in the laver of baptism, the fruit of His passion, torn from her tutelary care, and destroyed in the unnatural attempt to divide them, and to give to the world a portion of that which the Almighty jealously proclaims, in a voice of thunder, should be entirely, exclusively, and unreservedly His own.

The state of Catholic education during a recent disastrous period forms no rule for our guidance; as well might you say that man's aliment, in a time of plenty and prosperity, might be regulated by the privation to which he was obliged to submit in a time of famine. During the long interval to which I refer, the fountains of knowledge were partially poisoned or partially choked, like the wells of the ancient patriarchs in the land of Chanaan, which were filled up with stones while their descendants sojourned in the country of the stranger; on their return to the land of their fathers, they looked for the deep wells which they had dug, and on finding them, laboured to clear away the rubbish, and draw forth the clear and wholesome waters. It is thus the faithful and their pastors are now exerting themselves to remove the obstructions that rendered Catholic education inaccessible, and to open the fountains which, in more disastrous times, had been closed up. You, whose praise is in all the churches, will not fail, I am sure, to contribute effectually to this great work of the education of the young ones, and, in proportion as their numbers increase, to provide for their further accommodation. When I speak of your charity so widely known, I speak not without warrant: it is identified with works and monuments that speak louder than any attestation.

Your contributions, rich and exhaustless as the generous hearts from which they flowed, were, week after week, wafted to our shores, and poured on the bruised and bleeding members of Christ's body, first refreshing them by the unction of your bounty, and then spreading abroad the sweet odour of your good works and of their gratitude. But other sadder and more incontestable monuments tell the charity of this place, in which so many of its pastors laid down their lives, martyrs of mercy to the poor and to the desolate. Any further exhortation to such a people would be superfluous; and I have no doubt but you will be all anxious to secure the prayers of the poor, who, in the strong language of an ancient father, are called the patrons of souls, and equally of the poor little innocents who, refreshed by your bounty, will be the friends through whom you may be received into eternal tabernacles. Amen.

## CHARITY SERMON FOR CHILDREN.

"Fear not, little flock, for it hath pleased your Father to give you a kingdom."—S. LUKE, xii. 32.

To him who, without a superior guidance, looks abroad on society, it would seem that a large portion of God's creatures are abandoned by His providence, and doomed to unmerited and irremediable misfortune. The disproportioned share of the ills and blessings of life would appear a stumbling-block in his way, and his piety would be shocked by the reflection that the laws of justice are often reversed in the capricious distribution. Perplexed by a problem which often eludes the force of reason to resolve, he might entertain a secret distrust in the providence of the Almighty, and exclaim with the Royal Prophet: "My steps had well nigh slipt, because I had a zeal on occasion of the wicked, seeing the prosperity of sinners. . . . And they said, behold these are sinners, and yet, abounding in the world they have obtained riches. Then have I in vain justified my heart, and washed my hands among the innocent, and I have been scourged all the day, and my chastisement hath been in the mornings."[1] The difficulty which he found in exploring this mysterious subject is strongly expressed in the following language: "I studied that I might know this thing. It is a labour in my sight: until I go into the sanctuary of God, and understand concerning their last ends."[2] It was reserved for our Divine Redeemer to smooth the path which was obstructed by many a stumbling-block, not only to the pagans, but to God's chosen people, and accordingly the clear and simple words of my text, pointing to the heavenly inheritance of the little ones of this world, as well as many other passages of similar import, have unveiled to us the mysterious truth which the wisdom of man could not comprehend. To fortify His disciples against the casualties of life, to inspire the humble and forlorn children of the world with confidence, He tells them : "Fear not, little flock, for it hath pleased your Father to give you a kingdom." It is to the development of this important truth I purpose to devote the present discourse, in order to interest you in supporting those who are the heirs of so valuable an inheritance. Yes, in endeavouring to awaken a generous compassion for the children whose cause I advocate, I shall not be so much promoting their interests as the interest and happiness of those who strive, by a sympathy with their lot, to associate themselves with their elevated destiny.

---

[1] Ps. lxxii. 2-14.   [2] Ib. 16, 17.

Notwithstanding the full and explicit revelation by which Christ manifested His wisdom, and in which, to use the words of the Apostle, "We behold the glory of the Lord with face uncovered,"[1] are not there still some weak Christians who are scandalised, that "the ways of the wicked prosper:" persons who might be compared to the Jews, of whom the same Apostle says that the veil which darkened the ancient law was drawn over their hearts, hiding from them the full view of the glories of Christ's kingdom. If there are any who, repining at the inequality of the conditions of mankind, should desire to destroy the mutual dependence of its members on each other, they know not the first law by which the harmony of society is sustained. Where the most perfect order reigns, it is produced by the revolution of dependent bodies round a common centre; and thus, too, in society, God has ordained that its order should be preserved by an endless chain of mutual duties and obligations, connecting together its different parts, and ultimately fixed to the eternal throne of the Almighty. Such is the first link from which the order of society is drawn, and should it once be snapped asunder by the rage of substituting a delusive system of equality in its stead, the shock is instantly felt, the parts, having lost their principle of cohesion, naturally fall asunder, and are broken again into smaller and more repulsive fragments, until this endless partition of individual interests terminates in its dissolution. To obviate such disastrous consequences, God has wisely ordained that all the members of society should tend to a common centre of union, and be cemented by one principle of authority. From the nature of authority springs the necessity of subordination; subordination

---

[1] 2 Cor. iii. 18.

supposes mutual dependence; dependence a variety of ranks rising above each other, and from this diversity of ranks and conditions it necessarily follows that some will abound in affluence and wealth, whilst others are exposed to the chances of destitution. Could we, then, suppose that all the members of society were reduced to the same condition, what would be the result but the realisation of the lively image of St. Paul of a body all feet, or all hands, or all ears, a hideous and misshapen mass, without symmetry or form, not only unsightly to the eye, but, like every monstrous production, bearing the symptoms of a premature destruction. To impeach, then, the wisdom of God for the elevation of a few, would be the same as to arraign the wisdom which constituted the head with the nobler organs to direct the other members of the human frame. Is it, however, to be imagined that I am the advocate of the extremes of wealth and destitution, which so frequently meet our contemplation ? No ; they are the evidence of a diseased state of society, which renders some members emaciated, whilst others are swollen to a disproportioned size by the interception of that general nutriment which should circulate for the common benefit of all. It is not, then, the inequality of the members of the human race but their disproportion that is liable to censure. The one is the natural arrangement of Providence, the other the artificial production of the human passions and the melancholy monument of the tyranny of the stronger over the weaker members which were placed under their protection.

Since, then, there are unfeeling members, dead to every sympathy for their fellow-creatures, has God made no provision for the poor, in protecting them from their hard-heartedness? Yes, He has taken the weaker members under His own special protection. He has addressed Himself to the fears and self-interest of those in whose breasts the feelings of pity might be extinguished, by solemnly assuring us that without charity every other office of religion is vain, and that mercy to others was a necessary condition to obtain salvation. Thus the Prophet Micheas, addressing himself to God, in the name of the sinful people of Judea, in order to ascertain the terms of reconciliation, asks: "What shall I offer to the Lord that is worthy? Wherewith shall I kneel before the High God? Shall I offer holocausts unto Him, and calves of a year old? Shall I give my firstborn for my wickedness, the fruit of my body for the sin of my soul?"[1] After which interrogatories, the Prophet concludes: "I will show thee, O man, what the Lord requireth of thee: verily, to love mercy, and walk solicitous with thy God."[2] And again, when some of the people sent for the priests, to know whether they should sanctify themselves by fasting, as they had hitherto done, the Lord speaks thus, through Zachary: "Say to all the people in the land, when you fasted and mourned, did you keep a fast unto Me: and when you did eat and drink, did you not eat for yourselves and drink for yourselves? Thus, then, saith the Lord of Hosts: judge ye true judgment, and show ye mercy and compassion every man to his brother; and oppress not the widow and the fatherless, and the stranger, and the poor. But they would not hearken, and they made their heart as the stone of adamant, lest they should hear the words which the Lord sent in His Spirit, and accordingly the indignation of the Lord of Hosts fell upon them."[3] Finally, when the people of God, who relied chiefly on their repeated fasts, thus expressed their wonder that His wrath was not still appeased: "Why have we fasted, and Thou hast not regarded?

---

[1] Mich. vi. 6, 7.   [2] Ib. 8.   [3] Zach. vii. 5-12.

Why have we humbled ourselves, and Thou hast not taken notice?" He replies: "Behold, in the day of your fast your own will is found;" continuing in the following beautiful language: "Is this such a fast as I have chosen: for a man to afflict his soul for a day, and spread sackcloth and ashes? Wilt thou call this a fast, and a day acceptable to the Lord? Is not this rather the fast that I have chosen: loose the bands of wickedness; undo the bundles that oppress; let them that are broken go free, and break asunder every burden; deal thy bread to the hungry, and bring the needy and the harbourless into thy home; when thou shalt see one naked, cover him, and despise not thy own flesh. Then," continues the Prophet, "shall thy light break forth as the morning, and thy health shall speedily arise, and thy justice shall go before thy face, and the glory of the Lord will gather thee up. Then shalt thou call, and the Lord shall hear; then shalt thou cry, and He shall say, here I am. When thou shalt pour out thy soul to the hungry, and shalt satisfy the afflicted soul, then shall thy light rise up in darkness, and thy darkness shall be as the noonday. And the Lord will give thee rest continually, and will fill thy soul with brightness, and deliver thy bones, and thou shalt be like a watered garden, whose waters shall not fail."[1]

After such repeated and cogent exhortations to mercy, you cannot be indifferent to the fulfilment of this virtue. The writings of the Apostles abound with similar exhortations. "Loving one another," says St. Paul, "with the charity of brotherhood . . . rejoice with them that rejoice; weep with them that weep, being of one mind one towards another."[2] It is this view of the Apostle that will teach the rich why they received their wealth,

---

[1] Isa. lviii. 5-11.   [2] Rom. xii., 10, 15.

and reconcile the poor to their condition; and while it affords instruction to both, will illustrate the mysterious ways of Providence, whilst it impresses on the poor that, as in the human body there are members whose office is more toilsome, it teaches the rich that they, as fellow-members, are bound to alleviate their sufferings. Let not the children of affluence fancy that they are solitary beings, unconnected with the rest of society; nor let them fancy it is through neglect God has consigned to poverty so many of their fellow-creatures. No; but because He reserves them for a richer inheritance. Besides the evidence of this truth furnished by my text, St. James writes: " Hearken, my dearest brethren, hath not God chosen the poor of this world, rich in faith and heirs of the kingdom which God hath promised to those that love Him."[1] If, therefore, their lot is suffering, it is because they are destined to tread in the path which Jesus Christ has trodden, and because, as He assured the mother of the sons of Zebedee, we must first drink of the cup of His afflictions, if we wish to participate in the honours of His kingdom. What! Think you that the Redeemer, whose power stretched out the heavens in all their magnificence, and who still clothes the lilies of the field with glory more than that of Solomon, would have abandoned His own members to unremediable destitution? Could he not, after the example of Elias, in his pilgrimage to the holy mountain, sustain their faltering steps as they journey on through life, or multiply their scanty meal, like the loaves in the desert? Yes; why, then, has He plunged them in poverty? In mercy to the rich, whom, as the Gospel says, He has appointed stewards, to give them food in due season. Yes, without this opportunity, what means would have

[1] S. James, ii. 5.

been left to the rich of expiating their own sins, or of obtaining the divine mercy? Possessed of the gifts of fortune, which, if abused, only stimulate their sensual appetites, they might, like the rich voluptuary in the Gospel, repose in the enjoyments of this world until, like him, the torments of hell might awaken them from their dream of guilty dissipation. To save them from such a fate, spectacles of woe are continually presented to their eyes, reminding them that they are but the accountable stewards of their wealth; while the Gospel exhorts them to make unto themselves friends of the mammon of iniquity, assuring them that their mercy to the poor will be the condition and the measure of God's mercy to them. What a union of mercy and of wisdom in the economy of God! Foreknowing the advantages of afflictions, He has ordained that a large portion of His elect should be cast into its furnace, in order that their virtue might be purified, while, like the Hebrew confessors of old, they walked unhurt and triumphant through its fiery ordeal. And again, to counteract the danger of riches, He has ordained that the superfluous wealth, which either swells the tide of our passions, or, if suffered to stagnate, only engenders corruption, should be diffused through channels of benevolence, possessing the double virtue of washing away our guilt, whilst it relieves the children of misfortune. God has thus made the rich the ministers of His temporal, and the poor of His spiritual graces. Nay, He has made the wealthy more indebted to the poor than the poor to the wealthy, since the one, by giving that which the moth may corrupt, or any casualty take away, receives in return, as St. Bernard remarks, the friendship of those who are pronounced the heirs of the kingdom of heaven. He has thus wisely intertwined the destinies of the poor and the rich, that, as St. Paul says, there might be " an equality, from the abundance of the one supplying the wants of the other."[1] Sublime and merciful Spirit of the Christian religion, which hast descended from heaven! how illustrative of the origin from which Thou art derived, accommodating Thy graces to the different conditions in life, leading the poor man to heaven by patience, and the rich man by charity; raising what is low by a participation of what is elevated, warming what is cold, and dilating what is contracted; smoothing the inequalities of life, without destroying its gradations; fitting the different parts of society to the peaceful discharge of their respective functions, harmonising by grace the discord which nature would excite among the members of Christ's body, and cementing the head with the remotest members by the universal circulation of the vital principle of charity.

It is to the practice of this heavenly virtue your attention is now solicited. Among the various channels through which this charity may be dispensed, I know none more useful than those of religious education. In rearing the youth of the country to habits of industry and virtue, you are relieving society from the evils which ignorance and idleness generate. You become at once the benefactors of society and the co-operators of their salvation. If youth, then, be the season to mould the infant mind to those habits of virtue which its manhood will not outgrow, can there be a work more worthy of the charity of the human heart than to plant those seeds of virtue, which must thrive under the influence of a Christian education? You cannot, then, require any lengthened exhortation to animate you to push forward

[1] 2 Cor. viii. 14

the work you have so auspiciously commenced. It is not necessary for me to stop to remove those obstructions which a cold and calculating selfishness would interpose before the generous current of your feelings. Tell me not that you have rents and taxes to pay. I know it. But if, as S. Chrysostom remarks, the temporal penalties you would incur by neglecting those debts make you so punctual in discharging them, shall not the fear of the eternal punishment to which you would expose yourself make you solicitous to pay the debt of charity? Tell me not that you have many children to provide for. "Alas!" says St. Augustine, "how many unnatural fathers are there who, while they affect to provide for their children, are only treasuring up their children's destruction and their own: men who mistake their avarice for a paternal piety, thus indulging the meanest of the vices which, though called in Scripture the root of all evil, is never visited with due execration, because it passes for a prudent thriftness." Avarice, a vice which, according to St. Gregory, runs counter to nature itself by gathering strength and inveteracy from that decay which extinguishes every other passion—a vice which spoils every virtue, shrivelling up the soul of its victim into a sordid selfishness, leaving him a solitary through life, without the benefit of his self-denial, alike incapable of feeling or reflecting the happiness of society until he dies, cursed by many, blessed by none; nay, covered with the curses of his own children, whom, as St. Augustine says, he would disinherit, could he carry his mammon with him to the grave. If, then, you have many children, you have, says St. Cyprian, given so many hostages to heaven; and you must labour to be faithful to the redemption of your pledges. Forget not, then, by your charity to present a peace-offering for their sake. "For by such sacrifices," says the Apostle, "God's favour is obtained."[1] You will thus become, like Job, the high-priests of your own families, "who, rising up early, offered holocausts for each of his sons, lest, perhaps, they had sinned and offended God in their hearts."[2]

Having thus endeavoured to show that the usual apologies which are offered ought in reality to be rather incentives to charity, surely you require no further stimulus to animate you in your career of benevolence, or to induce you to water the seed which yourselves have planted, and to cherish their growth until they thrive and flourish by your cultivation. Yes, the little children are so many shoots growing on that portion of His vineyard which Christ has let out to you to be cultivated, and on you depends, this day, whether their opening blossom shall be rudely blown away by the storm, or whether, protected by your care and watered by your bounty, each one of those goodly shoots shall spring forth into the majestic tree mentioned by the Psalmist, planted by the running stream, spreading forth its leaves to the sun and clothed with fruit in due season. Which of those images are you determined to realise? Good and evil are now before you. Choose, then, between good and evil. Whether will you suffer them to languish by your neglect or thrive by your bounty? Choose, then, between the alternatives of vice and virtue, and decide whether you are to contemplate the picture of happiness or of desolation. To you those tender and helpless innocents turn this day, entreating you by all the ties of our common nature, nay, adjuring you by all the charity of our common Redeemer, to rescue His members from that doom of sin and misery which must await them, unless saved by your interposi-

[1] Heb. xiii. 16.  [2] Job, i. 5.

tion. In the language of the Prophet, they cry to the Father of mercies, "Remember, O Lord, what is come upon us; consider and behold our reproach. We are become orphans without a father; our mothers are as widows."[1] Go, then, forlorn of earth, all the enclosures that guarded your innocence are neglected; all the fences that were drawn around your virtue are fallen; go, then, without a friend to protect or a fence to guard you, to familiarise your hearts to vice and your ears to profaneness, the victims, perhaps, of some hard-hearted libertines, who, like the hoary hypocrites mentioned in Scripture, inflict on society the vices which they feign would punish, and which they only falsely deplore, until, plunging deeper and deeper into guilt, you drag with you into the abyss into which you are fast rushing the unfortunate individuals who, in the strong language of St. Athanasius, were guilty of your murder by criminally neglecting to arrest your melancholy career.

But no; your Heavenly Father has heard the voice of your lamentation, and He has provided for your comfort and support in the hearts of the benevolent. Yes, He has provided for their support. For the Prophet assures us "that they shall not hunger nor thirst; for He that is merciful to them shall be their shepherd; and, at the fountain of waters He shall give them to drink."[2] And what are those fountains of waters out of which they shall drink? They are the hearts of the merciful which the Wise Man likens unto fountains whose waters shall not fail. Open, then, those fountains of mercy with which God has enriched you, and let the desolate souls of your fellow-creatures rejoice. Fear not that your charity will exhaust your resources; for the hearts of the merciful are as fountains of water. Touch them not, you perceive no increase. Draw from them, you feel no

[1] Lam. v. 1, 2, 3.   [2] Isai. xlix. 10.

diminution. Fortunes may be wasted by luxury, families may be ruined by dissipation; one house may succeed another with the quickness of the clouds that are seen shuffling on our mountains. But who are they of whom the Prophet says that he saw them exalted like the cedars of Lebanon, and lo! when he passed by, he could could not discover a trace of their existence. Were they the merciful? No; but the profligate oppressors of the human race, whose memory perished in malediction from the earth like a vision of the night or a vapour of the morning. Whereas, it is said of the charitable, "These were men of mercy, whose goodly deeds have not failed, good things continue with their seed and are a holy inheritance. Their children, for their sakes, remain for ever; their seed and their glory shall not be forsaken; their bodies are buried in peace, and their name liveth unto generation and generation."[1] Do you, then, by your goodly deeds and works of mercy, be equally instrumental in bringing down the blessings of God on your posterity. You will thus faithfully discharge the trust which God has placed in your hands as stewards of His property. To use the familiar language of our Redeemer, by administering to the little ones food in due season you will be making unto yourselves friends of the mammon of iniquity. Their prayers will ascend to heaven in your behalf, and Isaias assures us "that God will not despise the prayers of the fatherless." And when the day shall come, when, stretched on the bed of death, your spiritual enemies shall surround you, and straiten you on every side, then the Lord Himself, because you have "understood concerning the needy and the poor, shall help you on your bed of sorrow."[2] Yes, when presenting the hideous catalogue of your sins

---

[1] Ecclus. xliv. 10-14.    [2] Ps. xl. 1-4.

your enemy shall strive to surround you with darkness and despair; the charity of this day shall open a vista of light and of hope through which you shall behold the prayers of those children like the ministering spirits, seen in the vision of the patriarch, ascending to heaven, and bearing to the throne of the Almighty their supplications for your sins, and descending again with the consoling assurances of forgiveness and mercy. Amen.

## CHARITY SERMON FOR WIDOWS AND ORPHANS.

"Shut up alms in the heart of the poor; better than the shield of the mighty and better than the spear, it shall fight for thee against thy enemy."— ECCLUS. xxix. 15, 16, 17.

OF all the duties which it is incumbent on man to discharge, there is none more frequently or forcibly inculcated in the inspired writings than that of mercy to the poor. In the Old Testament we find that the destitute were placed under the peculiar protection of the law of Moses, and in no instance does the wisdom of that legislator appear more conspicuous than in the regulations by which he provided for their necessities. In the lives of the ancient patriarchs their compassionate tenderness for the afflicted is recorded by the inspired writers as a peculiar topic of praise; and in the last instructions which the holy Tobias bequeathed to his son, he recommends the practice of mercy as he valued his acceptance with the Almighty. In the words of my text, its efficacy is set forth in the most consolatory language, assuring us that in the hour of our need it will bring us more aid than the arms of the mighty; and that when human strength will decay it shall be the shield of our protection. It was reserved, however, for the Christian religion to promulgate to all mankind the necessity of this virtue in language too clear to be mistaken, and to develop it into further obligations which were hitherto but little known. It was reserved for that Gospel which, in a peculiar manner, was preached for the benefit of the poor, to take that forlorn class under its special guardianship, and to spread its cheering and vivifying influence over those wastes of human misery where it was never felt before. Yes, those who were hitherto depised as the outcasts of the human race have been ennobled by its merciful spirit in the eyes of mankind, and the wealthy of every age have striven by their charities to earn the prayers of those who are peculiarly favoured of heaven. Not content with erecting asylums of charity for every species of misfortune with which man is afflicted, the Catholic Church has, by its emissaries of mercy, visited the abodes of the widow and the orphan, and descended into the prisons to light the dreary dungeons of the victims of crime. It is to co-operate with this merciful spirit you are called upon this day, and brought to assist in bringing hope and comfort into the cheerless mansions in which many of your fellow-creatures are immured.

Had man retained his original innocence we should not witness those extremes of power and dependence, of enjoyment and privation with which the face of society is so much disfigured. Perfect equality would then have reigned among the happy children of the same indulgent Father, with the exception only of those claims to veneration which are inspired by age or merit, and which the human heart never refuses to superior wisdom or virtue. But the introduction of sin destroyed this primitive simplicity and innocence of man, and the act of disobedience by which he aspired to knowledge and to freedom was the cause which plunged him into the depth of ignorance and servitude. Thus, then, man is born the victim of misery, and the violence of his passions has served but to aggravate the evils of his bitter inheritance. Without some shield to protect him against the casualties of life or the tyranny of other men's passions, he should be the most helpless and wretched of God's creatures, and accordingly we find that in the days of paganism, notwithstanding the humanising influence of letters and the enactments of legislation, the greater portion of mankind languished under the despotism of the worst passions of the human heart. The happiness of the many was sacrificed to the cruel caprices of the few, the rights of humanity were utterly neglected, and the ignorance of the pagans in matters of faith was equalled by the corruption and hardheartedness of their morality. "Proud and dissolute," as they are represented by St. Paul, "full of iniquity and covetousness, without affection, without mercy."[1] The rich treated the poor with all the scorn and contumely of a degraded caste, converting them into instruments to minister to their own appetites. Retaining of humanity nought save its form, all the feelings of nature were trodden out of their hearts by habits of oppression, until the unhappy victims of their cruelty might have cursed, with Job, the hour of their nativity, and have wished the erasure from the records of time of the day on which they were born.

Not so among the happy people who, amidst the general corruption, had preserved the knowledge of

---

[1] Rom. i. 31.

God's laws. Like the merciful Being from whom it emanated, the Jewish law breathed the tenderest compassion towards the poor and the afflicted. Nay, a portion of the tithes of every family was reserved for their relief; and in gathering in the harvest the widow and the orphan were not forgotten. "When thou hast reaped the corn in thy field, and hast forgot and left a sheaf, thou shalt not return to take it away: but thou shalt suffer the stranger, the fatherless, and the widow, to take it away: that the Lord thy God may bless thee in all the works of thy hands. If thou have gathered the fruit of thy olive-trees, thou shalt not return to gather whatsoever remaineth on the trees, but shalt leave it for the stranger, for the fatherless, and the widow. If thou make the vintage of thy vine-yard, and thou shalt not gather the clusters that remain, but they shall be for the stranger, the fatherless, and the widow."[1] Such is the charitable solicitude that was recommended by the Old Law for relieving the miseries of our fellow-creatures. Recommended, have I said ?—no, but commanded, since the passages I have cited are concluded by this emphatic precept, which awakens compassion by the recollection of similar misery, " Remember that thou also wast a bondsman in Egypt, and, therefore, I command thee to do this thing."

And has the Almighty abandoned the care of the widow and the orphan under the New Law? After having guarded them with such tender solicitude under a less perfect covenant, can we suppose that He has neglected their protection under the Christian dispensation? No; He who lived with the poor, conversed with the poor; and whose sufferings engaged His most active sympathies while on earth did not forget them ere

[1] Deut. xxiv. 19-21.  [2] Ib. 22.

His ascension into heaven. He therefore entrusted them to the care of the Church, that chaste spouse which He purchased with His blood, and whose breasts, to use a lively illustration of a holy father, are the exhaustless source of the support of His children. Charity, then, comes to us not only recommended by the grateful feelings which it diffuses over the human heart, but enforced by the positive precepts of our Divine Redeemer, and sanctioned by His entire authority. If you doubt it, hear the awful sentence which Christ will pronounce upon the reprobate in the last day: "Go, ye cursed, into everlasting fire prepared for the devil and his angels." And why this tremendous sentence? "Because," He says, "I was hungry and you gave Me not to eat; thirsty, and you gave Me not to drink; a stranger, and you took Me not in; naked, and you clothed Me not; sick and in prison, and you did not visit Me." And the reprobate shall exclaim: "Lord, when did we see Thee hungry, or thirsty, or a stranger, or naked, or sick, or in prison, and did not minister to Thee?" Then He shall answer, pointing to the poor: "Amen, I say to you, as long as you did it not to one of those least ones, neither did you do it to Me."[1] Can you think any longer that to succour the distressed and to assuage their afflictions is not a precept, or that it is what you are at liberty to fulfil, or to violate? " I might think so, too," says St. Gregory of Nazianzen, " were I not terrified by the language with which Christ shall confound the reprobate, since that cannot be any other than a precept, for the omission of which they are lost for ever."

Let those, then, who arraign the dispensations of heaven stand before the tribunal of Christ, and learn whether God Himself could have more mercifully pro-

[1] S. Matt. xxv. 41-45.

vided for the wants of the poor than by transferring on the rich the obligation of relieving them, under the awful penalty of their own reprobation. Or could the Redeemer breathe a more tender compassion for their lot than by identifying them with Himself, and pronouncing that He was relieved or insulted by the mercy or the cruelty that was shown to His creatures? In pronouncing the verdict of the reprobate, Christ alludes only to their hard-heartedness, assigning it as the sole cause of their condemnation: "Because I was hungry and you gave Me not to eat." As if He were to say: Because the poor, who were the members of my body, were hungry and you gave them not to eat, thirsty and you gave them not to drink, strangers and you took them not in, sick and in prison and you did not visit them; go into everlasting fire: go and abide by the sentence which you have pronounced upon others. It is written: "With the same measure you shall mete to others, it shall be measured to you in return;"[1] and as your unfeeling hearts were strangers to the kind impulses of mercy, its heavenly Spirit shall never mitigate the sentence which pronounces you accursed for all eternity.

You perceive, then, that if God requires of you to do charity to the poor, it is less for the purpose of relieving their temporal misfortunes than of averting the sentence of your own eternal ruin. It matters but little what this obligation may be called: it is of little importance whether it may be named justice or charity. It is sufficient for us to know that it springs from the will of the Almighty, and that it cannot be violated without forfeiting our own happiness. Let none, then, boast of the profession of the Christian religion, without the practice of this virtue, since without its influence the

[1] S. Matt. vii. 2.

soul of religion is gone. "For religion, pure and undefiled with God," says the Apostle, "is to visit the fatherless and widows in their tribulation."[1] If this were not true religion, if mercy were not an imperative duty, the neglect of which shall condemn the wealthy of this world, what means the awful denunciations of the same Apostle: "Go now, ye rich men: weep and howl for your miseries that shall come upon you. Your riches are putrified, and your garments are moth-eaten. Your gold and silver is rusted, and the rust of them shall be for a testimony against you, and shall eat your flesh as fire. . . . You have feasted upon earth, and in luxuries you have nourished your hearts in the day of slaughter. . . . You have stored up to yourselves wrath against the last days?"[2] With what reason, then, does St. Paul exhort Timothy: "To charge the rich of the world not to be high-minded, nor hope in uncertain riches, but in the living God, who giveth us abundantly all things to enjoy. To do good, to be rich in good works, to distribute readily, to communicate to others, to lay up a store for themselves, a good foundation against the time to come, that they may obtain true life?"[3] Let it not be imagined that we magnify the virtue of charity beyond its proportioned limits, and forget the other virtues that are so strongly recommended. No; St. Paul expressly tells us: "He that loveth his neighbour hath fulfilled the law;" and after enumerating the commandments, he concludes: "And if there be any other commandment, it is comprised in this word: Thou shalt love thy neighbour as thyself."[4] What wonder, then, that the efficacy of charity should be so much magnified, when, if well regulated, it comprises the other commandments? Nay; Christ Himself,

[1] S. James, i. 27.   [3] 1 Tim. vi. 17, 18, 19.
[2] S. James, v. 1-5.   [4] Rom. xiii. 8, 9.

in crowning the virtues of the just on the Last Day, alludes only to their works of mercy, not because their other virtues were of no value, but because their charity embraced them all; and when time shall be no more, the other virtues shall be lost in the depths of charity, like those magnificent floods that are seen distinct and separated through the regions which they traverse, until their names and properties are mingled together in the immensity of the ocean.

Those, then, to whom God has given the gifts of fortune are called on, as they value His favour and their own happiness, generously to share a portion of their wealth with the indigent objects that claim your compassion. They are children of the same Father; they have been purchased by the same redemption; and, after being purified by the trying afflictions of this life, they are destined for the same everlasting inheritance. Without the guilt of extravagance or dissipation, many of them have been reduced to their present forlorn and desolate condition by a train of misfortunes which it was not in their power to control. The consequence is, that they must perish or be rescued from their fate by your seasonable interposition. Let not your charity, then, be confined to words: it must manifest itself by the more unequivocal proofs of practical deeds of mercy. Insult them not by such ironical commiseration as that mentioned by the Apostle: "If a brother or sister be naked and want daily food, and one of you say to them: Go in peace, be you warmed and filled; yet give them not those things that are necessary for the body, what shall it profit?"[1] Yet such would be your conduct if, with a verbal admission of the existence of distress and much apparent sympathy for human suffering, you were

---

[1] S. James, ii. 15, 16.

to withhold all practical relief from its victims. Follow the advice of the Wise Man, who tells us: "Honour the Lord with thy substance, and thy barns shall be filled with abundance."[1] Do not expend in the service of your passions the wealth which you received for the nobler purpose of charity and benevolence, lest you should incur the reproach of the prophet Osee to the unfortunate city of Jerusalem: "And she did not know that I gave her corn, and wine, and oil, and multiplied her silver and gold, which they have used in the service of Baal. Therefore will I return, and take away my corn in its season, and my wine in its season, and I will set at liberty my wool, which covered her disgrace. . . . And I will cause all her mirth to cease, and her sabbaths and her solemnities."[2] What an awful warning to those who may have hitherto forgotten the end for which wealth was given, ministering to their vanity out of the just possessions of the poor! The just possessions of the poor! Yes; startle not at the position, since I should repeat a large portion of the inspired writings in developing still further this important truth. "Defraud not the poor of alms,"[3] says the Wise Man, to show the injustice of which we are guilty by the detention of what is necessary for their relief.

But I shall not detain your patience longer. I shall trust to the impression which the simple and heart-rending consciousness of the distress of your fellow-creatures must make upon you. You who breathe the wholesome air of heaven, and value such a blessing, think of the doom of those who, for want of necessary raiment, are doomed to the solitude of their chambers, inhaling a noxious atmosphere. You who revel in the luxuries of life, or, at least, who have never felt the

---

[1] Prov. iii. 9, 10.    [2] Osee, ii. 8-11.    [3] Eccl. iv. 1.

privations of its enjoyments, stop your ears for a moment to the sounds of merriment that charm you into a forgetfulness of other's woes, and listen to the solitary sighs of the widow or the feeble cries of the desolate orphans, that are idly wasted within the walls of their melancholy dungeons. Tear from your eyes that film of vanity and trifling, which, to use an idea of the inspired writings, gives to man an erroneous estimate of things by fascinating his senses, and descend in spirit into the varied recesses which misery inhabits in her most appalling forms, and tell me then, can you sit with an unfeeling insensibility at the board of luxury, and shut your heart against the distress that surrounds you? No; such opportunities of mercy cannot be rejected without serious danger. Should you leave the present objects that solicit your charity unrelieved, you risk the loss of God's grace—nay, what the avaricious may value more, the loss of that very wealth which they fear would be diminished by their bounty. What! lose their wealth by the very gripe with which they strive to secure it? Yes; and as St. Chrysostom well remarks: "Were we favoured with a view of the secret engines that sap the most prosperous fortunes, we should find the sighs, and tears, and imprecations of the poor among the most frequent and efficient instruments of their ruin." But why quote St. Chrysostom when the inspired writer tells us: "Injuries and wrongs will waste riches, and the house that is very rich shall be brought to nothing by pride: so the substance of the proud shall be rooted out. The prayer out of the mouth of the poor shall reach the ears of God, and judgment shall come for him speedily."[1] Your fortune, then, instead of suffering from your charity, is, if you are deficient in

---

[1] Ecclus. xxi. 5, 6.

this virtue, in danger of being transferred to more faithful stewards. "Make, then, to yourselves friends of the mammon of iniquity, that, when you shall fail, they may receive you into eternal tabernacles."[1] The poor are called by St. Gregory the porters of heaven, and you may justly fear that your prayers will not find favour with the Almighty if you close your ears against their eloquent supplications. Perhaps you may think this is an assertion not sufficiently warranted. If you think so, the Book of Proverbs will tell you: "He that stoppeth his ears against the cry of the poor, shall also cry himself, and not be heard."[2] Stop, then, your ears; if you will, you stop the ears of the Almighty against your own prayers; dole out a miserable pittance of relief; and if you have an iron heart, that never gave back a single tone of compassion or of mercy, go and boast of its firmness; but while you triumph in your tranquillity, recollect, too, that, like the treacherous calm that precedes the storm, your tranquillity may be but the prelude of your reprobation and your fall. Your prayers, then, alone will not be sufficient: they will not reach heaven without some medium to convey them; and if they are compared to the smoke of the incense which is grateful to the Lord, good works may be called the censers which send forth their odour to heaven. Recollect the heavenly vision in which Cornelius was assured that his conversion was owing to his prayers and his alms that were remembered in the sight of God.[3] You, too, may have sinned, and may need reconciliation. Enlist, therefore, the powerful suffrages of the friends of the Almighty in your behalf; and as the prayers of the people had the effect of saving the life of Jonathan, which was forfeited to the law, so shall the united

---

[1] S. Luke, xvi. 9.   [2] Prov. xxi. 13.   [3] Acts, x. 31.

supplications of those you shall have relieved go forth to heaven, and change the sentence of your condemnation into one of merciful acquittal. Amen.

---

## CHARITY SERMON FOR FEMALE PENITENTS.

"Deliver them that are led to death, and those that are drawn to death forbear not to deliver."—PROV. xxiv. 11.

WHATEVER might be the difference of opinion regarding the claims of other objects to the sympathies and active benevolence of the charitable, no one will dispute their titles to pity who have been conducted by their misfortunes to the very brink of death. A child abandoned to the miseries and perils of orphanage is an object that excites a just and lively compassion, and an appeal on the dangers that beset its tender and unprotected age is sure to engage all the efforts of the affluent and the charitable in providing the enclosures of education for its protection. The cries of distress in any shape or form are never addressed in vain to the Christian who has not extinguished by habitual cruelty that fellow-feeling which spontaneously prompts us to the relief of our suffering brethren. If misery, then, to use the thought of an eloquent pagan, displays, wherever it presents itself in human form, its title-deeds to the kindred sympathy and solace of every human heart, what must be the paramount claims of those objects who are victims to whatever is at once most pitiable and most frightful in human wretchedness? Virtuous and industrious families, fallen from comfort by sudden reverses of fortune, and pining in solitude, while a sense of dignity and shame conceals their sorows and their tears to their tenements of woe, are doubtless objects which should melt the most obdurate with compassion. Their case is not still comparable to that of my unfortunate clients. Though doomed to misery, they are not led to death; though consigned to anguish, they have still the consolation to think that it will soon pass away; whilst those for whom I claim your interposition have been led to death, and, if not rescued, must be again drawn to that death which, instead of bringing oblivion to their misery, will only awake that sense of torment which shall last for ever.

In the brief but comprehensive sentence, Do unto others as you would wish to be done by,[1] impressed on the human heart, and again revealed by the Redeemer in letters of light to the whole world, have the moralists and preachers of every age found a fruitful and inexhaustible theme when enforcing the obligations of charity. To the same divine precept shall I be content to confine myself in directing your attention to the claims of my penitents. Let the most obdurate and callous among my hearers suppose that when he first set out on his journey through life, when his steps were as yet feeble, and while he was unacquainted with the perils of the way, that he had the misfortune of falling in with robbers, who stripped him of the robes with which he was clothed in baptism, and after having rioted on the spoils of which they rifled him, abandoned him in the midst of the road, covered from head to foot with the wounds which their cruelty had inflicted. Suppose that, in that fallen and forlorn condition, when unable to rise or make any exertions of his own, some hard-hearted creatures were to pass, who, without any feeling for his lot, pursued their course, leaving

[1] S. Luke, vi. 31.

him to that inevitable death to which, under such circumstances, he should soon fall a victim;—what, I ask you, would be the judgment which you would pronounce upon such an individual? Would it not be that of our Redeemer: "With what measure you mete, it shall be measured to you again;"[1] and as mercy is the reward of him that "showeth mercy," would not your heart, by the same just process of reasoning, consign to a different doom him who was steeled against its divine influence? Yes; and this judgment, however severe, would be but a development of that simple truth with which I preface this discourse, and which, as far as regards our conduct to others, may be the perfect standard of Christian morality. It is in vain, then, for the cruel and the hard-hearted to endeavour to soothe their consciences by the fancy that they have been guilty of no injustice, if that conscience reproves them with having refused to the distress of others that measure of merciful relief which they should have reasonably expected in their own.

What, think you, was the amount of the crime against which the Royal Prophet thundered this dire imprecation: "May his children be fatherless, and his wife a widow?" What was the additional guilt that called forth this additional malediction: "Let his children be carried about, vagabonds, and be cast out of their dwellings?" Not content with this measure of vengeance, the Prophet still proceeds: "May there be none to pity or none to help his fatherless offspring." As if the evils of one generation were too limited for the enormity of his sins, he pursues his memory to after times: "May his posterity be cut off, and in one generation his name be blotted out." After pursuing his posterity until they utterly disappeared, and finding

[1] S. Matt. vii. 2.

nothing in the descending series on which to wreak his revenge, he returns back upon the innocent authors of his existence: "May the iniquity of his father be remembered in the sight of the Lord, and let not the sin of his mother be blotted out." It was not, however, enough that his sins should once experience the anger of the Almighty; but as if they were possessed of fuel for eternal vengeance, he adds: "May they be before the Lord continually."[1] What crime is it of which the Prophet wrought up the punishment to such a climax of horror? It must, you will say, be incest, or murder, or sacrilege, or blasphemy, or some dark and mysterious combination of sins that are not only unutterable, but from the idea of which the imagination recoils. No; it was neither incest, nor murder, nor blasphemy, nor sacrilege; but "because he remembered not to do mercy." What, then, must be the enormity of that guilt which could thus have compelled the most tender-hearted of all the prophets to ransack all the treasures of God's vengeance—nay, to explore the past as well as the future—and to gather, as if into one burning focus, all that was scorching in God's wrath, and to fix it with a collected intensity on the head of the devoted wretch who, without any deliberate cruelty being imputed to him, had merely forgotten to do mercy?

Again, the Prophet Osee, pursuing the same train of thought, says, in the name of the Almighty: "For I desired mercy, and not sacrifice,"[2] to show us that it is in vain we strive by all the solemnity of divine worship to appease the wrath of heaven, if we refuse to show mercy to our own fellow-creatures. How beautifully and feelingly is the same truth unfolded in that instructive parable in which the Redeemer of the world exhibits the cruelty of the man who brought his fellow-

[1] Ps. cviii. 9-15.  [2] Osee, vi. 6.

servant to a rigorous account for the debt he owed him, after receiving from their common master a generous remission of his own. The master's indignation was naturally kindled against a wretch who refused to extend to another the kind compassion which he himself had experienced; and he concludes his reproaches on his cruelty by the touching language: "And should you not have pity on your own fellow-servant?"[1]

But it is needless to multiply further instances in enforcing the obligations of compassion and of mercy. No; I shall not exhaust your patience in illustrating a truth which cannot be controverted without controverting every part of that twofold covenant which God has given to man, since whatever may be the clearness or obscurity of Scripture, the characters of mercy are like illuminated letters, striking the reader at the first glance, whilst they cast their lustre over every page of the sacred volume—a truth which, with more force than writing, speaks through every monument of benevolence and mercy which Christianity has profusely strewn over the face of the earth—nay, a truth that is so inscribed on the nature of man that it cannot be erased until you tear out at the same time the human heart, with these bowels of mercy which God planted there at the moment of his creation. No; I shall not detain you by any lengthened disquisition on a truth which meets the eye wherever it looks abroad, lest I should resemble those tedious writers who would fain conduct us by their feeble lights to the throne of the Divinity, whilst His glory, in the language of the Psalmist, breaks forth in the splendour of creation. No; the obligations of mercy admit of no debate: it is not a subject of doubt or controversy; its rights are respected amidst the rage of disputation; it is, perhaps, the only solitary virtue on which the most

[1] S. Matt. xviii. 33.

adverse have covenanted to agree; and surely it is a consoling reflection that, amidst the strife of contending tenets, this daughter of heaven is seen traversing the world, revered by persons of every creed; and, while she goes round performing the offices of mediation, like those heralds of peace whose persons are deemed sacred amidst the wars of contending nations, still breathing peace over the troubled elements of society, and striving to mitigate the angry passions which she cannot entirely subdue.

Having briefly endeavoured to impress upon your minds the cogent obligations of mercy, it is, I trust, unnecessary to detain you long by its obvious application. Through this zeal and piety of your pastors, seconded by the pious generosity of the faithful,[1] an asylum has been established for reclaiming the fallen; and you surely will not fail to uphold an institution in which their shattered virtue may be repaired? Impressed with its advantages, and the consciousness of their own danger, others are eager for admittance within its enclosures, and demanding, with all the importunity of souls, sensible that they are perishing, to be rescued from the gulf into which they are about to be plunged. With all the fervour of primitive times, they are thronging round the porch of the temple, and entreating you, with all the eloquence of tears, that its portals should be thrown open for their admission. Repulse them not, but rather stretch out a helping hand to assist their return, for probably they shall never be able to entreat you more. No; the vessel of their innocence has been long since wrecked; and while numbers of their companions have sunk before their eyes, they have been tossed upon the breakers, and at length drifted to

---

[1] Westport, where the sermon was preached.—ED.

the shore, where they are seen with wasted strength grappling with some rock, and with fainting voice imploring succour; and will you imitate the barbarians, who, instead of rescuing them from the perils of the deep, loosen their feeble and precarious hold, and fling them into the precipice? Shall it be adduced as an apology for such cruelty, that they, as having first exposed themselves to danger, are not entitled to compassion? Shall it be advanced by those who fancy that they are zealous for the glory of God, because they have no feeling for the weakness of their fellow-creatures, that they are not objects of pity, since they strayed through the perverseness of their own will? Perhaps they have. So did Magdalene. They have extravagantly wasted a stock of virtue which a more prudent and reserved line of conduct would have improved. And so did the prodigal son, who strayed from his father's house and squandered all his substance. They have, perhaps, knowingly and deliberately violated the precepts of the law, and incurred all its penalties. So did the woman found guilty of adultery, whose transgression the Redeemer rebuked by telling her to sin no more. Find me one who himself needs not mercy, and let him tear up again the wounds which penance has nearly closed by the sharpness of his reproaches. But are there really such as are guilty of the sin against the Holy Ghost as to envy God's creatures the pardon of their transgressions? If there be any who, with the ungenerous disposition with which the young man in the Gospel repined at the joy with which the father cheered his brother's return, repine at the favours with which penitents are healed; let them at once arraign the Almighty for having pardoned the thief upon the cross, and for having converted the persecuting Saul into a vessel of election. Let them, with the malignity of the Jews, entertain rancour towards Jesus for having raised Lazarus from the tomb, and restored her lost child to the widow of Naim. Let him at once clothe the Almighty with terror and with darkness, which would appal the human heart and chill its warmest affections, while he strips Him of the endearing title of Father and the corresponding attribute of mercy, without which the world would have been a hideous mass of corruption out of which virtue had departed, were it not for that heavenly Spirit of mercy that is always moving over the abyss, and quickening it with the warmth of life by the vigorous infusion of its graces.

But I will not do that injustice to this congregation as to suppose that there is one individual actuated by the feelings to which I have given utterance. On the contrary, I believe that you are individuals whose generous natures are so improved by the influence of religion as to melt into tenderness at the misfortune of others, and to make sacrifices of your own comforts in your endeavours to relieve it. Yes; I know I am speaking to Christians, who feel, with St. James, that religion pure and unspotted with God is to "visit the fatherless and widow in their tribulation."[1] Such are they who solicit your charity this day. Many of them are fatherless, perhaps, but all of them assuredly the children of tribulation. They have drunk deep of sorrow, until they drank all its bitterness; they have borne indignities and persecution in silence, until they almost sank under its exhaustion; and, like the bondswoman whom envy had banished from the heart of the Patriarch, they have wandered through a desolate wilderness, without a roof to shelter them, mingling their tears with the rain and their sighs with the winds of heaven, and, like her, perhaps, in the last agony of despair, meditating a mur-

[1] S. James, i. 27.

derous deed against nature's instincts, when the angel of heaven pointed to a fountain for her refreshment, and cheered her despair with the promise of a holier kingdom. Thus they, too, having been early seduced or banished from their Father's home, have wandered since through a dark and dreary desert, without any light to cheer or a fountain to refresh them; and with feet torn with the thorns on which they were doomed to tread through their sinful way, are now fainting under the twofold affliction of wounds and weakness, and ready to expire unless you assist in recruiting the one and healing the other. O yes! in the language of Scripture, they are covered "with wounds and bruises, which are not bound up, nor dressed, nor fomented with oil."[1] To you, then, this day is consigned the merciful task of dressing and binding up the wounds, with the pain of which they so long smarted, and mitigating with oil these sores and bruises which were rendered sharper by being exposed to the wind of heaven. On you devolves the Christian duty of reassuring their fainting spirits by directing them, like the angel I have just alluded to, to those running fountains that traverse this wilderness of life, and are continually gushing forth from the hearts of the merciful. Yes; the hearts of the generous are never-failing fountains, and riches in the hands of such individuals partake of the qualities of living wells that are always fed by inexhaustible resources. Open, then, those sources of mercy, and give joy to those who were long strangers to such a feeling. Should, however, there be any still callous to the calls of charity, and insensible to the obligations which mercy imposes, let him, at all events, look to himself, and guard his own home from the demons that might destroy its purity and happiness. Though he should cast

---

[1] Isai. i. 6.

away, through avarice, the bowels of compassion for more distant objects, he cannot divest himself of a parent's solicitude for the virtue of his child, so well painted by the Wise Man, who represents the "father waking for the daughter when no man knoweth, and the care for her taketh away his sleep, when she is young . . . lest she should be corrupted in her virginity."[1] No; though he should be steeled against every other feeling, he cannot be insensible to the dread of having shame and dishonour brought upon his own house, and being made, in the language of the inspired writer I have already quoted, "a laughing-stock to his enemies, and a by-word in the city, ashamed before the multitude, and a reproach among the people."[2] It is incumbent upon you all to raise the broken fences, and to protect the sanctuaries of your own homes against the tide of vice and immorality which is threatening to overflow the most sacred recesses of society. Yes; the contagion is fast spreading; the rude and insolent clamour of profligacy is heard in the streets; virtue is abashed and forced into secrecy by its violence. It is, then, your duty as men and as Christians, when vice becomes fearless, to display a corresponding heroism in the cause of virtue; and to rush, if necessity demands it, into the flames to rescue the struggling victims from the ruin with which they are menaced, nor to pause in the pious work until you place them in peace and safety on the summit of the holy mountain. Amen.

[1] Ecclus. xlii. 9, 10.   [2] Ib. 11.

## LAYING THE FOUNDATION-STONE OF A CHURCH.

"How lovely are Thy tabernacles, O Lord of hosts! My soul longeth and fainteth for the courts of the Lord."—Ps. lxxxiii. 1.

IT is not of any ordinary building your venerable Bishop has been just now laying and blessing the foundation. The intense interest which the undertaking has inspired is attested by the solemnity of the rites by which it has been ushered in, as well as by the ardent devotion with which such multitudes have thronged together to witness the sacred ceremony. It would seem as if you had even now felt the mysterious change which this spot had already undergone. Like the neighbouring grounds, it was hitherto trodden without emotion, but now it is approached with awe and reverence. The mearings for the courts of the Lord have been fixed; the vast area of His lovely tabernacle is viewed by every eye with rapture and delight; its foundations have been dug and sprinkled with the mystic waters, impregnated with salt, on which, like the salt cast by the Prophet into the barren fountains of the gardens, the benediction of heaven has descended, removing from its precincts every noxious and corrupting influence. Its corner-stone has been fixed, ready to connect the dependent portions of the edifice, and in it has been deposited a variety of emblems significant of the time and the object of its erection—old coins, with their respective inscriptions referring to the past, and parchments of which the transcripts will guide the future annalist of this diocese to the year in which it was founded, of the episcopal administration of your distinguished Bishop, of the monarch's reign who holds the sceptre of those realms, and of the present Pontiff who sways the hearts of millions of his spiritual subjects. Yes; all these mute symbols, so full of meaning and instruction, convey to the pious Christian impressive lessons, which no tongue could impart, of the mysterious majesty of the place which the Almighty has chosen for His future dwelling. But, above all, that cross, pronounced in the sacred Scriptures a badge of malediction and of shame until it was converted by our Redeemer's death into the banner of His triumph and glory, shows that Christ is now the exclusive owner of this place, and the planting of His standard proclaims aloud that He has ratified, through His authorised minister on earth, the covenant by which this place is now consecrated to the erection of a temple—one of the many mansions found in the kingdom of His Church, manifesting the magnificence of its Founder, and the profusion of the blessings with which He gladdens His faithful people.

Taking the ritual of the Church for my guide, I could not select a more appropriate text on this occasion than the very first verse of the sublime canticles you have heard now entoned, re-echoed from afar, by which every heart has been so sensibly affected. Long, however, before it was recited and sung by the Royal Psalmist, it was uttered on a most solemn occasion by a prophet, or rather a soothsayer, of a quite different character. When the Israelites were on their way to the promised land, they caused much uneasiness and annoyance to the nations of Chanaan, one of whose kings sought to purchase the services of Balaam, the famous seer, in order to curse this obnoxious people. Having ascended to the summit of a lofty mountain, and turning his face to the desert, he lifted up his eyes, and beheld the vast hosts of Israel spread over the wilderness, through their different stations, with their leaders, of tens, and of hundreds, and of thousands, under their respective ensigns and standards, in an unbroken circle of tents, from east to south, and from west to north, surrounding the tabernacle, with a precision of order such as the military camp of the most skilful of ancient or modern camps never surpassed, and probably never equalled. Struck at once with the amazing spectacle, which combined so much of strength and order, we are told that the Spirit of God came rushing upon him, seizing his entire soul and subduing every mercenary feeling; and then, forgetful or unmindful of his false and hostile mission, his tongue gave expression to the dictates of his heart, breaking forth into the rapturous language of my text: "How beautiful are thy tabernacles, O Jacob! and thy tents, O Israel! As woody valleys, as watered gardens near the rivers, as tabernacles which the Lord hath pitched, as cedars by the water-side."[1] He then follows up his prophetic vision of the triumphs of the Christian Church, with its widespread dominion and continuous duration, in a strain of inspired imagery as just as it is beautiful, all illustrating the harmonious gradation of its hierarchy, as well as the inexhaustible riches of those hallowed temples around which they are arrayed. It is no wonder that the Church should be thus represented under the figure of a camp, being the kingdom of Christ, to whom the nations were given as an inheritance, having no limits but the boundaries of the earth. "Who is she," asks the writer in the Canticles, "that cometh forth as the morning rising, fair as the moon, bright as the sun, terrible as an army set in array?"[2] exhibiting another striking illustration of the compact discipline by which the spiritual authority of

[1] Numb. xxiv. 5, 6.  [2] Cant. vi. 9.

the Church is wielded, and the consequent triumphs by which its incessant combats with the powers of darkness are crowned. In fine, the Church is represented under the figure of the city of God by one Prophet, Isaias; the city of the great King by another, the Royal Psalmist; by our Lord Himself, the city on the mountain-top; and I should be repeating a large portion of the prophetic writings if I were to cite the various passages which exhibit the empire of Christ under the same emblem of a fortress, ever engaged in the extension of its spiritual conquests, and, at the same time, in the protection of its acquisitions against the jealous and mutinous subjects who would fain raise up a rebellion within its walls. And it is after this model, so often displayed in the predictions of her own prophets, that the Church has been constructed by its Divine Founder, having Christ Himself for the corner-stone, the Apostles for its foundations, and the entire edifice, as the Apostle says, so compacted and so fitly joined together in its various parts, as to be equally proof against the hostility of those who would attempt to storm it by violence, or to take it by the more slow, and dark, and treacherous operations of the mine. By both external foes and intestine traitors it has been incessantly assailed, from its first establishment until now, and over both its victories have been equally signal and decisive. Though it wanted not, ere it reached and subdued the promised land of the Gentiles, some of those seditious defections on the part of its own children, such as Moses encountered from the envious Levite and his ambitious companions, who disputed with Aaron the exclusive honours of the priesthood, and though its altars were adorned with the plates into which the forbidden censers of those insurgents were beaten, and though in its tabernacles was deposited the rod of

Aaron, which budded and blossomed amidst the barren rods of his sacrilegious rivals; and though these monuments of its early sufferings in the desert are yet visible in God's Church, attesting, to the end of time, the protection of heaven which shielded the lawful priesthood, as well as the vengeance which overtook its attempted usurpation—still it was only at a later period, and when encouraged by powerful allies, that the banners of heresy and schism were daringly displayed. The first three hundred years of the existence of the Church were years of terrible conflicts with the confederated idols of the earth, defended by powerful emperors, the avowed patrons of the worst passions of the human heart by which those licentious idols were adored. Amidst the rage of the storm, the jealous murmurs of the schismatic and disobedient could scarcely be heard, and the selfish and ambitious had little to tempt them, when even the standard of revolt could not claim exemption from the penalties by which the faith of the Catholic Church was proscribed, and the persecutions by which so many of its intrepid martyrs were crowned. Well did they exemplify the beautiful language of the liturgy that has been now entoned: "Blessed is the man whose aid is from Thee, O Lord! Better is one day in Thy courts than thousands of days. I have chosen to be abject in the house of my God, rather than to dwell in the tabernacles of sinners."[1] Yes; the vivid sense of beatitude beyond this life, for which they panted, was the secret of their courage; and all the fleeting enjoyments of this perishable world were deemed as nought compared to the happiness of residing in the tabernacles of the Lord for ever.

Of all the nations that have been given to Christ as

---

[1] Ps. lxxxiii. 5-10.

His inheritance, and associated to the kingdom of His Church, some at an earlier and others at a later period, there is none that obeyed the merciful call with such cheerful promptness as our own, or one that has clung to the revered object of its love with a grasp so tenacious as death itself could not loosen. Though in the mysterious dispensations of His punishments and rewards no one can question the Almighty, no more than the potter's clay can ask of its maker, "Why hast thou formed me thus?"[1]—and though nations, like individuals, have no right to boast of gifts not their own, but for which they are beholden to the bounty of heaven—it ought to be a subject of unceasing thankfulness to us that God has never in His anger departed from our temples, or taken away His Holy Spirit from the hearts of our people. Those who were earliest favoured with the blessing have long since fallen away from the faith, and whole regions to whom the Gospel was preached by the Apostles and Evangelists have been for ages buried in idolatry. The portions of the vineyard that were planted by St. Peter and St. James have alone hitherto escaped the fury by which so many fair and flourishing gardens have been destroyed. A neighbouring church, though cultivated by the labours of zealous missioners, has had, too, the misfortune of becoming a prey to the boar of the forest, by which its sacred enclosures have been broken and its treasures have been rifled. How singular, then, has been the prerogative of St. Patrick, that the fruits of his labours have remained as enduring as those of the most favoured of Christ's Apostles! and how specially blessed must have been that people, whose faith and fortitude have been as unconquerable as those of Rome, and whose

---

[1] Rom. ix. 20.

fidelity has been no less striking than that of the kindred people of Spain, though subjected to as harassing a persecution as the others had suffered from the sanguinary fury of the Moors! Deep and grateful must have been the soil on which the seed cast by St. Patrick fell, to be productive of fruits so vigorous and so lasting; and the varied monuments of religion with which the land is interspersed are but faint emblems of their steady and ardent devotion, which no hostility could extinguish. Whatever portion of the island you traverse, you are sure to meet conspicuous memorials of the religious feelings of the people, not only in the ruins of those churches, colleges, and cloisters which they erected in after ages, but in the mountains, lakes, and holy springs which an unbroken tradition has converted into consecrated records of his life. Thus the lofty mountain on the shores of the Atlantic, on whose peak the eagle, who gave it a name, had so long fixed his nest, was thenceforward changed into the appellation of Croagh-Patrick, and is frequented to this day by multitudes of pious pilgrims. The wells and fountains in which he immersed and baptised thousands of converts who thronged round him as he went along, are still remembered and enclosed with a devout reverence . . . . .

## THE DEDICATION OF A CHURCH.

*"And he brought me again to the gate of the house, and behold waters issued out from under the threshold, . . . came down to the right side of the temple."*—EZECH. xlvii. 1.

AMONG the various images under which the abundant and continual graces of God's Church are represented, that of the fountain gushing forth from the threshold of His temple, and refreshing the earth with its waters, is one of the most just and familiar, as well as one of the most cheering and consoling. In describing the Catholic Church, the wisdom of its design, the vastness of its extent, the solidity of the structure, and the beauty of its decorations, the Prophets of the Old, and the Evangelists of the New Law have copiously employed their inspired eloquence. All creation lay before them, from which to borrow the most appropriate objects of their comparisons, such as the sun and the moon, the running stream, the smiling valley, or the lofty mountain; yet creation itself failed to give an adequate idea of that spiritual edifice and its treasures, which can only be viewed in its proper light when creation shall have passed away and time shall be no more. Yet though inadequate to bring to the mind a full idea of those blessings, they were a help to raise it towards their contemplation. Those material objects, adapted to understandings that receive their knowledge through the senses, were suitable vehicles for conveying information to the soul. They were, as St. Paul expresses it, that glass through which we imperfectly see God in this life: and a glass, too, thickly smoked and dimmed, since no mortal eyes could view such ineffable light without being overpowered by its splendour. Do not, then, be surprised at the profusion of imagery with which the sublimest truths of our holy religion are so deeply shaded. They were not exclusively the mediums of instruction in the Old Law; they passed, too, into the service of the New, as is abundantly shown by our Redeemer's parables, clothing its mysteries, but with far more of the light which the descent of the Holy Ghost has thrown around them. Hence those magnificent types, the city of God, the city of the great King, the empire of Christ, and the mountain of the Lord of hosts, so familiar with the writers of the ancient law, but which the followers of the Gospel have not discarded. In the former they were surrounded with darkness, and the lightning, which suddenly broke from them, only increased the terror in which they were shrouded; whereas now, instead of inspiring fear, they resemble those bright and moving clouds that are seen flitting over a lovely scenery, and giving additional beauty to the Church, whose charms they partially unfold. With the imposing and majestic figure of the exterior of God's church or temple, every mind is almost full; and its likeness to an army in battle array, drawn up in ranks against the enemy, might be well suited to times of war and persecution, or perhaps to a less favoured region, where the spirit of the ancient covenanters may be still found to linger, and where those who are engaged in building the temples of the Lord, if not under the necessity of grasping the trowel with one hand and the sword with the other, are often assailed with the odious impeachment of meditating treason against an earthly monarch whilst erecting His own temples to the God of heaven. Leaving, then, those more brilliant views of the Church to more exciting times or circumstances, I will, on this occasion, confine myself to the more peaceful, and quiet, and refreshing image of your temple, implied by my text, pouring forth a continuous stream from the altar to its threshold, and thence gladdening all around with the diffusion of the waters of life and benediction.

Whilst the simple and unlettered, as well as the most intellectual and refined, are forcibly struck with those characters of magnificence which the finger of God has drawn of Himself in the outstretched heavens, it is in the minute works of creation, almost impervious to the naked eye, the infinite wisdom and power of the Divinity are so wonderfully displayed. The vast and immeasurable expanse of the vault of heaven, studded over with countless globes of light and fire, are, after all, but the natural creations of that Being whose power has no limits, "who beheld and melted the nations, and of whom it is written that the hills of the world were bowed down by the journeys of His eternity."[1] But what excites astonishment is the perfection with which beings not larger than atoms are not only indued with life, but furnished with all the exquisite and complicated machinery of the largest animal organisation. And thus it is, too, with the Church. That its hierarchy should lift up their heads round the chief temples of the Christian world, like the cedars of Lebanon, and that they should be objects of veneration, clothed in all the dignity of the priesthood of Aaron, is what should be expected. But what is still more calculated to impress us with awe and gratitude is the complete development of the merciful plan of redemption in all the smaller churches scattered over the earth, making each and every one of them a perfect type of

---

[1] Habac. iii. 6.

her who is His own bride, and furnishing them with such perfect organisation, in harmony with the Head, as to convey to the end of time, in the localities in which they are planted, the fulness of all the blessings which were purchased by our Redeemer's death.

To instance the blessings which this Church shall henceforth provide for the infant portion of this flock, you have but to transport yourselves to those times of paganism when the power of the father over the family, if father he could be called, was absolute; when, as a grim and unfeeling tyrant, he measured all his duties by an odious economical calculation, consigning to death every child for whom he fancied he could not provide, or whose infirmities might render it a burden to the State. Or, again, to come to our own times, fancy yourselves in one of the large cities of China, listening, at the early dawn, to the bustle and clamour of cruel waggoners carting whole piles of infant children, picked up the previous night in the streets, where they were abandoned by their cruel mothers; follow them to the banks of a neighbouring river, where, as would be done to a litter of animals either unnecessary or too numerous for domestic use, they are promiscuously flung into the stream, where the creatures who scarce opened their eyes to the light are sure to find a double death, passing from a life of which they but tasted into eternal darkness, whatever may be one's opinion of further and severer punishment. Contrast such sad and appalling scenes of everyday occurrence with the group of matronly young women who will henceforth flock to this temple, bearing in their arms the young heirs of a heavenly kingdom, and caressed with all the affectionate reverence due to the lawful claimant of such a high destiny. Look at the priest pouring over their heads a portion of that mystic font on which, on Easter

Saturday, he invoked the Holy Spirit "that moved over the abyss,"[1] giving it fecundity, thereby washing away original sin, rescuing them from the dominion of Satan, and regenerating them in baptism, and you will then understand the purifying virtue of the stream flowing through this temple.

But the benefits of this fountain are not confined to that stage of our existence; they are felt through every portion of our after life, when, with the growth of years, the passions, too, begin to wax strong, threatening to extinguish the graces of baptism; when, notwithstanding the pious assiduity of parents and of pastors, their precepts are overborne by the violence of bad example, and the thoughtless victims of delusion fall in the slippery paths which they were often cautioned to avoid; then the same merciful spirit of the Church comes to their aid, inviting them to the chairs of penance that are ranged along the walls of the temple, which are asylums to protect them from the pursuit of their enemies, rather than tribunals for their condemnation. Different from the criminal courts of the world, the sorrowful confession of their guilt becomes a pledge of their pardon, rather than a warrant for their punishment. Into the sacred fountain that flows from the altar, the infirm and the palsied are let down, while the angel of the Lord is agitating the healing waters; quickened by their efficacy, they again come forth, sound and vigorous, casting away all the bandages of their wounds and of weakness, "and like the roe on the mountain,"[2] exulting in their entire freedom, and showing the virtue that went forth from the fountain, giving health to everything with which it came in contact.

Thus regenerated with the waters of baptism, and restored to its forfeited grace by the waters of penance,

---

[1] Gen. i. 2.   [2] Cant. viii. 14.

the children of the Church require still the spirit of strength, of discipline, and of association to shield them from further harm and to facilitate their future triumphs. This want is supplied by the chrism, mixed with balsam, that is blessed by the Bishop on Holy Thursday, the anniversary of the institution of the Holy Sacrifice of the Mass, and applied to their foreheads, possessing a virtue far more powerful than the oil which anointed the wrestlers in the ancient contests. Bearing on their foreheads the profession of their faith, and the sacred symbol of the courage which it inspires, they go forth like an army drawn up in battle array, carrying aloft the banners of the Church, and covered with the shields that hang in thousands from the towers of the temple. Thus equipped, they are proof against the fiery darts of the enemy; and let persecution rage in its most undisguised fury, as it has often done before, or let it assume the more treacherous form of affected kindness, as it does now, those youthful champions, fortified by the grace of the holy unction, are sure to triumph over the ambushed foe, as in the open battle. What but the courage with which the imposition of the Bishop's hand had indued them, would have enabled them to sustain trying ordeals for their religion no less scorching than the furnace of Babylon, out of which that religion always came unsinged by their heat and more burnished by their activity? What but the divine influence of the words so often heard from God's altar, " Fear not those who can kill only the body,"[1] could have made our intrepid martyrs of former times smile in the midst of the tortures to which they were subjected, seized as they were with the more overpowering fear of Him who can cast body and soul into hell? Yes; it was the Holy Spirit from on high, invoked by the Bishop's

[1] S. Matt. x. 28.

prayers, and descending into their hearts at his invocation, that kept from being crushed, broken, and ground to atoms a people over whom such heavy and overwhelming engines of oppression had successively rolled, and not only not annihilated, but springing up again with a rapidity and force that appalled their tormentors. And is it not the same supernatural efficacy of this sacrament that cements and binds up together the comparative remnant that still survives the combined operation of famines and evictions, the latter so systematically and remorselessly carried on as to form the most excruciating, because the most lingering, of all the sufferings yet endured, and appearing to be the result of secret associations and a general combination among landowners to sweep away its ancient and indigenous Catholic population? And yet, though it was a design like this against an entire faithful race that drew from the inspired writer the memorable words, " Now I will arise, saith the Lord,"[1] no loud reprobation of such cruelty rings throughout the land; and the complaints appear confined to the abundant but silent tears of the widow, that flow down her cheeks and go up to heaven and cry against him that causeth them to fall. But the Church shall never cease to mix her sorrows with tears thus forcibly drawn from those who are driven from the country through hatred for their religion. The Almighty draws good out of evil, it is true, and makes of the sufferings of our people and the cruelty of their oppressors an instrument for propagating our holy faith among distant nations. But that should not justify us in being silent upon the manifest iniquity of their forcible expulsion. We should not be of those who have no reproaches but for the poor, and no forbearance but for the powerful. We should, in the spirit of the

[1] Ps. xi. 6.

Church, apply oil and vinegar judiciously tempered, with which she heals the festering wounds of her penitents, and not cast all the acid on the sores of the poor, reserving for the heads of their oppressors all the oil of our adulation. God's designs in the crucifixion of our Lord were designs of benediction and mercy to mankind: no one would, on that account, refrain from expressing horror and execration of the crime of His executioners. The expatriation of our people may eventuate in benefits to our religion; that is no palliation for the wickedness of those by whom they are disported; and though I rejoice as much as anyone in the extension of the Church, I will never be one of those who will turn the Catholic colonisation of other countries into an unprincipled apology for the Catholic desolation of our own.

These are not the only blessings of which the waters that flow from the sanctuary are productive. Their purifying influence is likewise felt in sanctifying the marriage union, in lightening its yoke, and in providing with tender solicitude for the religious education of its offspring. Outside the pale of the Catholic Church the relations of this contract are confined to mere family interests, or, at best, those of society and the State, and hence they partake of the corruption of our fallen nature, and are generally accompanied with much of the domestic and public calamities which that corruption, uncontrolled by religion, engenders. Not so the sacramental union blessed at the foot of the altar by the minister of our Saviour, whose first miracle was wrought at the marriage of Cana, at the instance of His Blessed Mother, as if to be a perpetual memorial that the higher and holier end for which marriage was instituted should never be forgotten. Destined, in the first instance, to give valuable members to society, but more particularly to train those members to be fit associates for the saints in heaven, this twofold destination is never lost sight of by the Church, to the latter of which she directs the contemplation of her children. The union of Christ with His Church is the picture drawn by an inspired pencil, which she holds up to both for imitation. The reverence of the spouse of the Canticles for her wedded Lord is to be the model of her reverence, and the chaste affection, over which a withering or discolouring breath never passed, is to be the measure with which he is to return such a hallowed and indissoluble attachment. Here, then, is the secret of that sweet and peaceful harmony with which the married pair in the Catholic Church journey to the end of life, amidst all its crosses and all its troubles. It is the benediction bestowed in God's temple, and received with a deep reverence, that hallows the cottage, that pervades the village, and that is so felt throughout the parish, especially in Ireland, that land of chastity, because it is the land of faith, that some years ago it appeared in evidence before the House of Commons, that in a remote parish, far from any contaminating intercourse, comprising a population of eight thousand souls, not more than one illegitimate birth for the space of several years was found to taint the purity of its atmosphere. Whether such a creditable testimony could now be given anywhere, I doubt much, or, rather, I do not doubt, especially where those exotic institutions have been introduced, which in the country of their origin first sprung up from unbelief and profligacy. The taint of their breath is growing and spreading with their maturity; and notwithstanding the purity of the soil into which they have been transplanted, they still develop enough of their native corruption as to make our country ever regret their transplantation. At the period to which I have just now alluded, the people were illiterate, because the opportunity of learning even the alphabet of their own language was tyrannically denied them. Since then the knowledge of letters has been fast flowing over the land. Still the lips of the priest guarded in safety the more precious knowledge of purity and virtue. Have the Gospel virtues kept pace proportionally with the march of this foreign civilisation? It is to be feared, or rather it is certain, that they have not. Are the fathers and mothers of the present day, or, at all events, as things are going on, will the fathers and mothers of a future day be as solicitous to place beyond the reach of temptation the faith of their sons and the virtue of their daughters, as in those not very remote when the opposite vices were deemed utter strangers? They will not; nay, surrounded with such dangers, they cannot; for know that the literature of which our enemies boast, and of which your children partake in the eagerness with which they hunger for science, is not the unalloyed literature which a Government boasting to be Liberal should give to a people whom, with a singular want of truth, they boast they have made free; but it is a literature infected with maxims which must exercise a baneful influence on the growing generation. It is such a literature as the persecuting King of Antioch strove to establish in Jerusalem, with the assistance of Jason, the brother of the high priest, who so cordially entered into the views of the stranger, that the people of Jerusalem were thenceforward to go by the name of Antiochians; and the better to reconcile them to this change, a plan of academic exercises was set up for the choicest of the youth, with houses for their corrupt training, such as the Apostle forbids Christian ears to hear or Christian tongues to utter. Wherever the yoke of the Church is cast aside, the yoke of marriage soon shares the same fate. Since the rupture of England with the Catholic Church, the yoke of marriage has been reluctantly borne; the traditions of the old faith, however, were so strong that it still was borne, notwithstanding the mutinous clamours of the profligate for the licence of divorce. Those clamours have at length prevailed; the sacred yoke of marriage, lasting during life, has been broken and flung to the winds. The proximity of the countries, and the frequency of their intercourse, and, above all, sympathies of the corrupt with such enactments, will not fail to recommend to the teachers of those foreign Lyceums the study of those recent experiments that have defiled our legislation, and that threaten Ireland with the flood of legal immorality that has already inundated England. Think you that such examples and such sanction will not have their perverse influence in the schools placed exclusively under masters selected by such lawgivers, in infecting a vitiated literature with a still fouler corruption? Alas! the horror for vice will wear away with familiarity, the spiritual dangers to which the child is exposed will disappear in the splendour of those honours which a mother's fondness sees reserved for her son in the distance; and though all would shrink with horror in seeing them cast into the flood like the Chinese infants, or into the fire like the children of our Pagan ancestors, to many of the unfortunate frequenters of those forbidden colleges the difference of their treatment will be only in the manner, doomed to a more tardy, yet not less cruel immolation.

The contrast between the licentiousness of morals that accompanies a defection from the faith and the habitual innocence with which the faith is accompanied, only furnishes a stronger reason for clinging to those temples within which that faith and that purity are so jealously preserved. They become invested with more than usual interest, since on Sundays, besides the stated functions of divine worship, they are converted into schools, into which are seen thronging crowds of children, as if to the breasts of an affectionate mother, to appease that hunger and that thirst for pure spiritual nourishment which may have been denied them during the week.

Still, all those graces to which I have adverted are only so many rivulets, whereas it is in the great source of all spiritual blessings that abides within it, the immense and untold treasure of God's temple consists. It is the holy sacrifice of the Mass, daily offered by the priest for the sins of the people, that invests it with a mysterious splendour and beauty far surpassing that glory which, at the time of its dedication, filled the temple of Solomon. It is this continued residence in our tabernacles of Him whose delight is to be with the children of men, that brings those children in such multitudes around them, filling their souls with ineffable consolations. Yes, how intense is their feeling of the real presence of Christ in the Eucharist is strikingly manifested by the profoundness of their reverence to the Blessed Sacrament at the moment of elevation, when they appear to pour out their hearts, in homage to His divinity, at the foot of the altar, a homage which can only be compared to the ecstasies of love and reverence with which the prostrate spirits cast their crowns before the throne of the Lamb, ejaculating, at the same time, honour and glory and benediction to Him that liveth for ever and ever. Such ardent feelings, at once the effects and the evidence of this faith of the real presence in the adorable Sacrifice, can never be enkindled within any temple, or any heart, out of which that presence and that faith are gone. This is the great secret of the animation of our temples in the stillest hours of their solitude; this is the reason why they are continually opened to the visits of those who desire to snatch an hour from the anxieties or the more dangerous caresses of a deceitful world, to talk to their beloved, and find in that conversion a foretaste of happiness, which all the enjoyments of life cannot give. With the Holy Sacrifice of the Mass offered within it, the lowliest chapel in the land, and the least adorned, is rich beyond conception; without that sacrifice, the most magnificent temple that the genius of art ever conceived, or the resources of wealth ever erected, is a cold, cheerless, and unanimated structure, with no light to gladden its worshippers, because the source of light and life is not there; and with no floods of benediction issuing from its threshold to water the valley of thorns, because the springing well of benediction has been dried up. Hence those Catholic temples, in which the solemnities of the mystic sacrifice have ceased, appear joyless and deserted, the melancholy apparitions of their former selves; and as well might you imagine that the elaborate process of embalming might restore life in the image of the departed mummy, as to think that any aromatics could preserve the identity of those temples out of which the Holy of Holies is gone. It is no wonder, then, that when the Sacrifice of the Lamb was banished from the temple, with Him was banished, too, the joy and the happiness of the people, and, that prophecies ominous of public disasters went forth throughout the land, like the sepulchral voice, proclaiming woe, woe, which as the melancholy precursor of its ruin, and that of the nation, was continually issuing from the deep recesses of the temple. When the people, though not the original projectors of the impiety, lent their co-operation to this expulsion of the Holy One from His own sanctuary, the spiritual ruin of the country, as in the instance of that beyond the channel, was complete, and it will be a great mercy should He ever return to bless those tabernacles from which He has been so wantonly and so sacrilegiously excluded. The Irish people were not guilty of such a crime, and, therefore, no such direful spiritual maledictions fell upon the land. If the Almighty was deprived of the sacrifice offered by His Divine Son, in whom He is always well pleased, in His own temple, and if the unholy one was placed in His stead, the people were rather the victims than the agents of this desolation. When our Lord was banished from the tabernacle, they followed Him into the desert, and, though He had no fixed place on which to lay His head, He received at their hands a fealty and a homage not inferior to that which encircled Him in the most sumptuous temples. The continual presence of their God under the Eucharistic veil diffused joy over their path, and turned the wilderness itself into a smiling garden. The monuments of those times have not yet passed away. No; they are as prominent and permanent, too, as the rough features of the wilds in which the priest and the sacrifice found shelter. They have in some instances been considerably defaced, and their meaning entirely mistaken by substituting in some places a foreign dialect for the old native language of the country. Whether this has been done by accident or design, would be here a superfluous inquiry: it was more probably the result of a combination of both. That the enemies of the Catholic religion should not be desirous to preserve the memorials of their own cruelty, or of the fortitude of its devoted champions, it is not uncharitable to conjecture; and hence the false English version of names and localities, celebrated for Christian heroism, which our own language places in proper historical light. How much of the truth of history is lost by this deceitful medium; how much of the sweet odour of our religious traditions evaporates in passing into a vase not so suitable for its reception, may be illustrated by the examples of places I happen to know, designated in all official documents, *Moss* Hill, *Moss* Vale, and *Moss* Brook, whilst they are called by the rural annalists of the country, *Mass* Hill, *Mass* Vale, and *Mass* Brook; and that the latter are the correct interpretations of those names is evident from the corresponding Irish names still spoken by the people, and Cnoc ᴀn Ꭺꝓoɪn, Ᵹleᴀn ᴀn Ꭺꝓoɪn, Sputᴀ́n ᴀn Ꭺꝓoɪn unfold to us those magnificent spectacles of a priesthood and of a people well worthy of each other, the one offering up the sacrifice in the cavity of a hill, or in the depth of a valley, or under the projecting bank of a dried-up brook, whilst some of his flock kept watch and ward on the neighbouring heights, to save him from paying the forfeit of his felony in offering up the sacrifice of propitiation, among other good ends, for the pardon and salvation of his pursuers. How consoling it is now to see, at last, the exiled priest and the exiled sacrifice restored, and the people, with a rapturous delight that can scarcely find utterance, rivalling each other in giving them a suitable welcome, and adorning with befitting dignity the sanctuary of our Redeemer! Nay, such is their love for the beauty of God's house that, like the Hebrew people after their return from captivity, they have interrupted the building of the walls of the city, and I trust it is only temporarily, until they shall have first completed the temple of their God. This is in accordance with our Redeemer's advice: "Seek first the kingdom of God and His justice, and all those things shall be added unto you."[1] Yes, when the temple of God is finished, you will apply yourselves with fresh energy to

---

[1] S. Matt. vi. 33.

raising the suspended edifice of justice, whch alone gives to nations their stability, and I trust there will not be one of the stones, so long dispersed in unsightly squalor and dirt over the land, that will not be skilfully fitted in its proper place, forming a goodly structure of religious and social freedom, delightful to contemplate, and beneficial to enjoy.

Having thus given necessarily only a cursory glimpse of those rich treasures that adorn the temples of the Catholic Church; having directed your attention to the varied qualities of the waters that are issuing from its sanctuary, regenerating the infant, purifying the adult, confirming the infirm and the faltering, and sanctifying the marriage union, by lightening its yoke and easing its burden; having particularly dwelt upon the living fountain of grace that is flowing from its altar through the Holy Sacrifice of the Mass, allow me to congratulate you on the dedication of this church in the very centre of your town,* after so long an interruption, and to express a hope that the Almighty will pour His choicest blessings on those who zealously assisted in bringing it to a completion. Though the sins of the people may provoke the wrath of the Almighty, still the Blood of the Lamb that was slain, daily offered on its altar, will cry out louder than the blood of Abel, and appease the divine anger. Should the bolts of His wrath threaten to descend and destroy your town, like those metallic rods that bear away the electric fluid, the temple of God will prove a safe conductor to avert from His people the gathering vengeance of heaven. Henceforth this church is to be in a peculiar manner a house of prayer, from which the supplications of the faithful are continually to ascend to the throne of God, bringing down the assurance of His choicest blessings. The dedication

* Ballinrobe. Dedication of the New Church, Pentecost Sunday, 1863.—ED.

of the temple of Solomon closed with a pledge that the humble and penitent prayers of the people would be always heard by the Almighty; and let us hope that the prayers of the faithful will not find less favour in His sight under the more powerful covenant of the New Law. On the anniversary of this great festival the Holy Ghost descended on the Apostles, and the form of tongues of fire which He assumed was expressive of the fervour of divine love with which their hearts were inflamed. Let us, then, pray that the same Divine Spirit will come down on us, elevating what is low, warming what is cold, healing what is infirm, and purifying what is corrupt. Let our constant prayer be that, after having enriched us during life with the graces of His church, He may still grant us the last and, if not the greatest, certainly the most necessary then, the grace of extreme unction at the trying hour of our death. It is then, when human nature becomes weak, and our spiritual enemy becomes strong and furious, the love of the Almighty for the children of the Church is so signally displayed in supplying them still with those waters of life that flow from under the threshold of His temple. Let us, then, fervently pray that it may be our happy lot again to be anointed with the oil of strength, and again to be refreshed with the bread of life at that hour of awful conflict, on which an eternity of unspeakable happiness or misery depends; that, like Joseph, our last sickness may be consoled with the presence of our Divine Redeemer and His Blessed Mother, that we may derive confidence from the powerful intercession of the one, and the atoning passion of the other; that we may be filled with the humble hope of having the justice of our Judge satisfied by the mercy of His own mediation, and of hearing from His lips the gladdening invitation to enter into the joy of the Lord. Amen.

## THE DEDICATION OF A CHURCH.

"And I saw a new heaven and a new earth, for the first heaven and the first earth was gone ... And I John saw the holy city, the New Jerusalem, coming down out of heaven from God, prepared as a bride adorned for her husband, and I heard a great voice from the throne saying: Behold the tabernacle of God with men, and He shall dwell with them, and they shall be His people."—Apoc. xxi. 1, 2, 3.

THESE words are but a brief extract out of the Epistle read in the Mass on the feast of the Dedication of of the Churches of Ireland. And the first words that are read in the same Mass, after the priest ascends to the altar, are those remarkable ones of the trembling Patriarch Jacob: "How terrible is this place! This is no other but the house of God and the gate of heaven."[1] One of those passages is from the Book of Genesis, the first, and the other from the Apocalypse, the last of the inspired writings, and each of them is equally suitable on this occasion, and equally significant of the holy import of the magnificent liturgy of this day. In the text from Genesis we are impressed with a sense of the sacred terror that surrounds the sanctuary, being the house of God and the gate of heaven. But again, we are reminded, in the passage from the Apocalypse, of the same heavenly kingdom, which, when time shall be no more, is to be the eternal inheritance of God's own people. It is not by any casual coincidence that passages so remote in point of time have been brought together to illustrate and enforce the same important doctrine. No; there is conspicuous here the same exalted wisdom which shines through the arrangement of the appropriate Epistles and Gospels of all the Sundays and festivals of the year. Guided, therefore, by the sacred landmarks

[1] Gen. xxviii. 17.

that are fixed by the Church in the performance of all its sacred offices, I shall offer you some brief and simple reflections on the solemn ceremony of the dedication of churches, on the merit and reward of promoting such works, as well as on the dangers to families and to States, even in this world, when the holy interests of God's temple are despised or neglected.

It is not casually, then, but for the wisest purpose, that the Church has introduced into her liturgy the two significant passages regarding God's temple, to which I have just alluded. Going back at once to the infancy of creation, and proceeding without pause to the time when it shall have passed away, she teaches us how fleeting and evanescent is the intermediate interval—that interval which the world so much prizes for its history of wars, and conquests, and revolutions, that are continually flitting before us, without leaving a trace of their existence; and therefore she directs the attention of her children to the stone pillow of Jacob, as well as to the heavenly city of the Apocalypse—the beginning and the end—the alpha and the omega, as it is called in Scripture, of all the scenes of this busy world, without attaching any serious importance to those perishable interests that occupy so much the cares and solicitude of mankind. We are forcibly reminded of the solemn truth that we are but strangers and pilgrims here below, having no permanent resting-place, and looking forward to that city not built by mortal hands, which its architect has destined for us as our eternal abode. Of this everlasting city our temples are the emblems, and hence the extraordinary zeal and solicitude displayed, especially during the earlier ages, in their erection. Filled, nay, overpowered with the idea of the immensity and majesty of God, which Solomon himself could not sufficiently express when exclaiming in rapture that heaven and the heaven of heavens could not contain Him, they, too, felt their utter inability to give suitable spaciousness to the house in which God Himself condescended, in a peculiar manner, to reside. Feeling that they were, in the language of St. Paul, "fellow-citizens with the saints and the domestics of God,"[1] they justly concluded that no arch could be too vast, no walls too lofty, no decorations too rich, and no furniture too splendid for the service of those temples, which, in their brief passage through life, fixed their attention on their eternal tabernacles to which they were journeying. Hence those magnificent churches which rose throughout Europe in the middle ages almost with the celerity of magic, some of them, yet standing, attesting in their unviolated integrity, and others in the colossal fragments of their ruins, how familiar with eternity were those great minds whose images were impressed on such massive structures. Religion was then the master impulse that put society in motion. It then held that paramount rank worthy of the heavenly origin from which it was derived. Arts, sciences, policy, and commerce, all held their subordinate spheres round that fixed and hallowed centre to which all the fleeting interests of earth were tributary; and no matter how elegant might be the private, or sumptuous the public palaces of the great, they were always overshadowed by the towering splendour of the temple of the God of heaven. The reason is obviously shown in the words of our Redeemer: "Where thy treasure is, there too thy heart shall be;"[2] and that their hearts and their treasure lay in the House of God they sufficiently proved by the ample funds which they bestowed on its decoration. They recognised in it the likeness of the Holy City, the New Jerusalem mentioned

---

[1] Ephes. ii. 19.     [2] S. Luke, xii. 34.

in my text, coming down from heaven, adorned as a bride; and on this bride, like the chaste Spouse in the Canticles, called a closed garden and a sealed fountain, they lavished the choicest ornaments, as evidence of their holy affection. Do not, then, be surprised at the splendour of those stupendous edifices, or at the miraculous wonders that often accompanied their erection. They should surprise, indeed, if raised by those whose feelings were engrossed by secular pursuits, or by those whose energies are kept captive by those riches from which they cannot disentangle themselves, handing down from one generation to another enormous masses of wealth, as valueless to themselves and to society as if it were a treasure as yet hidden in the bowels of the earth, or cast by the force of a tempest into the bottom of the ocean: but, built by those who were quickened with the hopes of a happy resurrection, and who panted for its enjoyment, they were the natural effects of corresponding causes, and the sublime creations of a vigorous mind, sustained by a faith which no obstacle could subdue. Hence the frequent instances of providential interference that signalised and rewarded their unfaltering confidence in heaven. Hence the mountain, realising the literal language of the Scripture, was moved out of its place, in obedience to the confident prayers of one, and the grave itself gave up its tenant, to give testimony in favour of the rightful claims of another, from whom a portion of land belonging to his cathedral was sacrilegiously attempted to be wrested. There may be those animal men mentioned by St. Paul, who understand not those things that pertain to the Spirit of God, who would fain controvert these wonders. They may controvert them as they will, as they have controverted the miracles that ushered in Christianity itself: but, as St. Augustine remarks, those miracles could not be denied without the admission of a greater one, to wit, the easy reception of a religion that at once proclaimed war against the pride of the human intellect and the corruption of the human heart, without any miraculous agency to advance it. Thus, if they controvert those miracles to which I have alluded, they cannot controvert at least the striking illustration of that more wonderful spirit of omnipotent faith, then prevailing, that could remove all the mountains which the calculating spirit of the world still throws in the way of religion, and still subdue, by an appeal to times and witnesses now no more, that selfish and rapacious spirit which often prompts the great ones of the world to covet and to seize the small remnant of the pious donations of the people. It was the influence of that ardent faith and generous devotion to which I allude, that appeared to exempt our own happy country from much of the evils entailed by sin on our common race, and make it amidst the surrounding nations a kind of earthly paradise. It was from this spirit sprung those numberless *Kills* and *Cluans*, the former signifying church, the latter, places of religious seclusion, which were so thickly scattered throughout the land, as to be intertwined with its topography. If it was truly said of Judea that it was a holy land, through which you could not walk without meeting at every step the tracks of God's agency, where every monument was a memento of His mercy or His power, in a similar manner it could be told of this Island of Saints that its very atmosphere breathed holiness, and that every spot over its varied surface was redolent of piety. Its title deeds to this distinction rest not on the flattery or fiction of its writers. No; they are wrought into the entire texture of our history; so that to deprive us of that richest treasure, the odour of a good name, the former appellation, by which our parishes and townlands were baptised, should be erased, and the face of the country undergo a strange revolution. On another occasion like this I directed the attention of my auditory to the dazzling evidence of its ancient prominence in society, which the hundreds, nay, the thousands, of its affixes of *Kill*, or church, continue to convey. Now I will confine myself to the no less significant names of *Cluan*, connecting them with some of the brighest and most exalted names in the ancient annals of our Church. Thus, St. Finian and Cluanard, St. Brendan and Cluanfert, St. Jarlath and Cluanfois, St. Coleman and Cloyne, or Cluan, emphatically so called, and St. Kieran and Cluanmacnoise, have been so united, that as long as those names now fixed remain, the memory of those eminent men, whom they educated and formed, shall never pass away. No; the very scenes of their education, the peace and the solitude of which they are so expressive, were well adapted to an extraordinary development, and, like those lone and lordly trees of the forest, that grow and expand, remaining fresh and vigorous while generations of forced and elaborate culture decay and perish, thus those mighty men are seen standing after the lapse of ages, spreading their reputations far and wide, and sheltering with their holy patronage the children of the land of their nativity. From those Cluans and their academic solitudes sprung a number of other eminent scholars, who, like Samuel, were nurtured within the solitudes of their temples, until, like him, they were fitted to convey lofty lessons of justice to the rulers of the world, and of duty to their people. Among such were St. Fechin More and St. Coleman of Lindisfarne, or of Boffin of Mayo; the two Columbs, one with an Irish and the other with a Latin affix, to distinguish them by the peculiar names of Columbkil and

Columbanus, the former the Apostle of Christianity
among the Picts of Scotland, the other the herald of
the Gospel in Gaul and in the midst of the Appenines,
and both speaking with courage and intrepidity before
kings without ever being confounded. Yet in no nation,
either of Picts, or Franks, or Germans, or Italians,
could those devoted missionaries ever find a more
faithful people than at home; and whilst the fruits of
several of them have decayed; whilst the faith, which
Columba planted, has long since perished round the
environs of Iona; and whilst the once favoured sub-
Alpine regions appear to be weary of the blessings
which St. Columbanus brought them, the faith which
they left in Ireland, to be reared and cultivated by the
companions of their cloistered lives, is yet, thank God,
as fresh and pure, and cherished in the inmost affections of the people of Ireland, as in those far gone days,
when those great Apostles departed from its shores
to enlighten the distant regions of Europe. Among
those great and holy men who were content to confine
their labours to their own country, by diligently cultivating the portion of the vineyard which was assigned them,
was Nathy, the patron saint and first prelate of this diocese,* the disciple of St. Finian, the master of St. Fechin,
the student of Cluanard, the teacher of Achonry, and one
of that brilliant clustre of saints to whom I have just
referred, who have cast a rare effulgence over the close
of the sixth century of our era, in comparison to which
the saints of other nations and of other times, appear
like the stars in the firmament, some of brighter and
others of a feebler lustre, whilst the collected splendour
of the Irish saints, particularly these, may be well compared to that broad and effulgent zone that girds the
heavens, and flings on every side a steady and unfailing

* Achonry.—ED.

lustre. Amidst the broils of contending chieftains, and the rapine and plunder of the Danish pirates, who soon after infested the country, the torch of the true faith was constantly kept burning in the churches of this diocese, as well as of the kingdom, to the time of that eminent man,[1] who had to experience and deplore the violent tempest of anarchy and schism that swept over the Church in the sixteenth century, despoiling the temples, and leaving their endowments a prey to every sacrilegious invader. In him the Irish Church found a pillar of light to direct her children at that stormy period; and, after acting a distinguished part in that great Council of all the churches that assembled in Trent, to animate, to guide, and to sustain the nations now reeling from the shock of the recent religious revolution, he returned to his suffering flock, among whom his life was prolonged to the close of the unauspicious reign of that unfortunate queen, that was so fatal to the religion of England, and so trying to the fidelity and heroism of thousands of devoted martyrs in Ireland—a queen who was flattered and idolised by contemporary courtiers, as she has been accused and stigmatised by a distant and disinterested posterity, on whom I shall forbear bestowing those harsh epithets which her character has well earned, and whom historians of cool and dispassionate judgment have not hesitated to compare with the worst woman that ever wore a crown or wielded a sceptre. To the people who wept over his tomb while he was gathered to his fathers, he had nothing to leave of the splendour of the temple which he witnessed in his younger days but its nakedness and its desolation. But he left a far more precious legacy than its material riches, to wit, the odour of a goodly name, cherished to this day, of whom it could be said, like the high priest,

[1] Eugene O'Hart, O.P., Bishop of Achonry.—ED.

the son of Onias, "that he took care of his people, that he shone in his days as the morning star in the midst of a cloud, and as a bright fire burning frankincense; as a massy vessel of gold, adorned with every precious stone, and as a cypress-tree rearing itself on high, when he put on the robe of his glory, and was clothed with the perfection of power; and when he went up to the holy altar he honoured the vesture of holiness."[1]

Such was the great and saintly prelate, raised up by God in those evil days, and whose sacred fame could well compensate his successors for the many material privations to which they were doomed from that period. But it has at length been deemed high time to clear away all the unsightly rubbish that has been necessarily accumulating round the site of the temple; and accordingly, whilst his predecessors have been labouring with all the zeal and energy which the circumstances of the time could permit, to rear the rural churches, to your present venerated Bishop[2] has fallen the laborious but still the consoling lot of conceiving, nay, of executing, the project of restoring in a befitting form the cathedral of his diocese. But what were the revenues on which he purposed to draw for the erection of this holy edifice, and what are the resources on which he relied for the final accomplishment of all its fittings and decorations? He had no royal treasury at his command; no royal floats were ready to waft the lofty timbers of some distant forest for the laying of the roof of this temple; nor did the public exchequer enable him to line the road with the lengthened suite of mules and horses, laden with hewn masses of stones from the quarries of the neighbouring mountains. No, nothing of all this. Yet, with unhesitating confidence, he commenced a work of

---

[1] Eccles. l. 4-12.    [2] The late Most Rev. Patrick Durcan.

immense magnitude and toil; and he was right, since he might calculate on more prompt and steady success than those who can command the public taxes. He calculated on that spirit of zeal as sustained as it is enthusiastic, which is ever all-powerful, but especially in the infancy of religion, or at a period not unlike infancy, when, after long and dreary disasters to religion, the national spirit is awakened in celebrating its joyous revival. Yes, there is, then, about it some of the energy of a giant refreshed from a long slumber, and coming forth clad in the might and agility that belong to the glories of resurrection. It is from the impulse given it by such a spirit that the second temple of Jerusalem was seen to rise a beautiful object from the rubbish in which it was so long buried. "Then rose up the chief of the fathers of Judah and Benjamin, and the priests . . . and everyone whose spirit God hath raised up, to go up to build the temple: and all they that were round about helped their hands with vessels of silver and gold, with goods and with beasts and with furniture, besides what they had offered on their own accord."[1] In this inspired language we find a correct historical anticipation of the zeal for religion, and the generous sacrifices for restoring the beauty and splendour of God's house, that distinguish the priesthood and the people of Ireland. The chief of the fathers has now, as well as then, but to arise and to select their aid, and the faithful priests, whose spirit God hath raised up, throng around, proffering their assistance; and the varied contributions of their numerous and devoted flocks, from the gold and silver vessels of the wealthy to the slender offerings of the poor, mark a holy rivalry in their united co-operation. Now, as on that occasion, temporary obstacles may be

---

[1] 1 Esdras, i. 5, 6.

thrown in the way of the completion of such a holy work by the enemies of our country, or of its faith, still no enduring impediment could obstruct, much less utterly defeat its progress, because your spiritual chief and his brethren and all the people stood as one man to hasten them that were doing the work in the temple of God.

You will not, then, require of me any further argument to prompt your zeal in prosecuting to its entire completion the work of this temple to-day so auspiciously dedicated. There are no members in the community, whatever may be their profession, their calling, their rank, or station in society, that are not bound, even for the attainment of their own laudable ends, to make the temple of God the chief object of their solicitude. As for the clergy, it will be admitted that this is their paramount duty. Like another Samuel, the sanctuary should be their habitual home, feeding its hallowed fires with an unfailing supply of fuel, that when they go forth from its sacred hearth they may scatter its living coals amidst a chill and corrupting world. To review the various gradations of society, and to point out the peculiar and personal interest which they should take in the glory of God's house, would, at this advanced stage of my discourse, be too heavy a task for your attention. There is one divine virtue, at least, in the praise of which all are unanimous, and the cultivation of which seems to be an object of general desire—I mean mutual charity. If you wish to preserve and propagate its spirit, you will be solicitous to sustain and decorate the temples of the true faith, in which alone it has been enshrined, since as well might you expect that beauty and symmetry, and, in short, all that mysterious harmony of form which unites the members of the human frame, could be found after the spirit has abandoned the lifeless clay, as to think that the grace and loveliness of that charity which binds mankind together could survive when the Spirit of faith and religion are forced to flit from among their earthly habitations. You cannot, then, but feel a lively zeal and interest, warmed with a domestic affection, in seeing this house duly decorated and embellished, being in reality a temple of peace and concord, as well as the temple of the true religion. It is enough for mankind to be six days of the week engaged in all the distracting duties and vexatious annoyances incident to their several stations in society. They should, on Sundays and on great festivals, have an opportunity of uniting in one permanent and all-engrossing pursuit; and, as the larger as well as the lesser rivers, down to the smallest streams, all flow with different currents and distinct channels into one ocean, so should it be with man. For six days they may pursue a separate course, and occupy a distinct station in life, but on the seventh they should all unite in the same broad channel of prayer, and join in offering their solemn acts of thanksgiving and adoration to the Almighty. And then your good Bishop, in finishing this temple, where the most blest and fortunate, as well as the most forlorn and unhappy, may associate in finding that peace which the world cannot give. Even the most passionate and successful suitors of fortune find at last—and it is a happy discovery—that the fondest objects of their pursuits have flitted from them, like shadows which children vainly endeavour to grasp, and, resigning such foolish illusions, they will rather seek to be lowly in the house of God than to dwell in the tabernacle of sinners. How often, too, will this other class, whose sorrows and misery bow them to the earth, find under the wings of the sanctuary that shelter and protection which is denied them by the world; and when, perhaps, some victim of its cruelty, like the unfortunate maid who was banished from the house of the Patriarch, deprived of every hope and every tie which bound him to life, shall be sinking into the arms of despair, he may receive consolation by beholding the temple at a distance, as she did when the angel beckoned to her in the desert, and, hastening forward, may be refreshed with those waters of mercy that are continually gushing from the sanctuary of God's mercy. To none, however, is a zeal for the temple of God more important than for those whose lives are engaged in the profession of arms. What, it may be asked, is it sought to give to the most destructive of all occupations additional force? No; but it is meant to mitigate the evils of which that blind and brutal monster, war, is so generally productive, and to confine, by the moral influence of religion, within certain bounds, the fury of the worst of all the plagues which sin has inflicted on the world. It is meant that war should not be deemed matter of mere brutal courage, and the soldier a mere irresponsible machine; that, like every science, war and its votaries should be regulated by the principles of truth, and justice, and honour: such as signalised those campaigns that were undertaken for holier motives than a lust of plunder and dominion. We require the soldier to be animated by the pure and lofty spirit that strung the courage of the Machabees when fighting for their realm and for the temple; the courage that led the armies of the West to rescue from profanation the sepulchre of our Redeemer, the chivalry that saved Europe from the slavery, the barbarism the infidelity, and the profligacy of the Mussulman, when its nations were roused and united by the appeal of the common father of the faithful. Such Christian courage, in short, as has been so often displayed by the faithful soldiers of our own country on those trying occasions when, as duty could not be doubtful, success or defeat were not made a matter of sordid calculation, and when the most brilliant success that crowned the aggressive victor could not be as honourable as the discomfiture of the fallen in the cause of their country and of religion. If that chivalrous spirit that loves to espouse the right, though it should be the weaker side, is now so rarely to be found, it is because the zeal for God's glory, and the beauty of His house has waxed cold among men, and it is vain to hope that it shall be ever warmed into generous action, unless its heat be kindled and sustained from the fires of God's temple. Domestic life, with all its endearments, is no less prized by our people than by any other upon earth. Why, then, are ties of kindred and of home so easily and so suddenly snapt asunder by the Irish Catholic as to court the most dreadful dangers? It is for the very reason that his family affections are so dear to him that he resigns them when the still holier attachment to his religion and his God commands the sacrifice, and that this gentle son, who loves his mother with all the artless simplicity of a child, is seen, at the call of a higher duty, to be transformed into a warrior, and to spring with the swiftness of an eagle, and the courage of a lion, to every field where the faith of his youth is to be vindicated, and the rights of the head of the Church, the common father of the Christian world, to be guarded.[1] Calumny itself could not impeach the courage of the Irish soldier, when fighting for his faith or for his country, unless designedly blinded. I can conceive that the persistent maligners of our race might not be satisfied with the feats of valour performed by the Irish Catholic soldier in a service in which he is assailed by

---

[1] Allusion here to the corps of Irish Pontifical Zouaves.—Ed.

conflicting feelings, if not unmanned by conflicting duties—a service, in which the brightest triumph must be darkened by the saddening conviction that the blow struck for the freedom of another country was only to bind in faster fetters the religion of his own. I can well conceive our enemies not to be entirely content with such cold and reluctant duty; though, under all the circumstances, it should, instead of censure, draw forth their gratitude and admiration. But to accuse them of cowardice when fighting for the Pope, to arraign their valour when combating for their temples and their altars, is to arraign their fidelity to their religion, a virtue that could never have been denied them. And the reason this flood of calumny has been let loose upon our soldiers is this, because envy feared how painful might be the contrast between the feats of an Irish soldier in a service which persecutes his faith, and the feats of the same soldier when he feels that his power will crown with additional triumph the object of his dearest affection. Let us recollect that it was on the wicked profaners of God's temple, and the persecutors of his priesthood, the most signal chastisements have been inflicted; but that it was in protecting the same temples, and the rights of the same priesthood, the most striking manifestations of God's interposition have been displayed. It was after rifling the temple of Jerusalem, and defiling its altar that the impious King Antiochus felt the hand of the Lord heavy upon him: driving at a furious pace, in haste to repeat the same sacrileges of which he was already guilty, he was flung from out of his chariot, and so bruised that a loathsome disease was the consequence of which the noisome exhalations were tormenting to himself and intolerable to the entire army.[1] In like manner, Heliodorus, at the insti-

---

[1] 2 Mach. ix. 9, &c.

gation of another king, went to rob the sacred treasures of the same temple; but his sacrilegious attempt was checked by the terrible apparition of a young man mounted on a furious horse, whose forefeet smote the robber on the forehead, whilst two angels laid him, almost gasping for death, upon the floor.[1] But to come down to Christian times, and to pass over several instances of the manifest interposition of the Almighty on behalf of Christendom, suffice it to advert to the fate of another impious tyrant, who, like Antiochus, breathing fury against God's temple, proudly boasted that he would feed his horse with a measure of oats at the altar of St. Peter.[2] And yet six years did not entirely elapse, when this conqueror, who, from the rapidity of his movements, received the surname of The Lightning, fell into the hands of Timur,[3] another Mahometan tyrant still more triumphant, and was carried about in an iron cage, a spectacle to the world of the folly of human pride, of the limits of human power, and the utter inability of both to cope with the eternal counsels of the Almighty. At a later period, towards the close of the sixteenth century, when the same Turkish race, the enemy of civilisation as well as of religion, threatened to overrun Europe, they were defeated, and their fleet scattered in the Gulf of Lepanto—a victory which was ascribed to the powerful intercession of the Blessed Virgin, and the tidings of which were brought at the very moment to the Pope[4] by a miraculous message, surpassing any modern telegraph in the quickness of its communication. The modern revolutions that are now convulsing Italy, and threatening to subvert the order of the neighbouring States, are not improperly

---

[1] 2 Mach. iii. 25.
[2] The Turkish Sultan Bajazet I. towards the close of the 14th century.—ED.
[3] Otherwise Tamerlane.—ED.     [4] St. Pius V.

compared in the pastorals of some of the French bishops, with the anarchy that accompanied the armies of the Turks. Nay, these wars, carried on in the heart of Christendom, and waged against the Holy Father by some of his own ungrateful and unnatural children, are in some degree far more formidable than the invasions of the Saracens, before which Europe so often trembled, inasmuch as intestine quarrels are always more rancorous than wars with foreign enemies, and the hostility with which her schismatical children pursue the Church that bore them, is far more deadly and more poignant to their afflicted mother than the worst persecutions with which pagans and infidels ever assailed her. The prayers of the Church are not less necessary nor less efficacious now than in those times. The intercession of the Holy Mother of God is surely not less powerful, nor the faith of the people in that intercession less strong and lively, than it was then. This Sunday happens, I hope by a favourable coincidence, to be in a special manner the feast of her holy patronage. These festivals are as pillars of light which the Church intersperses through the desert of life to afford guidance and repose in our dreary pilgrimage. Let us, then, implore the Virgin that she look down with particular favour on the temple this day dedicated to the honour of the Almighty, that all who come to worship here may, like Moses, who stripped off his shoes because the ground on which he trod was holy,[1] leave outside its threshold all worldly thoughts by which the sanctity of this temple could be defiled; that she may guard with equal solicitude the purity of those other temples belonging to its worshippers, namely, their own bodies, called by St. Paul the temples of the Holy Ghost;[2] that she may inspire them with holy thoughts to preserve them undefiled; that, when

---

[1] Exod. iii. 5.    [2] 1 Cor. vi. 19.

this and all the material temples shall have passed away with this world, the temples of our bodies, after having been dissolved by death, shall be raised up again, bright, glorious, incorruptible, and immortal, through the merciful power of our Redeemer, who, by dying for us, destroyed our death, and renovated our life by His Resurrection, to whom be honour, and glory, and benediction for ever. Amen.

---

## THE CONSECRATION OF A CHURCH.

"And the children of Israel, the Priests and the Levites, and the rest of the children of the captivity, kept the dedication of the house of God with joy."—1 ESDRAS. vi. 16.

SUCH is the language in which we are told by the inspired historian of the dedication of their temple after the return of the Jews from their captivity. Humbled by seventy years of a severe foreign bondage, the penitent Hebrews sighed for their ancient residence of Sion, and longed to pour forth their sorrow for their sins, and their gratitude for their deliverance in the temple of their fathers. Accordingly, the Almighty lent a favourable ear to their petitions, and mercifully solaced all the hardships of their exile with the certain hope of its speedy termination. While the spirit of the people sunk under the accumulated evils they had endured, and their hearts were sore because their hopes were so long protracted, God, by the assurance of His prophet Jeremias thus cheers their despondence: "I will save thee from a country afar off, and thy seed from the land of their captivity, and Jacob shall return and be at rest, and there shall be none whom he may fear."[1]

Never was prophecy more faithfully fulfilled. The language of my text speaks the evidence of its accom-

[1] Jer. xxx. 10.

plishment. "And the children of Israel, the Priests and the Levites, and the rest of the children of the captivity, kept the dedication of the house of God with joy." It is to solemnise a similar dedication you are assembled here this day : not the dedication of a temple confined, like that of Judea, to the worship of one people, but the dedication of a church, consecrated to the Redeemer, at whose altar all the nations of the earth have knelt, realising the prediction that His reign should extend to the extremities of the world, and that "a pure oblation should be offered in His name from the rising of the sun to the going down thereof."[1] Yes, we are come to offer our homage to Him who has thrown down the wall that separated Jews and Gentiles, and who has been deservedly called the corner-stone, uniting into one solid and harmonious structure the loose and discordant materials of all the ancient temples. It is a scene worthy of all the reverence of the human heart, it is one to which human tongue cannot do justice; nor should I presume to explain the nature of that homage which is due to the Almighty, had He not condescended in time to come out of the mysterious darkness in which He was shrouded from eternity in order to dwell in human tabernacles, and prescribe the forms of worship by which He was to be adored. Guided, therefore, by the revelation of His own wisdom, I shall briefly sketch the necessary obligations of that worship which creatures owe to the Supreme Being, as well as the conditions with which it ought to be accompanied in order to render this religious homage, which is proffered upon earth, acceptable in heaven.

Of all the feelings of our nature there is none more reasonable or spontaneous than that which prompts us to break forth into grateful acknowledgments to the Author of our being. It is a feeling which springs with

[1] Malach. i, 11.

all the rapidity of instinct from the human heart, and to which our cooler reason gives its most solemn approval. Hence the uplifted hand, the suppliant knee, the downcast face, the beseeching eye: hence the upright form and lofty forehead fixed on heaven, denoting at once man's august origin and end; and hence every feature of the human countenance, flexible to every impulse of that spirit which was breathed into it by its Divine Author, while it is moulded to the varied expressions of thankfulness or of supplication. Hence the high antiquity and universal prevalence of public worship, coeval with the origin of the human race, and co-extensive with its diffusion, leaving no interval of time or place to which the light of history can lead us, in which you cannot trace the vestiges of its existence. You can discover the evidence of this religious feeling in the festivals and sacrifices of every nation of the globe. Nay, it is reflected in the variety of monuments that are still strewn over its surface, from the rude stone on which the Patriarch offered his early worship to the Lord to the splendid cathedral of St. Paul or the golden roof of the Vatican. Contemplating the splendour of the heavens, which, in the inspired language of the Psalmist, announce the glory of God,[1] man viewed through the magnificence of the firmament, a faint image of its Author, and bowed, in affection or in fear, to the mysterious Being whose terror spoke in the thunder, or who, to use the milder illustration of St. Paul, showed himself in showers and the fruitfulness of the seasons. The individual who could refuse to acquiesce in this general sentiment was supposed to offer violence to the dictates of his own mind. Hence it was expressed in the religious institutions of every people, and all creation might be deemed as one magnificent temple continually

---

[1] Ps. xviii. 1.

resounding with the praises of God, whilst the sun, the moon, the seas, the floods, the forests and the mountains, were, in the language of Scripture, as so many ministers swelling the pomp of divine worship and hymning, with silent but harmonious accord, the power and the wisdom of their Maker.

In the manifestations of this homage there was, it is true, among the pagan nations a strange and fantastic variety. In proportion as they were removed from the fundamental source of religion, the public worship was gradually corrupted. The light of reason was overcast by the baleful influence of the passions. Vice assumed the name and usurped the honours of virtue; man sunk in sensuality, adored under some personified form the foulest idols of the human heart; "the glory of the incorruptible God was changed into the likeness of corruptible man,"[1] and a crowd of false and inferior deities obscuring the throne of the Almighty, intercepted those honours which were due to Him alone. Yet, in despite of the superstition with which it was mingled, the influence of religion was not entirely extinguished; no; since it cannot be extinguished without the extinction of the human heart, out of which a feeling of religion spontaneously grows. The stream of morality was corrupted, it is true, among the nations through which it spread; yet, amidst the mass of impurity which it accumulated from the influx of the human passions there were some untainted properties by which you could trace its pure and primitive fountain. These properties were the dogmas of a general belief, originally derived from the Divine source of revelation, and which were transmitted over the earth without being lost in the tide of superstition with which they were conveyed. Yes, they were the precious relics of the treasure of important

[1] Rom. i. 23.

truths originally imparted to man, and which all the wasteful extravagance of his descendants could not utterly destroy. If the pagans then had their victims, it was in imitation of the sacrifice of Abel, of which it is said that "the Lord had respect for his offering,"[1] and of which the tradition spread abroad among the nations, though its origin might have been disfigured by fable, or lost in the remoteness of time. By a similar sacrifice the patriarch, who was rescued from the flood, commemorated his gratitude, and his piety was rewarded with the assurance that the same vengeance would never be inflicted on his posterity. If sanctuaries were set apart for the exclusive purpose of divine worship, we can trace the practice, if not higher, at least to the vision of the patriarch who poured oil upon the stone on which he slept, thus consecrating the spot which the presence of the Lord had rendered holy. Thus we will find all the leading rites and dogmas of religious worship bearing the stamp of their derivation from heaven; and whilst the subordinate ceremonies that were mingled alike with every system of truth or error, might be said to resemble those light and looser materials, which, when torn from one edifice, are not easily distinguished in the other to which they are transferred; those few original dogmas stood amidst the wreck of religion as lofty columns of a marked and definite order, attesting by their loneliness the vastness of the ruin, and directing the curious and the contemplative of every age to explore their original destination.

Were we, therefore, confined to the knowledge which our reason and history supply, we should be taught the necessity of solemn public honours to our God. But, instead of being obliged to extract the particles of truth from the mass of errors with which they were mixed,

[1] Gen. iv. 4.

we have a safer and more summary process in following the guidance of that law which, to use the language of the Apostle, "shone like a taper in a darksome place,"[1] and which was fed by fresh accessions of prophetic light until it broke forth in the full splendour of the Christian Church.

Amongst the Jewish people, to whom God had specially revealed His will, the public worship was celebrated with the most imposing solemnity. Having assumed towards that people the more accessible character of a tutelary Monarch, He ordered a tabernacle to be constructed for His residence, and Moses, following the model that was shown him on the mountain, erected a tabernacle which was at once the court of the Supreme King and the sanctuary of the Divinity. On the decoration of this portable temple the wealth and ingenuity of the citizens were cheerfully expended. The number and ornaments of its pillars, the costliness of its hangings, the richness of their embroidery, the variety of utensils that formed the furniture of the tabernacle, together with the graving of works of gold and silver with which its walls were profusely overlaid, are all recorded in Exodus with a minuteness of detail which would be fatiguing to your attention.[2] Such was the eagerness of the people to pour their offerings into this temple, particularly of the females, who stripped their persons of their most precious ornaments of jewels, in order to consecrate them to God, that Moses found it necessary to interfere, and moderate their generous devotion. Yet, that the beauty of His house was not unacceptable to the Almighty, we learn from the sacred text, which assures us "that after all things were perfected a cloud covered the tabernacle of the testimony, and it was filled with the glory of the Lord."[3] To all, but the priests of

[1] 2 S. Pet. i. 19.     [2] Exod. xxxvi. seqq.     [3] Exod. xl. 32.

the race of Aaron, was the ministry of the tabernacle inaccessible, and only once in the year, and then, robed in the vesture which God Himself had prescribed, were they permitted to cross the sacred threshold of the sanctuary in which the Divine Majesty visibly resided. No foreign ceremonies were adopted into the Jewish ritual. No strange divinities were associated to the honour of the God of Israel. No; He tells us Himself He is a jealous God, and could not share with any rival the honours of His throne. If any, therefore, had sought to infect the purity of divine worship by the introduction of idols they were sure to expiate their treason and idolatry with their blood. The reason of this severity will appear obvious to him who considers the state of Judea as well as the surrounding countries at that time. It was essential to the preservation of the hereditary records of religion. Encircled, as was the land of Judea, by the frightful mass of error which had already overspread the earth, it was necessary to arrest it by the most formidable barriers. Hence all the terrors that guarded the purity of the Hebrew worship; and had these been removed, the tide of idolatry rushing in on every side would not only have swept away the tabernacle of religion, but would have also buried in its ruins the divine records which lead us back, with unerring step, to the history of creation and the origin of mankind.

Such was the first temple which God commanded to be erected and consecrated to His honour. This shifting tent was well adapted to the wants of His people while they were yet journeying in the wilderness, or engaged in war with His enemies. However, it seemed an unsuitable residence for the Divine Majesty after they had reposed in the secure possession of the promised land. Hence the pious King David conceived the design of erecting a temple worthy of the God of Israel. He lamented the indignities to which the ark was exposed by falling into the hands of the Philistines, though God, by the most signal chastisements, had avenged its profanation. He was afflicted that, without any shelter but that of skins, it was exposed to the inclemency of heaven, whilst he himself reposed in a house of cedar. Accordingly, he meditated the erection of a magnificent temple; but the work, which was conceived by the piety of the father, was reserved to be executed by the wealth and wisdom of the son. Solomon, grateful for the gifts with which he had been enriched, as well as by the assurance of the Almighty to perpetuate the royal honours of his house, resolved to execute the project of his father; nor did he cease his solicitude until he illustrated his reign by a monument which at once displayed the ardour of his zeal and the extent of his resources. The magnificence of this house may be well conceived from the vastness of the preparations. "The king," says the sacred text, "numbered out seventy thousand men to bear burdens, and eighty thousand to hew stones on the mountains, and three thousand six hundred to oversee them. . . . . For the house," said he, "which I desire to build is great, for our God is great above all gods. Who then can be able to build Him a worthy house? If heaven and the heaven of heavens cannot contain Him, who am I that I should be able to build Him a house, but to this end only that incense may be burnt before Him?"[1] It was thus the pious monarch expressed the inadequacy of his own power to give sufficient dimensions to a house that was destined for the residence of the King of heaven. Its length, including the porch, was eighty cubits; its breadth, twenty; its height, an hundred and twenty; and he overlaid it

[1] 2 Paralip. ii. 2-6.

within with pure gold. He paved also the floor of the temple with precious marbles, and graved cherubims on the walls, anxious to compensate for the littleness of the structure by the richness of its interior and the variety of its decorations. Having completed an edifice which surpassed all the temples of antiquity, not less in the splendour of its architecture than in the purity of its object, he perfected the work by a solemn dedication of seven days. From the entrance of Emath to the torrent of Egypt, Israel poured in its vast population to assist at the solemn ceremony. "So great was the multitude of victims, says the inspired writer, that rams and oxen were sacrificed without number. The priests brought in the ark of the covenant and laid it in the holy of holies, under the wings of the cherubim. . . . . Both the Levites and the singing men . . . clothed with fine linen, sounded with cymbals and psalteries, and with divers kinds of musical instruments, and lifted up their voice on high: the sound was heard afar off: so that when they began to praise the Lord, and to say: Give glory to the Lord, for He is good, for His mercy endureth for ever, the house of God was filled with a cloud."[1] Solomon, seizing this assurance of the divine favour, poured forth before the Lord his fervent supplications for its continuance. His prayer was graciously accepted by the Almighty: "A fire came down from heaven to consume the holocausts, and the house was filled with the majesty of the Lord."[2]

Whilst the service of the temple was faithfully performed, so long did the Almighty manifest a peculiar solicitude for His people. But as their piety grew remiss, He gradually withdrew His protection, until their infidelity was at length punished by a severe and protracted exile. After their return from bondage, their

[1] 2 Paralip. v. 6-13.   [2] 2 Paralip. vii. 1.

temple was restored and dedicated with a solemnity similar to that of the former, and remained, until the coming of the Redeemer, the centre to which all the true worshippers of Israel brought their offerings.

But it seemed inconsistent with the benevolence of the Deity to reside exclusively on Sion, and the time was at length filled up which was to diffuse the blessings of the true worship among the nations of the globe. Accordingly the wall of separation, that lay between the Jews and Gentiles, was levelled, and the inhabitants of the remotest regions were invited to offer their united thanksgivings to their common Redeemer. The call was quickly obeyed: the nations bowed their necks to the meek yoke of the Gospel. Temples in honour of the one God rose on the ruins of idolatry, and the cross, once the badge of shame, but now the symbol of glory, glittered in triumph over the fallen temples of paganism. The revolution, which this holy religion wrought in the morals of mankind, corresponded with the divinity of its origin. Wherever it was preached the face of nature was changed. Kindness succeeded to cruelty, temperance to licentiousness, humanity to oppression; in a word, peace, and charity, and self-denial, and all the social and domestic virtues followed in its train. It mitigated the cruelty of war, it lightened the load of despotism, it eased, nay, loosened the chains of the captive, and bound in strong fetters the tyranny of the human passions. Nay, all the arts, which contribute to the improvement and embellishment of social life, received fresh impulse from the Christian religion. Architecture, and painting, and music, which were hitherto degraded by ministering to idols, were now transferred to the nobler service of the one God. Instead of inflaming the passions by immoral representations, the pencil was now employed in tracing the horrors of sin, or the triumphs of virtue, whilst it exhibited to the eye the images of the dying Redeemer or His heroic followers, who bore in safety, through every combat, the sacred symbol of the cross. Music, too, was ennobled in its object, and its sublimest inspirations seem to have lain concealed, until they were drawn forth to entone the praises of the Almighty, or the magnitude of His mercies to fallen man. In short, the human mind was elevated to a loftiness of conception which it knew not before. Every object on which it was employed bore the impression of that vigour which the Christian religion imparted. The proudest monuments of the pagan artist shrunk into insignificance before the nobler designs of the Christian; the successors of the crucified fisherman called forth genius which mocked the combined powers of the Cæsars to command; and the pilgrim, not only of religion but the arts, ceases to be struck with the celebrated relics of the ancient shrines of Pæstum or of Rome, as soon as he crosses the threshold of the sacred temple, whose lofty dome draws up the soul to heaven, and whose vista, still stretching like an unrolled volume as you advance, naturally reminds you of the hidden immensity of that Being to whose honour it was reared.

Why have I dwelt upon those advantages of Christian worship? To show its indissoluble connection with the best interests of society, and to convince you that in promoting the one you are likewise contributing to the happiness of the other. Yes, religion is not only the herald that announces the happiness of another world: it is likewise the most efficient instrument in forwarding the interests of this. Without subverting, it regulates the dependencies of society. It humbles the proud and elevates the lowly by the recollection of a common origin. It knits the most distant members of the human race through the bond of a common redemption. It softens into smooth and smiling elevations those high ascents of rank, which otherwise would be barren, rugged, and inapproachable; and while the peer and the peasant kneel in the presence of their common Sovereign, all the artificial little distinctions of life disappear in the immeasurable distance between them and the Divinity. Often has the lust of revenge been subdued by the contemplation of a crucifix; often has the toll of death from some neighbouring steeple arrested the force of some lawless passion; often has the image, nay, the name of the saint whose feast we celebrate this day (for to the Savoy peasantry there is a charm in the very name of Francis of Sales), often has the name of this saint, passionate by nature, but by grace a prodigy of meekness, converted into lasting friendships the feuds of those Alpine villages, which no secular power could appease. In short, if a country were to be civilised, or a city to be erected, a house of divine worship must first consecrate the spot, in order that the people may find, under the tutelary influence of religion, the guardianship of their laws and the bond of all their covenants.

You are, doubtless, the friends of society. You, therefore, feel an anxiety to forward its best interests. If so, I call on you this day to promote an object with which those interests are interwoven. Yes, religion is the spirit by which the existence of society is sustained. And if that spirit were once extinguished, it would present nought but a loathsome and hideous mass, festering with the wounds inflicted by the passions, and falling asunder under the weight of its own corruption. It is, therefore, no wonder that Christ characterised His holy religion with the names of " spirit and of truth." " The hour cometh," says He to the Samaritan woman, "when the true adorers shall adore the Father in spirit and in truth: for the Father also seeketh such to adore Him."[1] Different from the false religions which disfigured the earth, and whose fatal effects were felt in the demoralisation of mankind, His religion came in spirit and in truth, and diffused, at its coming, through the diseased frame of society, a tone of healthiness and animation. Wherever the same spirit of truth in religion and sincerity in its profession sways the human heart, it has a corresponding influence, nor shall it cease to invigorate those public and private virtues on which the safety of society reposes. Truth, then, is the first condition which Christ requires in His worship. The reason is obvious. Our belief will have a corresponding influence on our practice. Hence the Pagans, having conceived erroneous notions of the Divinity, incorporated those impure notions with the public worship. The infection soon spread to the practice of their lives, and hence, as error was mingled in its source, the stream of public morals became necessarily corrupted. To save society from consequences equally disastrous, the Spirit of truth, free from any admixture of error, must continue to preside over the adoration of the Deity. Though the heart is the principal seat of religion, still, without the aid of an external ministry, it might soon be extinguished. Our best affections are often volatile, and hence, without being regulated by proper instruction, our religious feelings might be exalted into a fiery enthusiasm, or subside into utter indifference. Hence the necessity of Christian temples to guard the sacred fire of religion; hence the necessity of that authorised ministry, from which the Spirit of truth promised not

[1] S. John, iv. 23.

to depart, [1] to keep perpetual vigil round it, lest it should be blown into a destructive flame by the violence of fanatics, or again be suffered to go out through the perverse negligence of insidious infidels, thus leaving society without sufficient heat for the development of the virtues, like the chill and darksome regions of the North, where vegetation dies, because they are almost bereft of the light and warmth of the sun of heaven.

And is it only after the lapse of eighteen centuries that we are building for the first time temples to the Lord, to preserve the sacred fire which He brought down from heaven? No; the topography of the land, marked as it is with the repeated names of kils or churches, attests the contrary. And there are still more sensible monuments than names. Yes, through the expanded arch, the lofty steeple, the lengthening nave, the branching tracery, and the clustered columns, together with other fragments of Gothic architecture that are strewn over the land, you may perceive a magnificent, though a shattered, image of the ancient piety of our people. But Ireland, like Judea, was punished for her sins, and accordingly "her sanctuary was made desolate, her festivals were turned into mourning, her Sabbaths into reproach; her honours were brought to nothing, her temples became as a man without honour, and the vessels of her glory were carried away captive." [2] Then our priests, like their Hebrew predecessors, snatched the fire from the altars of our falling temples, and hid it in a valley, and, like the tabernacle which was rescued by the prophet from the ruins of Jerusalem, the ark of our religion was preserved amidst the caverns of our mountains. [3] What wonder, then, that this fire which was hid in a deep pit did not guide by its light, or warn by its influence!

[1] Isa. lix. 21.   [2] 1 Machab. i. 41.   [3] 2 Machab. ii.

Do I allude to those scenes in order to stir up in my hearers any painful recollections? God forbid. From the lips of the minister of religion no accents but those of charity should fall; and were this divine virtue to be exiled from every other assembly, it should find an asylum in God's temple. No; I allude to them in reference to the subject which I have pursued in this discourse, to show the indissoluble alliance between the interests of society and religion. Divine worship cannot be violated without the frame of society being torn; and it is remarkable in Scripture, that whilst the sanctuary was laid waste, the land was said to enjoy the Sabbath of her desolation.[1] If, therefore, I have glanced at the evils that accompanied the ruin of the asylums of religion, it is only to make you appreciate the blessings that must spring from their restoration. And if I have glanced at the disasters of Judea, whilst its worship was profaned, it was only to contrast them with the happiness it enjoyed when a more mild, as well as a wiser, policy restored Zorobabel to the honours of the temple. Yes, it is to congratulate those who perceive that in promoting the glory of God they are forwarding the best interests of the people, and that in laying the foundations of God's house they are laying the foundations of their own as well as of the nation's prosperity. If, then, I allude to those scenes that are past, it is to awaken in our souls livelier feelings of joy by a recollection of those sorrows with which it was contrasted. Yes, there is in the bottom of the human heart some mysterious abyss, in which the feelings of joy and sorrow are found to commingle. What wonder, then, if some transient grief should float across the present joyous solemnity, when it is said of the dedication alluded to in my text "that

---

[1] 1 Machab. vi. 49.

one could not distinguish the voice of the shout of joy from the noise of the weeping of the people."[1] But the Levites stilled all the people, saying, "Hold your peace, for the day is holy: and be not sorrowful."[2] Yes, this day is holy; be not sorrowful, but rather rejoice that the sacred fire which was hitherto hidden amidst "thick water" is at length brought out and deposited in our temples, and that, like the sun mentioned in the sacred text, which was hitherto in a cloud and suddenly shone forth to light the mysterious fire and consume the sacrifice, the spirit of charity, too, has at length broken forth from the cloud that overcast it, dissolving the thick water which had almost chilled the warmth of the human heart, and kindling there, once more, its holiest affections. Need I give any further proof of the sacred influence of that spirit than the congregation here assembled this day, composed of individuals of every class, forgetting every sentiment that could alienate and divide, and merging every feeling in promoting the glory of God and the peace of mankind? If there is any heart that has not hitherto yielded to its influence, it must be softened by the ceremony of this day. Yes, the prayers of the people here assembled will ascend to heaven and bring down fire, not such as was invoked by the terrific zeal of the disciples on the sinful cities of Judea, but such a fire as burnt the sacrifice of Solomon, consuming every corrupt affection of our souls, and leaving there a holocaust agreeable in the sight of heaven. Vouchsafe, then, O God, in whose hands are the hearts of Thy people, to give this happy consummation to the ceremony of this day. Send forth that Spirit which, to use the language of Scripture, once renewed the face of the earth, and elevate what is low, purify

---

[1] 1 Esdras, iii. 12.   [2] 2 Esdras, viii. 11

whatever is corrupt, and expand whatever is narrow and contracted in our affections. "Lend, O Lord a gracious ear to the supplications of Thy servant, and accept the prayers which he prayeth to Thee this day. If heaven shall be shut up, and there shall be no rain because of the sins of Thy people, and they praying in this place shall do penance to Thy name, and shall be converted from their sins by occasion of their afflictions, then hear Thou them in heaven, and forgive the sins of Thy servant and of Thy people. And if they sin against Thee, for there is no man who sinneth not, and Thou being angry deliver them to Thy enemies; then, if they do penance in their heart, and make supplications to Thee in their captivity, and knowing the wounds of their own hearts, shall spread forth their hands in this house, saying: 'We have sinned; we have done unjustly; we have committed wickedness;' then hear them in heaven, in the firmament of Thy throne, their prayers and their supplications, and forgive Thy people, and give mercy to Thy inheritance."[1] Amen.

## THE CONSECRATION OF A BISHOP.

"And going preach, saying, the kingdom of heaven is at hand."—
S. MATT. x. 7.

WHILST your attention is fixed on the solemn ceremony before you; whilst the enthronement of the young pontiff forms a centre whence circulates through every spectator a lively and contagious interest; whilst the future cares and anxieties of his union with his see are forgotten in the splendid ritual of his spiritual espousals; whilst,

[1] 2 Paralip. vi.

in short, in the lustre of the ring, the richness of the robes, the majesty of the mitre, and the solemnity of the crosier, you behold nought but those pleasing images of power, which shall ever have attractions for the vain of the world, and which often throw over the high places of the sanctuary a bright and fascinating cloud, which often conceal, until they are ascended, the depths and the dangers of the precipices beneath, allow me to awaken you, if possible, from the delusion which the scene before you may have for a moment cast on your reflection, and to conduct you where he has doubtless been conducted in spirit during the days of his preparation for the sacred office he is about to assume. Allow me, then, first to place you in the midst of a large and populous city, where all its ills and diseases are accumulated together in loathsome confusion; where the lame, the blind, the deaf, the dumb, those whose features are defaced by cancer, as well as those whose limbs are shaking with palsy, are laid before the portals of his house, whilst you distinctly hear the first salutation with which he is greeted on the day after his investiture. Behold the habitual levee that are to besiege your morning hours, that are to occupy a large portion of the day, and the solicitude for whose infirmities is frequently to intrude itself on your midnight repose. Again, follow your prelate to an extensive pasturage, covered with immense flocks, of which the guardians are comparatively few and the fences neglected, whilst the wolf prowls around the enclosures, threatening to devour the tenderest lambs of the fold. You then hear him accosted by the Supreme Shepherd, who tells him that the sole care of his future life is to consist in feeding the flock, in guarding it against the foe, in repairing the broken fences, and reproving the negligent shepherds, and if through his fault one of the flock were to perish, its price shall be demanded at his hands. Finally, accompany him to an extensive district, where the fields are already whitened with a rich and abundant harvest, where the master of the field puts a sickle into his hand, telling him that, in consequence of the season being far advanced, and the reapers few, he must toil with unremitting diligence, and bear up against the heat of the sun and the weight of intense labour, until the master shall see every sheaf of the harvest carefully deposited in his barn. What, you will doubtless ask, is the purport of those imaginary scenes, or why transport my auditory from the pleasing enjoyment of the present to fix their attention on such serious and painful prospects? If they appear fanciful, the fancy is not mine. They are literally the parables of Him who sought access to the human heart through the means of familiar comparisons, and which the Church has wisely extracted out of the Gospels. They were all, as we learn from the corresponding Gospels of the Evangelists, uttered on the occasion on which He chose His Apostles, and sent them into the world, and impressed those parables on their attention, lest they should ever forget, amidst the ease and the caresses of the world, that their ministry was one of care, of anxiety, and of toil.

To those qualities, then, of physician, of pastor, and of labourer, under which the Redeemer portrays the true character of an apostle, I shall confine myself in this discourse. In his character of pastor the people shall be informed of their obligations towards their bishop; in the same character of pastor, as well as those of physician and labourer, the bishop shall be respectfully reminded of the weighty responsibility of his own. On the occasion of uttering the parable to which I have just turned your attention, Christ recounts the names of the Apostles to whom He gives this important commission: "Go and preach, for the kingdom of heaven is at hand."

Our reason teaches us to respect every delegated authority in proportion to the dignity of him from whom it is derived. Behold, then, in the text just quoted the title to your respect and obedience possessed by the Apostles and their legitimate successors. Commanded by the Redeemer to go and preach, the Apostles went forth with the seal of His authority impressed on the charter of their delegation. Unlike municipal functionaries, who receive the ensigns of office from the secular source of princes or of people, the Apostles were assured, and the assurance was fulfilled, that they should receive from Christ Himself the keys of the kingdom of heaven. Why deduce from this circumstance the unbroken perpetuity of the apostolical authority in the Church? Because, different from the kingdoms of earth that rock before every passing breeze, and that are often upset by the violence of revolutionary storms, thus showing in their cumbrous materials the congenial frailty of the artificers by whom their foundation was laid, the kingdom of Christ, established by infinite wisdom and power, is pronounced by the prophet to be coeval with its founder. "Look upon Sion, the city of our solemnity," says Isaias, "a rich habitation, a tabernacle that cannot be removed; neither shall the nails thereof be taken away, neither shall any of the chords thereof be broken."[1] If order be essential for upholding the most limited and fleeting dominion, it cannot be supposed that a kingdom which was to stretch to the extremities of the world, and to endure through the viscissitudes of ages should not be regulated by that disciplined order which would enable the chiefs of the Church to wield its

---

[1] Isa. xxxiii. 20.

strength against the formidable array of power, by which that kingdom was to be continually assailed. Hence the same prophets who foretold the establishment of the perpetual kingdom of the Church, announced in like manner that it should be perpetually governed by rulers; and if they clothed the Church under the imagery of a shepherd's tabernacle, they have designated its rulers under the appropriate appellation of pastors. "And I will set pastors over my flock," says Jeremias, "and they shall feed them, and they shall fear no more, and not be dismayed."[1] Here, then, is the distinct announcement that the inhabitants of the kingdom established by Christ, and preached by His Apostles, are to be continually fed by faithful pastors, and, of course, that the authority of the first rulers still resides, by virtue of its regular transmission, in the persons of their successors. But should you deem not the language of prophecy which shadowed the future government of Christ's Church sufficiently clear and conclusive, listen to the words of the Redeemer on an occasion of the deepest and most touching interest. The last solemn instructions of every legislator must have a peculiar force. Just as the Redeemer was returning from the earth to take possession of that kingdom which He conquered by His sufferings, whilst His hands were yet stretched out to bestow on His beloved Apostles His last benediction, and in the same breath with which He breathed on them the plenitude of His power, He says: "All power is given to Me in heaven and on earth: Going, therefore, teach ye all nations, baptising them in the name of the Father, and of the Son, and of the Holy Ghost: teaching them to observe all things whatsoever I have commanded you: And

---

[1] Jer. xxiii. 4.

behold I am with you all days, even to the consummation of the world."[1] What, then, is the import of the words, "I am with you?" That they are emphatic, and fraught with mighty meaning, is clear from the previous word "behold," with which the Redeemer roused the attention of his Apostles. Yes, "I am with you" is language expressive of Christ's own aid and presence in every difficulty and danger. They are the words with which God Himself rebuked the timidity or strung the courage of Gideon, and of David, and of Jeremias, and of Isaias, and of other holy and intrepid men, encouraging them not to be dismayed, and assuring them of safety through the most fiery ordeals, as long as they were covered with the shield of His protection. But how long has He promised the aid of His presence? "All days," all seasons, all time, "even unto the consummation of the world." Here is the promise from which we deduce the continuous providence of the Redeemer over the Church which He has founded, as well as His protection of the rulers to whom its government is confided. Here is the infallible pledge of that order which shall regulate its movements by day as well as by night, founded on the same word by which the heavens were first formed; resting on the veracity and the power of the incarnate Son, "the figure of the Father's substance, and the image of His glory,"[2] who first launched into the immeasurable solitudes of space the countless bodies that are since revolving in their orbits, sustained by the word of His power. As sure, then, as the morning sun is to gladden creation by its light, and that any darkness that may obscure it is soon to pass over, it is equally certain that His Church will continue to enlighten mankind, without ever being long obscured by the errors that may float

---

[1] S. Matt. xxviii. 19, 20.   [2] Heb. i. 3.

across its surface; nay, more, when the heavens and earth shall pass away, unsustained by the power that first called them into existence, the Church in its renovated form shall attest for all eternity the power and the wisdom of Him, one iota of whose word shall never pass away.

A body with whom Christ promises to abide is entitled to your veneration, and to show that the present bishops of the Church are entitled to a share of that reverential feeling, it is only necessary to show that they form links of the apostolical chain through which the virtue of Christ's promise is conducted, and exhibit proofs of that virtue in the uninterrupted continuity of His protection. Fortunately for the children of the Church in whose favour the Apostles and their successors have been appointed the trustees of Christ's precepts, the claims of the rightful heirs are as clear as the legacy of the true religion is valuable. Shall it be necessary for the sincere inquirers after truth to discuss the different pretensions of the confused and adverse names that claimed, and still may claim, the possession of Christianity? Is he to listen to Arius, inviting him to follow him to the remote East; or to Calvin, at a more recent period, raising his standard in the West; or turn to Pelagius in the North; or again to pursue the fleeting systems of Donatus in the South? Is he thus to obey every capricious individual who beckons him to follow in adverse directions, distracted by opposite counsels, the sport and plaything of every wayward breeze that blows from the four quarters of the heavens, always inquiring, and never finding, until at length, with a mind as unsatisfied as when he first set out upon such religious inquiries, he sinks under the exhaustion of his frustrated efforts to discover those simple truths which Christ came to reveal to the humble and the little ones? God forbid; I tell all such persons, in the language of the Apostle, to "avoid foolish questions, and genealogies, and contentions, and strivings about the law."[1] It is unnecessary to entangle yourselves in such perpetual and intricate discussions, while you can trace the visible and palpable apostolic line in the descending series of their episcopal successors, and say, in the language of Irenæus to the sectaries of his own time: we confound all those who gather not with Christ by the uninterrupted succession of our bishops. How summary this argument; yet, you must perceive, it is strong as it is simple. The presence of Christ was to protect His Apostles and those who were to succeed them in their sees until the consummation of the world. Therefore, to assure ourselves of this presence guiding them in their ministry, and confounding the pretensions of all others, we have only to trace back the succession of our bishops, and show, as Tertullian says, the first to have been either an Apostle or one of the men who was engrafted on the apostolic trunk, and thus derived the vigorous nutriment of sound doctrine from the vivifying virtue of the apostolical seed. With this unbroken succession of the Bishops is identified the continuous and unbroken stream of the pure doctrine of Christianity, since, as the same holy Father remarks, no other doctrine can be true but what the Church received from the Apostles, and the Apostles from Christ, and Christ from His Father, who revealed Himself only to His Son, on whom He poured the fulness of His wisdom. What, therefore, was His doctrine must be still derived from those Churches which the Apostles founded, and which are so many fountains, of which the pure waters are conveyed through the channels of a legitimate succession. They, then, who are instructed by

---

[1] 1 Tit. iii. 9.

those pastors stand, to use still the language of Tertullian, on a firm foundation; they are in possession; they are the heirs of the Apostles; they drink out of the sealed cistern flowing within the enclosures of Christ's garden, which has never been troubled with the impure currents from abroad; whilst, as St. Cyprian says, no matter how specious the arguments of those who are without, the stream of continuity once broken, its contents must necessarily be mixed up with a large infusion of exotic errors.

Whether, then, that doctrine is imparted by written or oral communication, it is from the apostolical churches and those who preside over them its purity is derived. Alas! that it should be even thought that ink or paper placed the doctrine of Christ and its true interpretation beyond the pale of the authority of its legitimate expounders. Should any doubts arise regarding the meaning of Christ's discourses, and doubts did often arise, even in the minds of His own disciples, to whom but to Himself did they appeal for its genuine interpretation? And, think you, if for the purpose of a more extensive diffusion of those discourses He had put them to writing during His life, would He have forfeited the right of being their only authorised interpreter? Would not he that despised Him when expounding His own writings, despise Him that sent Him, as well as when giving His oral instructions; and if he that despised His Apostles despised Christ Himself, think you that the Romans, that the Hebrews, or the Ephesians, could have been free from the contempt of not hearing St. Paul if, as soon as his Epistles reached them, they abjured his authority as teacher, and became themselves the expounders of his written Epistles? Your reason revolts at such a thought. Nay, more, can you imagine that the Christians of those infant churches ever submitted those writings to their own exclusive judgment, or when the inspired men who gave them passed away, that the faithful of Crete or Ephesus ever interpreted them but under the guidance of Titus or of Timothy, whom he constituted first his co-operators, and then his successors in the divine ministry? No; as well might the children of a rich and bountiful father take the written record of his last testament into their own hands, renounce the authority of the witnesses to the deed, as well as of the judge who would award the property, until they should waste it in unnatural litigation, as that the heirs of the Christian religion could discard its apostolical trustees, and then fritter it away in intestine contention. It was not to have their authority superseded by the private interpretations of those Christians that those Epistles were written to them; no, but it was rather to guard their meaning, as well as to communicate more, that St. Paul established Timothy at Ephesus, in order that the things he heard through many witnesses, the same he might commend to the faithful men who shall be fit to teach others: "continue thou, then," he adds, "in the things thou hast learned, and which have been committed to thee, knowing of whom thou hast learned."[1] And in similar language he speaks to Titus: "For this cause I left thee in Crete, that thou shouldst ordain priests in every city, as I also appointed thee;" and then concludes: "These things speak, and exhort and rebuke with all authority."[2] Here, then, is the model of that order which has been perpetuated by the Redeemer sending the Apostles as He was sent by the Father, and they again constituting pastors to ordain others as they themselves were appointed, and commanding those pastors not to dispute, but to

---

[1] 2 Tim. ii. 2, iii. 14.   [2] Titus, i. 5, ii. 15.

preach with all authority what they receive through the testimony of many witnesses, and to commend the same to faithful men, who would be competent to preach it to others without any adulteration. These pastors are the pilots who are to conduct the faithful to the haven of their happiness; the Church is the bark, the world the sea, through which they are steering. In this perilous voyage should any attempt to dispense with their aid, they are exposed to imminent danger. They may possess the chart or the written word, but, wanting the knowledge which it requires, and deprived of a guide, they can have no security, whilst those who rely on their authority enjoy the most assured confidence; if ignorant, they may and must trust to those who have conducted thousands the same way; and if enlightened, they are still more confident when they see those pilots, instead of concealing, spreading the chart of their salvation before their view, and discover, in proportion as they study it, the most admirable accordance between the instruction of the chart and the skill of their conductors. Behold, then, the pastors of the Catholic Church; far from refusing to the faithful access to the sacred volume, they confidently refer them to it as the written depository of their heavenly commission. And to show that they inherit the same commission, they have only to unfold the catalogue of their bishops, and trace it to an apostolical origin.

In order to ascertain who are those faithful men duly appointed, we have only to trace back the succession of our bishops. But, as it might be tedious, says St. Irenæus, to trace them all, it is sufficient to trace the series of the Bishops of Rome, at once the greatest and most ancient of all the churches . . . with which, on account of its more powerful principality, all the churches of the world must be in communion. How simple and how safe the way in which the Catholic walks: whilst others wander to and fro amidst devious paths entangled as a labyrinth, they have only to grasp the clue supplied by the line of their bishops until they find it spring from the great and central apostolical tree of Rome; some nearer the root, as those of Italy and Spain, others at a higher distance, like those of Ireland; some at still remoter intervals, like those of Germany; and others, like those of America, branching from near its top, still green and vigorous like the palmy monarchs of their own forests, and enabling thousands to find repose under the amplitude of its shade. Yes; some of the goodly branches which it bore in its early growth have withered like the rods of Core as soon as they were cut from this apostolical stem, and deprived of its nutriment, while all that have clung to it are still seen sound and healthful as the rod of Aaron, and bearing evidence by the abundance of their fruit, as well as the beauty of their foliage, of the vigorous principle from which they draw their growth.

In the preceding part of this discourse you must perceive the duties you owe to your new pastor. If deriving descent from an illustrious race, or participating in its riches, form any claim to veneration, how strong must be his titles who can say with the psalmist: "I have taken root among an honourable people,"[1] and who, by being legitimately called as Aaron was, belongs now to that royal priesthood so styled by the Apostle of which the founder was Christ, and the branches adorned with the most brilliant verdure. Do you imagine that I mean, by reminding him of the lofty lineage of the race into which he is adopted, to fill his mind with any vain complacency, or to induce him to imitate those, who fancy that, because their ancestors

[1] Ecclus. xxiv. 16.

were noble they may be worthless, and claim from the title-deeds of their hereditary honours a patent for personal degeneracy? On the contrary, I remind him of it to fill him with humility instead of inspiring him with pride. If I point to the elevation on which he is placed, it is to warn him of the dangers of the precipice below. If I remind him of the important situation of a pilot, it is to make him fearful for the safety of those whom he is appointed to conduct through the troubled and perilous ocean of this life. And if I call his attention to those holy men of heroic might and high renown whom he has succeeded, it is to remind him and us all, by the condition of our feebleness, when contrasted with "those men of great power, who show forth the dignity of prophets, who, by the strength of their wisdom, instructed the people in holy words and gained glory in their generation."[1] If I remind him that he is the first of that chosen body who are selected from among the people, it is not with a view of inspiring him with a love of ease, but rather to enkindle his courage and prompt him to action, since no one is fitted to lead others to the field, or inspire them with powers, who does not himself share in the burdens and the labours which he imposes. If in the willing veneration of the world he sees his own dignity reflected, it is not to fill him with complacency, but rather with alarm; it is not that vanity may be gratified with salutations in the streets, or the first seats in every assembly, or the sound of those pompous titles that the profane delight in; it is to remind him that he is allowed the honour of the first place because he is charged with the heavy duties of the last, that it is not to be ministered unto, but rather to minister to the others, he has taken on himself the holy office of the sanctuary, that the higher

[1] Ecclus. xliv.

he ascends in the hierarchy the heavier and the more painful are the obligations of his servitude, impressing us with the justice of the title adopted by one of the sainted successors of St. Peter, the servant of the servants of God, and which, from being so significant of their harassing duties, has been adopted by all the succeeding Pontiffs. In short, if I impress on him that he is master of the house, it is not that he may lord it over the domestics; it is not that he may, to use the Scripture language, be a lion in the house, scaring away peace from its threshold by the caprice and turbulence of an overbearing temper, but that he may cultivate the arts of peace, that, like a faithful steward, he may distribute, among the family, food in due season, and that, should they be sick and infirm, he may, instead of irritating their wounds by his harshness, endeavour to heal their disorders by infusing, into the wholesome acid of sound discipline, the oil of charitable and paternal counsel. He is a pastor, it is true, appointed to watch the fold and forming one of that body whom the Holy Ghost has constituted to rule the Church of God. Melancholy however, would be the lot of him who would rather dwell on the flattering idea of ruling, rather than the serious obligation of feeding the flock, which is conveyed in the appointment. Should any, losing sight of the cares, the toils, and anxieties of the pastoral office be so unfortunate as to turn it into an engine to minister to their avarice, their sensuality, or their pride, let them ponder well the bitter reproaches of the prophet: "Wo to the shepherds of Israel that fed themselves. Should not the flocks be fed by the shepherds? You eat the milk, and you clothed yourselves with the wool, and you killed that which was fat: but my flock you did not feed. The weak you have not strengthened, and that which was sick you have not healed, that which was broken you have not bound up, and that which was driven away you have not brought again, neither have you sought that which was lost: but you ruled over them with rigour and with a high hand. And my sheep were scattered because there was no shepherd, and they became the prey of all the beasts of the field. My sheep have wandered in every mountain and in every high hill, and my flock were scattered upon the face of the earth, and there was none that sought them. Therefore, ye shepherds, hear the word of the Lord: As I live, saith the Lord God, forasmuch as my flocks have been made a spoil, and my sheep are become a prey to all the beasts of the field, for my shepherds fed themselves and not my flocks. Therefore, ye shepherds, hear the word of the Lord . . . Behold, I myself come upon the shepherds; I will require my flock at their hand, and I will cause them to cease from feeding the flock any more, neither shall the shepherds feed themselves any more. And I will deliver my flock from their mouth, and it shall no more be meat for them: and I will visit my sheep, and I will bring them out from the people, and will gather them out of the countries, and will feed them by the rivers in all the habitations of their own land."[1] Behold in these denunciations the punishments that await bad pastors who for ever are lording it over the feeble flock, but never protect them from the prowling foes that are panting for their destruction. Whereas, to use the beautiful language of the pastorals of St. Gregory, they should cherish the weak with all the tenderness of a mother, and rebuke the audacious with the authority of a master, accommodating his manner to the various tempers of men; now, like St. Peter, deprecating every homage from those

---

[1] Esech. xxiv. 2-14.

who, like Cornelius, were filled with religious respect for his person; and again, like the same Apostle, wielding the thunders of God's vengeance against those who, like Ananias, insulted by his lying hypocrisy the Holy Ghost; consoling the poor in their lowly condition in language that breathes the beatitudes that were delivered to them on the mountain, and "charging the rich of the world," to use the expression of St. Paul, "not to be high-minded;"[1] in a word, as St. Bernard says, displaying their authority in subduing the wolf that invades the fold, rather than annoying the timid flocks that are placed within its enclosures. Should any be so infatuated as to feel complacency in their power, let them hear the words of Wisdom: "Power is given you by the Lord, who will examine your works and search out your thoughts. . . . Horribly and speedily will He appear to you: For a most severe judgment shall be for them that bear rule. For to him that is little, mercy is granted, but the mighty shall be mightily tormented. For God will not except any man's person, neither will He stand in awe of any man's greatness: for He made the little and the great, and He hath equally care of all: But a greater punishment is ready for the more mighty."[2]

In fine, the bishop is to be an assiduous and indefatigable labourer, as appears by the different characters by which the Apostles are designated. I shall not now dwell on the various mystic functions that are assigned them in the inspired writings, now represented as fishermen gathering the elect into their nets, again as hunters chasing from every hill and from every mountain those monsters of vice that turned the earth into a moral wilderness,[1] and all which types are significant of solici-

---

[1] 1 Tim. vi. 17.      [2] Wisd. vi. 4-9.

tude and of toil. I shall confine myself to the familiar parable of the vineyard and the field, to which the Church is so often likened, and its apostles to husbandmen, whose duty it is to fence it, to work it, to weed it, and to gather in the fruit in due season. The office, then, of the ministry is not a place to indulge ease or indolence, but requires the most unremitting correspondence of mental attention and corporal labours. To every bishop a portion of that vineyard is let out by the Master of the field, who requires of him the strictest fidelity in his stewardship, and will reward or punish him according to the measure of his negligence or his zeal. Should it be found secure in its enclosures, and to have thriven under the episcopal cultivation the spiritual steward will have the consolation of hearing: "Well done, thou good and faithful servant; because thou hast been faithful over a few things I will set thee over many things, enter thou into the joy of thy Lord."[2] Should he, however, be a bishop under whom the crop had withered, and his portion of the field had languished, how applicably might its state be described in the words of the Psalmist: "Thou, O God of hosts, hast planted a vineyard, and wast the guide of its journey: Thou plantedst the roots thereof, and it filled the land. . . . The shadow of it covered the hills, and the branches thereof the cedars of God. It stretched forth its branches unto the sea, and its boughs unto the river. Why hast thou broken down the hedge thereof, so that all they who pass by the way do pluck it? The boar out of the wood hath laid it waste, and a singular beast hath devoured it. Turn again, O God of hosts, look down from heaven and see and visit this vineyard."[3]

I trust that these and such similar reproaches as I had

[1] Isai. xiv. 16.  [2] Matt. xxv. 21.  [3] Ps. lxxix. 10-15.

occasion to introduce into this discourse, shall be never applied to the ministry of him whose consecration forms the interesting ceremony of this day. Still the possibility of their future application shows that his situation is not one which can be contemplated without feelings of terror. Were the youngest, the vainest, the worldliest, and the most aspiring in this assembly seriously to reflect on the situations which I have attempted to describe, and to imagine themselves charged with all their responsibilities, they would find the pleasing fascinations of dignity dispelled from their eyes by the painful realities of duty. The hands that are now clothed in silk and gold, they should behold weary with probing the wounds of others, and almost unable, from the frequency of the office, to hold up the cup from which they were wont to pour the wholesome mixture of wine and oil on the ulcers of their patients. Instead of their eyes being dazzled with its ornamental covering, they might then behold a forehead furrowed with age and care, and embrowned with the incessant action of the autumnal sun, from the reaping and gathering of many a harvest. In the room of the decorated sandals they might then behold the feet of the pastor worn by incessant walking, as well as the thorns which he had to encounter through the various departments of his fold; and in the gilded crosier, the emblem of awe and authority, they might behold the staff on which the pastor, feeble from age and faltering from fatigue, strives to support the footsteps that are tottering under the load of some strayed sheep of which he went in quest through the fastnesses of the mountains. Such, at least, are the images that presented themselves to him during the hallowed days of his retreat; nor should I be surprised if he trembled lest the magnificent robes in which he was arrayed might not prove like the garlands which used to deck the victims for sacrifice. Yes; they are the emblems of his immolation, showing that, on this day every feeling and every attachment that might breathe of the world is consumed as an acceptable sacrifice on the altar of religion. Be not, therefore, dismayed at the prospect of the perils that shall encompass your ministry. If you be weak I shall draw from that very weakness a consoling assurance of your strength, and if you are fearful your fears will form the groundwork of the most assured confidence. Trust not to yourself, but to the promises of Him who sends you, telling you He will be with you all days to the term of your life, as He will with those who come after you to the consummation of the world. What, then, have you to fear? You are not more weak or timid than the Apostles. You are less skilled in knowledge than those who boasted they knew nothing but Christ crucified. You are not more destitute of that credit which rank and wealth confer than those who proclaimed they had not gold or silver to distribute; yet, strong in the mighty Spirit of Him who was always with them, they went forth and achieved the conversion of the world. Why, then, be disheartened, or rather, why not be elated, like St. Paul, at the thoughts of our own infirmities, knowing that no natural power could compass what is required of us to achieve, and, consequently, casting all our confidence on Him, "who has chosen the weak things of this world to confound the strong, and the foolish things of this world to confound the wise, and the things that are not, to confound the things that are, that no flesh might glory in His sight?"[1] Behold, then, the true cause of all their triumphs—the utter annihilation or sacrifice of self-love in their hearts, which could oppose any obstacles to the will of the Almighty. Hence, they were like the

[1] 1 Cor. i. 27 seq.

mustard seed, which must first perish before it can spring up into a luxuriant return. Hence, they were justly compared to clouds moving over the earth as it pleased the breath of the Holy Spirit to waft them, and filling every land over which they passed with the fertility of their waters. Go you, in like manner, bearing the same commission, and inspired with the same confidence. Announce with a trumpet voice their sins to Israel, that it may please God in His mercy to rouse them to repentance, or that, if they be not converted, their blood may not be demanded at your hands. "I charge thee before God and Jesus Christ, who shall judge the living and the dead, by His coming, and His kingdom: Preach the Word, be instant in season, out of season, reprove, entreat, rebuke, in all patience and doctrine. Be thou vigilant, labour in all things, do the work of an Evangelist, fulfil thy ministry, be sober."[1] "For a bishop must be without crime, as the steward of God: not proud, not subject to anger, not given to wine, no striker, not greedy of filthy lucre, but given to hospitality, gentle, sober, just, holy, continent:"[2] bearing the burdens of others, and instructing as spiritual men such of his brethren as may be overtaken in any fault, considering lest himself also be tempted.[3] It is thus you will inherit the merciful spirit of that priesthood of whose first great Pontiff it is written that "we have not a high-priest who cannot have compassion on our infirmities, but one tempted in all things like as we are, without sin."[4] For it behoved him in all things to be made like to his brethren, that he might become a merciful and faithful high-priest with God, to make a reconciliation for the sins of the people, for in that wherein He Himself hath suffered and been tempted He

[1] 2 Tim. iv. 1-5.  [2] Tit. i. 7-9.  [3] Gal. vi.  [4] Heb. iv. 15.

is able to succour those who are tempted. With this high-priest as your model, as far as human weakness can imitate divine perfection, mingle the mercy of a parent and a brother with the exercise of the pastoral office. Allow me, then, to conclude this tedious discourse in the language of the two greatest of the Apostles, embracing the respective duties of the people and the pastor, exhorting the one, in the words of St. Paul: "Obey your prelates and be subject to them, for they watch as being to render an account of your souls, that they may do this with joy and not with grief."[1] And you now associated to a share of the apostolic office: "Feed the flock of God which is among you, taking care of it, not by constraint, but willingly, according to God: not for the sake of filthy lucre, but voluntarily. Neither as lording it over the clergy, but being made a pattern of the flock from the heart. And when the Prince of Pastors shall appear you shall receive a never-fading crown of glory."[2] Amen.

[1] Heb. xiii. 17.     [2] 1 S. Pet. v. 2.

## PROFESSION OF A NUN.

*"For they are virgins: these follow the Lamb wherever He goeth.—* APOC. xiv. 4.

AMIDST the group of varied and magnificent visions that rose and passed in rapid succession before the prophetic eye of St. John in the island of Patmos, there is none which exhibits the beautiful features of the Catholic Church more strikingly than the one I have just selected. In glancing at the other parts of this mysterious picture we feel we cannot remove the obscurity in which they are shrouded, or relieve our minds from the terror in which they are invested. But no sooner do we contemplate this peaceful and hallowed scene of thousands of virgins of either sex, forming the nearest and most effulgent circle of the sainted spirits by which the throne of the Lamb is surrounded, and filling the soul with the harmony of their heavenly canticles, than our fears give way to the joy which such a scene inspires. This is a scene of which, before the coming of our Divine Redeemer, the world could not form the faintest idea. Far from aspiring to the practice of this pure virtue, the world was steeped in the indulgence of sensuality; and though some were not insensible to the charms of virginity, it was deemed a state of perfection almost beyond mortal attainment. Even among the Jewish people, though held in estimation, it was in a degree far inferior to that in which it ranks among Christians, and a portion of the veil which was spread over the entire law hung over this virtue in like manner, hiding from the view the splendour of those attributes belonging to this divine virtue, which it was the prerogative of the Catholic Church, and the Catholic Church alone, to unfold. Yes, every cause must be productive of corresponding effects, and though human nature, laden with its primitive corruption, could never exhibit the heroic virtue to which I propose to point your attention, the descent of the Spirit of God purified the entire mass; and from the time that a Virgin Mother gave to the world the mysterious birth of her Virgin Son, the same Divine Spirit has marked its peculiar complacency for this virtue by enduing thousands with constancy and courage to consecrate to God the virtue of their virginity. In union with this, and as handmaids of purity, are seen the kindred virtues of poverty and obedience, to which those young females are now to devote themselves; and it is on the subject of this sacrifice of themselves I propose to address you, in order to give instruction to some of my hearers on duties from which these have already drawn the sweetest consolation.

In the sacrifice which is made by the religious are comprehended the three vows of poverty, chastity, and obedience. Disobedience was the bitter source from which sprung all the disorders that dispeopled heaven of its first inhabitants, and that has entailed upon the earth the countless evils by which it continues to be afflicted. The virtue of obedience, therefore, is the first and most important of all the obligations contracted by religious, and the very foundation by which every religious community is sustained. It repairs the frightful breach caused by the turbulence of self-will, and restores that order and symmetry and peace that mark the movements of bodies that are guided and controlled by a wise intelligence. Had not man's will, in the perverse exercise of its freedom, violently forced itself from the path of obedience, the moral world would have exhibited the same silent harmony which we admire throughout all nature, when all the heavenly bodies in their respective orbits obey with wonderful harmony the first law imposed on them by their Maker. It is no wonder that perfect obedience, or the utter annihilation of individual will, which caused man's misery, should be made the first step in leading him back to the happiness from which he strayed. Hence St. Jerome remarks that self-will and Christian virtue are like numerical quantities, so placed in relation with each other that, in proportion as you subtract from your own will, you add to the stock of human perfection; and St. Bernard, who, like the holy Father just mentioned, was the oracle of the Christian world in his day, and who illustrated in his own person the precept of obedience, of which he eulogised the value, following up the same thought of St. Jerome, breaks forth into this strange language: destroy the perverseness of self-will and hell itself is annihilated. Deeply had those holy men sounded the bottom of the human heart, and seriously did they meditate those inspired writings from which they drew their wisdom, and which tell us "obedience is better than sacrifice . . . because it is like the sin of witchcraft, to rebel, and to refuse to obey, like the crime of idolatry."[1] And why the grievous crime of idolatry? Because, says St. Gregory, such self-willed subjects make an idol of their own presumption, to which they offer worship. And, therefore, St. Basil, who is justly reputed one of the fathers of monastic life, ordains that all religious guilty of disobedience should be separated from the body, like persons covered with a leprosy, lest they should spread over the community the contagion of their disorders. You may confound this obedience,

[1] 1 Kings, xv. 23.

says St. Gregory, with a degenerate spirit; if you do, you must labour under the most melancholy error, since it is this virtue that enables those who practise it, to become the greatest of all conquerors in triumphing over those lofty spirits, who may have owed to their disobedience all the horrors of their fall.

The total abandonment of worldly wealth and the adoption of rigid poverty might appear to the world a severe sacrifice; not so, however, to those who laid, in the vow of obedience, the foundation of Christian perfection, since it is much easier to renounce our possessions than to renounce ourselves; and he, that resigns by obedience his own will, lays the axe to the root of numberless vain and noxious deceits. As the Catholic Church proposes as a model the obedience of our Redeemer, who was obedient even unto the death of the cross, she proposes to us likewise Him who when He was rich became poor for our sakes, that through His poverty we might become rich in spiritual grace. Witnessing the passionate eagerness which the children of the world pant for the acquisition of wealth, and weeping over the sad disorders of which it is the source, she draws around the inmates of religion the secure fence of voluntary poverty. Impressed with the truth of the words of St. Paul, "for they that will become rich, fall into temptation, and into the snare of the devil, and into many unprofitable and hurtful desires, which drown men into destruction and perdition: For the desire of money is the root of all evils, which some coveting have erred from the faith, and have entangled themselves in many sorrows."[1] Stripped of all heavy and unnecessary incumbrances, and girt for the journey, they meet with less impediments in their passage; and as poverty is

[1] 1 Tim. vi. 9.

one of the surest titles to the kingdom of heaven, according to the language of St. James, who says that God has selected the poor for His sacred inheritance, the religious are placed in that position that they may say with St. Paul: "I esteem all things as nought, that I may gain Christ."[1]

In fine, to complete the sacrifice of themselves, they dedicate their virginity to God, in order that henceforth, freed from earth and its temptations, they may, in the language of St. Paul, "think on the things of the Lord, and be holy in body and in spirit."[2] By this religious immolation they literally enter into espousals with their Divine Lord, as is beautifully expressed in the language of their dedication; they thus put the last crown on their consecration by a virtue, which is deservedly called by St. Cyprian the queen of all the virtues. Such is a simple summary of the obligations contracted by those holy females on this solemn occasion, and such is the heroic sacrifice, they lay on the altar, of all that the world most values and adores.

What folly, exclaims the votary of pride, of wealth, of sensuality, thus to resign all the fascinating prospects of youth and fortune! No doubt it is egregious folly in their eyes, and so was a God, incarnate and crucified, to the proud understanding and corrupt hearts of the Gentiles, as it is still to practical unbelievers. Believe the one; is not the other a natural and obvious consequence? And if the Son of God, in the intensity of that charity with which He sought to restore fallen man, was content to hide the splendour of His glory under the lowly vesture of our nature for more than an average of the life of man, is it to be wondered that for a similar

---

[1] Phil. iii. 8.   [2] 1 Cor. vii. 34.

term of human life thousands would be found to forego the united lustre of beauty, rank, fortune, all but feeble and glimmering shadows, in order to be associated with their Redeemer in that glory which He purchased for them by His sufferings on the cross? It is no wonder, then, that those who have no lively faith in the mystery of love which the cross reveals, would wonder at such sacrifices as this day displays; whilst those who, like St. Paul, are lost in the contemplation of the length and breadth and height and depth of the charity of Christ, are not at all surprised at any corresponding elevation of love to which God's creatures are disposed to rise. Hence, while all the secular pomp and official homage, which awaited the vestal virgins of pagan Rome, could not win three individuals to make the painful sacrifice, the Christian world has witnessed monasteries of either sex multiplying with such amazing rapidity, and casting their colonies so profusely over provinces and kingdoms, that we are told by St. Chrysostom, in one of his homilies, that the numbers of those holy cenobites who led the lives of angels upon earth were equal to the married population. Nor was Europe less distinguished for the multitudes and fervour of the children who fled from the contagious atmosphere of the world, and sought shelter for their virtue amidst the holy solitudes of the desert or the cloister. The same spirit of retirement and religious seclusion accompanied the progress of the Gospel throughout our own sainted Island. St. Bridget, the shining light of the Irish Church, was nearly contemporary with St. Patrick, having received the veil from St. Mel, one of the disciples of our great apostle, and during her own life she had the satisfaction of seeing the conventual life, which she may be deemed to have founded, propagated and fixed over part of Ireland. It is not for me to attempt to describe the flourishing state of the monastic institutions in this country, which kept proportionate pace with its growing reputation for sanctity, for charity, and for learning. Yes, and strange as the assertion may appear to some, they will always flourish in proportion as sanctity, charity, and learning will be valued in every country. They are not those institutions of a passing nature, springing from caprice, and which, after having had their ephemeral existence, may be consigned to decay. No; they have sprung out of the very bosom of Christianity; they have been rocked in its cradle; they have grown with its strength and expanded with its maturity; they have experienced every vicissitude of prosperous or adverse fortune, which cheered or sunk the children of the Catholic Church; in short, they are intertwined with and form a portion of its constitution, and it is only when that Church shall cease to have mortal existence, that the monastic orders shall entirely disappear from the earth. And why? because they are animated with the immortal spirit which enlivens and informs Christianity itself; the obedience which, like the primitive spirit that moved over the deep, breathes, over the mutinous elements of human strife, its peaceful influence; the poverty, which Christ bequeathed as the precious inheritance of His elect; and the chastity, of which He illustrated the value in the mystery of the Incarnation, and which elevates the lot of the lowly children of earth to the condition of angels, giving them, by anticipation, the enjoyment of their happiness.

In proportion, then, to the prevalence of the spirit of the Catholic Church in any country is the progress of those institutions to which it gives rise. Hence the number of monastic houses spread over Ireland, and hence its topography, like that of

Judea, is marked with the monuments of religion. Whether you traverse the centre of the island, or wend your circuitous way around its extremities; whether you visit the islands on its lakes or penetrate into its deepest valleys, you find at every step, living, speaking, attestations of that spirit that once filled the breasts of its people. These monuments were razed, their inmates were banished, the matin hymns as well as the vesper canticles with which they resounded were hushed, and the unsightly fragments, that are strewn in such profuse ruin, tell of the violence and rapacity to which they owed their extinction. But, like the transient sleep and silence of Him to whom they owe their existence, they are once more exhibiting throughout the country the glories of a resurrection. And under their renovated form they are shaped, by the wise influence of the Catholic Church, to the shifting wants and necessities of society. When thickly planted throughout the country, they were as so many beacon towers throwing around them the light and warming vigour of their charity. It was not, then, necessary that the consecrated virgins should be going forth from their peaceful solitudes, to diffuse that mercy which went forth from those asylums which they inhabited. But when those beacon fires that cast their brilliancy over the land were extinguished, a thick darkness succeeded, and with the long-continued darkness a corresponding chill and coldness that blighted the growth of the virtues of charity and mercy, and prevented them from ripening into full maturity. Such is the state of society that succeeded the suppression of those sainted asylums of peace, of prayer, of learning, and of charity. To repair the evils you have had abundance of expedients. You have had schools without religion, dispensaries without mercy, poor-houses without charity, until Christendom, almost crushed by the iron weight of expensive machineries, unrelieved by the spirit of religion, is, in the strong language of St. Paul, heaving under the incumbrance, and longing for sending forth those cheap protections of the poor, those spontaneous productions of the Catholic faith and civil freedom, where the measure of relief has no other limit but a boundless charity, and the recompense of those who dispense it, is regulated by the poverty of the Gospel. Yes, not only Ireland, but England, and every country in Europe on which the light of the Catholic Church is reviving, sighs for those institutions, and it is from the consciousness of their decrease, and the inadequacy of all other remedies, however expensive, that those monastic institutions are now springing up over the land. There is not an infirmity, to which our fallen nature is subject, that has not found its appropriate remedies in the institutions of the Catholic Church, where numbers are employed in instructing the ignorant, feeding the hungry, clothing the naked, visiting the sick, consoling the disconsolate, raising the dejected, loosening the captive, and, in short, going around like angels of mercy, mitigating the evils under which humanity is festering. It was to break the fetters of the captive that the Order of Mercy was first instituted. When the fairest provinces of Spain groaned under the yoke of the Moors, and the children of the Catholic Church were carried away captive in order to be educated in an abhorrence of their country and their faith, the Mother of God inspired some holy persons with the heroic resolve of devoting their labours, their fortunes, nay, their liberties, and, if necessary, their lives, to the redemption of those unfortunate victims from the horrors of their temporal and spiritual captivity.

The history of those Orders furnishes many authentic details of religious suffering, such as could be only equalled by the heroism of the first martyrs, and which could not be endured unless fortified by the same spirit with which the courage of the first martyrs was sustained. It is to break a similar yoke, or, at least, to lighten its pressure, that the Sisters of Mercy are sent by Divine Providence into this favoured district. And the inhabitants will, no doubt, feel and exhibit corresponding gratitude to the pious, the enlightened, and solicitous pastor who sought, and who succeeded in finding, such seasonable assistance in the spiritual difficulties under which this as well as all parts of Ireland yet labour. It is a cheering dawn after such a long and dreary darkness. It is an auspicious festival on which the spiritual immolation of those virgins is perfected. No doubt their mission is under the guidance and patronage of the holy Mother of God, who first inspired the institution of their Order. What more appropriate day could have been selected for this dedication to the Order of Our Lady of Mercy than the Sunday of the Feast of the Rosary, marked with so many historical monuments of her miraculous interposition? To pass over other interesting records, I shall only allude to the signal triumph gained by the Christians on the first Sunday of October, in the year 1571, over the formidable armament of the Turks in the Gulf of Lepanto. Having assembled on this occasion the most formidable fleet which they could equip, they carried terror and dismay into the very heart of Europe, and the western nations trembled lest the Mahometan power, which so often had been checked, should at length bury in the tide of its barbarous conquest every vestige of Christianity and civilisation. St. Pius V., the then reigning Pontiff, cast himself and the interests of the

Catholic Church on the protection of the Blessed Virgin, and ordered public prayers and processions in her honour, in order that the pure worship of her Divine Son should not be supplanted by the blasphemies of an impostor, who impiously profaned the sacred character of prophet by assuming so holy and incongruous a name. The prayers of the Church were crowned with signal success; and it is recorded that at the very time in which victory declared in favour of the Christians the Pope was favoured with a miraculous revelation of the event, who imparted, at the same time, to others, the joyous communication. From that period the first Sunday in October is consecrated to a grateful commemoration of this event, and his successor ordained, that on every recurring anniversary, should be celebrated the Festival of the Rosary.

It is, then, an auspicious day, and besides your own pious prayers and those of this vast congregation here assembled, you will doubtless share in the treasures of grace which the accumulated supplications of the faithful all over the earth will not fail to bring down on this holy festival. She will be your help and succour in all your sorrows and necessities. If you are in trouble, invoke her aid; if overspread with sorrow, invoke her light, which, like the morning star, diffusing calm over the deep, will dissipate every darkness and restore a heavenly light to your minds. She is not only your patron, but also your model, held up by the Church, as St. Ambrose says, as a mirror to all virgins through which they may contemplate the virtues they are to practise. Hence appropriately is she represented in the inspired writings under the figures of a fenced garden, a sealed fountain, and after her the Church itself is likened with the same images, adorned with virgins whose virtues, like the sweetest flowers, spread their fragrance throughout the entire atmosphere. Yes, it is only within the garden of the Catholic Church, fenced by its discipline, and watered by the untainted fountain of its pure doctrine, and warmed by the genial heat of the grace with which it abounds, have sprung up in every age, and will still spring up, those choicest flowers, fairer than the lily, and more fragrant than the most exquisite spices that bloom under an eastern sun. And of this fair garden there is not a fairer portion than our own sainted island, which appears to be so congenial to the growth of those virtues, that even among the ruins of their habitations, though their inmates are so long gone, there still lingers the odours of their sanctity. Yes, the soil of Ireland is peculiarly favourable to the growth of those virtues, and the very atmosphere is redolent of their sweetness and purity. They may be trodden under foot, as they have been trodden when the fences were broken, and the beasts of the forest have been let in to rifle them; but with the return of the spring and the repair of the enclosures, and the cultivation of the husbandman, the lily will again display its beauty and give forth its fragrance. The discipline by which it is guarded may appear sharp and repulsive; but let it be recollected that the most fragrant of flowers grow amidst the thorns, or in the solitude where they are not sullied by the noisome breath of society.

What a heroic mission do those young females undertake! It may be said that they have no distant countries now to traverse, no tyranny to endure, and no captives to redeem, as had some of their predecessors in similar monasteries. They have the same painful and perilous functions to discharge. How often are they obliged to go and bring the light of religion to a poor soul that, until the moment of sickness, sat in the darkness of wilful ignorance, notwithstanding the frequent opportunities of instruction? How often will they be obliged to seek them in the far countries of sin and sorrow into which they had wandered, striving to touch them, in the accents of mercy, with a sense of the happiness which they had forfeited, and of the misery into which they had fallen, and to strengthen their tottering steps with courage, and fill their desponding souls with consolation, as they rise to come back to the house of their Father? How often will they be obliged to weep over the chains in which the captives of sin are bound, imploring Him, who restored to his disconsolate mother her young child who was stretched upon the bier, to restore to the life of grace some young and thoughtless sinners over whose spiritual death the Church, their tender mother, had been shedding tears of compassion? These are the holy objects of the mission which those pious Sisters have to discharge. They are to realise the parable of the Gospel, carrying, like the wise virgins, their lamps copiously furnished with oil, diffusing along their path its heat and lustre. Such continual diffusing of light requires fresh and continuous supplies of the unction of grace that it may not be exhausted. Offer, then, my dear Christians, your united prayers that they may persevere to the end, fulfilling the high and holy duties which they have been called to perform : solicitous in prayer, fervent in watching, with loins girt and the lamps in their hands trimmed, furnished, and burning with the oil of charity and good works, that when the Bridegroom knocks they may receive Him, not only without terror, but with joy, and be admitted to share with Him the wedding feast, and sing canticles in heaven with those countless virgins that are privileged to follow the Lamb wherever He goeth, for ever and ever. Amen.

## THE SYNOD OF THURLES.

> "And the angel said to her: Fear not, Mary, for thou hast found grace with God. Behold, thou shalt conceive in thy womb, and shalt bring forth a Son: and thou shalt call His name Jesus. He shall be great, and shall be called the Son of the Most High, and the Lord God shall give unto Him the throne of David, His father: and He shall reign in the house of Jacob for ever, and of His kingdom there shall be no end."—LUKE, i. 30-33.

OF this magnificent and merciful prophecy, which the angel of the Lord announced to Mary, the humble Virgin, she beheld the completion of a considerable part before her triumphant assumption into heaven; and the rest has been, and ever shall be, further developed in the extension and stability of Christ's kingdom of the Catholic Church, until its term on earth shall expire with the world itself, thenceforward to continue in heaven its eternal duration. Of this great kingdom of the Church, which was thus heralded by one of those pure spirits that minister around the throne of the Most High, our nation and people have, from their first annexation to its dominion, formed a goodly and a faithful portion; and in this episcopal senate, assembled under the auspices and control of the successor of St. Patrick, clothed with the delegated dignity of the Holy See, you have a fair sample of those grave legislative assemblies by which the permanent government of this spiritual kingdom is secured. This kingdom of Christ's Church, planted on earth for the restoration of fallen man to the divine inheritance which he had forfeited, and destined to sustain a perpetual conflict with the old enemy, stung with rage and envy that his spoil should be wrested from him, has not been unprovided with the means necessary for a warfare so holy and so arduous; nor have its chief watchmen been left without sufficient aid to secure the protection of their respective wards against the untiring assaults of their sleepless and treacherous enemy, by which it shall not cease to be assailed. What, then, is the nature of the government of this kingdom; who are the chief legislators on whom its administration devolved; and what is the source and sanction of the laws by which the evils of disorder and confusion are avoided, and the blessings of union and strength are secured? Those appear to me the appropriate topics on which to dwell during the auspicious continuance of this national council.

Scarce did our Divine Redeemer come forth from the seclusion of His private life when He called His Apostles, and sent them forth with the commission: "And going, preach, saying : The kingdom of heaven is at hand."[1] How analogous the words of this His first commission to His Apostles with the language in which the angel shadowed forth to the Blessed Virgin the nature of His spiritual kingdom! In whatever form, then, the Church's authority is exercised, its pastors are entitled to the respect and obedience of the faithful, when bound in communion with the chief pastor, to whom, in the person of Peter, He confided the care, and solicitude, and government of His entire fold. But it is through the medium of its congregated councils, through those acts that embody the varied wisdom, and that reflect the condensed authority of its bishops under its venerable head, the majesty of this kingdom is particularly displayed. Although the Apostles were endowed with individual infallibility, being under the immediate inspiration of heaven, yet, when a great controversy arose regarding the retention or abolition of some of the ritual observances of the Old Law, they adopted the

[1] S. Matt. x. 7.

measure of communing with each other in council, where, after much disputation, Peter arose, declaring that the yoke of circumcision should not be imposed on the Gentile converts. In the free deliberation of its members, and the final and irreversible decision of their chief, and the full and entire acquiescence of all, in that decision, this Council of Jerusalem has been looked to as a sacred model for all future councils, combining all the weight derived from the lights and the virtues of the members that compose them, and deriving incontestible claims to reverence and submission from their obedience to the head of the Universal Church, the Bishop of Rome.

No matter from what quarter the wind of error was blowing, it was to the successor of St. Peter every eye was turned against the danger of the rising storm. No matter in what region of the earth the standard of revolt was unfurled, it was to the same successor of St. Peter the adjuration of the Church was sent forth, to strike the guilty and irreclaimable insurgents with the sword of the sanctuary. Travel down the long period of the Church's history, from St. Peter to the present Pontiff who blesses the world with the wisdom and benevolence of his reign, and stretch your vision across the broadest expanse that was ever found within its ample boundaries, and you encounter the Roman Pontiff in every movement of the one, and at every step of the other, not annoyingly, but propitiously; now animating the assembled fathers at Nice, with a St. Michael's fidelity, again to smite the ancient fiend, who, in the person of Arius, renewed, against the divinity of the Son of God on earth, the same impious war for which he was hurled out of heaven; again sustaining, against a similar assault on the glory of the godhead in the person of the Holy Ghost, the faithful bishops at Constantinople;

and, finally, encouraging the zealous fathers of Ephesus to vindicate for the Blessed Virgin the rightful title of Mother of God, contained in my text, of which, being next in hate as she was in dignity, the same untiring enemy of mankind sought to rob her. The Pope is everywhere, and his voice is heard, and his influence felt, and his authority owned, not only in those august œcumenical assemblies, as they are called, impersonating the entire Church, and over which the ruler of the entire Church should preside; but whenever the faith is endangered, or its intrepid champions exposed to peril, or the holy discipline of the Church attempted to be changed or trampled on, then you find him protecting the great Athanasius from the fierce confederacy of the heretics of his time; or, St. Chrysostom, against the enemies raised up by his eloquent assertion of morality and virtue; and proclaiming, as in the former case, for the instruction of all synods and assemblies, however numerous or exalted their members, that it is interdicted by ecclesiastical rule to any churches to make laws without the authority of the Bishop of Rome. The readers of Protestant historians, who associate the names of Gregory and Innocent, or Sylvester, with despotism and usurpation, may fancy that this domination was the offspring of the Middle Ages. Little do these shallow Sciolists, who calumniate these Pontiffs, know their characters—persons who were by nature the meekest of men, and generally seated with a sincere reluctance on the Pontifical throne. They remind us of the language of Jeremias, which we read as applied to St. John, in the liturgy of this day—men, who interposed the apology of their own feebleness as unable to utter the first unformed sounds of infants; but when called by God, and filled with His spirit, those infants of embarrassed speech spoke in the presence of kings and were not confounded; and from the position and grace of their office, became as vigorous as giants in defence of the trampled liberties of the Church. Yes; to preserve, then, the images and language, they were converted into walls of brass and pillars of iron, and chosen quivers; and, like those walls, they stood firm and unmoved against the rushing tumult of their foes, and like the chosen quivers, they sent forth those burning shafts whose light and fire came from heaven. No matter where held—whether at Arles in France, or Toledo in Spain, or Carthage in Africa, or Constantinople in the East—they acknowledge the authority of the Bishop of Rome with as profound a reverence as those held in his own presence within the sacred walls of St. John of Lateran, not only on questions intimately and essentially connected with the faith, such as withdrawing the flock from poisonous practices, and leading them to the pure and wholesome fountains, but on all the duties of man, from the throne to the cottage, was the authority of the Pope recognised and revered, since there is not a solitary duty or obligation of any class or person from the humblest to the most elevated in society, placed beyond the sphere of his all-comprehensive jurisdiction. Hence the frequent and necessary interference of the Roman Pontiff in guarding the sacred rights of marriage against the inroads of immorality, and the holy institutions of celibacy against concubinage; and hence his frequent wrestling with the powers of this world, and the carnal weapons of lust, and avarice, and pride, by which they sought to tarnish the glory of the sanctuary.

Those were intrepid Pontiffs who wrestled with the monstrous iniquities of their times ; they labuured incessantly to extend freedom to the slave, education to the ignorant, comfort to the disconsolate, and, in a word, to realise the benevolent mission of

Him of whom they are the successors. To give light to those who sat in darkness, and liberty to the captive, the stagnant masses of ignorance and corruption which, if left unmoved, would have spread destruction all around, were stirred and agitated by the wholesome breath that went forth from the centre of Christianity; and in this salutary motion of its waters the evils of society, if not healed, were considerably mitigated. From the same centre issued the impulse to which Europe was indebted for the erection and support of its schools and colleges, which sprung up with amazing rapidity and success, encouraged and sustained everywhere by episcopal synods and councils, and such would they have continued if a fatal check had not been given to those salutary institutions. On the lamentable causes by which they were checked, I need not occupy your attention long. They are associated with those disastrous revolutions by which the peace of the Church all over Europe was shaken, and its authority forcibly transferred to mere secular agencies. Suffice it to observe that the great schism, which towards the close of the fourteenth century distracted Europe, enervated for a time the influence of the Roman Pontiffs, and, with it, the beneficient action of episcopal councils. The Papal pretenders who transferred, the second time, their seat to Avignon, which, on the first occasion necessity might have justified in the legitimate Popes, chiefly relied on the French kings for the maintenance of their schismatical power, and, in return, as will ever happen to feeble usurpations, made large and unwarrantable concessions of ecclesiastical authority to those kings by whom these uncanonical pretensions were sustained. Behold, the latter source of those royal invasions of the spiritual jurisdiction by which the Church began to be enslaved, and to which some of the intoxicated slaves were taught to give the name of liberties. For those invasions of the Papal authority a sanction was sought in the Councils of Bâle and Bourges, and the consequence was that the venerable ecclesiastical hierarchy of France, so renowned in its early history, was, by persevering violence, pushed out of the canonical track of its predecessors. As an incontestable instance of this anomalous course, witness the convention of disastrous celebrity, held towards the close of the seventeenth century—neither a diocesan synod, nor a national or provincial council; no, but a nondescript clerical aggregation of an utterly strange and novel character, accommodated to the secular influence from which it sprung, moving, as a necessary consequence, out of the fixed orbit of regular ecclesiastical bodies, and like all such eccentric, though brilliant aggregations, threatening disorder and ruin in their career. The disorders with which the uncanonical assembly was fraught, were not slow in their development; for revolt, in the first instance, becoming daily more organised, and then heresy, and next infidelity, followed with regular and rapid succession in its train.

For nearly three entire centuries, from the close of the Council of Trent to the present propitious period, has the Church been in fetters throughout almost all Europe, and incapable of that free and harmonious action which, through its canonical councils, always regulated by the Popes, it exercised in the preceding ages. With the authority of the bishops thus shackled, the charitable and intellectual institutions, which they were wont to foster and to guide, fell almost exclusively under the control of secular agencies, and their step-dame influence was felt in the comparative neglect of the orphaned children who, no longer guarded by a mother's care, were allowed, nay, led to stray beyond the fences of religion and of virtue. Then was there a minister of this, and a minister of that duty, once, more appropriately as more effectually, discharged by the Church, which now became enfeebled by the partition of its functions, and their entire subtraction from its merciful control. Then, instead of a body remarkable for its strength and beauty derived from the variety of its members, and the compactness with which they were knitted together, represented in the inspired picture of the Church given us by the Apostle, and exhibiting in its living symmetry the Divine Spirit from which it came forth, the Church, bound and manacled, was subjected to a dissecting process, and those parts which, when united, were so sightly and so firm, became, when loose and scattered, bereft almost of the energy of life and the comeliness of their form. Between virtue and knowledge, between morality and science, an unnatural divorce was attempted, as if they had not flourished in all their vigour when wedded together under the tutelage of the Catholic Church. Of the shoots of the tree of knowledge, bitter experience has taught the fruit to be the knowledge of evil as well as of good: whereas, it is only when engrafted on the stem of faith, and watered with the dews from heaven, it becomes so rich and fragrant as to give a foretaste of eternal life. Science itself is subjected to minute analysis for the purpose of resolving it into independent sources, as if all knowledge could not be traced to its own heavenly origin, or as if the various colours and names it assumes from the refracting mediums through which it passes, were not, like the variegated rays of the sun, all derived from the great original and eternal light of the Word, "which enlighteneth every man that cometh into this world."[1] It would seem as if one distinct domain, and that sufficiently limited, had been assigned to the Church,

[1] S. John, i. 9.

whilst a larger one of indefinite extent is claimed for secular science, over which, it is contended, she should exercise no control.

Thus, in the transmission of errors the Manichæan heresy is renovated in another form, and two distinct and independent principles are asserted to rule over the intellectual world, even in a state of antagonism with each other. The existence of any such co-ordinate principle in science, as fraught with evil and with discord in the intellectual as it would be in the material world, the Church has never recognised. But, holding her high and sacred position, as the noblest emanation of God's infinite knowledge that ever came down on this world, she has not ceased, and never will cease, to exercise her reasonable dominion over all the subordinate sciences, allowing the human mind the fullest scope in their cultivation and development, provided they came not in collision with those sacred truths that are entrusted to her custody. Privileged to teach all truth unto the end of time, and to exercise full authority in its propagation, she never can allow the interference of any teaching that would tarnish the lustre of revealed truth or arrest its diffusion, being " mighty to God unto the pulling down of fortifications, destroying counsels, and every height that exalteth itself against the knowledge of God, and bringing into captivity every understanding unto the obedience of Christ."[1] Yes; this supreme dominion, given her to make captive every human intellect, she can never abdicate, and the loftiest as well as the lowliest of the secular sciences are so many handmaids in harmonious accordance, whose legitimate office is to move and to swell the majesty of her train. It is true that some of them forcibly and un-

[1] 2 Cor. x. 4, 5.

naturally arrayed themselves against the queen from whom they derived their light; but the world is impatient to have them again restored to their allegiance. For more than fifteen centuries the entire dominion of the civilised world belonged to her, the well-earned fruits of her early conquests, its science, its arts, its civilisation, its history, its laws, and its institutions, for promoting the welfare of mankind; and am I to be told that the treasures of her wisdom and trophies of her authority—those arsenals of her munitions, and records of her power—are to be rifled and given over to some of her insurgent and disobedient children against that very Church by which they were created? "The heavens shew forth the glory of God, and the firmament declareth the work of His hands;"[1] and is it then dutiful on the part of God's rational creatures to suffer that, through their perversion of science, the heavens, the mute heralds of God's glory, should be made speak a different language, and bear, through the construction of their interpreters, false witness against their Maker? As well might you hail the progress of the horde of licentious anarchists, who lately seized and held possession of Rome, and, after banishing its Pontiff, exercised a despotism as destructive as it was loathsome—rioting amidst the ruin which they were creating, until, in their disastrous progress, the bronze statues of saints and martyrs should be recast in pagan moulds, and the Christian marbles should be chiseled into pagan forms, until the inspired productions of Christian artists should yield to those idols of a licentiousness which the Apostle forbids us to name, and until the glorious worship in St. Peter's should be replaced by the impure divinities of the Pantheon. As the destruction of those monuments, or their appropriation to other purposes, would be a disaster

[1] Ps. xviii. 2.

which not only the friends of religion but civilisation should deplore; and, as the return of the Roman Pontiff was hailed with universal joy into the capital of his dominions, so should it be a subject of deep regret that the historical records of any Christian nation should be in the hands of enemies, and of joy that they should be restored to their rightful owners, who alone can place them in a proper light.

It is a consolation that, out of the mass of disorder the Almighty sometimes draws out good; and, as an illustration, at the very time the anarchists of the world are proclaiming, in the exile of the Roman Pontiff, the fall of the Apostolic See, scarcely do they indulge the short-lived triumph, when his welcome is enthusiastically greeted, not only by Rome, but by the Christian world, and all the fettered churches of Europe are set free. Again, thank God, the song of jubilee is heard; because, all over the world the captive hierarchy is set free comparatively. No longer are the Bishops of France interdicted by royal edicts or parliamentary ordinances from holding their august councils according to the canons of ancient times. No longer are the Bishops of Germany imprisoned, so as not to be able to obey the impulse of their piety in paying their homage at the shrine of the Apostles. No; their bondage is loosened; and, within these two years, what a consoling spectacle to behold the Bishops of France and Germany, assembled in all the majesty of their ancient synods, running a race of emulation in restoring the institutions of past times, and rivalling each other in their devotion to the chair of Peter! How magnificent the destiny of this glorious Church, and how the amplest limits of the Roman empire shrink in the comparison of the vaster extent of its spiritual successor, and how narrow the boundaries of the Ganges or the Euphrates, over which the great Roman orator anticipated his fame would be wafted, in comparison with the wilderness of space that stretches to Baltimore on one side and Australia on the other, where, within those later years the bishops and archbishops of worlds unknown to the ancients, assemble and solemnly utter the profession of the same faith of Rome, and obedience to the same authority of the successor of St. Peter! And shall Ireland be last in this universal rivalry of faith and devotion? Shall she be palsied near the brink, whilst all the others are walking forth in gladness, and bounding with energy and strength from the virtues of the agitated waters? Oh, no! The hierarchy and people who are here assembled, are living illustrations of the faith, and of the powers by which it has been protected: the one coming forth as from the crypts of the catacombs, arrayed in splendour; and the other thronging around them with the devotedness of children. The pastors and the flocks are worthy of each other;—the former multiplied to their entire number from the disastrous time when only two bishops could be found in the land, and the latter, though thinned by years of the severest suffering, still forming by their numbers as well as their fidelity, the crown and glory of their pastors. Such a glorious exodus reminds me of the inspired language applied to the Church, comparing it, in its beautiful array, to the tribes of Israel. She is still, and shall ever be, faithful to her title of being one of the most devoted daughters of the spouse of Christ. The majestic spectacle which you contemplate, proves that of her sacred hierarchy no one has been diminished, of her power not one sceptre has been broken, of the hairs of her head, not one has been singed in the fiery ordeal through which she has traversed. That excites the consoling hope that she is to share in the rewards of those who have "come out of great tribulation and have washed their robes in the blood of the Lamb,"[1] and who sing benediction, and glory, and wisdom, and thanksgiving, and honour, and strength, to our God for ever and ever. Amen.

---

## THE OPENING OF THE TUAM SYNOD, 1854.

"For where there are two or three gathered together in My name, there am I in the midst of them."—S. MATT. xviii. 20.

WE cannot more appropriately open the solemn council on this great Festival of the Assumption of Our Blessed Lady than in the language of our Divine Redeemer, which St. Celestine addressed to the bishops some fourteen hundred years ago, when convoking the Council of Ephesus. The presence of the Holy Ghost, observes the pious Pontiff, is attested by the numerous assemblage of His anointed priesthood; for, if the presence of the Holy Spirit be not wanting when only two or three are assembled in our Saviour's name, how much more securely may we not calculate on His presence and protection when those are assembled in His name, and in greater numbers, with whom, through the Apostles, He has promised to abide to the end of time, teaching the things which He has commanded, and dispensing the graces of the sacraments which He has instituted. Never, continues the holy Pope, was Christ, whom they were commanded to preach, wanting in sustaining the

[1] Apoc. vii. 14.

doctrine of His own preachers, whether it was promulgated by the Apostles themselves, or by those to whom their divine commission had descended. In the solicitude of the pastoral office all those have participated, who, at different times have been seated on the chairs of the Apostles, and by the hereditary right of their legitimate succession, associated to a share in the consoling privileges, as well as in the awful responsibility, which their exalted ministry involves. It was not enough that the Apostles went forth casting the seed of sound doctrine, and watering it abundantly with their blood. No; it was still necessary that this seed be fostered and preserved, and the care of its cultivation and protection to the end of time devolves in a special manner upon those who, notwithstanding the diversity of places over which they may be scattered, are bound, by their joint solicitude and labour, to transmit in its integrity to others the rich treasure which has reached them through the series of their apostolical predecessors. It is to fulfil our portion of this common duty we are assembled here on this occasion—bishops, priests, and people—in the name and to the glory of our Lord and Master, Jesus Christ, relying firmly on His own promises, that He will vouchsafe to us His divine assistance, and that He will not fail to listen to the prayers of the assembled thousands of the people, ascending to the throne of mercy, to bring down on our deliberations the blessings of heaven.

To impress adequately how much we need the divine assistance and the prayers of the people, through which it is conveyed, I need but glance at the figures under which the pastors of the Church are represented in the inspired writings, and at the mystic functions that are assigned to them, all, expressive of incessant solicitude and toil. In one place, they are represented as fishermen, casting forth their nets into the deep, and gathering in the elect from its waters; in another, under the apparently strange figure of persons engaged in the chase, driving from every hill and from every mountain those monsters of wickedness and infidelity which sometimes turn the earth into a wilderness. Again, the Church is likened to a field, and the pastors to husbandmen whose daily duty it is to work it, to weed it, to build or repair its fences, and to gather in the fruit in due season. Nor are we to omit a passage of the Psalms which so strikingly sketches the arduous contests that must engage the chiefs of the Church in guarding the deposit of the faith, and repulsing the assaults of its enemies. "Surround Sion," exclaims the Royal Prophet, "and encompass her; tell ye in her towers; set your hearts on her strength, and distribute her houses, that ye may relate it in another generation."[1] Illustrating the comparison of "a city seated on a mountain,"[2] the Church has never ceased to attract the attention of the world, and if it has everywhere scattered the benefit of its light, it is no less certain that it has encountered bitter hostility from every quarter; and if, as we are told by the inspired writer, the most ordinary life partakes of the military character, how much more so was the life of the chief pastors of the Church a continual succession of vigils and of warfare, incessantly labouring to encompass the walls of this outspread city—now sending forth from its towers the voice of their warning, and again assigning to such of their associates as were distinguished for their fidelity and prowess those portions of the breach through which, if neglected, a stealthy or a daring foe might securely enter. How strikingly are those and several

---

[1] Ps. xlvii. 13-14.   [2] S. Matt. v. 14.

such representations of the zeal, the toil, and struggles of its pastors exemplified at different periods in the annals of the Church.

In the Apostles, their first vocation was changed and exalted into that of fishers of men casting their nets without tiring, until they were nigh breaking from the multitude they had taken. In some of the subsequent fathers and champions of the Church we discover those mighty men of renown, who pursued and wrestled with those monsters that profaned the earth by warring against heaven. Such were St. Athanasius and St. Hilary in their days, who moved from kingdom to kingdom animating the faithful against the blasphemous heresy of Arius and his followers, who sought to tear the Son of God from His eternal throne. Such, too, were St. Cyril of Alexandria, and St. Celestine, from whom I have already quoted, who vindicated the honour due to the Blessed Virgin, of which Nestorius, a prelate, backed by the temporal influence of the imperial court of Constantinople, sought to rob her by denying that she was the Mother of God. If the Apostles have been justly considered fishermen in gaining countries to the Church, and those fathers, I have alluded to, likened to courageous combatants in protecting the faith, well might St. Celestine be entitled to the praise of both; since, whilst he preserved the east from a heresy that was aimed against the Blessed Mother of God, he swept the western seas with the nets of the fishermen, and brought our own nation from its depths to the pale of the Catholic Church. Never was a more precious gem yet drawn from the bosom of the ocean, for since it caught first the gleam of the faith which revealed its richness and its beauty, its solidity has been proof against all force; and, no matter how thick the darkness, it could not obliterate or tarnish its lustre. Not, indeed, that it was not sufficiently tried in the most fiery ordeals—not that Satan had not often sought to sift its followers as wheat, as he once attempted on Simon, but the same power that fortified the faith of Peter fortified likewise that of Ireland, because it was indissolubly bound to the same rock; and hence those gates of hell, which could not prevail against the one, have been, from their connection, equally powerless against the other. In a long-continued contest, in which Satan and his followers have put forth all their strength for the upturning of our Church, it is not to be imagined that it should have escaped utterly unharmed. It was a contest for life or death, for the light of faith or the darkness of infidelity; and, like the serpent, who leaves his body without defence when his head is in danger, the Irish people cheerfully sacrificed their bodies, their lands, their immunities—nay, more, all the material interests of their Church, and, what is more painful to a sensitive and intellectual people, they bore the forced privation of literature and science, in order to preserve the rich jewel of their faith, the hidden treasure of the field, with which neither the wealth nor wisdom of the world could be put in competition. In other countries even successful assaults upon religion were but of short continuance. In some the tidings that announced the approach of the aggressor, were at the same time the harbingers of his triumphs; and the faith and courage of the vanquished sunk at once, without an effort to rise from under the first tide of barbarous conquest that passed over them. In others, for example, nearer home, the feeble faith of the chief pastors of the Church, long dimmed in a tainted and corrupt atmosphere, paled before the more dazzling glare of mere secular honours, for which they panted, and when the few intrepid shepherds were stricken down by violence—

when the tall and majestic trees of the forest fell beneath the axe of the woodman, and the more numerous mercenaries yielded to the allurements of the world, then were these flocks scattered without leaders, a prey to every ravenous beast, never perhaps again to be gathered unto the fold of the one shepherd, unless through a singular miracle of God's mercy. Not so with the faith, and pastors, and people of Ireland. They were doomed to suffer from more than one tyrant, and these terrible trials were not confined to the term of a century. No; without taking any liberty with the stubborn faith of history, the ten persecutions that afflicted the early Church might have been said to have been acted over again in our own devoted island, and with an intensity proportioned to the narrower range of space and time over which they extended. From the last and worst of the Henrys to the second of the worthless Georges, the grim portraits of ten active or acquiescent royal persecutors of the Irish people, for no other cause but attachment to their creed, stand out before us, without including the truculent and remorseless Cromwell in this ominous number, and as if to show how far, like another Job, the patient fortitude of a nation, faithful to its religion, could rise when sustained by the finger of God, the disastrous reign of the cruellest of all these monarchs was permitted by a mysterious Providence to stretch over almost a half century, exhibiting an epitome of the most savage and revolting atrocities of them all.

It was no wonder if, during such a lingering contest that would have exhausted the energies of the most devoted heroism, a contest which might be likened to the couch of slowly burning fire on which St. Lawrence, the martyr of this week's liturgy was stretched, several of those mighty men who were appointed to surround Sion, and encompass its walls, should have gradually disappeared. It is no wonder if our churches were then defaced, if their towers had fallen, if our sanctuaries were left desolate, if our Sabbaths were made a reproach, and our festivals turned into mourning, if our temples became as a man without honour, and if the vessels of their glory were carried away captive. Then were literally fulfilled our Redeemer's own words, that, "The foxes have holes, and the birds of the air nests, but the Son of Man hath not where to lay His head."[1] Then was He again forced to fly into the desert, not from fear that the multitude might proclaim Him King, but from fear that His followers should be subjected to the tragic execution acted on Calvary. It was no wonder if the solemnities of our worship then ceased, and if the voice of the organ and choir were silent; the heavenly canticle that commanded the sun, the moon, the stars, the sea, the rocks, the rivers, and the mountains, to praise the Lord, seemed then under an interdict; not only the cunning of the artist, but the materials which he fashioned, were all impressed into the service of heresy; the musical metals themselves were forbidden to intone the glories of their Maker; and if, perchance, their seditious tongues were heard to issue from any obstinate tower, summoning the scattered flocks to the temple of God for sacrifice, or penitence, or prayer, they were sure to be taken down by some sacrilegious hand, and, like muffled felons, consigned to some neighbouring morass in solitude and in silence. Then, too, were our apostolical candlesticks, which so long spread their broad and united effulgence over the land, gradually extin-

[1] S. Matt. viii. 20.

guished and taken away; and on two occasions, within the disastrous interval I have mentioned, there were to be seen but two or three of those solitary episcopal lamps, ebbing out as if the last remnant of the sacred oil that fed them; yet, with the flickering flame which they cast around the hallowed spots where they remained, burning them into so many "gossens" of light and gladness, amidst the gloom of despondence which was setting in over the entire country.

And why do I dwell with such marked and special emphasis on these two periods of our history, when our bishops residing in Ireland were so few, and barely sufficient by the imposition of their hands, enfeebled by age and embrowned by labour, to propagate the ministry of the priesthood; when they were obliged, like St. Athanasius, to snatch a hasty sight of their flocks, and then to fly, to found, perhaps, as did our own Archbishop Florence Mac Conry, the University of Louvain, colleges in foreign lands, from which the exiled youth of Ireland might bring home the sacred fire of religion and learning, and scatter it among the people, chilled and almost benumbed to death by the cold and creeping influence of heresy, which threatened to seize and extinguish their constitution. I do it to bear solemn and authentic testimony to the singular merits of such a nation, and to animate, by the recollection of the devotedness of their predecessors, the faith of the children who have succeeded such a religious race. I do it to carry out the spirit of my text, to show that the Holy Ghost resides among those who are truly gathered together in His name, not only actively and infallibly guiding the teachers of God's Church, but infallibly guiding their flocks also, and making their docile hearts the passive depositories of His truth and graces, even when they may be for a short time, from some necessity, deprived of the tending care of their pastors. I do it to show, on opening this council, how great is our reliance on the prayers of all the faithful who are here assembled in the name of our Divine Redeemer. At any time and on any occasion, our confidence in the humble supplications of the people would be great, knowing their mighty efficacy. How much more so when they are offered under the shadow of her protection who was seen, on the anniversary of this day, taking possession of the kingdom which her Divine Son had prepared for her; while the heavenly choirs were heard, thus greeting her advent into heaven: "Who is this that cometh up from the desert, flowing with delights, leaning upon her beloved?"[1] And well, too, in the dawn, I hope, of more prosperous times, may we repeat the same significant anthem, which may apply to the Church, the spouse of our Lord, as it does more directly to the glories of His Mother. In no nation among those by whom, according to her own prediction, she was to be called Blessed, is the honour of the Holy Virgin cherished with more zealous reverence, or her intercession sought and relied on with more affectionate devotion. We require no new or strange theories on this point; for it is not yesterday nor to-day the name of Mary has become among us the source of so much attraction to the homage of every Christian heart. No; her name and worship were wafted to Ireland with the first tidings of salvation by which our shores were gladdened, and that amidst circumstances which left an ineffaceable impression. Events of an exciting character never fail to lend a peculiar colour and complexion to the minds of contemporaries.

When St. Patrick was on the eve of starting from

[1] Cant. viii. 5.

Rome for the conversion of our country, he was no stranger to the blasphemies by which the Holy Virgin was assailed, nor to the zeal and grief of the Pontiff who laboured so much to vindicate her insulted dignity. Landing in Ireland in the very season when the assembled Fathers of Ephesus hurled their condemnation against her impious assailants, our Apostle must have been imbued with a deep sympathy in the triumphs of the Church, and the discomfiture of its enemies; and he must have listened with devout rapture to the echoes of the enthusiasm which went round the Christian world when the people of Ephesus, still remembering the virtues of the Virgin who so long sojourned in their city, with the beloved Apostle to whom she was commended by her Divine Son, rose up in the majesty of their mighty faith, seconding the zeal of their bishops, and drowning the hoarse and dissonant murmurings of a courtly and corrupt and heretical faction, in the loud enthusiastic concert which proclaimed that Mary was the Mother of Jesus, and, for the same reason, Mother of God. Mother of God! What an assemblage of ideas, of sanctity, of influence, and of mercy, do these words, Mother of God, convey? And what wonder that her name, her honour, her patronage, and her invocation should have been, from its origin, bound up with the framework of our religion, nay, inscribed on our soil, and intertwined with the household salutations of our venerable language? Yes, the religious statistics of Ireland can attest the numberless churches that have been dedicated to Mary in every diocese in Ireland, and through the massive fragments of their ruins strewn over the land, you can behold, as through a broken mirror, an imperfect image of the ancient piety of our people. Nay, more, the ordinary social greetings of the natives bear the impress and breathe the fragrance of the doctrines of the incarnation, which you look for in vain in any other country, and, unlike the constrained and unmeaning conventionalities of *fine day that*, the most refined form of ordinary salutation, it appears, that can be found in our imported speech—polished it may be, but cold and icy as it is polished—our own native tongue sends, warm from the heart, that heavenly phrase with which the angel of the Lord introduced his divine embassy, reflected again back with additional fervour by invoking on the person uttering the salutation the joint benediction of God and His Virgin Mother. There is, rely on it, in such pious forms of salutation a training to a high and Christian urbanity which all the faithless literary institutions of the world cannot supply; there is that ordinary aliment or daily bread which the sustenance of faith requires; there is a fashioning of the young and tender mind to purity by setting the spotless mirror of purity always before it; and there is in it that fragrant virtue, which is never found to flourish, save in the garden of the Catholic Church, watered by the graces coming through the Virgin Mother, to whom so appropriately belongs the beautiful appellation of the "sealed fountain."

With such evidence, then, furnished by their topography and language, of the singular veneration of our people for the Virgin Mother of God, it is not necessary that I should specially impress on you to mingle, with your prayers for us, a prayer, too, for her powerful intercession. To her this temple is specially consecrated. Nay, though several festivals to her honour are interspersed throughout the entire year, it is to this great feast of the Assumption of her body and soul into glory that our Cathedral church is peculiarly dedicated. It is but right, then, that on such a great and solemn occasion as this, we should implore her interposition in her own temple—a temple which, were I to be silent, would not fail to attest the traditionary reverence of Ireland for the Mother of God, raised, as it has been, by the munificent piety of the clergy and people of this diocese, with my revered predecessor at their head, one of the men whose praise is in the churches, who showed forth the dignity of prophets, powerful in instructing the people. As language is too feeble to convey any adequate idea of her bliss and glory, the Church applies to her some of the most beautiful images in which the Divine Wisdom celebrates its own praises: "I was exalted like a cedar in Libanus, and as a cypress-tree on Mount Sion: I was exalted like a palm-tree in Cades, and as a rose-plant in Jericho: as a fair olive in the plains, and as a plane-tree by the water in the streets, was I exalted. My branches are of honour and of grace, and my odour like the odour of the sweetest balm and cinnamon."[1] Yet not all these figures could adequately express the graces with which she has been adorned, the glory to which she has been elevated, the extent of merciful patronage with which she has been invested, or the odour which her name and virtues have spread throughout the world. No; nor the still more exalted image of St. John, comparing her to a "woman clothed with the sun, and the moon under her feet, and on her head a crown of twelve stars."[2] Yet all those high prerogatives of the Queen of Heaven are still the gifts of the Almighty flowing from the immensity of His goodness, as experienced in the angelic anthem that welcomed her advent to heaven: "Who this ti that cometh up from the desert, flowing with delights, leaning upon her beloved." Yes, leaning upon her beloved, who looked to the

---

[1] Ecclus. xxiv. 17-22.   [2] Apoc. xii. 1.

humility of His handmaid, and exalted her to the dignity of a queen, arrayed in gilded garments, enriched with varied embroidery. And were I now, in invoking the intercession of the Blessed Virgin, to turn to her image there, her head enwreathed with a diadem, some, perhaps, would feel, or affect to feel, scandalised, as if we were addressing ourselves to senseless representations. Should any entertain such a feeling, they will I trust, be instructed by the following historical incident: When Leo, the tyrannical emperor of the East, had ill-disguised his want of reverence for our Divine Redeemer by making war upon the crucifix among other images, a pious bishop, knowing his heart was steeled against all persuasion, called to mind the apologue with which Nathan reached the heart of David, and accordingly made use of a similar argument. Admitted to the presence of the emperor, he showed him a coin impressed with the imperial image, then flung it on the ground and trampled it under foot. The emperor was suddenly enraged, and felt himself treated with the utmost ignominy. And he was right: he forgot for a moment his false logic regarding the unfeeling materials of images; nature asserted her dominion over him, convincing him that, in the insult offered to his senseless likeness on the coin, the imperial majesty was obviously outraged. The bishop's argument succeeded, who promptly observed: "If you feel insulted at your image being thus trampled on, how is it that you have no feeling of insulting the God of heaven, whilst you insult, break, and scatter in fragments the symbols of our redemption, the venerated image of His crucified Son?" I need not pursue the application of this historical incident to the image of the Blessed Virgin. All the honour that is due to the Blessed Mother of God is given because her merits are all derived from the inexhaustible source of our redemption. On her Divine Son she leaned in her sufferings; by Him she was sustained, and on Him, her Beloved, she leans now in His glory. Of our Church it may be likewise said that she is going up from the desert, wherein she so long sojourned, continuing to lean exclusively on Him whose arm sustained her in her trials through the wilderness, where " He has been the guide of her journeying."[1] In her more prosperous career she surely stands not in need of any other aid, or of any other counsel, than the outstretched arm that protected her in her dangers and in her weaknesses, and those, that should be inclined to lean on the hollow support of the world, would find they were only leaning on a reed, which every breath was sure to sway, convinced of the truth of the inspired maxim, that it was better to trust in God than in princes. We will, then, trust in the promises of Him who has founded His Church and protected it, beseeching Him, in the prayers of the liturgy, on this solemn occasion: "Aid us, O Lord, by Thy presence; pour Thy spirit into our councils, and be Thou the sole suggestor of our judgments; guide us in the ancient paths, and let not ignorance mislead us, or a regard for gifts or persons betray us from the right course. And Thou, O Blessed Virgin, Holy Queen, Mother of mercies, our life, our sweetness, and our hope, turn thy compassionate looks on us, and obtain for us the grace of treasuring up the words of thy Divine Son, as thou didst treasure them in thy heart, that they may be a light to our path and a lamp to our feet in all our trials; that, after sharing in the sorrows which thou didst share with thy suffering Son, we may, with thee and all the saints, be sharers, too, in His everlasting glory." Amen.

[1] Exod. xiii. 21.

## TUAM SYNOD, 1858.

"Pass not beyond the ancient bounds which thy fathers have set."
—Prov. xxii. 28.

It is the melancholy lot of those who are placed beyond the pale of the Catholic Church to be continually carried about by every wind of doctrine, whilst the spirit of union, which it breathes, is found among the faithful children who have remained within its sacred enclosures. The peace which our Divine Redeemer left to His Apostles as His parting legacy has descended with the doctrine which He commanded them to preach, and has continued in the Church as the uniform handmaid of that power which He promised to exercise for its protection. Within, where the apostolic authority is felt and acknowledged, you are sure to find harmony in the profession of the same one faith, as well as that settled peace of which according dispositions must ever be productive. Whereas, outside the bounds of its acknowledged sway, nought is to be heard but the loud and incessant din of the strife of contending sectaries which cannot be appeased amidst the reign of anarchy and disorder. From such a contrast, between the wildest uproar from without and the most tranquil order from within, we may infer the importance, nay, the necessity in Church government, of the caution of the Wise Man conveyed in my text, of not crossing the mearings that have been fixed by our Fathers. It is this reverence for ancient usage, this zeal for the traditionary doctrines once delivered to the saints, this solicitude for walking in the same paths in which our holy predecessors have trodden; yes, this sensitive

---

im his origin, his duties, or his end, was obliged owledge its utter incapacity for the performance duous a work. Nay, though reason had, then as since, achieved the most brilliant triumphs in d in civilisation, so far was it from elevating man cale of moral perfection, that he sunk to a degree al sensuality from which, without supernatural never could arise. This appears from the ng picture left us by the Apostle in his Epistle Romans, of the revolting profligacy of the pagans, he describes as "filled with all iniquity and malice, nication, full of envy, murder, and contention, who d the glory of the incorruptible God into the s of the image of corruptible man, whom God ed up to a reprobate sense,"[1] because they aggra- all the grossness of their natural corruption by cked refinements of a licentious reason. This vivid tion of the hideous profligacy of the heathens, up to shameful affections, a description that has escaped being tolerable to pious ears, though left one whose tongue, like that of the prophet of as touched and purified by a burning coal from n, too clearly shows the unfitness of philosophers, t or modern, to be the teachers of morality—an which the Catholic Church founded, instructed and ted by our Divine Redeemer, is alone competent charge. Our religion, then, being a code of laws, recepts, and counsels, not discovered by reason, vealed by our Redeemer, its perfection is to be trans- d pure as it was received. "All power," He says, ven Me in heaven and in earth. Going, there- teach ye all nations, baptising them in the name Father, and of the Son, and of the Holy Ghost.

[1] Rom. i.

apprehension of disturbing with rash and irreverent hands, those striking landmarks of doctrine and discipline, and of jurisdiction that stand out before us in our retrospect of the past: it is, in short, all this, forming a feeling analogous to a sense of an awful trust, that swayed so powerfully the greatest of our predecessors, and enabled them to hand down to us the precious deposit which it is our duty to transmit with a like fidelity to after generations. It is on the peculiar nature of this deposit, and on the most effectual method to preserve and perpetuate it in its integrity, I now purpose to engage your attention.

Invested as we are, with a local and subordinate portion of that legislative authority that resides in the Church, and met for the purpose of framing statutes for the good government of our flocks, our office would be but ill understood by those who would compare our functions with those of secular legislative assemblies. Appointed as they are to provide for the growing wants of society, that is ever changing, a wide latitude is allowed to secular legislators in the enactment of their laws, as well as in the discussion of those principles of public weal on which they may be founded. Not so with ecclesiastics: they have laid before them a model from which they are not permitted to depart, and, like Moses in the promulgation of the commandments, their entire solicitude must be turned to the exact copying of the pattern which has been shown them on the mountain. In vain, then, would the world expect that the Church should keep pace with its shifting progress, or that its laws should bear the impress of those improvements which society continually undergoes. On the contrary, let society still go on progressing with a celerity unexampled in the past; let further secrets of nature, hitherto hidden, be successfully explored, and

Teaching them to observe all things whatsoever I have commanded you, and behold I am with you all days, even to the consummation of the world."[1] From these words it appears that the Apostles were commanded to teach the nations to observe all the things which He had commanded them, and that they and their successors might be faithful witnesses as well as fearless judges of the doctrines they were commanded to promulgate, He promises to be with them all days, fortifying their intellect and their courage at every period, to the end of time. This has been the model of teaching shown to the Apostles on the summit of Mount Olivet, and which has been since copied by their successors in the ministry to the present day. In accordance with this spirit, St. Paul writes to Timothy: "Thou, therefore, my son, be strong in the grace, which is in Christ Jesus. And the things which thou hast heard of me by many witnesses, the same commend to faithful men who shall be fit to teach others also."[2] "Continue, thou, in those things which thou hast learned, knowing of whom thou hast learned."[3] The Apostle here directs the peculiar attention of his disciple to the substance of the doctrine which he taught him, the source from which he derived it, the witnesses through whom it was transmitted, and finally exhorts him to choose faithful men, who, by reason of their fidelity, as witnesses, rather than their sublimity, as disputants, will be peculiarly fitted to teach others.

As the perfection of our religion consists in being transmitted pure, as it has been revealed, the duty of thus transmitting it must be performed by those to whom it has been entrusted. It is, then, from those churches over which they presided, and into which, as so many

---

[1] S. Matt. xxviii. 19, 20. [2] 2 Tim. ii. 1, 2. [3] 2 Tim. iii. 14.

wells, they poured their apostolical doctrine, we must draw it in order to distinguish it from the errors with which heretics sought to mingle and infect it. Such is the maxim of St. Irenæus, Bishop of Lyons, who thus writes: "The tradition of the Apostles promulgated throughout the world, is rendered venerable in the Church to those who are desirous of the truth, and we can number those who were appointed bishops in the churches by the Apostles and their successors, to our time, who neither taught nor knew such frantic opinions. If the Apostles knew any mysterious truths which they secretly taught the perfect, they must have communicated them principally to those to whom they entrusted the churches. Wherefore," he concludes, "we should hear those ancients in the Church who derive their succession from the Apostles, and who, according to the will of the Father, inherit the gift of truth with the succession of episcopacy." In order, then, that we should not cross the ancient boundaries of the true faith, or stray into the regions of error, we have only to consult those who, by virtue of their episcopal succession, derived their doctrines from the churches which the Apostles had founded and taught. If our confidence be strong when reposing on the truth of the doctrines transmitted in one, how much more so when fortified by the united traditions of several churches; and it is on that account the practice has prevailed from the earliest times, of several bishops meeting occasionally together to collect the traditions of their respective churches, and to impress the seal of their authority on the sacred treasures of divine doctrine. In acting thus they followed the advice of the Wise Man: "Stand in the multitude of ancients that are wise, and join thyself from thy heart to to their wisdom.... Despise not the discourse of them that are ancient and wise: for, of them thou shalt learn

## TUAM SYNOD, 1858.

*"Pass not beyond the ancient bounds which thy fathers have set."*
—PROV. xxii. 28.

IT is the melancholy lot of those who are placed beyond the pale of the Catholic Church to be continually carried about by every wind of doctrine, whilst the spirit of union, which it breathes, is found among the faithful children who have remained within its sacred enclosures. The peace which our Divine Redeemer left to His Apostles as His parting legacy has descended with the doctrine which He commanded them to preach, and has continued in the Church as the uniform handmaid of that power which He promised to exercise for its protection. Within, where the apostolic authority is felt and acknowledged, you are sure to find harmony in the profession of the same one faith, as well as that settled peace of which according dispositions must ever be productive. Whereas, outside the bounds of its acknowledged sway, nought is to be heard but the loud and incessant din of the strife of contending sectaries which cannot be appeased amidst the reign of anarchy and disorder. From such a contrast, between the wildest uproar from without and the most tranquil order from within, we may infer the importance, nay, the necessity in Church government, of the caution of the Wise Man conveyed in my text, of not crossing the mearings that have been fixed by our Fathers. It is this reverence for ancient usage, this zeal for the traditionary doctrines once delivered to the saints, this solicitude for walking in the same paths in which our holy predecessors have trodden; yes, this sensitive apprehension of disturbing with rash and irreverent hands, those striking landmarks of doctrine and discipline, and of jurisdiction that stand out before us in our retrospect of the past: it is, in short, all this, forming a feeling analogous to a sense of an awful trust, that swayed so powerfully the greatest of our predecessors, and enabled them to hand down to us the precious deposit which it is our duty to transmit with a like fidelity to after generations. It is on the peculiar nature of this deposit, and on the most effectual method to preserve and perpetuate it in its integrity, I now purpose to engage your attention.

Invested as we are, with a local and subordinate portion of that legislative authority that resides in the Church, and met for the purpose of framing statutes for the good government of our flocks, our office would be but ill understood by those who would compare our functions with those of secular legislative assemblies. Appointed as they are to provide for the growing wants of society, that is ever changing, a wide latitude is allowed to secular legislators in the enactment of their laws, as well as in the discussion of those principles of public weal on which they may be founded. Not so with ecclesiastics: they have laid before them a model from which they are not permitted to depart, and, like Moses in the promulgation of the commandments, their entire solicitude must be turned to the exact copying of the pattern which has been shown them on the mountain. In vain, then, would the world expect that the Church should keep pace with its shifting progress, or that its laws should bear the impress of those improvements which society continually undergoes. On the contrary, let society still go on progressing with a celerity unexampled in the past; let further secrets of nature, hitherto hidden, be successfully explored, and brought out to public admiration; let the mysterious bond that links all the distant bodies of the universe, be so unveiled as to be made, if possible, palpable to our senses; let the rapidity of communication, nay, of written and material correspondence, further outstrip in speed, as it has already literally outstripped the course of the sun in the firmament, or the voice of the thunder in the clouds of heaven: the Church, instead of toiling after such prodigious labours, or fearing to be distanced in the noisy race, silently pursues its majestic mission of guarding the treasure of divine truth which heaven has entrusted to its keeping, and views the most brilliant discoveries in nature, as but so many faint reflections of the Eternal Word, the uncreated Wisdom, the figure of His Father's substance, and the splendour of His glory, conceived in His first generation long before the huge bulk of the hills above, or the hollow abyss of the seas made their appearance, and from whom, born in time and in the flesh, from the womb of the Blessed Virgin, her own origin and lustre are derived. All those amazing developments of the laws of nature are calculated to benefit man, and excite his admiration for the power, and his gratitude for the beneficence of the Almighty, the Church contemplates with the utmost satisfaction. Yet, though instead of checking, she would rather guide and regulate our intellect in such adventurous discoveries, it is not to be imagined that she could be ever eclipsed by their brilliancy, or drawn by their attraction from her own steady course. No; the course of the Church is altogether distinct from that which reason is pursuing in such material discoveries; not less distinct are the laws by which their respective functions are guided. The Church was founded by our Divine Redeemer to conduct man to heaven at a time when human reason, exhausted by fruitless efforts to teach him his origin, his duties, or his end, was obliged to acknowledge its utter incapacity for the performance of so arduous a work. Nay, though reason had, then as well as since, achieved the most brilliant triumphs in arts and in civilisation, so far was it from elevating man in the scale of moral perfection, that he sunk to a degree of brutal sensuality from which, without supernatural aid, he never could arise. This appears from the appalling picture left us by the Apostle in his Epistle to the Romans, of the revolting profligacy of the pagans, whom he describes as "filled with all iniquity and malice, and fornication, full of envy, murder, and contention, who changed the glory of the incorruptible God into the likeness of the image of corruptible man, whom God delivered up to a reprobate sense,"[1] because they aggravated all the grossness of their natural corruption by the wicked refinements of a licentious reason. This vivid description of the hideous profligacy of the heathens, given up to shameful affections, a description that has hardly escaped being tolerable to pious ears, though left us by one whose tongue, like that of the prophet of old, was touched and purified by a burning coal from heaven, too clearly shows the unfitness of philosophers, ancient or modern, to be the teachers of morality—an office, which the Catholic Church founded, instructed and protected by our Divine Redeemer, is alone competent to discharge. Our religion, then, being a code of laws, and precepts, and counsels, not discovered by reason, but revealed by our Redeemer, its perfection is to be transmitted pure as it was received. "All power," He says, "is given Me in heaven and in earth. Going, therefore, teach ye all nations, baptising them in the name of the Father, and of the Son, and of the Holy Ghost.

[1] Rom. i.

Teaching them to observe all things whatsoever I have commanded you, and behold I am with you all days, even to the consummation of the world."[1] From these words it appears that the Apostles were commanded to teach the nations to observe all the things which He had commanded them, and that they and their successors might be faithful witnesses as well as fearless judges of the doctrines they were commanded to promulgate, He promises to be with them all days, fortifying their intellect and their courage at every period, to the end of time. This has been the model of teaching shown to the Apostles on the summit of Mount Olivet, and which has been since copied by their successors in the ministry to the present day. In accordance with this spirit, St. Paul writes to Timothy: "Thou, therefore, my son, be strong in the grace, which is in Christ Jesus. And the things which thou hast heard of me by many witnesses, the same commend to faithful men who shall be fit to teach others also."[2] "Continue, thou, in those things which thou hast learned, knowing of whom thou hast learned."[3] The Apostle here directs the peculiar attention of his disciple to the substance of the doctrine which he taught him, the source from which he derived it, the witnesses through whom it was transmitted, and finally exhorts him to choose faithful men, who, by reason of their fidelity, as witnesses, rather than their sublimity, as disputants, will be peculiarly fitted to teach others.

As the perfection of our religion consists in being transmitted pure, as it has been revealed, the duty of thus transmitting it must be performed by those to whom it has been entrusted. It is, then, from those churches over which they presided, and into which, as so many

---

[1] S. Matt. xxviii. 19, 20.   [2] 2 Tim. ii. 1, 2.   [3] 2 Tim. iii. 14.

wells, they poured their apostolical doctrine, we must draw it in order to distinguish it from the errors with which heretics sought to mingle and infect it. Such is the maxim of St. Irenæus, Bishop of Lyons, who thus writes: "The tradition of the Apostles promulgated throughout the world, is rendered venerable in the Church to those who are desirous of the truth, and we can number those who were appointed bishops in the churches by the Apostles and their successors, to our time, who neither taught nor knew such frantic opinions. If the Apostles knew any mysterious truths which they secretly taught the perfect, they must have communicated them principally to those to whom they entrusted the churches. Wherefore," he concludes, "we should hear those ancients in the Church who derive their succession from the Apostles, and who, according to the will of the Father, inherit the gift of truth with the succession of episcopacy." In order, then, that we should not cross the ancient boundaries of the true faith, or stray into the regions of error, we have only to consult those who, by virtue of their episcopal succession, derived their doctrines from the churches which the Apostles had founded and taught. If our confidence be strong when reposing on the truth of the doctrines transmitted in one, how much more so when fortified by the united traditions of several churches; and it is on that account the practice has prevailed from the earliest times, of several bishops meeting occasionally together to collect the traditions of their respective churches, and to impress the seal of their authority on the sacred treasures of divine doctrine. In acting thus they followed the advice of the Wise Man: "Stand in the multitude of ancients that are wise, and join thyself from thy heart to to their wisdom.... Despise not the discourse of them that are ancient and wise: for, of them thou shalt learn wisdom and instruction of understanding, for they have learned of their fathers."[1] In accordance with this method of consulting the ancients who have learned of their fathers, so suited to an hereditary deposit, the Catholic Church has not failed from the time of the meeting of the Apostles in the Council of Jerusalem, to manifest the utmost solicitude for the due celebration of ecclesiastical synods. Of those some consisted of the bishops of one or more provinces, and others of several nations representing the entire Church, all, however, requiring, for the sanction of their proceedings, the approval of the successor of St. Peter, on whom our Redeemer conferred the supreme power of governing His spiritual kingdom, and keeping its several parts in their respective positions, firmly bound together. With what force and beauty is this figure of the unity of Christ's Church carried out by the Apostle in his Epistle to the Ephesians, telling us that "He gave some apostles, and some prophets, and some others evangelists, and others pastors and doctors, for the edifying of the body of Christ, who is the Head from whom the whole body, compacted and fitly joined, by what every joint supplieth,"[2] is clothed with a strength and symmetry by the spirit that pervades and invigorates all its parts, so as to be proof against dissolution.

Of those important and learned assemblies, some had for their immediate objects the protection of the faith against errors by which it was assailed, or the vindication of discipline against abuses by which it was gradually enervated. The beauty of God's house, the majesty of divine worship, the decent uniformity of the ceremonies by which the sacraments were administered, the diffusion of a Christian education, and the protection of

[1] Ecclus. vi., vii., &c.  [2] Ephes. iv. 11, 16.

the cloisters, within which the evangelical counsels flourished, were the subjects to which the assembled bishops most generally turned their attention. Nor were the occasions rare when the remonstrances of those assemblies were raised against the oppressors of the poor and the despoilers of God's temple, but oftener against those insidious foes who, in every age of the Church, labour to subject its ministers to the influence of a secular policy, and to crush that evangelical freedom which the Apostle asserted even in his chains, and which is the soul breathed into it by its Divine Founder, for ever preserving it from corruption. In the eventful annals of the Church there are not found any chapters more interesting than those that record the struggles of its holy and intrepid pastors against the encroachments by which the civil power so often sought to make it its footstool; and as long as the bishops of any country were both able and willing to meet in council, so long were they able to present a wall of brass within which the sacred interests of faith and morality, and mercy to the poor, were guarded. The rights of the Church were at length overborne by violence in this struggle. The apostles of peace were stigmatised as the fomentors of discord, the best friends of society were represented as its bitterest foes, their stated assemblies were scattered or suppressed, and with the discontinuance of those synods discipline lost much of its force, and the Church was shorn of that external beauty which it derives from the splendid liturgy of its altars. Civil order did not long survive the shock which the Church had sustained; and with the dispersion of the stones of the sanctuary, the strongest and most ancient of the social fabrics of Europe were shaken to their centres. If the Church suffered, its sufferings were shared in turn by the powers that inflicted it, until they were taught by the experience of reciprocal disasters, to adopt the wise counsels of tolerance and peace.

Since then, and the period is comparatively a brief one, a new order of things has sprung up with an amazing rapidity. The first feeling that naturally seized the pastors of the Church was deep sorrow, on witnessing the squalor that covered the face of the sanctuary in comparison to its former beauty. However, after indulging the first natural burst of anguish, they chid their grief and strenuously applied themselves to clearing away the rubbish, to raising the temple, to stimulating the artificers, until its walls are seen expanding into such proportions from without, and adorned, from within, with such grace and loveliness, as to cheer the souls of the people, nay, to console the grief of those who, if they did not witness the splendour of the former temple, have heard of its glory through the traditions of former times.

It is to assist in seconding a change so consoling, and giving it a fresh impulse that the venerable prelates of this province are assembled on this occasion under the roof of this holy temple. They come to take council together as inmates of the same household, as members of the same mystical body, as witnesses of the faith which they derived from their predecessors, and as legislators, too, having authority to enact such laws as will appear to them best calculated to guard that faith, with its free and unfettered action, as well as the pure morality which is sure to follow in its train. In short, they come together in order to walk more securely by their mutual aid in the old ways, resolved not to pass, themselves, or suffer others to pass, the ancient bounds which have been set by our fathers. In nothing, perhaps, does the wisdom of the Church shine forth to more advantage than in those provincial councils meeting at stated times, and regulated by settled and canonical usage. Faith has no local limits; it is not regulated by the geographical latitude of countries, nor the civil boundaries of kingdoms, and therefore it is fitting that when obscured or assailed the different nations of the earth, under the guidance of the Holy Father, should sometimes assemble to illustrate and defend it. The exercise of that tyranny that has so often afflicted the Church, and involved whole provinces in one common persecution, is generally co-ordinate or co-extensive with the sway of the ruler or government that inflicts it, and therefore it is but natural and right, that the prelates of any such nation should take counsel together against a common injustice or a common oppression which, however different might be their ecclesiastical customs, or however co-ordinate and independent their ecclesiastical jurisdiction, still, as subjects of the same civil authority, equally affects them all; and hence those national councils or assemblies are not of such stated and normal recurrence in the Church as provincial synods, being brought together by the casual violence of a national schism or a national persecution. Such was the schism of the Donatists in Africa; such was the persecution of the Arian Vandal monarchs in Spain, and such, in fine, were the national calamities inflicted on our own country by the sanguinary efforts of the civil power to extinguish the faith in Ireland, and all requiring a combination of mutual energy to meet such calamities—an energy which was displayed in the extraordinary meetings which such exigencies required.

Not so, however, with provincial synods: they are of stated recurrence, and, with the high sanction of the holy Council of Trent, enter into the canonical constitution of the Church. No wonder; they are founded on two principles dear to the Church—the regulated freedom of its local authority and the uniformity of its local discipline. Were the manners, customs, and language of all the nations of the earth the same, no doubt the Church would not tolerate a difference of religious ceremonies more than of doctrine. But the manners, customs, and languages of nations being so different that they could never be recast into one mould, and being no obstacle to the profession of the same faith, or the acknowledgment of one authority, or the prevalence of essential discipline, she has exercised the wisest forbearance in the permission of very subordinate differences of practice, thus strengthening her authority by winning the attachment of widely different people. But that the same people should not be offended or scandalised by a capricious diversity of rites in the midst of them, she has partitioned nations and kingdoms into the smaller division of provinces, consisting of dioceses, supposed to be so similar in habits that the united authority of all could easily establish and maintain among them, that perfect uniformity in discipline and religious practice, which is the firmest bond of ecclesiastical as well as civil governments. Thus we have at once that perfect unity of faith and essential discipline, which the supreme authority of one head is so calculated to secure, and that difference of subordinate practices, arising from a diversity of local circumstances, which the wisdom of the same authority leaves to the experienced discretion of the local pastors; and hence the Church comes forth realising the image of the queen, mentioned by the Psalmist, robed in her majestic garment, of which the one unbroken ground is relieved by the richness of its embroidery and the variety of its border, diversified in its tint as it is seamless in its texture, and which it would be impious to strive to tear asunder, as it would be presumptuous to besmear with any strange dyes, which it refuses, in order to cover the entire with the same dusky uniformity of colour.

It is to contribute to the solid cohesion of the body under one head the vicegerent of Christ, and to the beauty of its parts, the venerable prelates of this province are here assembled. But as our collected efforts would be unavailing without the grace of Almighty God, for whose glory we are assembled, and as the prayers of the faithful are the ordinary precursors of that grace from above, let us send forth our fervent supplications to the Author of all good gifts, that He inspire us with wisdom to devise, and strength to carry out, what will most contribute to the exaltation of His Church and the sanctification of His people. And that those, our prayers, may go forth under the most favourable auspices, let us offer them under the patronage of the Holy Mother of God, the anniversary of whose glorious assumption into heaven will be celebrated on next Sunday, with the songs of men and angels. Nor let us forget the illustrious martyr of this day, St. Lawrence, whose praise is in all the churches, the fire of whose love was stronger than the burning embers on which his body was stretched, and who smiled amidst the slow tortures of the gridiron, as if enjoying, before leaving the earth, the beatitude of heaven. Let us ask their intercession, and the joint intercession of the patrons of our own dioceses, and the numberless saints which our Church has associated with the angelic hosts of heaven, that we, too, may walk in the old ways, guided by the bright landmarks of those who went before us, and that, to borrow the beautiful illustration of our own ritual, as we and our flocks are embarked on the same voyage, sharing the same dangers, and eager to reach the same goal in safety, it may be our lot to hear from our Divine Master the consoling words: "Well done, good and faithful servant: because thou hast been faithful over a few things, I will place thee over many things. Enter thou into the joy of the Lord."[1] Amen.

## FUNERAL ORATION ON DR. CANTWELL.

"And we will not have you ignorant, brethren, concerning those that are asleep, that you be not sorrowful, even as others who have no hope."— 1 THES. iv. 12.

SUCH are the significant words regarding the faithful departed which St. Paul addresses to the infant Church of Thessalonica. Such, too, is the consoling language which the Church has adopted into her liturgy for her dead, thus moderating the grief of her children, for the loss of friends and relatives, by the cheering hope of a happy resurrection. "For," continues the Apostle, "if we believe that Jesus died and rose again, even so those, God will bring with Him, who have slept through Jesus." We may have perceived what a complete revolution regarding the nature of death has been effected in the ideas and language of mankind by our holy religion. Instead of the ghastly idea of an eternal insensibility, or of some shadowy existence with which death was generally as-

[1] S. Matt. xxv. 21.

sociated, the light of faith reveals the resurrection of the body, a doctrine rendered familiar to us by the Apostles' Creed, but which, preached by St. Paul to the philosophers of Athens, was received by them with astonishment, if not derision. The bed of death which unbelievers shunned, and from which the voluptuous votaries of the world still shrink with horror, is, in the eyes of the true Christian, a couch on which the faithful sleep, resting from their labours, and awaiting the morning of a new life to awake to the enjoyment of never-ending bliss. The shroud, so unsightly and appalling to eyes that love exclusively to dwell on the fascinating scenes of fashion, becomes the wedding garment, in which the children of the Church are decked, expecting with impatience the joyous coming of the Bridegroom. The bier, with all its sable emblems of mortality, is contemplated as the victorious car on which Christ's faithful followers are borne to the goal of their souls; and their grave, a dark and dismal dungeon to those who have no hope, rises and expands into a triumphal arch, through which the Conqueror of sin and hell has conducted the captives, whilst His heralds proclaimed, in the inspired language: "O death, where is thy victory? O death, where is thy sting."[1] These are the reasons why the obsequies for the departed in the Catholic Church, mournful as they seem, furnish a subject of joy rather than of sorrow. The grave, bereft of its gloom, death, stripped of his terrors, and the friends of the departed soul presenting on the altar offerings to the Eternal Father, a merciful mediator on his behalf, all present to the survivors a group of consoling images never to be contemplated in those dark and dreary and chilling regions of unbelief outside the pale of the

---

[1] 1 Cor. xv. 55.

Catholic Church, on which the light and warmth of Christian hope never yet have shone.

These are the feelings that brought, scarcely a month ago, notwithstanding the severity of the season, such a number of his clergy and people to the obsequies of the illustrious prelate now sleeping in his grave. And it is to the influence of the same feelings we are indebted for this mournful and magnificent spectacle, amidst a drifting storm of snow, exhibiting such an array of priests and people, offering up their united prayers on behalf of that good father, to whom they are beholden for the profusion of blessings, of which his episcopal ministry was so fruitful. From me you cannot expect anything like an adequate portrait of your deceased prelate. To the learned and industrious annalist of this large diocese of Meath, who has already contributed so much to our ecclesiastical literature, I must leave the grateful task of devoting a luminous chapter to the life and labours in detail of one of the most illustrious prelates that ever adorned the Church, even of Ireland. He will record, on a scale commensurate with their importance, a series of events to which I can only glance, connected with which he held a prominent position. He will, no doubt, tell of his early life, tracing it back to that period when the footsteps of the apostle had yet scarcely left any deep or discriminating impression on the surface over which they bounded, and even then he, will discover some of those elements of his future character and career, a robust and well-built frame, and buoyant and playful temperament, united with habitual innocence, which guarded and preserved the vigour of the one and the cheerfulness of the other, thus fitting him, by their united development, for the labours and conflicts incidental to his protracted ministry. He will not pass unnoticed his younger years at the seminary of Navan, or his yet more brilliant career in the college of Maynooth, where he united labour with recreation, in accordance with rule, in such due proportions that one never trenched on the other, study forming his chief aim, and play, instead of degenerating into a loss of time, used as a relaxation, in order to give it additional force.

Having completed his college course before he reached the age for priesthood, he was appointed Dean in that establishment, and, by his efficient and considerate discharge of the duties of his office, he illustrated the maxim that they are the most safe to be entrusted with the exercise of power, who have given the most edifying and practical proof of obedience. The comparatively brief term of his collegiate office was succeeded by his appointment to the parish of Kilbeggan, where he dispensed those treasures of piety and knowledge which he laid up during his academic seclusion, and left proofs of his ardent zeal and indefatigable labours in the monuments which he erected.

Among the clergy who vigorously sustained the efforts of O'Connell during the stormy and eventful years, that immediately preceded the measure of our qualified emancipation, the parish priest of Kilbeggan was conspicuous. He communicated to others the generous flame which warmed his own heart, and so important were his services in the cause of an oppressed people, that they formed the link of an unbroken friendship between him and Ireland's Liberator. But it was on the occasion of his elevation to the episcopacy the talents and virtues, with which he was blessed, were displayed in all their beneficent lustre. In the annals of the ancient people of God, as well as in the more recent history of the Christian Church, we may observe how the Almighty, in His wisdom, extended to an unusual term the lives of some of his faithful servants, who were raised up to guide his people, or to repair the terrible evils inflicted by their enemies. Thus were the days of Moses, after being chosen to bring the Hebrew people out of Egypt, protracted to the period of forty years, whilst, amidst aggression from without and mutiny from within, he conducted them towards the Land of Promise. When, in the early ages of the Church, the Christians had only a respite from the cruelty of the Roman emperors, the din of the sectaries, which had been drowned amidst the storm of persecution, again broke forth with redoubled fury under their banners, which so troubled the minds of the people, and confounded the old landmarks of error and orthodox belief, that one of the eloquent Fathers of the time exclaimed that the world wondered to find itself Arian, or rather, to strip the phrase of its exaggeration, the world wondered to find itself represented as Arian through the clamorous insolence of that dominant faction; then, did the Almighty raise up in the young Athanasius, afterwards the distinguished Archbishop of Alexandria, a powerful vindicator of the divinity of Christ. After assisting at the great Council of Nice, of which he was as if the oracle, and which formed a model for the ecclesiastical polity by which the Church has so often baffled the designs of her enemies —and will continue to defeat their hostile aggession to the end of time—his years were extended to near half a century, now consoling and strengthening his own flock, and again doomed to exile and misery, his banishment was turned into a benefit to the Church, by teaching and consoling those, among whom he was doomed to wander. Thus, whenever Satan was let loose on the world, men, holy and intrepid witnesses of the faith, were raised up, like Enoch and Elias in their own time, to control his impiety, and so achieve his discomfiture. Thus, in our own time, and in this extensive, prominent, and central diocese, comprehending, if I may term it, an octarchy of episcopal churches, some of them the earliest endeavours of our great Apostle, St. Patrick, have appeared two men, Patrick Plunkett and John Cantwell, like pillars of light on the mountain-tops, diffusing their heat and splendour for the long period of eighty-four years over one of the widest ranges of ecclesiastical scope in Ireland. The term of their episcopate, including the brief reign of Dr. Logan, one of the mildest and most estimable of prelates, which formed a connecting link between them, extended over a period little short of a full century. And such a century of evangelical toil, so continuous and successful, of digging and of sowing, sometimes in tears, and of fencing and of weeding, and of reaping, and of gathering into the barns the fruits of their industry, was seldom seen. For eight-and-forty years did the former traverse the whole diocese yearly, visiting every parish, preaching to every flock, catechising and confirming the young, giving seasonable counsel to the clergy, and apposite instruction to all classes of the people. The time for gathering the dispersed stones of the sanctuary, and of erecting the fallen temples, had not yet arrived, and scarcely did it set in, when the latter, besides rivalling his predecessor in all the works of this ministry, began to run the course of a giant, encouraging the erection of churches of chaste design and ample area all over the diocese, so that to him might be applied an observation regarding a Roman emperor, that he found Rome built of brick, and left it built of marble.

He was not one of those Pharisees who could impose the load of grievous duties upon his clergy and his people, without putting so much as his little finger to lighten the heavier burden. No one ever better understood the value of that homage of the heart, and that prompt and implicit obedience, which is ever accorded by the generous on seeing the leader cheerfully sharing the labours of the humblest of that hierarchy, which has been compared by an ancient prophet to an army in the array of battle. Well did he study, and cheerfully did he fulfil the precepts of St. Paul to Timothy and Titus, which form such a complete epitome of the episcopal duties: "I charge thee, before God and Jesus Christ, who shall judge the living and the dead, preach the word: be instant in season, out of season: reprove, entreat, rebuke in all patience and doctrine. Be thou vigilant; labour in all things; do the work of an evangelist; fulfil thy ministry."[1] In the performance of those duties no one was more faithful or indefatigable. Like the commandments of the Old Law, he seems to have set them before his eyes, and to have meditated on them in the morning and in the evening, as he came in and as he went out, so that they became the habitual practice of his life. In fulfilling his ministry his vigilance never slumbered, his zeal never relaxed, his judgment, regarding the sound doctrine of Catholic education, never strayed, and his confidence in its ultimate achievement, when seriously and strenuously sought, never faltered. It is true that, in common with his brethren, he had often to exhort his people to patience and resignation. But if the occasion required, if any delinquents abused their wealth or power in the ruin of the humbler members of his flock, then would he, like the Apostle before Festus, discourse on justice, and chastity, and judgment, appalling the sinner from a continuance in his misdeeds, if not immediately succeeding in his conversion; whilst he sympathised with the severe sufferings of the poor, he neither forgot nor denied

[1] 2 Tim. iv. 1-5.

the sources from which they flowed; whilst he preached patience under oppression, he neglected not to admonish those by whom it was inflicted. He lamented the fate of the poor, driven from their fields to make room for cattle bloated to enormous dimensions; between the conflicting claims of his people he laboured to keep an equitable balance; nor was he ever known to reserve all his caustic reproaches for the bruised members of the one, and to pour, on the heads of their oppressors, all the oil of his adulation. Well may we rank him among those men of renown, who gained glory in their generation, men of great power and wisdom, who were feared in their days; of him might well be said, as was said of Simon, the high priest, that in his own sphere he took care of his nation, and that in his days he fortified the temple.

It was feared, I understand, by some of the bishop's friends, that there would not on this occasion be any memorial of his many virtues. That could never be; for if ingratitude were insensible to the obligation, or rather if modesty were to shrink from its performance, the walls of this beautiful church, one of the first monuments of his zeal, would not fail to proclaim his praise. "Blessed are they who die in the Lord," says St. John, "for their works follow them."[1] His numerous works follow him, and not only attest his merits upon earth, but have pleaded, I trust, for him in heaven. It is now thirty years since he consecrated this temple, the work of his hands, when, in accordance with his desire, I addressed some few words to the numerous throng that crowded the temple on the subject of its inauguration. It is a curious coincidence that, at a similar request of his respected successor on whom his mantle has fallen, and in accordance with the wishes of his respected clergy, it should be my lot to offer a like

[1] Apocal. xiv. 13.

poor but affectionate tribute over the tomb containing his body, lately the temple of the Holy Ghost. The coincidence of such scenes cannot but inspire deep and solemn emotions in the hearts of any who may share them, especially when coupled with the recollection that the numerous assembly of archbishops and bishops who hastened on that occasion, and assisted in the same work at the consecration of the cathedral of Tuam, and not only those, but all the members of the then Irish episcopacy have passed away, to mingle spirits with that heavenly host, composed of people of all tongues, and sexes, and nations, that were seen in the prophetic vision of St. John the Evangelist.

When we consider how the faltering confidence of Moses, in striking the rock a second time, was visited with a temporal punishment, as was the complaining of the king who felt an inordinate satisfaction in displaying the wealth of his palace and his kingdom, we must feel a lively gratitude to the Church for her solicitude in providing for her departed children the means of satisfying the divine justice for those sins into which, the most virtuous of the saints might have been betrayed, by surprise and inadvertence. Should any such arrears remain due by your departed friend and father, you will fervently pray that they may be cancelled by the holy Sacrifice of the Mass offered up on our altar; and that he, when released, if at all detained in prison, may pray that we who yet remain may labour to provide for our own passage, in order that our long-suffering Judge, who mercifully delays, because He is desirous to favour, and not to condemn, may discover naught that would hinder or retard us from entering into the joys of the Lord which He Himself has purchased for us by the effusion of His blood. Amen.

## ADDRESS TO THE THEOLOGICAL STUDENTS OF THE COLLEGE OF MAYNOOTH, 1822.

I REALLY know not how to address you. I must confess, and it is no affectation of modesty, that, arriving at this period of the year, which is about to close our labours, I feel more than ordinary embarrassment. It may excite surprise that one who has been so often accustomed to address with the confiding familiarity of colloquial language, should at once assume such solemnity of tone, and that the ordinary routine of business should be so suddenly invested with such serious and impressive interest. This is the very circumstance that accounts for my embarrassment. The subject itself is calculated to depress by its associations, and the consciousness that I have more than once dwelt on it, perhaps to satiety, embarrasses me more. On this topic I struggle between the difficulties incident to variety and sameness, and approach it with apprehension, lest, in attempting to be new, I should cease to be natural. Were it my first time I might, of course, tempt you to accompany me by holding out the hope of instruction or amusement; but it is hard to cure the distrust created by repeated disappointments, and sure I am that few are possessed of the powers of the prophet, who could so change the scenes or charm the senses as to cheat his companions into the persuasion that they were conducted by another guide, and that they were travelling another way.

I did, therefore, think to take leave of you without this formality; but I found on reflection that I had gone too far to recede. What is usually done is expected by the next generation, and a construction of slight or indifference might be put on the omission of a usual practice. Lest, therefore, my silence might be mistaken for sullenness, which surely I have had no reason to entertain, and conscious that ceremony is seldom resorted to except towards them for whom a respect is entertained, I have resolved to overcome all the difficulties that were suggested, and to say a few words of past or future occasions, which, however indifferent in themselves, might derive some value from the circumstance of their being a tribute of reciprocal regard and attention.

The freedom, with which I have occasionally animadverted upon any departure from decorum, when I conceived animadversion was due, is a proof that I have no secret arrears of misconduct to settle with any individuals. I am not one of those, who, at their parting would fain solicit an act of indemnity for the past; no, Gentlemen, as long as I continue I purpose to persevere in the same line of conduct. If I were even to take my leave for ever, an undeviating adhesion to my duty is the reflection that would give me most consolation; and what would gratify me next is, that I had to direct individuals, to purchase whose esteem it was not necessary to depart from that duty. The infliction of reproof might have excited a transient uneasiness in those who might have been its object; but now I am glad, not, because they were made sorrowful, but, because the rebuke, that inflicted pain, became the instrument of their correction.

Different modes of treatment are suited to different temperaments. Towards those who are insensible to the strong, though silent, influence of religion and propriety uniform rigour may well be adopted. But for me, I felt I had to address a body, whose love of good order seconded my own, and that in checking any casual manifestation of levity I was less the controller than the organ of your own sentiments. I should incur the reproach of my own mind if, through weakness, I should connive at any disorder; and I should be equally ashamed of the littleness of perpetually putting forward an authority which, if not necessary to exercise, it is prudence to conceal. If, therefore, the order of the class has not been disturbed by the exhibition of any scene, of which the recollection would embitter our feelings at the present moment, the praise is more due to a preventing attention on your part, than to any forbearance of mine; and as St. Chrysostom well remarks, in his treatise of the Priesthood: " One has but little merit for those virtues which have not been tried by the opposite temptations."

To this commendation, which I willingly give to the general propriety of your conduct, I must add the expression of an equal satisfaction at the zeal and success with which you have appeared to have prosecuted your studies. In almost all I observed a bent of mind which gave a decided preference to theology; and in many I was happy to find a spirit of inquisitive, and yet tempered criticism, united to a respectful though intelligent doubt. However, lest dwelling too long on your intellectual progress might seem to betray some complacency, I shall defer that topic to the occasion on which, I trust, you will acquit yourselves to the satisfaction of all the spectators. At the examination every individual will have ample room for the display of his talents; and you will be led from the commencement to the end of the treatise, without discrimination, as chance or memory may suggest. I am glad, indeed, to have as yet one or two tests to fix my own judgment in the adjudication of literary rewards. The ardent competition that has spurred the speed of the candidates, and the closeness with which some have pressed upon each other's footsteps, make it desirable still to lengthen out the ground to put their strength to a further trial. I wish I had it in my power to say, in recompense for your industry: "*Nemo non donatus abibit;*" but as that is impossible, I must confess I feel myself considerably embarrassed. In the ascending scale of merit there are some whose pretensions approach by such a trembling line, that one might be inclined to adopt the contrivance of some of the magistrates in the disturbed districts, who, unwilling to have their names appear first in certain requisitions, suffered their love of precedence to give way to their apprehensions, and condescended to equalise themselves by writing their signatures in the form of a circle. For the adoption of this plan, however, there is no precedent. I shall only observe that where there is a marked distinction, the associates shall not be multiplied, and that where no such difference is discernible, equality of merit alone, and not precedent or example, shall determine their number.

You may imagine that I mean to amuse you once more by bringing out the different feelings of the disappointed, by anticipating the various topics of reproach or consolation in which some congenial groups may indulge to soothe each other's disappointment, and ingeniously discover some latent cause for such preference or exclusion. No, Gentlemen, I will not disturb your gravity by such an exhibition, trusting that there is a reserve amongst you, which will not suffer you to be so buoyed up beyond a just standard, by these insidious compliments, under which insincerity may lurk for the purpose of, afterwards, exposing you to their derision.

I will content myself with making one serious reflection, less for the purpose of shielding myself against any distrust, which I am conscious you do not entertain, than for the purpose of giving just views to the inexperienced, and of directing those, whose lot it may be, on a future occasion, to dispense, in a more exalted theatre, the dignities of the Church.

The dispensation of justice is too sacred a trust for the intrusion of any other feeling. And the adjudication of literary rewards I look upon as a matter of the most rigid justice. My esteem for the body of the class indeed is great; but I trust I will not be considered disrespectful in saying, that there is not an individual, whom I do not consider as valueless, when compared with the strictness of my own obligation. Now there is no assignable reason to influence one except some individual partiality. If any might be so weak as to sacrifice justice to personal considerations, a little reflection would convince them of their folly. You could not expect even any particular gratitude from the individual, because, thankfulness on such an occasion is what a man of sense would not wish to have, and which a man of delicacy would forbear to express. When there is little expectation of gratitude there can be no temptation to confer a favour. It is a recorded saying of Louis XIV., founded on that extensive range of observation, which he acquired from his commanding position, that he never conferred a place but he made one man ungrateful and many discontented. Now, if such be the case with mere gratuitous favours, where there is no just cause for enmity, because no injury is done, and where in the other there might be some claim to gratitude as there was none in the distinction, how much more so in a matter of justice, when the excluded may labour under the illusion that he has been deprived of a right, and the other, of course, entertains the confidence that he has obtained only that to which he was justly entitled. I know there is generally a modesty about genuine merit, which, as it underrates its own deserts, may dispose it to entertain a kind sense towards those by whom it is requited. But if you were so weak as even to reflect on such a motive, your course should still be justice, for in that quarter you should look for thankfulness least, where the reward was least merited.

Though I have introduced the anecdote concerning Louis XIV. as applicable on this occasion, I should not wish to leave on your minds that dark view of the human character which it seems calculated to convey. This, like many other maxims, has only a partial reference to mankind; its truth with regard to him was founded on his particular situation. Too exalted for sympathy, that alternate influence of feeling, by which alone, separate minds may be commingled, and which must constantly seek the level, could never have reached his elevation. Hence his observation is founded on the principle which accounts for the infrequency of sincere friendships amidst the inequalities of life.

Of course I cannot plead exemption from the common lot of error; but, though my judgment may stray, no unworthy bias shall still incline its erring direction. And I think it superfluous to remind you of the higher motives which, I am sure, have influenced your exertions.

And before concluding the subject, I take occasion to congratulate those of the first year, on their diligence and attention. I refer to them on account of their circumstances on entering here. I might have mentioned before that their progress here should alone influence my judgment. I abstained lest the allusion might seem less encouraging than disheartening. But now as they have gone through their trial, I am glad that they have so felt the importance of their studies as to make it appear that the cloud, which seemed to hang round them on their entrance, was happily only artificial and transient.

Of the treatise, which occupied your studies during the year, I will not detain your attention in magnifying the importance or advantages. What one is as yet unacquainted with, he may well take on the credit of another. While the mind is yet void, it may be satisfied with the most clumsy and unfinished likeness. But were I now to attempt to delineate the Church, I should probably resemble those, who would fain continue the cold labour of dispensing lectures when the masterminds of some of their disciples had already caught those living and divine forms, to the apprehension of which they might have been stimulated by their professor's encouragement, but which their professor's mind could never have conveyed. You have explained the foundation, and contemplated the majestic edifice of the Church; and in the solidity of that foundation, and in the symmetry of that structure, you have, doubtless recognised the finger of the Divine Artist. You have been, during the year, slowly ascending the mystical mountain of the Lord, and the incessant glory that is still burning on its summit is a standing proof that it is still sanctified by the residence of the Almighty. Your study has not, I trust, been a barren and lifeless lecture, satisfied with the cold assent of the understanding, in which your piety had no share. We are the children of the Church, and we are told that "he that honoureth his mother is as one that layeth up a treasure."[1] It is through her you have been regenerated; it is in being members of her com-

[1] Ecclus. iii. 5.

munion that you found your hopes of salvation; it is to her service you are shortly to consecrate all the faculties of your being—and surely it is a service that would dignify the noblest exertions of man. In the language of Ecclesiasticus, we may say, "he that loveth her loveth life; and they that watch for her shall embrace her sweetness: they that serve her shall be servants to the Holy One, and God loveth those that love her. He that hearkeneth to her shall judge nations, and he that looketh upon her shall remain secure."[1] Your talents, then, cannot be consecrated to a nobler end. The moment one is consecrated to her service he should apply to himself the prophetic admonition: "Set thy face towards Jerusalem, and let thy speech flow towards the holy places."[2] And there is none who feels a lively devotion for her interests that would not gladly resign the most flattering prospects with which the world could tempt for the sake of following, even in the last place, in the train of the tabernacle.

After those reflections, suggested by the past, I shall now turn your attention to thoughts connected with the future. After long confinement to a place the duties of which he considers to be dull from their sameness, or painful from their rigour, one naturally looks for relief in a change of condition. In no other point of view can you look on the mission as a relaxation. If it be an uncomfortable truth that the life of man is a warfare upon earth, the metaphor is peculiarly applicable to a minister of the Gospel. It is remarkable that it is under the emblems of warfare the Prophet exhibits the gradations of the hierarchy, and that the Apostle represents the virtues by which victory is to be secured. It would, therefore, be a preposterous idea to separate great labour from the functions of the priesthood. The high

[1] Ecclus. iv. 13-16.   [2] Ezech. xxi. 2.

places of the world may be consistently aspired to by its votaries for the purpose of moving through a wider range of dissipation. Not so in religion. It reverses the principles of human ambition; and what Christ says: "He that is the greatest among you must be as if he were the least," is rigidly true. In religion, the higher you rise the more restraints it imposes. What may be allowed to an humble is denied to a higher ecclesiastic; the nearer you approach the centre the more glaring become your defects, and the narrower the circle of your enjoyments, until the first dignitary, the very centre of the Church, is restrained by regulations almost approaching to confinement.

These things I mention, not with a view to dishearten you, but to show how anomalous it would be to bring into the Church any of those views, which animate the candidates of the world in a competition for its honours, and to banish that worldly spirit with which any would attempt to infect the purity of your conversation. I trust that your speech will always desire to flow towards the holy places. I would not wish to offend by any ludicrous allusion; but, though you may not know, you may at least have heard of individuals, whose cast of conversation betrayed a tincture of worldly views which no refinement could dissipate, whose coarse anticipations of future enjoyment are easily seen through the thin veil of drollery under which they affect to conceal them, and who, on obtaining the object of their desires, often share the fate of the squire of celebrated memory, who panted for power only that he might more freely enjoy the good things of the world; but, on finding himself oppressed with the cares and fatigues of government, impatiently sighed for the tranquillity of his former life.

Those who are going on the mission will shortly find

themselves placed in a relation to which they have been hitherto unaccustomed. They will find themselves possessed of a portion of authority which it would be necessary to administer with a gentle yet firm hand. The instruments by which a priest should rule his people are represented by the Prophet Zachary under the emblems of two rods, the one called Beauty, the other a Cord,[1] and it is remarkable that he did not recur to the chastisements of the one until they became entirely insensible to the sweetness of the other. Character, or the good opinion of men, you are to value only as far as it may be subservient to your ministry and an auxiliary to virtue. The more you win the confidence of your flock the more extended will be your influence. Never, however, through a weak condescension, venture beyond the sphere of your duty. If you do, you will find it hard to return with safety and with dignity. You will find yourselves at the mercy of every accident, and doomed to be the victims of their caprices, which it was your duty to regulate and control. Before you dread the disapprobation of others you ought to reflect whether they are competent to pronounce on the good or evil tendency of your measures. And I cannot but here express my conviction, that the faults of many lean too much towards accommodation. It is to be regretted that there is too free an admission of the laity into the deliberations on religion; too great an indiscretion on the part of the clergy in gossiping over the foibles of their own brethren; and, in fine, too familiar a reciprocation of lay and clerical intercourse. The less, however, the number of your advisers, the more necessity of caution and deliberation on your own part; and thus, by promoting their interests, you will be able to secure their

---

[1] Zach. xi. 7.

attachment without compromising your own dignity. Let me, therefore, exhort you, rather to keep in view the precepts of the Gospel, than the practice of those, who would fain seduce you to a different standard. The examples may be rare; but is it not lamentable to reflect, that there are some, whose collegiate life gave presages of a useful ministry, losing the fruit of their retirement from the world, and sinking into those vulgar, as well as vicious habits which their influence might have corrected? The priest, according to the Apostle, ought to be the pattern of his flock. He it is, therefore, who is to guide and they to follow. And when you approach each other it should be by a connection resembling that golden chain mentioned in ancient story, with which you might draw them upwards towards yourselves without their being able to disturb you from your immovable position.

Though for the dignity of the priesthood, and a respectful discretion, I will not insinuate those greater faults, which, I trust, you shall never learn, even from the melancholy fate of others, let me caution you against ever suffering profane or licentious conversation. There are occasions when subjects of a delicate nature are introduced for the purpose of information; but these occasions should be rare, and the language should be cautious. But never ought such conversation be endured for a moment unless forced by necessity. Whatever may be the licentiousness of the world, it ought to be kept aloof from the minister of God. His general demeanour may be placid and engaging; but should the condescension of his manner be mistaken for weakness, then he must assume an austere deportment, and should licentious conversation presume to approach his sacred person, he must wear a cold severity of countenance, which, like the mystic head on the shield of Minerva, would chill its effrontery and appal its insolent approaches. It is one of the proverbs of Holy Writ that a sad countenance driveth away a back-biting tongue; and its effect in discountenancing licentiousness may be expressed in the well-known words, *timebat a facie frigoris ejus.*

The information you have acquired here will be more or less valuable in proportion to the use to which it is converted. Whatever might have been the indulgence of the people heretofore to their pastors, there is now among them, whether as a blessing or an evil, an eagerness for acquiring knowledge, which makes them impatient for instruction from the priest, and perhaps discontented when it is withdrawn. In whatever light it is viewed, whether as a blessing or an evil, this feverish disposition cannot now be allayed but by an increased exertion, on the part of the clergy, in administering wholesome knowledge. If you wish to be in reality useful and efficient ministers, you must divest yourselves of the erroneous notion, that to instruct well, a long and laborious preparation is necessary. Commence from the moment that you commence your mission. It requires no extraordinary talents to convey simple instructions to the poor. What to you is familiar by a long acquaintance with theology, and what might cost you much labour in collecting and arranging, might be entirely lost on the slowness of their apprehension. For them, it is not good to be learned or theological; nor would it be wise for a preacher to follow those inscrutable doctors whose ordinary path was a course which no human eye could follow. I do not mean, however, to recommend that careless manner which, by exciting the disgust, relaxes the attention, and, perhaps, excites the hostility of your hearers.

Whatever may be your talents, they will be unsuccessful if not improved by unremitting industry, and the richest stock of knowledge, if not repaired by occasional reading, would soon suffer a considerable diminution. I only mean that you ought not to defraud the poor of instruction because you have not arrived at that eminence, which the more you labour to acquire, the more sensible you will become of your distance from its attainment. I should not wish to be understood as repressing the proper energies of genius, if the exertions of this energy should be necessary. You may, in the course of your ministry, meet with opportunities, when the glory of God and the interests of religion may require of the most reserved to put forth the talent with which God has gifted them. For the Wise Man says that "better is the man that hideth his folly than the man that hideth his wisdom."[1] In such circumstances ornament and elevation would not be incompatible with an habitual simplicity and modesty of manner; and, prompted by necessity, you might stand forward in the richest attire of human eloquence, imitating the blessed matron of Bethulia, who, under the inspiration of the Divine Spirit, laid aside the weeds of her widowhood, and came forth arrayed in the vesture of her virginity, and because the power of her charms was chastened by the purity of her intention, she had smitten unto death the blasphemer of the God of Israel.

I have mentioned that the Irish mission has its difficulties; yes, but the Irish mission has its advantages, too. Unlike those countries over which the blessed feet of them who bring the tidings of peace have never walked, Ireland exhibits to its missionaries the monuments of their religion. While we see the edifices which arose

Ecclus. xli. 18.

during the more recent period of religious bigotry silently disappearing from the country, without leaving a single stone to tell that they ever stood, the ruins of the churches that were so richly strewed over the country, still restore to the eye of enthusiasm the full and perfect image of the ancient splendour of the Catholic worship. Those institutions are swept away, because resting only on the surface; the others are everlasting, because rooted in the very existence of society. Our people are Catholic; their habits are Catholic; nay, the Protestant churches of her cities, as well as the solitudes of her mountains, still breathe the living spirit of the Catholic religion. In the one you behold the broken reliefs of Catholic statuary, still revealing, in spite of every effort by which it was defaced, its original design; and in the other you are shown the hiding-place where, like Jeremias, her priests preserved the ark of their religion, until the tempest had blown, and in the language of the Psalmist, we have worshipped, in the spot which was trodden by their footsteps. Yes, Gentlemen, Ireland seems destined to be Catholic: her inhabitants are Catholic; the Catholic religion is inscribed upon the soil; it is intertwined with her society; it lives in the memory of the present, it loiters among the monuments of past times; and the very language of Ireland's topography shall ever preserve the ancient piety of its people.

Now, that this is our last lecture, you doubtless feel much pleasure in arriving at the term of your academic career. Yet, is it not a pensive pleasure, such as one feels in the stillness of a fine evening, when the joy that is awakened by the surrounding scenery is subdued into a solemn tone by its melancholy associations? The associations of a day like this are equally subduing. In every reflecting mind they show a consciousness of mortality, and beget that thoughtful cast of mind which would gladly retire from the bustle of life, to meditate on its own lot, and enjoy the delight of its own loneliness. It may be weakness, it may be melancholy, it may be a dread of dissolution; but whatever be its name, I cannot disguise my sensibility to the repeated recurrence of scenes of this nature. I rejoice that it is becoming stronger with years. It might be well for the spiritual interests of mankind if, on inclining into the vale of life, they became more sensible, at every step, of the rapidity and downward tendency of their motion, and that they were able to say with the Apostle, that as the outward man is corrupted, the inward man is renewed day by day, until what is mortal is swallowed up by immortality.

It is unnecessary, in conclusion, to exhort you to forget the little jealousies and trials which put your patience to the test during your residence here. You will soon learn that, like the rest of your collegiate exercises, they were only lighter trials by which you were disciplined to the endurance of greater trials. You may hereafter smile at the trifles that could have disturbed your quiet.

These reflections naturally lead me to another, which will not fail to affect every feeling and generous mind. In the annals of learning we find that an affectionate regard for the Alma Mater was a strong feature in the characters of those, who were either distinguished for the elevation of their genius or the generosity of their feelings. The opposite sentiment never influenced any but those who were too insensible to feel or too proud to acknowledge their obligations. Connections the most disinterested and lasting have been the result of academic education, and often are anniversaries instituted by the children of the same seminary, to seek respite from the cares and anxieties of the world amidst the fresher and probably more inherent recollections of collegiate life. This is the sentiment with which I would wish to inspire you all—a strong and lively zeal for the College which, not confined to a few accidental acquaintances, embraces, in its concern for the parent, all the interests of the children. We should be proud to say, *radicavi in populo honorificato*, and I trust that the strength and soundness of the root will be but evinced in the healthiness of the suckers it shall have successively transplanted. Indeed, I am glad that, in spite of the affectation of the cold and the fastidious, this feeling is becoming now more general: it may be checked by circumstances. The College, like our country, is endeared by distance, and time and experience will only increase your veneration. Let, therefore, your thoughts occasionally flow towards Jerusalem, and in these recollections you will find something of an exalting and classical nature that will prove a counterpoise to the sordid and depressing tendencies of the world. Do not imagine that I am selfish. No; I may soon probably stand in the same relation with yourselves. I, too, may be numbered among those who have been children of the College, and on the recurrence of this time my face may be probably turned towards the East, to offer up my vows for its prosperity, and to rejoice in its glory. These are the sentiments we ought to entertain; there is a generosity, there is a piety in the feeling that forgets the individual in the general interests of the community. If this collegiate spirit be cherished and perpetuated, we need have no apprehension for its welfare; it will produce a succession of men, by whose exertions its character will be exalted. We may have occasion to deplore the loss of some of its members, whom death may snatch away, but still the vivifying and regenerating principle will remain; and in deploring the loss of any individual one may console himself with the noble sentiment with which the Athenian matron chid her sorrow for her child—

"Athena has still many a nobler son to spare."

With better reason than the Apostle, ought I say, bear with a little of my folly; but with him, I may add, whether we be beside ourselves or whether we be sober, it is for you. In the spirit of the Catholic Church, whose doctrine of the Communion of Saints is in accordance with the immensity of its love, and hoping for a corresponding charity in you, with the same Apostle, I give thanks to my God in every remembrance of you, always, in all my prayers, making supplication for all with joy. And this I pray, that your charity may more and more abound in knowledge and in all understanding, that you may approve the better things, that you may be sincere and without offence unto the day of Christ, being filled with the fruit of justice, through Jesus Christ, unto the glory and praise of God.

## ADDRESS TO THE THEOLOGICAL STUDENTS OF THE COLLEGE OF MAYNOOTH, 1823.

I HAVE heard of a curious contrivance to which a preacher had once recourse to secure the attention, or rather to check the wanderings of his flock. Whether they were alarmed by the holy terrors of an eloquence to which they had been hitherto unaccustomed, and, like Festus, wished to defer their conversion, and hear the preacher at a more seasonable time ; or whether he was one of those who had long since worn away the freshness of novelty by the unvaried repetition of the same truths, the history does not mention, though the commentators have maliciously ascribed it to the latter; but certain it is that he found himself deserted by his congregation. To guard against the recurrence of a similar disaster, he pondered over in his mind a variety of expedients, until at length, having bethought himself of the mighty influence of music, he resolved by its aid to stimulate their indifference. He accordingly provided himself with a flute, and thus equipped, he mounted the pulpit, reserving, however, his instrument as his last resource. As soon as he commenced his trite, and, perhaps, his solitary sermon, which it is said the dullest of his flock could repeat, the people went out, and he was left alone, like the flower in the desert, to waste its fragrance on the breath of heaven. Immediately he sounds his instrument, at which he was, probably, a better proficient than at preaching ; and the people, struck with the strange sound of this novel kind of ecclesiastical trumpet, rushed eagerly into the church. The clerk, who got previous directions to station himself at the door, turned the key as soon as the people entered, and the preacher quietly resumed his discourse, rejoiced that he had succeeded in restoring once more, to the bosom of the church, his restless and schismatical congregation.

The drift of my apologue, to minds apprehensive as yours, it is unnecessary to unfold; I, too, having already addressed you so often, might require the aid of a similar expedient to sustain your weary attention.

Solemn as are the feelings which must be awakened by the conclusion of the year, yet that solemnity may be diminished by habit, and a parting address looked upon as an ordinary and matter-of-course ceremony. But there is still an inherent solemnity in such a scene which may well defy all the force of frequency to take away— a solemnity which, though it might be heightened by the feelings of an eloquent, yet still resist the dullness of the worst speaker; and I am sure, that the preacher, whose story I have just related, would have been spared all the trouble of his contrivance, had it been his lot to have addressed his parishioners for the last time. Independently of the uncertainty of death, it is certain that I address at least those of the third year for the last time, a word which is always accompanied with serious reflections.

You have often looked forward with impatience to the term of your studies, which you have reached at last; and the time which, while future, you saw advance with a heavy and killing slowness, now past, assumes a different aspect, and seems to outrun the following eye, in the rapidity of its flight, to mingle in the mass of departed ages. Without dwelling long on this subject, I am sure that your fancies catch more than I could utter, and that you feel that your joy, on having reached the goal, is saddened by the reflection that you have made equal advances to the grave. Thus it would seem, that Providence had wisely determined that every blessing should bring an antidote against its abuse, by reminding us that the same time, which is hurrying on to its possession, is silently abridging the period of its enjoyment. Perhaps the whole range of social life does not exhibit so sensible an illustration of the fleeting nature of human affairs, as such an establishment as ours. In the world, if we except those awful but rare visitations by which a whole people are swept away, there is seldom a chasm that could startle the serenity of the beholder. All its generations are so intertwined in all the gradations, from infancy to manhood, and from manhood to old age, that none is suddenly severed from the other; but while its members silently and imperceptibly disappear, society still presents the same unvaried uniformity, throwing over the celerity of its vicissitudes the illusion of an apparent repose. Not so here: the changes are visible and striking, every year witnessing the void occasioned by the departure of one series filled up by another that eagerly presses into its place and all pushed forward by the incursion of a new and strange generation that rushes with impatience to occupy the last vacancies. This is a circumstance which has not escaped your observation; but probably it has not struck all with an equally forcible impression. The affectation of sensibility, that is not felt, must ever be disgusting. But if you should feel surprise, why a truth, which may pass but lightly over the hearts of my hearers, should fall with a heavier impression upon mine, you will reflect that, as you are encircled in a group who are borne along by the same motion, as it equally affects all, you are less conscious of its rapidity, than from a position comparatively stationary, the ruins that pass before you seem to shift with quicker alternations.

In adverting to your conduct and progress in the course of the year, I shall not detain you long, nor shall I be suspected of insincerity in repeating the approval to which I have more than once given expression. Aware that with your general conduct I have not had any immediate concern, I have not travelled beyond the limits of my duty officiously to exercise an authority, which more properly belongs to others. And it is with equal pleasure I can state that, within the sphere of that duty I have had no complaints to prefer, and that we have been able to conduct our affairs without any foreign interference. In thus applauding your regularity, it is not mere commonplace, nor do I dread to share in the reproach of the prophet to the pastors who speak pleasing things, calling good evil and evil good, affecting to conceal what is known to their confusion, and cruelly palliating their disorders, which grew inveterate by connivance. The value of discipline in an ecclesiastical seminary is known by experience. Where there is not discipline there is not piety. It is better to prevent disorder by a temperate and wholesome rigour and a candid admonition, however painful to our feelings, than suffer it to grow unnoticed and unreproved. This is the process which the Gospel prescribes. In following it, it is true, you may give pain to the feelings; but it is a pain that is accompanied by a remedy : in neglecting it you suffer the disorder to fester, until, at length, it proves fatal through the cruelty of your indulgence. You have heard it said : It is good for a man to carry the yoke from his youth. Christ Himself tells us that His yoke is sweet and His burden light. And those who have profited of the restraints of discipline will find the truth of the words of the Wise Man, that those who put their feet into the fetters of wisdom, and their neck into her chains, will find that her fetters will be their defence, her bands a healthful binding, and her chains a robe of glory.

The number of students in the class has given you an opportunity of exercising those generous motives of conduct by which you must be actuated through life. Were the fear of having your indolence exposed the strongest motive to quicken your industry, it might still elude the most suspicious and unwearied vigilance. Much must, therefore, be left between you and your own hearts. One cannot feel much pleasure in recalling those precepts which were enforced early by terror. A more effectual method is the persuasion of their importance. The period is just approaching when the obligations of his profession will strike more forcibly upon every mind, and for the disposal of that time which could not come under a professor's observation I trust you will be able to stand the test of a well-regulated conscience.

As far, then, as I had an opportunity of judging, and it was pretty extensive, I must express my satisfaction at the uniform attention and success with which you have prosecuted your studies. I wish it were in my power to assign every individual an award equal to his deserts, if not to his expectations. But while the human mind is exposed to the illusions of error on the one hand, and vanity on the other, so long will it be exposed to all the bitterness of disappointment. To quench all hope would, indeed, be a gloomy consolation. Perhaps you have heard of the addition which Dean Swift made to the beatitudes. "Blessed," &c. Abstracting from its profaneness, there is some wisdom in the sentiment. Where there is such a variety of judgments, few would come to the same results in their calculation, and it would be absurd to attempt to gratify the hope of all, when some cannot be gratified but by the disappointment of others. The business of the year shall alone regulate its rewards; and, instead of presuming to fix the limits of anyone's career, I should feel particular pleasure in noticing and encouraging his progressive improvement.

The day of distribution is a day on which the different feelings of triumph on the one hand, and disappointment on the other, and of mirth among the neutral party, are mixed together in the most fantastic variety. While some are convinced that their labours have been rewarded, all the easy-going gentlemen of the house take ample vengeance on the painstaking students, whose hopes have been unfortunately frustrated. When I speak of disappointment I do not mean those who, though unsuccessful, might well compete with the more fortunate candidates whose place the professor finds it difficult to determine, being like him, who, residing on the doubtful confines of two countries, knows not to which he belongs, and who, therefore, may be placed on either side without exciting much surprise. But there are sometimes found persons, almost in every college, who, without any pretensions to distinction save that of an over sanguine imagination and an easy credulity, are amused with hopes of distinction which never entered into any mind but their own. They are instantly surrounded by a crowd of ambiguous friends who proffer their hollow consolations somewhat like the comforters of Job. They remind him of such and such an earnest for distinction which he had given, contrasting it with the less splendid display of another candidate, and then, with a far-sightedness surpassing that of the professor, they point out the secret and circuitous train of motives that operated on his exclusion, which would probably require all the ingenuity of an Italian politician to unwind. After having artfully worked upon his feelings, until he almost vows to give up the unproductive study of divinity, they retire with something of the self-satisfaction of the arch and insidious renard, whose insinuating flattery had so entirely subdued the tenacious nature of a bird notoriously unmusical, as to persuade it that it was one of the most tuneful creatures of its kind.

The College, I trust, is so much improved that what I describe from dull reality you will not be able to discover save in imagination. Do not, however, imagine that your professors estimate only those talents that obtain collegiate distinction. There are many who pass here apparently unobserved, and yet who prove some of the most useful individuals in the ministry. Of the polished and massy pillars, that contribute at once to its support and to its ornament, there are few in the Church, as in every other edifice. Its principal materials may be likened—some, to those interior abutments which, without attracting the public eye, uphold the principal weight of the building, and the others, to those lighter shafts figuring in the front, by which the solid parts of the structure are concealed, clothing its walls without sustaining any of its weight, and adorning its exterior by their graceful decorations.

Whatever may be the success of your collegiate career, I should caution you against the illusion of turning it into a saving bank, on which to draw for the future necessities of your character. It may give you a claim to a favourable introduction, but still it is only a pledge, which, if not redeemed by exertion, must be forfeited through your own indolence. I have often heard it made a subject of regret or of triumph, that the victors of the College were thrown into the background by the incessant and successful diligence of their former rivals. This must frequently occur. For different talents there are different tastes to appreciate them.

Besides, whoever contents himself with idly contemplating the honours which he has earned in his collegiate career, will soon find himself distanced in the competition, like the admirers of the faded ancient greatness of our country, who are feasting their eyes, and indolence, and vanity with the smoky images of their ancestors, while the brilliant success of a new candidate for fame obscures their dim and distant splendour. This obvious thought will teach you the necessity of persevering exertion. Reputation, like every other conquest, must be preserved by the same means by which it was acquired. You must, therefore, never relax, whatever may be the success of your first efforts. In the commencement you may experience a kind partiality; there is a certain generosity that gives credit to youth for the fruits of a riper age, kindly enkindling, by the breath of approbation, the full flame which otherwise might perish. But when that season is over, you may be assured the debt will be exacted with rigour, and that many, who might give credit for the future, are not equally disposed to appreciate past services.

If I have insisted on the necessity of this perseverance, it is less for the purpose of making you court the approbation of the world than of showing the dangerous fallacy of such a view. The man whose reputation attracts admirers, and whose company is courted to give animation to every circle, who is told that after the severity of his toil, he may now lawfully taste all the charms of repose, may live a little time on the repute he has treasured up; but he will soon find himself, not only a bankrupt in virtue, but totally rifled of the odour of his good name. The talents, which excited just admiration when enlisted in the service of religion, when profaned to the purposes of conviviality, excite disgust and alienation; the society which would have been still sought if it retained its dignity is now shunned when it is lost: as he becomes easy and obtrusive his friends gradually retire. Those, who were the most instrumental in destroying it, are the first to desert him when in the hour of his need: the strong man of Israel, now shorn of his strength, becomes a proverb among his enemies and the jest of the banquet; and the priest, whom the tears and benedictions of thousands would have followed to his grave, goes down abandoned and forlorn; and, perhaps, after a pious prayer for his salvation, the most indulgent wish that could accompany his departure, is a wish that he were forgotten.

If I have thus seriously concluded those reflections, it is to cure you of that ardent confidence with which young and generous minds may throw themselves on the world, until they are awakened from their delusion by the teaching of its desertion. It is to teach you to fix your hopes on Him, by whom a cup of cold water given in His name will not be unrequited. Reflect on this in time, if you wish not to swell the number of those who, in venting their complaints against the world's ingratitude, are only revealing their own ignorance and egotism, and paying the just forfeit of their erroneous estimate of human remuneration.

We have been this year engaged in the discussion of the most mysterious subjects of religion. Without occupying your time by pressing on your mind that in discussing the truth of religion, the evidence which results from the splendour of its miracles ought to dissipate the doubts that might be suggested by the darkness of its mysteries, I shall propose to your serious at-attention a few reflections suited to the occasion.

Man cannot reject the belief of mysteries without admitting one to which reason affords no solution. The intuitive and unremitting contest that is carried on between reason and the passions, and the alternating vicissitudes of their dominion, is a problem which, after having long exercised, at last eluded the ingenuity of man. Plato considered that this discordant state was the punishment of some original transgression. Cicero referred it to the cruelty of Nature, which he characterised with the name of stepmother, and Manes, as you all know, to two independent beings of equal power but opposite inclinations. Thus the mystery was acknowledged, and every attempt to explain it, only ended in thickening the confusion. Here, then, is a palpable mystery, inexplicable in its nature yet incontestible in its existence: here is that knot which, after having baffled human reason, required the aid of the Divinity to unloose. Original sin explains this frightful anomaly between man's strength and weakness, and this mutiny of the elements, of which he is composed, ceases to excite our wonder when we reflect that he is still stricken with God's vengeance for an original transgression. But original sin itself is a mystery that shakes our notions of justice. Yes, but you cannot reject it, without admitting another still more embarrassing. Man, born in original sin, is a mystery, and without original sin, is a greater.

Whatever system, then, you adopt—whether of natural or revealed religion—you must take your stand upon mystery, with this difference, that what in the one is dark, solitary, and unconnected, in the other becomes lucid, dependent, and consecutive. The state of man without original sin is a glorious truth, deduced from no remote principles, and connected by no dependent consequences; while the same state of man, with the light which revelation throws around it, forms the foundation on which is reared a majestic system of religion, mysterious, it is true, but harmonious in its mysteries; in which the attributes of the Divinity are reconciled, the contrarieties of human nature are explained, and God and man appear without the shadow of contradiction. Such is the simple plan, by which the perfection of religion is unfolded, a plan commencing with a palpable truth, which cannot be denied, because all have felt it: to follow it would be to develop all the parts of our religion. However, I shall only attempt to connect with it the subjects we have discussed this year.

An infinite injury required an infinite satisfaction. It is God alone that could pay it. The infinite satisfaction of one person to the infinite justice of another, reveals the plurality of relations or of persons in the Divinity; and the connection of suffering with satisfaction impossible in the Godhead conducts us to the knowledge of the Incarnation. If the Incarnation was a work worthy of the wisdom of God to conceive, and of His power to accomplish, the sacrifice of the Mass gives the merciful plan its full development and perfection. Before that time there was between God and man a distance immeasurable and impassable. To reconcile heaven with earth it behoved Christ in all things to be made like unto His brethren, that He might become a merciful and faithful high priest before God, that He might be a propitiation for the sins of His people. But if, when we were enemies of God, we were thus reconciled to Him through Jesus' Christ, who associated Himself with human nature when human nature was struck with the Divine malediction, how consonant is it with the same merciful plan that the same Victim would continue to offer Himself for our sins, still able and willing to procure our pardon—able, because of His divine power, and willing, because of His experience of human infirmity. While we assist, then, at the great sacrifice of the Mass, through what a train of grand and religious ideas are we conducted. From an oblation of bread and wine, by which we acknowledge, in the choicest gifts of earth, the bounty of heaven, we ascend to the period of its institution, and there behold Christ abolishing the bloody sacrifices, and inviting Jew and Gentile to share in this banquet of reconciliation. It recalls the memory of the Passover and the covenant of Abraham, the history of man's fall and the promise and accomplishment of his redemption, thus conducting the contemplative mind through all that is elevated and interesting in the history of religion, until at length it rests in the presence of its God—not that awful presence clothed in terrors, which forbids approach, but the presence of a God clothed in our own nature, inviting us to more familiar intimacy with an astonishing condescension, and literally realising, but chastening at the same time, those excesses of affection with which, in the language of Job, friends often desired to be incorporated with each other. In fact, in Him we find the consummation of all that we admire in the divine mysteries, Jesus Christ, true God and true man, united to the one by His divinity, to the other by His humanity, connecting the opposite extremes by His twofold nature, thus reconciling all things unto Himself, and making peace through the blood of His cross, and its mystic representation, both as to the things on earth and the things that are in heaven, thus proving what the Apostle says, that Jesus Christ is the Alpha and Omega of religion and of man, from whom all things proceed, and in whom all things must repose.

I find that I have nearly filled up the limits of our time, and I fear I have nearly exhausted the kindness of your patience. I imagined, indeed, that my address would be briefer on this, than on former occasions; but if, like the stream it has swelled as it descended, I believe that like it too, as it removes from the source, it has lost in its quality what it has acquired in the copiousness of its materials. I shall conclude by pressing on your attention the necessity of keeping alive by uniform application the knowledge which it cost so much of labour to acquire. On the necessity of attention to ecclesiastical studies it is almost unnecessary to enlarge to those who are destined to be the sole source of instruction to the ignorant. I have read, indeed, instructions, cautioning young ecclesiastics from burying in the solitude of study those talents which should be actively employed. I believe, however, that instances are rare in which a love of reading becomes a dangerous passion, and that in general it is more necessary to stimulate than to check the desire of knowledge. Independent of any conscientious motives, a love of study saves you on those occasions when your virtue would be exposed, or your character lowered, and will charm those heavy intervals, which those who are strangers to its delights, scruple not to murder either in melancholy or dissipation. I should not be an enemy to the temperate enjoyment of society; but it should be that virtuous society, which improves while it pleases, and which, while it solaces the fatigues of labour, never relaxes the energy of virtue. Such is the society recommended in Scripture. "Stand in the multitude of the ancients that are wise, and join thyself from thy heart to their wisdom, that thou mayest hear every discourse of God, and the sayings of praise may not escape thee."[1]

An extensive intercourse between the clergy would

---

[1] Ecclus. vi. 35.

be productive of much advantage. The little prejudices, that are fostered in less frequent intercourse, would be dissipated; the common fund of intellect and of knowledge would be enriched by the contributions of each individual; and all would derive strength and energy from mutual co-operation. Without this community of feeling, this concert of purpose, much of the most strenuous exertions must be abortive; and though some effect may be produced by single exertions, we know from long experience, that those are always weak who are divided. Besides, it is a melancholy truth that young men, of hope and promise, often sink beneath their level, and those talents, which would have ripened under proper cultivation, are chilled and contracted under an unpropitious influence. An intercourse with those, whose virtues are worthy of imitation, is calculated to counteract the effects of such untoward circumstances. It would thus always cherish the spirit of improvement, it would be a relief to the labours of the mission, and it would give you an opportunity of confiding to some enlightened and sympathising heart, those cares and anxieties, that are rendered lighter by participation. Such an interchange of civility, always under the control of decency and temperance, would oblige you to attend to domestic propriety so favourable to health and virtue; and you would find in such a society an element in which your spirit would still rise above the overwhelming influence of the manners that surround you.

I trust that the principle of mutual charity and co-operation shall be diffused from here, and circulated through the extremities of our national Church, connecting its remotest members with this common centre, and through it cementing them with each other. There may be some, who will not feel much disposed to recall the remembrance of the place of their education. Let them, however, not trust the sincerity of their feelings; time will work a change, and when pressed with the cares and fatigues of the mission, and thwarted in their exertions by a spirit, which neither kindness could conciliate, nor severity subdue, the hardships of their collegiate life will appear to have been exaggerated by their impatient inexperience. But whatever may be the accidents or imperfections of a college, there is not a feeling or a generous mind, that will not look back, with something of a sober reverence, to the place of his education. It is not, if you will, to its localities or to its inmates; these, of course, may pass away and leave no vestige of their existence; it is not its vicinity or its transient appendages; but still there would linger about its ruins something, I know not what, of a moral being, to which the memory would turn with fondness, and which would extract from every feeling heart a spontaneous veneration.

And now that you are on the eve of one of the most important changes of your life, may the Holy Ghost who descended on the Apostles diffuse His ample spirit over you, investing your hearts with His choicest gifts, and making you the heirs of their dispositions, as well as of their ministry. And when the days of Pentecost are over, like them it will be your lot to spread yourselves into different quarters of the Church. Before you separate, however, you ought to reflect on the sublimity with which religion invests the natural feelings of the human heart. Although remote from each other there is still a strong tie to connect you in the consoling doctrine of the communion of saints, a link which is not sundered by separation or even by death, but reaches to another world, embracing heaven and earth and purgatory in the amplitude of its connection. In that sacrifice, then the great centre of this connection, and of which the matter, according to St. Paul, is a mystic and significant symbol of the union of the faithful, you will have an opportunity of commemorating the companions of your collegiate life. "There is a man," says the Wise Man, "that is subtle and a teacher of many, and yet is unprofitable to his own soul."[1] It is a sentiment which ought to strike all with apprehension whose lot it ought to be to convey instruction to others. Conscious how I may stand in need of the like, I should solicit a share in your prayers if I were equally conscious that I had any claim to them; yet, I may be allowed to ask, from the kindness of your charity, what I cannot claim on any other title. However, if a like commemoration of those, who were my disciples, should challenge your regard, I faithfully pledge the assurance of reciprocal remembrance.

---

## ADDRESS TO THE THEOLOGICAL STUDENTS OF THE COLLEGE OF MAYNOOTH, 1824.

IN the memoirs of Captain Rock, that celebrated Irish chieftain, who is now invested with a classic immortality by our unrivalled countryman, who pours the magic of his own mind over every subject which he touches, there is an anecdote, of which I am reminded on the present occasion. He tells us that a Frenchman once borrowed a work, consisting of many volumes, from a friend, who, through archness or mistake, always gave him the same volume; and when he was supposed to have read the entire, being asked by his friend what he thought of the merits of the work, he replied, with great

[1] Ecclus. xxxvii. 21.

seriousness: "Il est assez bon, mais il me semble que l'auteur se repète." Were I to address persons whose hearts were as unimpressionable as those of the Frenchman, and whose memories were equally leaky, I should not fear, like his friend, to lead you again and again through the same discourse, content if, instead of discovering an identity, you should entertain some doubts of a possible repetition. However, I must say, in truth, the principal topics, which are suited to such an occasion, are but few in number and susceptible but of little variety. The scene itself is but the repetition of one which has often occurred, and naturally brings with it similar recollections. The office of praise or reproof, regret or satisfaction, must be the usual burden of his discourse who would address a numerous class at the close of the ecclesiastical year; and for the simple emotions of the heart nature has but few words, and these words are equally simple. He who should, therefore, affect to be elaborate on a subject, by its own nature so simple and confined, would probably share the fate of those, who are doomed to toil on every anniversary over an exhausted subject, until their productions wear the uniform features which mark a common affinity.

I care not how often I have to repeat it, I cannot resist, on a review of your conduct this year, the expression of my unqualified satisfaction. I am not anxious to give novelty to my language by mingling it with censure. I do not like the deep, elaborate contrivance of some refined amateurs of music, who strive to draw harmony from a judicious and well-balanced mixture of symphony and discord. No; I prefer the sameness of order to all such variety, and therefore I shall freely submit to the imputation of dulness while my theme is approbative.

I cannot part with such a number of young men, who

have been so long linked to me by a similarity of pursuits, without expressing my regret at the separation. If I were to dismiss you without a single allusion to the past, or a single anticipation of the future, I should be unworthy of the station which I occupy. I should think it unkind, now that we are to separate, not to bid an adieu to those who have sailed with me in the same bark, and though I cannot pretend to the age or the wisdom of the good Acestes, who warned his friends of all the perils that were to await them in the voyage, yet I hope it shall not be attributed to an overweening desire of instruction, if I should communicate some of those thoughts, which I have derived from the conversation or writings of others.

On the business of this year I shall not detain you long. The attention which you have paid to the subject, which occupied us this year, was proportioned to its importance. I am glad that in your conduct in the class there has been a corresponding decorum. The only regret which I feel is one, that the very large number in the class denies me the opportunity of ascertaining, with precision, the various degrees of merits by which they are distinguished. There may be some on whose deserts all may be agreed. With more frequent opportunities of comparison the task would be difficult; with the the few already exhibited, any decision would be presumptuous. Hence I am loath to declare, that in leaving the class my mind is as undetermined as your own, and that, so far from fixing any anticipated judgment, it is, to the last moment that any further trial is to be made, ready to receive any new impression. Without this complete indecision, your examinations would be vain, your trial at composition a mockery, possessing, perhaps, sufficient merit to entitle you to a favourable sentence; but, like the sufficient grace of the Jansenists never efficacious, because it should combat a stronger force. Such an unfavourable conviction, operating on the mind of any individual, would be a check upon his industry; whereas the contrary persuasion, that every effort will be attended to, would give a stimulus to exertion.

You are aware that, in the original plan, the object of compositions was to fix the doubtful claims of those whose pretensions might seem equal. But since the enlarged number of the class brought out a corresponding mass of talent, hence the number has been increased, and the selection itself considered a distinction. Were a professor to judge exclusively the relative merits of the compositions that come before him, without reference to the answers of the year, he would frequently depart from the general opinion of his class. Of the marked difference between the oral and written responses of some, you have a striking exemplification in the judgments passed on the compositions of certain individuals, those years back, which seemed to be in the inverse ratio with each other.

The relative superiority of speaking or writing is a subject of grave and serious controversy, which has a long time divided the learned world, and which I feel as unwilling, as I am incompetent, to decide. To avoid, therefore, any undue partiality for either excellence, I endeavour, in my estimate of merit, to blend both those qualities, unwilling to depress the talents of oratory or composition, but manifesting a preference when the readiness and profusion of the one would be seconded by the accuracy and precision of the other.

I have heard of a professor who, to reconcile his disciples to a disappointment, frankly confessed to them an instance of human infirmity of which he was guilty in his youth by giving way to temptations of vanity, from which, it is said, the most ordinary vigilance might have secured him. He mentioned that on a certain occasion he expected no less than ten or twelve premiums, but that, to his great mortification, his hope was disappointed in all. From the specimens which they witnessed, they were not disposed to sympathise much in the disappointment of his earlier days, especially after making a reasonable deduction from the accumulations of his advanced years. The cloud, which had so long hung in his mind over the character of him who had marred his expectations, was dissipated by one of those acts of tardy justice which occasionally occur, since all unanimously absolved the judgment of him who disappointed such unfounded pretensions; and though to forgive his professor was one of the most difficult and heroic victories of his life, it was confessed that his other afflictions must have been few, or that those foes, which he vanquished, must have been rendered more formidable by the activity of his own fancy.

However, to be serious, I feel all the difficulties of adjusting the nice shades of discrimination between such a vast number of persons, a task in which no one can plead exemption from error. But after resorting to every method of guarding against mistake, one at least has the satisfaction which arises from a conscious purity of motive. In the last trial of composition the name is covered with a seal, which is not broken until its merits are determined, without any reference to its author. Instead of being influenced by any previous opinions of his talents, I register my judgment before the name is disclosed, a judgment, which afterwards remains undisturbed through favour or affection; nor shall I, I trust, ever imitate those, whose first unbiassed judgment of an unknown writer would be found, with the fluency of mercury, to rise or fall in obedience to the warmth or the coldness of their feelings.

No; in a matter of justice, feeling is to be kept aloof, and all the little considerations, that enter into the spirit of management, must be disregarded. If a distribution were to be a matter of management, I have no doubt but a dexterous professor could manage the feelings, and, by a judicious balancing, produce that sort of harmony which arises from equal opposition. But the awkward artifice would be soon seen through; and could I suppose anyone capable of such motives, he would adopt the most effectual method of defeating his own purpose. Were I, abstracting from my duty as professor, to give my opinion of the Gentlemen in the class in any other relation, I have no hesitation in saying, that there are some in the class whose virtues and literary acquirements will confer as much lustre on religion, and perhaps more than those who are most highly distinguished. The Church is not confined to one species of excellence, and, as the Apostle well remarks, there are but few who excel in a variety of attainments. Hence a diversity of natural and divine graces, springing from one common origin, which imparts to one the word of wisdom, to another the word of knowledge, to a third the grace of healing, to another the discerning of spirits, to another divers kinds of tongues, and to another the interpretation of speeches, of all which gifts, it is as doubtful which is the most excellent, as of the organs of the human frame, which is the most perfect, and of which either would be as unequal to the support or ornament of the Church as any one of its senses would be to dispense with the aid and ministry of the others.

I have thus spoken to you at some length of a subject in which you must feel an interest, which, for the sake of religion, I should be sorry to see extinguished. I shall not affect the lofty indifference of those who have no regard for any station below their own, and whose philosophical contempt is sure to be as sorely avenged by the more mortifying disdain of others still more elevated. No; I should rather, if I may be pardoned an allusion to such a distant model, imitate the conduct of Benedict XIV., whose Bulls are distinguished beyond those of the other Roman Pontiffs, that while they convey his authority, they unfold more fully the reasons on which that authority was founded. It was not weakness that dictated such conduct to Benedict XIV. No; but, conscious of the integrity of his conduct, he knew that his laws would derive more force from an explanation of the motives on which they are founded. To explain the reasons of such laws bespeaks a confidence; to assign none excites suspicion in weak minds that they are indefensible. When, therefore, such explanation shall have failed, it will be full time for me to adopt the summary principle of *stat pro ratione voluntas;* and, to imitate those who, conscious they can assign no reason but caprice, attempt to spread the weakness of their motives behind the terrors of a mysterious and inquisitorial authority.

However, in addressing myself to ecclesiastics, it would be unreasonable to omit that higher motive which should animate every Christian, and without which human energy would languish. It was in addressing himself to Christians that St. Paul introduced this same argument, contrasting the rivalry of Christians, who may all be crowned, with the contests of the ancients, where only one gained the victory. Let those, then, who may be disappointed console themselves with the approbation of Him whose vigilance never slumbers, and whose judgment never strays, inviting us to a competition into which the spirit of jealousy never enters; holding out a reward, for which all may strive and which all may acquire, and where the completion of one man's hopes will not be the bitter fruit of another's disappointment.

Our College has been a theme that was always dear to my feelings, and which, I trust, I shall never cease to honour with a filial affection. But circumstances of recent occurrence now bring the subject more forcibly to my attention, and induce me to dwell a little longer on our national establishment. Need I allude to a random charge said to be made in a certain quarter on this College, which, under the mask of a regard for its character, contained some undefinable injurious insinuations.[1] I shall not be an indiscriminate panegyrist; it betrays the spirit of partisanship, which takes from truth all its dignity. I shall not, therefore, affect to admire everything about our College, nor shall I attempt to vindicate the conduct of any who might have reflected disgrace upon the institution. But, making full allowance for some cases of individual delinquency—and what institution can be free from such examples?—I believe that, through a hostile spirit, the faults of our clergy are magnified in number and aggravated in their enormity. Whether they receive a foreign or domestic education, our clergy seem fated to be calumniated. When driven from home they come back, if we are to believe our enemies, fraught with disaffection to the Government that persecuted them. And if they remain in their own country all the faults of the old clergy are instantly transformed into virtues, in order to mortify, by the invidious contrast, the spirit of our native ecclesiastics. Thus the versatile hostility of our enemies can shift with all the change of situation which the clergy

---

[1] The precursor of more recent charges respecting the ecclesiastical training of the youth of Ireland, which elicited from the Prefect of the Sacred Congregation de Propaganda fide, the late Cardinal Barnabo, the scathing letter of the 2nd June, 1873, published in the Acts of the Synod of Maynooth, p. 9.—ED.

undergo, reminding one of the unfortunate man in the fable who, whether he walked or rode, was equally sure of censure; or rather, illustrating a character still more familiar, I mean the inexorable pedagogue of Brown, Jones, and Robinson, who, instead of punishing because he discovered faults, laboured to discover faults in order to punish; flogging one because he could swim, and his companion because he could not, thus resolved at every hazard to gratify his natural cruelty, and converting what he pretended would have been the protection of the one into the aggravated guilt of the other. Thus it is with those who go forth from this College, who must be charged with the indiscretion of others, while they reflect lustre on their country. It is amusing to hear the mixture of praise and apology with which some affect to defend the College, whose officious and obtrusive advocacy it would indignantly disown. Under the affectation of regret for defects which are either exaggerated or for which it is not the College that is responsible, they badly conceal their uneasiness at its progress, and, by reluctantly meting out that "feeble praise which half bespeaks dispraise," they sufficiently betray their ungenerous feelings. Imagine not, Gentlemen, that the College is to be defended from every assailant; it must rest on its own respectability. Like every work that is destined for permanence, it must be the slow and silent production of time, *sicut arbor obscuro crescens ævo*, which, when it has attained its full strength, should any rude hand attempt to check its growth or warp its direction, in the resilience of its strength, would swing the unequal pressure, and assert its native tendency to the skies.

Do not imagine that I wish to nourish your vanity. No, but to excite your piety, since no one can be indifferent to the interests of an establishment so extensively interwoven with the interests of religion. The arrogance and pride of some of the young men from this house has been made a matter of frequent complaint. I have no doubt but there have been instances of a petulant and supercilious demeanour, which is often cured, because it brings with it its own punishment. Such individuals ought not to be spared. But what is remarkable is this, and I have had some conversation with a variety of characters, that I never knew the charge to be preferred by those who were distinguished for their humility. The Wise Man tells us that there are always quarrels among the proud. Hence the frequency of these contests with which some are opposed, while the meek and the generous, and the apostolical men command a submission bordering on reverence. Let those, then, who are so liberal of their complaints study whether, in exacting too much, they provoke not that pride of which they complain. There may not be among those from the College that frequency of visits, that assiduity of attention, that incessant and fatiguing cant, by which the pride of the higher orders is generally soothed; but if dignified seclusion, an unwillingness to waste one's time in idle gossip, an uncomplying disposition where religion would be compromised, and a complete contempt for that indescribable sort of character which is known by the name of *bonhomie*, be considered pride, long may the students of this College deserve the imputation.

God forbid that anyone should misapprehend my meaning, or that I should not inculcate that virtue which is the foundation of the Christian religion. But I have only remarked that this charge has been deepened by exaggeration. There is in some minds a confusion of ideas which would mistake true greatness for pride, and would call meanness humility. And, therefore, without questioning that there are instances when the charge is just, I am inclined to believe that it arises, oftener, from the sordid and cynical spirit which, while it trampled on the noble and generous pride of Plato, was showing the more disgusting exhibition of its own.

I trust, then, that you will so demean yourselves, as the Apostle says, as to leave no room for reproach among the gainsayers, and that no one will despise you on account of your youth. Your conduct shall be more narrowly watched than that of your predecessors. Faults, which the state of society would then have pardoned, would now in the eyes of the world be inexpiable. If the darkness of the times that are gone by, concealed the virtues of our clergy, it also protected some vices which the present enlightened period would reveal to public view. I believe it will be confessed, that it now requires more caution to conduct one's self in society than heretofore. For some time past, though the course through life was dull it was tranquil and secure; whereas the brilliant prospects, which now more frequently sparkle on its surface, ought to warn us of the danger which they generally conceal. The Catholic clergy are become, from the nature of their office and exertions, necessarily influential in the country; and much of the happiness of that country must depend upon their exertions. The existence of this College, under a proper direction, must always contribute to increase that influence by collecting here young men from all quarters of the country, and sending them forth forgetting everything that should divide, and breathing only the spirit which should unite them. Yes, the "*divide et impera*," the bane of every society, has been too long acted on; nor could our clergy counteract its pernicious effects. They themselves, though inculpably, I must confess, were the victims of its influence; and scattered in small establishments over the Continent, were incapable of that concert and union which early connections inspire. When here they might be brought to know each other; their asperities might be worn away by mutual contact, and their prejudices corrected by the infusion of a more liberal feeling. Such are the blessings which an institution like this will not fail to realise. Already has it created deep and extensive sympathies; there are few who are not interested in its prosperity. Those sympathies will be strengthening, and intertwining themselves with the whole Catholic people of Ireland. The birth day of the College, though now it scarce awakes attention within its walls, shall be hailed as a sacred anniversary among its children. The stone of its foundation will be deemed an emblem of the perpetuity of our religion, and the ring which encircles it of the circumference of our country, over which its spirit shall extend. The ingenuity of its sons shall create other interesting devices; and I trust it shall continue to prosper until a national soul is felt through every portion of our national College, and diffused to the extremities of the kingdom, returning again like the life-blood through every artery, without meeting one cold or mortified member to check it in its progress, until it circulates the warm and animating impulse through the entire frame of our national hierarchy.

When speaking of the College, and the noble object for which it was founded, no one can apprehend the danger of exaggeration. On other topics some might excite ridicule by an injudicious disproportion between the littleness of the subject and their thoughts. But on contemplating the magnitude of this institution, and the present and prospective interests which it involves, one's only apprehension must arise from the poverty or the coldness of his conceptions. From the busy interference of some with whom it has no connection, you would imagine the College was in their keeping, and that, like Mount Atlas, they were preventing it from tumbling on our heads. But it wants not now their kind solicitude. No, I trust that you all feel that the young College has burst its shell, and that it is plumed with strength; and that if, like the bird of Jove, its first rising be slow and solemn, it is only for the purpose of poising its weight and concentrating its vigour when it shall whirl its rapid and majestic flight towards the sun of science, and, with unwearied wing and unshrinking eye, still approach the luminary without being fatigued from its distance or oppressed by its splendour.

I could talk to you a great deal, and dispense a variety of formal admonitions on the dangers which you are to meet, and on the prudence with which you are to avoid them. But with a saint, who was asked by another to give him some lessons on the great affair of salvation, I answer, "Be in earnest," knowing that if he once felt an earnest zeal to accomplish that great object, all the darkness and difficulties in which he was involved would immediately disappear. It is thus with you; be in earnest about the magnificent designs of benefiting your country and your Church by your labours, and you will infallibly succeed. If, then, there should be any one that requires incessant vigilance to guard him against wrong, let him not enter into the Church, since even the eyes of Argos could not follow him everywhere. Nay, if there should be any, whose dispositions are not mischievous, but are of that passive kind as to require to be roused by incessant admonition, let him not enter, since no outward action could sustain his languid career against the *vis inertiæ* of his own indolence.

You must not only possess that singleness of eye which will direct you in the right way, but also the strong and ardent spirit of zeal; that *vivida vis animi* which agitates the living body, which no impediment can retard, and no exertion can tire, as independent of any impulse as it is impatient of any obstacle, borne along by the force of its own velocity, and kindling, as it moves, by the vehemence of its own action.

I perceive I have spoken to you at sufficient length, and if with more than usual seriousness, it was called forth by the seriousness of the occasion: and I wish I could feel some of the madness of St. Paul in speaking of the same religion which inspired that Apostle. I will not prolong your attention further: what each of you can do for the Catholic Church your own meditations will speak to you more than human tongue can utter. But as this is the last time that we are all to meet together here in the same circumstances, and since many, in leaving the hall to-day, will rub its dust off their feet for the last time—not, I hope, in malediction—I thought it but a small requital of gratitude to address to you these few words in return for your uniform respect and attention. And when I speak of that respect, do not imagine that I look on it in any other light than in that of an act of homage to religion. Woe be to the superior, who would attempt to support himself on any other basis! Were he to attempt to regulate subordination by any other standard, or intercept that respect which is referred to the place he holds, he would be soon a just victim of his own presumption. While, then, I value your respect, I value it because it is the spontaneous dictate of virtue, recognising in everyone, who occupies any station, a link of that great chain of mutual dependence which God has formed, and merging every subordinate consideration in a respect for established order. As you are, then, going to embark on the voyage of life, I should be insensible if I felt not an interest for those who have so long sojourned here. And if I cannot furnish you with the lessons that are derived from age, and the tried perils of the deep, to warn you of the dangers that await you on the way, I can offer a still stronger consolation which the Catholic only feels, since we can all invoke for each that Power who will not fail, as He has promised, to awake at our prayers, to rise at our prayers to rebuke the sea and still the anger of the storm. For those who remain still behind they will, I trust, endeavour to lay up a sufficient store of knowledge, as a chart to direct them when they follow. If the man in the happy valley felt weary of the insipidity of unchequered repose, it is not to be wondered if others, notwithstanding the tranquillity of this place, should wish to tempt the active scenes of life in spite of their dangers. If so, they shall not pine in the melancholy reflection, that they are left behind, until age or infirmity should unfit them for the labour. It may thus be our lot to be engaged in the same labour as we have shared in the same literary leisure. But whether or no, I shall always feel pleasure in recollecting my connection with such a respectable number of young men, whom I shall rejoice to see striving in the competition of virtue—nor shall I fear to be profane since the Scripture consecrates the word—and running the race of glory. If St. Paul, in the ecstasy of his revelations, thought he stood in need of the prayers of the faithful, it would be in us the height of presumption to think we stood in no need of such assistance. Since, then, we are the heirs of that religion which has for every pang its peculiar consolation, and which alone associates the heart to the empire of the understanding, I trust we shall not be unmindful of that Apostle's pious practice, which consecrates the best feelings of our nature: there is scarcely one of his letters which he does not conclude with a tender and solemn adjuration of mutual remembrance in their prayers.

I have only to remark, and I may now do so with freedom, since few will make the application to themselves, that I observed once or twice something like an indifference. I was unwilling to observe on it at the time, being one of those doubtful matters which you know not whether to ascribe to indifference or infirmity. However, ascribing it to the former, I did not wish to animadvert on it. Perhaps they were some who found the labours of study as unworthy of their talent, and who thought that their talents were wasted on a disproportioned object, like him of whom it is said that, while he made a poor fist of the distaff he could wield the thunderbolt. But you may perceive that I never wasted any time in the recommendation of theology to your attention, because such incessant recommendation betrays a consciousness that it requires extraordinary aid. If its importance is not otherwise felt than by the action of incessant terror it will be studied with little assiduity, and with less profit. Thanks to those who have rescued it from its barbarism, and invested it with becoming interest, such as it is now cultivated, or as it ought to be studied, it associates with it the knowledge of Scripture and of history, unlike the treatises of theology which were studied by some in former times, in which not a name was quoted more ancient than their own time. As if the whole circle of science and theology was confined to their own age, they quoted each other like oracles; but their forgetfulness of the ancients was amply avenged by the indignation of posterity, which has equally forgotten them of whom no relic exists save that mathematical improvement of the infinite series of argumentation which they imported into theology without the aid of a binomial theorem to resolve it, and who in transforming the plainest sense into the profoundest mystery, realised the boasted powers of the philosopher, in Lucian, set up to auction, who could change a man into a horse by the single touch of a syllogism.

---

## ADDRESS TO THE THEOLOGICAL STUDENTS OF THE COLLEGE OF MAYNOOTH, 1825.

You have often heard of the charms by which men are so attached to life, that even when every rational hope of remaining longer is gone, they still cannot endure the idea of their departure. I must confess I have laboured under a similar illusion, and, though my judgment assured me of the certainty of speedy separation, yet it was one of those scenes which my feelings forbade my fancy to anticipate. It may excite surprise that one can feel regret in quitting a place which he willingly resigns; and the least expression of reluctance to exchange one's situation may appear affected or unnatural, to those who have only carelessly viewed the surface of life without reflecting that some of its most tempting honours are like the sunny apples of Istkahar, of which naturalists say they are all sweetness on the one side, but all bitterness on the other; the sunny side is pleasing to the view, the bitterness is not felt if not tasted. Hence the incredulity of mankind with respect to dangers which they never tried; and hence the lessons of moralists, on the illusions of life, are often treated with the same heedlessness as the cautions of age are received by the thoughtlessness of youth, disregarded until time confirms their wisdom, when the adventurous incredulity of the next generation avenges the indifference, with which they received the precepts of their fathers.

But let the charms of life be what they may, let it possess all the reality with which the fancy of some invests it, I defy any individual, possessed of a heart, to make such a transition without the most serious emotion. Before you approach such a period in your existence, you may be tranquil, when you pass it you may experience a similar calm; but the passage itself like the narrow straits that are always vexed by the contending currents of opposite seas must be agitated by the swell of contending feelings which rush from the contrary directions of the past and the future. If, therefore, I should appear melancholy, it will not wear the air of mystery or affectation to those who have explored the recesses of their own heart, and who can find, in that single volume, an epitome of all the passions of mankind. May it not be that my regret at departure proceeds from a selfishness, which would fain disguise itself under the appearance of a generous and disinterested sensibility; may it not be from the consciousness that so much of the happiness of life is flown, accompanied by the pensive thought which must steal over the most sanguine mind, that, even when one seems to be mounting the ascent to elevation, he is only approaching nearer the goal of his existence. . .
. . . . . . . Yet when I look back upon those

epochs, they seem to touch each other so closely as to leave but few landmarks of the distance which we traversed; so that he who would close his years in a College would startle at the insidious celerity with which they steal away, and exclaim with the prophet "My generation is at an end, and it is rolled away from me as a shepherd's tent."[1] However we may be surprised at this peculiar swiftness of a collegiate life, it is still natural; the sameness of its course seems to shorten its duration, as the eye, ranging over a smooth and unbroken expanse of water, is less sensible to its extent than if it were chequered by a variety of objects.

Of the many topics that crowd on my mind on this occasion, it is difficult to ascertain which deserves the preference. However, before I advert to any other subject, it is just that I should make some observations on your conduct and progress during the year. In the prosecution of a task of daily recurrence, it is not to be expected that languor is to be relieved by continual novelty, or that the attention is to be roused by powerful excitements. A remark of a celebrated periodical writer might be equally applicable to professors and students, "that he who is consigned to a stated task must often bring to his subject an attention dissipated, a memory embarrassed, a body languishing with disease, and a mind distracted with anxieties." We must therefore occasionally experience inequalities, and feel those fluctuations of talent and of temper that are incident to life. On a fair estimation, then, of the conduct of the year, I must express myself in terms of unqualified satisfaction. Nay, when I consider, on the one hand, the irksomeness of some hours, together with the coldness and constraint that are the proverbial appendages of the schools; and, on the other, the life and vitality natural

[1] Isai. xxxviii. 12.

to young and ardent minds, I must confess the impression I have received is that of edification.

. . . . . I have often wondered that persons who did not seem unacquainted with the character of our people, would not avail themselves, with more success, of such a noble instrument for government. Treat them with kindness, with candour, persuade them by proofs that will satisfy their judgment, that you are interested in their welfare, and whether in the civil or military or ecclesiastical department, a silken cord would lead those who could never have been driven. They require no management, no intrigue, no mysterious artifices of a weak and tortuous policy to direct them. He, who fancies he cannot govern without hiding himself in such a labyrinth, becomes generally the victim of his own rashness, since it would require the clue of Theseus to disengage himself from the labour in which he is involved. Give them but the exertions of your body and the straightforward purpose of your mind, you need fear no embarrassment, and their preventing gratitude will supply the want of your exertions. Hence, when I hear of discontent in the country, and magistrates continually demanding serious enactments, I should inquire with St. Bernard whether they did not provoke what they complained of, and perhaps without the same generous motive to palliate their conduct, I might be reminded of the story of putting the bowl into the sack of Benjamin, and then accusing him of theft. . . .

I will not hesitate to say that it is his virtue, that has given the Catholic priest such an ascendancy in society. Possessed of the same affections he pours into a wider channel those charities which others confine to their own kindred, and hence the mutual affection with which his generous devotion is requited.

It is this reciprocal kindness that has given the priest an appellation so expressive of the love, which he feels for the children of his adoption. Nay, the influence of this virtue is felt in the secret reverence of the Protestants for the virtues of a Catholic priest. In the ministers of their own Church they may admire the frivolous accomplishments of the world; seldom, however, are they struck with the sterner features of religion. They see the Catholic priest practising a virtue which they deem almost unattainable, from which he derives in their eyes a loftiness of character which extorts their reluctant homage. The charm of this character dissolves the strongest prejudices, and gives access to every society; yet in the most familiar moments his character is not forgotten, if he forgets it not himself, and that virtue, to which he has consecrated his life, throws round him a mysterious circle which rejects familiarities, and invests him even in the midst of the world with the loneliness and sanctity of an anchoret. Nay; what, perhaps, you have not sufficiently considered, this virtue alone vindicates the claims of the Catholic Church to the appellation of sanctity. You have heard of the contrast frequently made between the virtues of Catholic priests and Protestant ministers. Yes; but the name of virtue in both churches has a different signification. You have been told that there are few scandals among Protestant ministers; they are not much exposed to fall who are placed upon a level. You are reminded of the falls of Catholic priests; the magnitude of the fall proves the height of their elevation.

I will not conclude without adverting to the College, a theme too important to be omitted on the present occasion. It was long a subject of neglect or obloquy;

lately it has extorted the praise of numbers who were not at all partial to its fame. . . .

There is, however, one peculiar advantage in our national establishment, to which, perhaps, you have not sufficiently adverted, and which ought to make it dear to the lovers of literary merit and of ecclesiastical freedom. By collecting all the youth of Ireland into one large theatre they are placed in some measure before the public, and their future destinies will be under the equitable control of public opinion. What a stimulus to emulation! Heretofore, scattered in smaller communities, their relative merits were not recognised; like objects seen through the fragments of a mirror, they presented different aspects, according to the medium through which they were viewed. Hence that sort of religious clanship, that ecclesiastical feudalism which, in an unworthy contest for the ascendency, not unfrequently forget public interest. Whereas, before a national tribunal all may be viewed from one common point of observation, and he that would have towered in a smaller community, would be taught to shrink into his natural dimensions.

Let, then, in the language of Scripture, your thoughts occasionally flow to this place; nor do I offer any violence to your feelings in such a recommendation. Be the accidents or imperfections of the College what they may, yet the parent has this claim on your filial piety. . . . After having long sojourned here with you, we shall also engage together in ecclesiastical labour. The College shall not have a sincerer worshipper, nor one more interested in its prosperity; and I can say with sincerity, that there are no hours of my life to which I shall turn with a fairer retrospect, than those which I have spent in cheering the literary labours or sharing the innocent relaxations of the children of the College. If I have obtained any portion of the public approbation, or if my mind was ever kindled, I shall not easily forget those whose generous breath fanned the feeble flame, which otherwise might have perished. If I have had any talents I was long unconscious of them, until, like the fabled nymph who accidentally saw her likeness in the waters, I viewed some faint image of my own mind in the mirror of your approbation. The likeness, however, did not please me, and it then became my study by patient toil to improve it, until it should be presented to the public in a form worthy of the approbation of those, who viewed the rough outlines with such partiality.

I perceived early in life a sullen and apparently an irreconcilable schism between literature and theology. In tracing their history, I found they were originally united; and it was in some measure my ambition to restore the ancient alliance. In the interval of this schism I found some venerable names, such as Bossuet, who strove to effect a reconciliation, but whose labours, like those of Cardinal Bessarion, were rendered ineffectual by the perversness of the age. In this attempt I had to address myself to them separately, and to make repeated overtures to either, insisting, however, that theology should form the leading figure, and literature should be the humble minister of its train. I have striven to forget those who forgot the ancients themselves, in whose barren works you look in vain for any expanded views of the sacred writings, or any historical illustration. Yes, historical illustration: you will find it the richest source of truth; and though you should read only for amusement, like Assuerus, who took up the annals of his country to solace the weariness of a sleepless night, like his lecture, it may in the hands of Providence be instrumental in bringing about the salvation of your people. Never waste your time upon those who will not reward your labours, who, instead of learning, give you their own crude fancies, and who, in their zeal to protect the majesty of truth, never suffer you to approach its sacred precincts without passing through a fierce file of syllogisms, and making your obeisance at every step; and when at length you are permitted to enter the presence-chamber, you wonder how the insignificance of the personage could require such a formidable and gorgeous retinue. These are not the models I have studied. No; though I might despair of imitating him, I still learn to admire the writings of St. Jerome, who illustrated the image of our national poet by pouring into the sweet and majestic strain of his diction the mingled streams of sacred and profane learning.

Though dispersed through Ireland, however, as long as the College exists, the name to which it is consecrated will always remind us of the exalted model to whose virtues we should aspire. As he is the common patron to whom all Ireland pays its vows, the College dedicated to his name should be the common temple, to which all should bring their offerings. You need not fear those sceptics who would rob us of his existence; as long as the religion of Ireland and the College stand, they will speak their refutation. I have often smiled at the superfluous labours of antiquarians in proving the existence of a man which is inscribed on all the monuments of our country. They remind you of the darkling labours of the metaphysical writers, whose faltering lights, in leading us to the throne of the Divinity, are lost in the splendours of creation. . . . It is time that I should conclude, because I must have worn out your patience. I have only to say that, though absent from the College, I shall be present in spirit. I know, too, that the more immediate instruments are not always the most powerful agents, and that the finest instruments are often rendered abortive when employed by clumsy hands. I know the College; nor shall I fail to make use of my experience in my intercourse with the different authorities by whom it is regulated.

As for literary composition, I fear that the care of refitting a portion of our national Church, which, alas, has not yet cleared away all the rubbish of its desolation, and gathering the scattered furniture of the sanctuary, shall divert me from my favourite pursuits. However, when I reflect on the labours of St. Augustine, while the Church of Africa was wasted by the Vandals; how St. Leo found leisure amidst the calamities that afflicted Rome; how St. Gregory could snatch some intervals from the cares which so perplexed him that he knew not whether he was a temporal prince or a spiritual pontiff; how St. Athanasius could give to the world his sublime conceptions on religion, while he was wandering over Europe or hiding himself in tombs and cisterns—I do not despair, without insinuating a presumptuous comparison, of being able to achieve a project which I have long since meditated.[1]

As we are now on the eve of Pentecost, I shall pray that the Holy Ghost, who descended on the Apostles, may diffuse His ample Spirit over us, investing us with His choicest gifts, and making us the heirs of their zeal as well as of their ministry. There is a singular affinity between our destinies, as it will be my lot, as well

---

[1] His work on the "Evidences and Doctrines of the Catholic Church" soon afterwards published for the first time, is here alluded to.—ED.

as yours, to receive on this occasion the Sacrament of Holy Orders. The Church, to secure reverence for the sanctuary, has thrown a splendour round her ceremonies, which strikes the world with emotions of awe and admiration. It is the majesty of religion, and not the sense of individuals she wishes to consult. While, therefore, we are robed in the ornaments of the priesthood we ought to tremble, lest we should be like the victim led to the altar, unconscious that the waving honours, in which he prides, are the very symbols of his destruction.

THE END.

M. H. Gill & Son, Printers, Dublin.

www.ingramcontent.com/pod-product-compliance
Lightning Source LLC
Chambersburg PA
CBHW031948290426
44108CB00011B/724

* 9 7 8 3 7 4 2 8 3 7 4 1 7 *